1-2-3® QuickStart

A GRAPHICS APPROACH

Developed by Que® Corporation

Text and graphics pages developed by
David P. Ewing and Katherine Murray

Que® Corporation
Carmel, Indiana

1-2-3® QuickStart

Copyright © 1988 by Que® Corporation

All rights reserved. Printed in the United States of America. No part of this book may be used or reproduced in any form or by any means, or stored in a database or retrieval system, without prior written permission of the publisher except in cases of brief quotations embodied in critical articles and reviews. Making copies of any part of this book for any purpose other than your own personal use is a violation of United States copyright laws. For information, address Que Corporation, 11711 N. College Ave., Carmel, IN 46032.

Library of Congress Catalog No.: 88-61788

ISBN 0-88022-386-3

This book is sold as is, without warranty of any kind, either express or implied, respecting the contents of this book, including but not limited to implied warranties for the book's quality, performance, merchantability, or fitness for any particular purpose. Neither Que Corporation nor its dealers or distributors shall be liable to the purchaser or any other person or entity with respect to any liability, loss, or damage caused or alleged to be caused directly or indirectly by this book.

91 90 89 88   8 7 6 5 4 3 2 1

Interpretation of the printing code: the rightmost double-digit number is the year of the book's printing. For example, a printing code of 87-4 shows that the fourth printing of the book occurred in 1987.

This book covers Version 2.01 of 1-2-3.

Trademark Acknowledgements

Que Corporation has made every effort to supply trademark information about company names, products, and services mentioned in this book. Trademarks indicated below were derived from various sources. Que Corporation cannot attest to the accuracy of this information.

COMPAQ is a registered trademark of Compaq Computer Corporation.

dBASE, dBASE II, dBASE III, and dBASE III Plus are registered trademarks of Ashton-Tate Corporation.

IBM Personal System/2 is a registered trademark of International Business Machines. PS/2 is a trademark of International Business Machines.

Lotus 1-2-3, Jazz, Symphony, and VisiCalc are registered trademarks of Lotus Development Corporation.

Publishing Director
David P. Ewing

Product Director
David P. Ewing

Editor
Terrie Lynn Solomon

Technical Editor
Timothy S. Stanley

Production
William Hartman, Dennis Sheehan, Cheryl English

Proofreaders
Lori Lyons, Carrie Marshall

Indexer
Sherry Massey

Composed in Garamond by
Hartman Publishing

Page Design by
William Hartman, Hartman Publishing

Acknowledgements

Que Corporation thanks the following individuals for their contributions to this book:

Bill Hartman, of Hartman Publishing, for the excellent design of the pages and graphics in this book, for his willingness to make numerous modifications and additions to the book without complaint, and for the many evening and weekend hours he spent completing the project.

Kathy Murray, for her excellent developmental work on this book, including organizing the chapters and topics within each chapter, developing concepts for many of the graphics, and for preparing the text for editing.

Terrie Lynn Solomon, for her skillful editing, her dedication to ensuring the correctness of this book, and her management of the final production stages of the project.

Tim Stanley, for his technical review of the text and graphics in this book, and his much needed assistance with creating screen graphics.

Joanetta Hendel and Stacey Beheler, for their assistance with organizing the many parts of this book project and for their invaluable support to the developmental and editing staff working on this book.

Dennis Sheehan and Cheryl English, for their skillful paste-up and photographic work and for their willingness to assist with the final production stages of the project.

Randy Strong, of TANGO Press, for the effort and time he gave to ensuring timely and high-quality production of the final pages of this book.

Contents

Introduction
Using this Book 2

An Overview of 1-2-3
What Is 1-2-3? 8
The 1-2-3 Electronic Spreadsheet 10
1-2-3 Basic Concepts 16
1-2-3 Formulas and Functions 20
Spreadsheet Commands 24
1-2-3 Graphics 28
1-2-3 Database Management 34
Keyboard Macros and the Lotus Command Language 38

Getting Started
Introduction 42
Starting 1-2-3 44
Exiting 1-2-3 50
Learning the Keyboard 54
Learning the Screen Display 60
Using 1-2-3's Help Feature 64

1-2-3 Basics
Introduction 68
Moving Around the Spreadsheet 70
Entering Dates and Formulas 78
Using Mathematical Operators in Formulas 84
Using Functions 88
Entering Labels 92
Editing Data in the Worksheet 96
Managing Files 100

Creating a Worksheet
Introduction 132
Selecting Commands from Command Menus 134
Using Ranges in the Worksheet 138
Using Worksheet Commands 160
Moving the Contents of a Cell 192
Copying the Contents of a Cell 196
Saving Your Files before You Quit (/Quit) 212
Accessing DOS from 1-2-3 216

Printing Reports

Introduction 218
/Print Printer and /Print File 220
Printing Reports 224
Hiding Rows, Columns, and Ranges 232
Controlling Paper Movement 236
Adding Headers and Footers 242
Printing Cell Contents and Clearing Print Options 250
Preparing Output for Other Programs 254

Creating and Printing Graphs

Introduction 256
An Overview of Creating a Graph 258
Selecting a Graph Type 266
Specifying a Data Range 272
Enhancing the Appearance of a Basic Graph 278
Preserving the Graph on Disk 302
Accessing and Exiting PrintGraph 306
Printing Graphs 310

Managing Data

Introduction 332
What Is a Database? 334
Creating a Database 338
Modifying a Database 346
Sorting Database Records 350
Searching for Records 360

Understanding Macros

Introduction 388
What Is a Macro? 390
The Elements of Macros 392
Planning and Positioning Your Macro 396
Documenting and Naming Your Macros 400
Executing Macros and Using Automatic Macros 404

Appendix

Installing 1-2-3 412

Conventions Used in this Book

A number of conventions are used in 1-2-3 QuickStart to help you learn the program. One example is provided of each convention to help you distinguish among the different elements in 1-2-3.

References to keys are as they appear on the keyboard of the IBM Personal Computer. Direct quotations of words that appear on the screen are spelled as they appear on the screen and are printed in a special typeface. Information you are asked to type is printed in italic; if the context indicates clearly what is to be typed, no special typeface is used.

The first letter of each command from the 1-2-3 menu system appears in boldface: **/R**ange **F**ormat **C**urrency indicates that you type */rfc* to select this command if you are entering it manually. The first letter of menu choices also appears in boldface: **C**opy.

Words printed in uppercase include range names (SALES), functions (@PMT), modes (READY), and cell references (A1..G5).

Conventions that pertain to macros deserve special mention here:

1. Macro names (Alt-character combinations) appear with the backslash (\) and single-character name in lowercase: \a. In this example, the \ indicates that you press the Alt key and hold it down while you also press the A key.

2. 1-2-3 menu keystrokes in a macro line appear in lowercase: /rcn.

3. Range names within macros appear in uppercase: /rncTEST.

4. In macros, representations of cursor-movement keys, such as {DOWN}; function keys, such as {CALC}; and editing keys, such as {DEL}, appear in uppercase letters and are surrounded by braces.

5. Enter is represented by the tilde (~). (Note that throughout the text, Enter is used instead of Return.)

When two keys appear together, for example, Ctrl-Break, you should press the two keys simulatneously. Other key combinations, such as Alt-F10, are performed in the same manner.

To the Reader

1-2-3 QuickStart uses an exciting new approach to introduce the fundamental concepts of 1-2-3 to beginning users. Throughout the book, each 1-2-3 topic is presented in several pages of easy-to-follow text, followed by two or four pages of graphics. The graphics illustrate the topic discussed on the text pages.

Whether you need to create and update financial spreadsheets, develop and maintain a 1-2-3 database, or produce reports and graphics, *1-2-3 QuickStart* is the book for you. The text sections help you understand exactly how to get started quickly with 1-2-3, while the illustrations and captions in the graphics spreads explain and call attention to specific program operations.

After you become familiar with 1-2-3 commands, the keyboard, and the process of creating and printing spreadsheets, databases, and graphics, you can use the graphics in *1-2-3 QuickStart* for reference when you need to be reminded of the steps and sequence of commands. Become productive with 1-2-3 quickly and easily with *1-2-3 QuickStart!*

Introduction

1-2-3® QuickStart is a unique book on 1-2-3. Instead of presenting information exclusively in a text format, *1-2-3 QuickStart* teaches you how to use 1-2-3 by showing you how to perform various tasks. The entire *QuickStart* concept rests on the use of graphics as a method of teaching. In most books, when you read about a concept, you have to visualize the concept in your mind, and then decipher it. With *1-2-3 QuickStart*, we do the visualizing for you.

The book is not entirely graphics, as you will soon see. We've used text to highlight specific elements, to explain steps in a graphic, and to give information about concepts that are too abstract to be explained in a graphic.

How Is This Book Organized?

1-2-3 QuickStart varies from traditional books in more ways than its text-to-graphics ratio. Chapters don't begin on right-hand pages, as they do in other books. Each page in *1-2-3 QuickStart*—whether it's a left or right page—is part of a two-page spread.

Each spread is designed to illustrate a specific topic; often one text spread and one graphic spread is used to discuss the topic fully. Some discussions merit more than two spreads—for these more complex discussions, you will find references to other Que books in which you can find more information.

▼

Learning any new program can be an intimidating experience. Mastering a program as complex and powerful as 1-2-3 often requires a considerable amount of time and effort.

1-2-3 QuickStart is designed to help you shorten your learning curve by allowing you to turn to the topics you need quickly.

The highlighting rectangle on the right side of this page shows the current chapter; the rectangle at the top of this page shows the current topic. By watching the position of these rectangles, you will always know your location in this book.

▲

How Do You Use This Book?

To help you find your way around in *1-2-3 QuickStart*, the chapter titles are listed down the side of the page. The current chapter title is enclosed in a rectangle. The chapter title also is displayed in the upper-left corner of the spread. Across the top of the page, the topics discussed within that particular chapter are listed. Again, a red rectangle is used to call attention to the current section.

Using This Book

1-2-3 QuickStart was designed to help you learn the basics of 1-2-3 as easily as possible.

The QuickStart approach gives you the power of accessing whatever information you seek by using the top right and right margins to show you the sections and chapter titles. This helps you to know, at any given time, where you are within a particular chapter.

Text and graphics are integrated to help you learn 1-2-3 by whatever method is easiest for you.

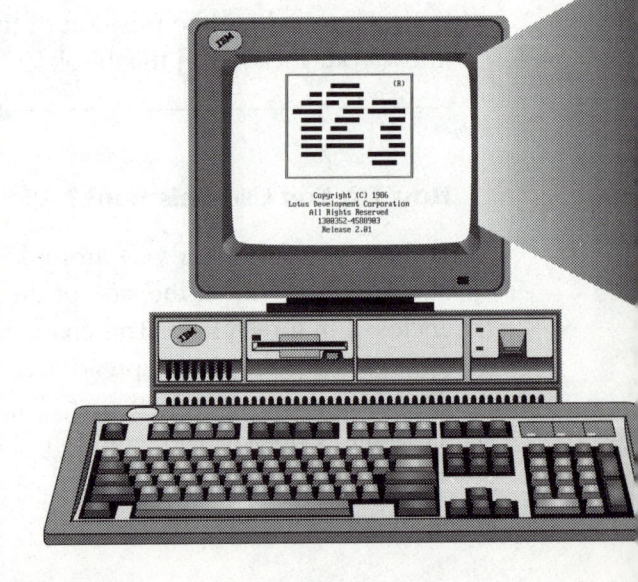

Using this Book

Introduction

An Overview of 1-2-3

Getting Started

1-2-3 Basics

Creating a Worksheet

Printing Reports

Creating and Printing Graphs

Managing Data

Understanding Macros

Appendix

Topics

On the top right margin of the spread, the topics within the current chapter are listed. You'll notice as you flip through the book that the topics change from chapter to chapter. The red rectangle is used to highlight the current topic.

Chapters

The names of chapters are listed across the right margin of the spread.

The current chapter title is enclosed within a rectangle. As you move from chapter to chapter, the rectangle moves to reflect your location in the book.

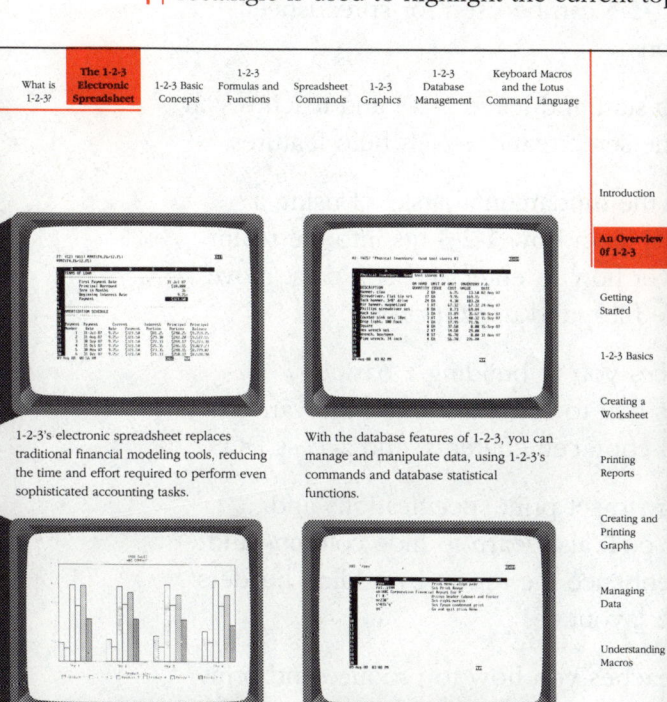

1-2-3's electronic spreadsheet replaces traditional financial modeling tools, reducing the time and effort required to perform even sophisticated accounting tasks.

With the database features of 1-2-3, you can manage and manipulate data, using 1-2-3's commands and database statistical functions.

1-2-3's graphic capabilities let you create five different graph types.

Using 1-2-3's macros and command language, you can automate and customize 1-2-3 for your particular application.

5

Using This Book

What Does This Book Contain?

The chapters in *1-2-3 QuickStart* are organized to take you from basic information to more sophisticated tasks, including printing reports and creating graphs.

"An Overview of 1-2-3" shows you the wide range of 1-2-3's capabilities. You'll explore how 1-2-3 can be used for spreadsheet, graphics, and database applications.

"Getting Started" explains how to start and leave 1-2-3 and teaches you the basics about the keyboard, the screen, and 1-2-3's help features.

"1-2-3 Basics" teaches you about the fundamental tasks of using a spreadsheet. In this chapter, you'll learn how 1-2-3 fits into the realm of integrated software and discover how to enter and edit data, move around in the worksheet, manage files, and use functions.

"Creating a Spreadsheet" introduces you to building a basic spreadsheet. This chapter teaches you to use ranges, use the various worksheet commands, move and copy cell contents, and access DOS.

"Printing Reports" shows you how to set print specifications and organize your data for printing. You'll also learn to hide columns and rows, control paper movement, enhance the report by adding headers and footers, and change the page layout.

"Creating and Printing Graphs" teaches you how to produce and print graphs with 1-2-3. This chapter takes you from selecting graph types to adding titles and legends to printing with PrintGraph. In addition, this chapter teaches you to set and change print specifications and preview graphs before printing.

"Managing Data" explains how to use 1-2-3 for data management. You'll learn to create and modify a database and sort and search for specific records.

"Understanding Macros" gives you an introduction to the concept of the keyboard macro. This chapter teaches you to plan, position, name, create, and edit a simple macro.

This book concludes with one appendix ("Installing 1-2-3") and an index. As you'll notice from the index, each topic is referenced in only one or two places. This apparent "lack" of cross-referencing actually means that we've done our job well; we've grouped all information about a particular topic in one section—or chapter—of this book.

Who Should Use This Book?

1-2-3 QuickStart is designed to be a quick guide for new 1-2-3 users. Whether you are just sitting down with 1-2-3 for the first time or are trying—for the umpteenth time—to learn enough about 1-2-3 to use it efficiently, *1-2-3 QuickStart* gives you enough information to get you going quickly. By presenting topics in a text and graphic format, *1-2-3 QuickStart* highlights important concepts and takes you through important information by providing steps and explanations interwoven with graphics.

What Do You Need To Use This Book?

There are no prerequisites to using this book, or, for that matter, to using 1-2-3. This text assumes of course, that you have the software, the hardware, and a desire to learn to use the program.

1 An Overview of 1-2-3

Before you put your fingers to the keyboard and start using 1-2-3, you need to know the range of capabilities 1-2-3 gives you. If you are inheriting a spreadsheet that someone else created, coming up to speed with 1-2-3 may require little more of you than simply entering data. If, on the other hand, someone has handed you the 1-2-3 package and said "Prepare a forecast for product A," your task may seem a bit intimidating. For that reason, whether you are an experienced spreadsheet user or a novice, this chapter will show you the wide range of capabilities offered by 1-2-3 and will help you understand how 1-2-3 will fit into your day-to-day tasks.

As you read through this chapter, ask yourself which of the 1-2-3 features you'll be using most often. Will you be maintaining an accounts receivable spreadsheet? Perhaps your department is in charge of setting up a database to track inventory. Will you be responsible for printing reports and graphs? Whatever the application, read the appropriate overview sections closely, and look for chapter references at the end of those sections for the chapters in this book that deal more specifically with that topic.

Whether you are an experienced spreadsheet user who is just new to 1-2-3 or you are a complete computer novice, you will find that 1-2-3 is not a difficult program, per se. Like anything else, your point of reference means everything. If you start by learning the basic concepts of 1-2-3 and then gradually build on your expertise, bit by bit, you'll be amazed by how easily you'll learn the program. If you opt to jump right in and start using string functions right away, you may find yourself running into snags. In this book, we take the easy, step-by-step approach.

Key Terms Used in This Chapter

electronic spreadsheet	The 1-2-3 spreadsheet is known as the electronic replacement for the accountant's pad.
cell	The intersection of a row and a column in the 1-2-3 spreadsheet.
cell pointer	The highlighted bar that allows you to enter data into the spreadsheet.
formula	A formula, such as +A1+B1+C1, performs an action on a specified cell or range of cells.
function	A function is like a "shorthand" method of using formulas. For example, instead of typing the formula +A1+B1+C1, you could use the SUM function @SUM(A1..C1).
command	A command is used to carry out an operation on the spreadsheet.

What Is Covered in This Chapter?

In this chapter, you will learn about the following:

- How 1-2-3 functions as a spreadsheet
- Basic spreadsheet concepts
- The graphics capabilities of 1-2-3
- How 1-2-3 handles data management tasks

9

The 1-2-3 Electronic Spreadsheet

1-2-3 integrates graphics and data management with a first-rate spreadsheet. 1-2-3's overall design, built-in functions, and commands are based on the conventions used by early spreadsheet programs. Although those conventions are still part of 1-2-3, today they are greatly improved, making 1-2-3 the most popular business software ever developed.

At the most basic level, 1-2-3 can be defined as an integrated program that can produce

- Financial spreadsheets
- Database applications
- Reports
- Graphs
- Macros

What are the conventions that make 1-2-3 an excellent spreadsheet program? First, 1-2-3 is designed as an "electronic" replacement for the accountant's columnar pad, pencil, and calculator. Second, 1-2-3 understands relationships among all of the numbers and formulas in a single application and automatically updates values whenever a change occurs. Third, 1-2-3's commands simplify and automate all the procedures related to creating, changing, updating, printing, and graphing spreadsheet data.

Basically, 1-2-3 is an electronic version of the accountant's columnar pad, pencil, and calculator. Spreadsheets give users the freedom to create, change, and analyze financial models with a minimum of time and effort.

The electronic spreadsheet is the foundation of the 1-2-3 program. The framework of this spreadsheet contains the graphics and data-management elements of the program. You produce graphics through the use of spreadsheet commands. Data management occurs in the standard row-column spreadsheet layout.

The importance of the spreadsheet as the basis for the whole product cannot be overemphasized. All the commands for the related features are initiated from the same main command menu as the spreadsheet commands, and all the commands are in the same style. All of 1-2-3's special features originate from the spreadsheet. For instance, in data management, the database is composed of records that are cell entries in a spreadsheet. Similarly, macros and Command Language programs are statements placed in adjacent cells in out-of-the-way sections of a spreadsheet. And all the commands for displaying graphs refer to entries in the spreadsheet and use these entries to draw graphs on the screen.

The typical electronic spreadsheet configures a computer's memory to resemble an accountant's columnar pad. Because this "pad" exists in the dynamic world of the computer's memory, the pad is different from paper pads in some important ways. For one thing, electronic spreadsheets are much larger than their paper counterparts. 1-2-3 has 8,192 rows and 256 columns!

The 1-2-3 Electronic Spreadsheet

The 1-2-3 spreadsheet replaces the accounting tools ordinarily used for financial tasks. The pad, pencil, and calculator have been replaced with a screen, cursor, and coprocessor that together give you more power, speed, and accuracy for all your spreadsheet operations.

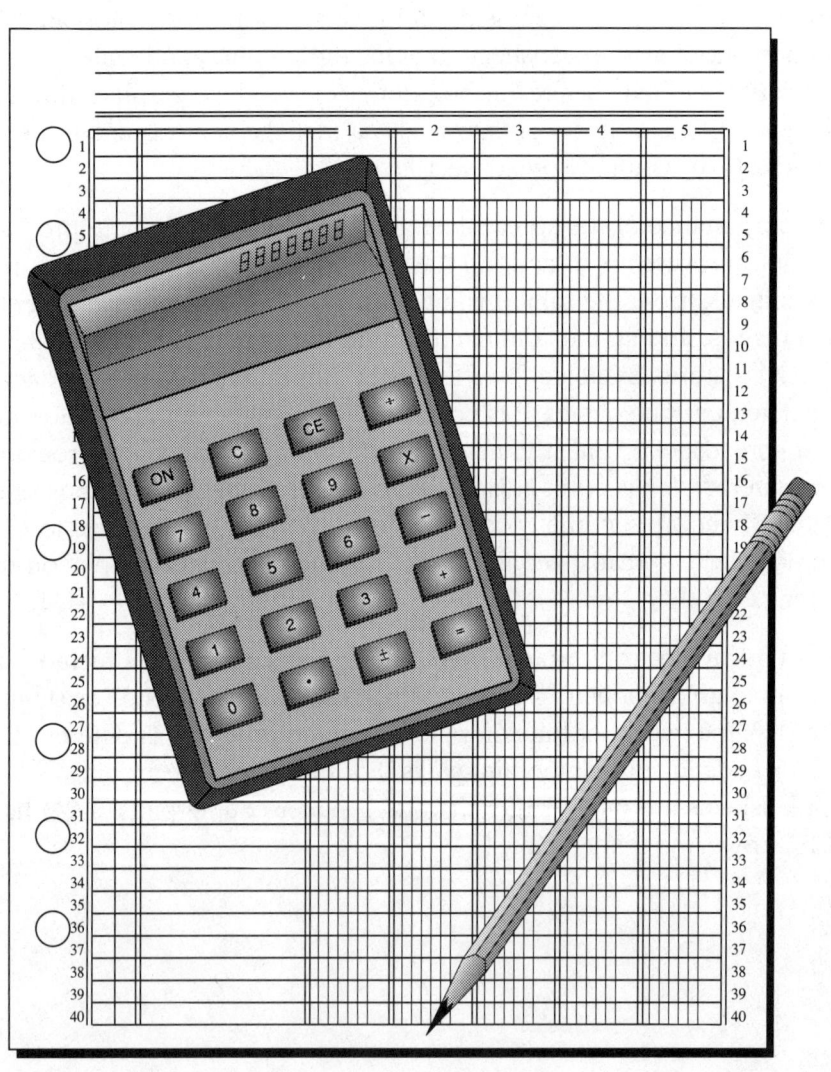

What Is 1-2-3?	**The 1-2-3 Electronic Spreadsheet**	1-2-3 Basic Concepts	1-2-3 Formulas and Functions	Spreadsheet Commands	1-2-3 Graphics	1-2-3 Database Management	Keyboard Macros and the Lotus Command Language

Introduction

An Overview of 1-2-3

Instead of writing data by hand on a pad of paper, you type data in columns.

Getting Started

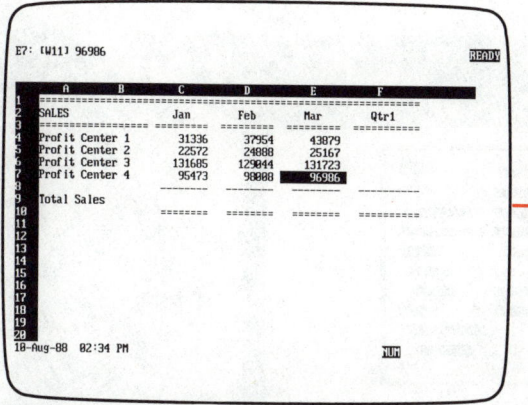

1-2-3 Basics

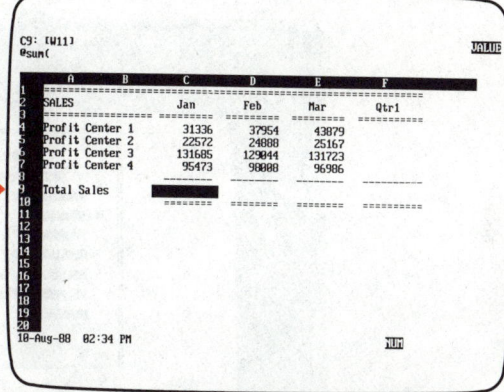

Creating a Worksheet

Printing Reports

No more pressing buttons on the calculator or trying to remember complex formulas.

To sum a column of data, for example, you simply type @ s u m (.

Creating and Printing Graphs

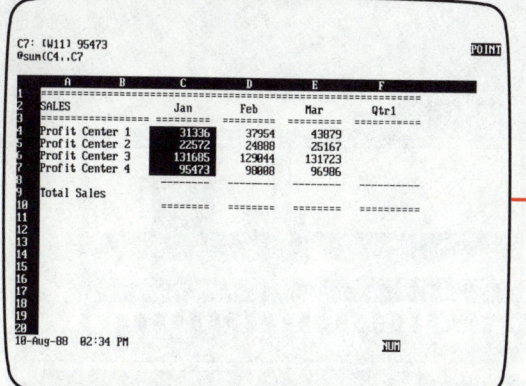

Managing Data

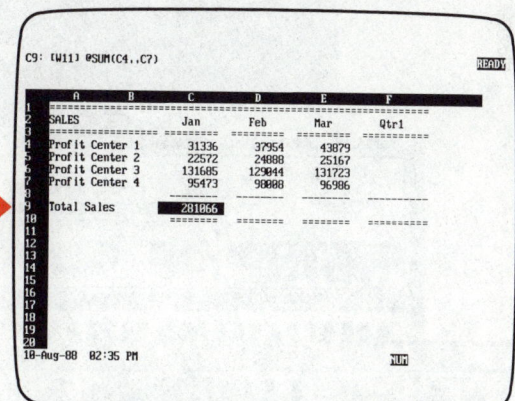

Understanding Macros

Move the cell pointer to C7, press . (period), and move the cell pointer to C4.

Finally, type) and press ↵Enter.

Appendix

13

The 1-2-3 Electronic Spreadsheet

What is 1-2-3?

1-2-3 is an integrated spreadsheet program that is capable of much more than just number crunching.

| What Is 1-2-3? | **The 1-2-3 Electronic Spreadsheet** | 1-2-3 Basic Concepts | 1-2-3 Formulas and Functions | Spreadsheet Commands | 1-2-3 Graphics | 1-2-3 Database Management | Keyboard Macros and the Lotus Command Language |

Introduction

An Overview of 1-2-3

Getting Started

1-2-3 Basics

Creating a Worksheet

Printing Reports

Creating and Printing Graphs

Managing Data

Understanding Macros

Appendix

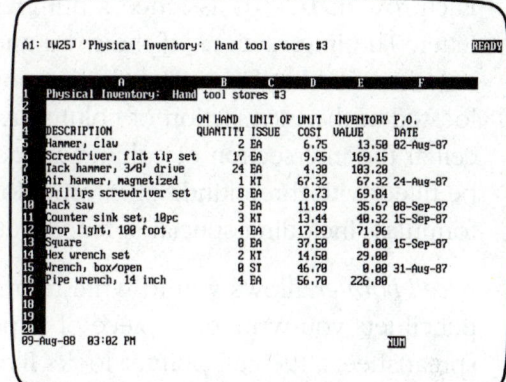

1-2-3's electronic spreadsheet replaces traditional financial modeling tools, reducing the time and effort required to perform even sophisticated accounting tasks.

With the database features of 1-2-3, you can manage and manipulate data, using 1-2-3's commands and database statistical functions.

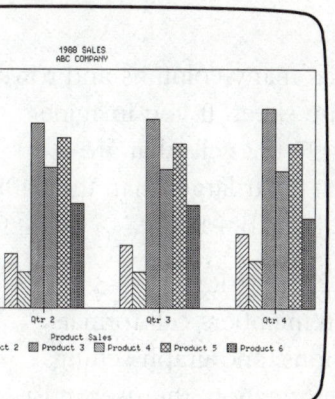

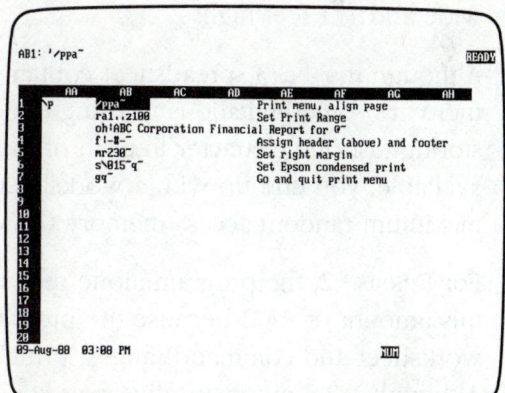

1-2-3's graphic capabilities let you create five different graph types.

Using 1-2-3's macros and command language, you can automate and customize 1-2-3 for your particular application.

15

1-2-3 Basic Concepts

Each row in 1-2-3 is assigned a number, and each column is assigned a letter. The intersections of the rows and columns are called *cells*. Cells are identified by their row-column coordinates. For example, the cell located at the intersection of column A and row 15 is called A15. The cell at the intersection of column X and row 55 is called X55. Cells can be filled with three kinds of information: numbers; mathematical formulas, including special spreadsheet functions; and text (or labels).

A *cell pointer* allows you to write information into the cells much as a pencil lets you write on a piece of paper. In 1-2-3, as in most spreadsheets, the cell pointer looks like a bright rectangle on the computer's screen. The cell pointer typically is one row high and one column wide.

With 8,192 rows and 256 columns, the 1-2-3 worksheet contains more than 2,000,000 cells. Each column is assigned a letter value ranging from A for the first column to IV for the last. A good way to visualize the worksheet is as one giant sheet of grid paper that is about 21 feet wide and 171 feet high!

Although the 1-2-3 spreadsheet contains that many columns and rows, there are some limitations to using the entire sheet. If you imagine storing just one character in each of the 2,097,152 cells that are available, you end up with a worksheet that is far larger than the 640K maximum random-access memory (RAM) of an IBM PC.

For Release 2, the program alone requires 215K of RAM. 1-2-3 needs this amount of RAM because the program remembers cell formats, worksheet and command ranges, print options, and graph settings. Although 1-2-3 automatically saves some information, the user must also save some information in 1-2-3.

Key 1-2-3 concepts to remember:

- The 1-2-3 spreadsheet contains 8,192 rows and 256 columns.
- Each row on the 1-2-3 spreadsheet is assigned a number.
- Each column on the 1-2-3 spreadsheet is assigned a letter.
- A *cell* is the intersection of a column and a row.
- Cells are identified by their column and row coordinates (such as A2, B4, and F10).
- The *cell pointer* is the highlighted rectangle that allows you to enter data into the spreadsheet.

Because the 1-2-3 grid is so large, you cannot view the entire spreadsheet on the screen at one time. The screen thus serves as a window onto the worksheet. To view other parts of the sheet, you scroll the cell pointer across and down (or up) the worksheet with the arrow keys. When the cell pointer reaches the edge of the current window, the window begins to shift to follow the cell pointer across and down (or up) the spreadsheet.

To illustrate the window concept, imagine cutting a hole one inch square in a piece of cardboard. If you placed the cardboard over this page, you would be able to see only a one-inch square piece of text. Naturally, the rest of the text is still on the page; it is simply hidden from view. When you move the cardboard around the page (in much the same way that the window moves when the cursor-movement keys are used), different parts of the page become visible.

1-2-3 Basic Concepts

The 1-2-3 spreadsheet contains 8,192 rows and 256 columns. The section of the worksheet you see on-screen is actually only a portion of the entire spreadsheet.

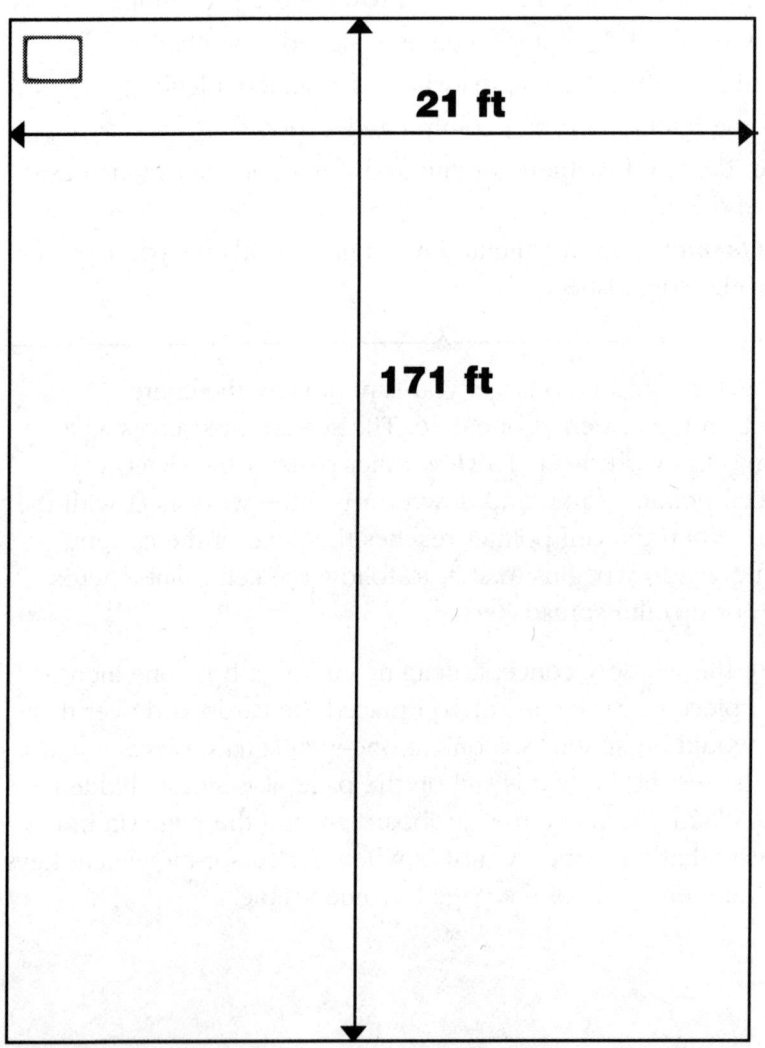

Spreadsheet total size.

| What Is 1-2-3? | The 1-2-3 Electronic Spreadsheet | **1-2-3 Basic Concepts** | 1-2-3 Formulas and Functions | Spreadsheet Commands | 1-2-3 Graphics | 1-2-3 Database Management | Keyboard Macros and the Lotus Command Language |

Introduction

An Overview of 1-2-3

Getting Started

1-2-3 Basics

Creating a Worksheet

Printing Reports

Creating and Printing Graphs

Managing Data

Understanding Macros

Appendix

The default 1-2-3 worksheet displays eight columns (each nine characters wide) and twenty rows. You can change the number of columns displayed, however, by narrowing or widening one or more of the columns.

19

1-2-3 Formulas and Functions

Electronic spreadsheets allow mathematical relationships to be created between cells. For example, if the cell named C1 contains the formula

    +A1+B1

then C1 will display the sum of the contents of cells A1 and B1. (The + sign before A1 tells 1-2-3 that what you have entered into this cell is a formula, not text.) The cell references serve as variables in the equation. No matter what numbers you enter into cells A1 and B1, cell C1 will always return their sum.

Playing "What If"

1-2-3 allows you to play "what if" with your model. After you have built a set of mathematical relationships into the worksheet, you can recalculate the worksheet with amazing speed, using different sets of assumptions. If you use only paper, a pencil, and a calculator to build your models, every change to the model will require recalculating every relationship in the model. If the model has 100 formulas and you change the first one, you must make 100 calculations by hand so that the change flows through the entire model. If you use a spreadsheet, however, the same change requires the press of only a few keys; the program does the rest. This capability permits extensive "what if" analysis.

1-2-3 Functions

As you know, you can create simple formulas involving only a few cells by entering cell addresses with the appropriate operator (+, -, /, *). 1-2-3 functions are the tools for creating complex formulas. Spreadsheet functions are shortcuts that help the user perform common mathematical computations with a minimum of typing. Functions are like abbreviations for otherwise long and cumbersome formulas. You use an @ symbol to signal 1-2-3 that an expression is a function. For instance, the SUM function in 1-2-3 is written as @SUM(A1..C1).

1-2-3 offers all the spreadsheet functions you would expect to find in a powerful spreadsheet program—and then some. The following list describes each of these function types.

Mathematical functions: For business, engineering, and scientific use. Includes mathematical functions, trigonometric functions, a random-number-generator function, and functions for rounding and determining remainders.

Financial functions: Basic financial functions for net present value and internal rate of return calculations, plus a complete set of functions for annuity, compound growth rate calculations, and depreciation.

Statistical functions: For calculating the sum, average, minimum, maximum, count, variance, and standard deviation of a range of values. Also includes database statistical functions.

String functions: For manipulating strings.

Date and time functions: For manipulating dates and times.

Special functions: For changing numeric entries to strings (and vice versa) and managing the use of both numbers and strings in your worksheets.

1-2-3 Formulas and Functions

1-2-3's "What If" Capability

One of the biggest benefits of 1-2-3 is the program's "what if" capability. You can forecast sales for two products over the next six months and recalculate the revenue totals for different discounts.

50% Average Discount

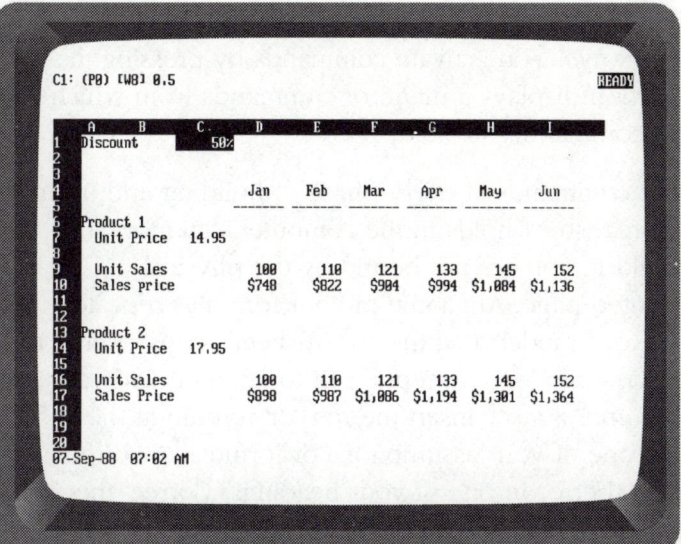

You can enter 50% into C1, and 1-2-3 will calculate the total sales.

55% Average Discount

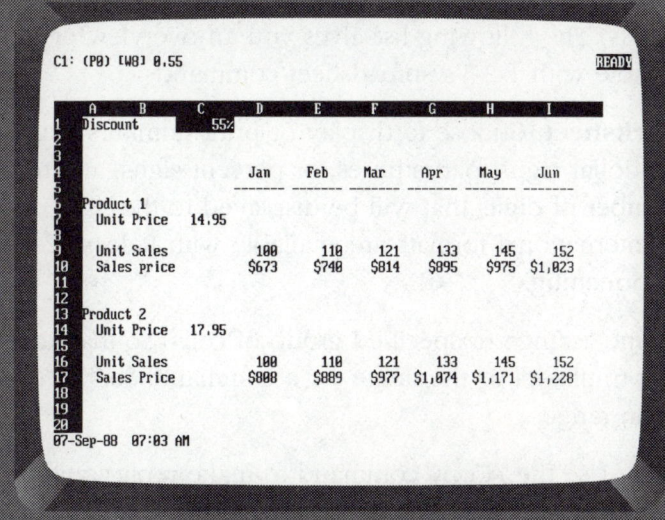

You can change 50% to 55%, and 1-2-3 will recalculate sales price figures.

Spreadsheet Commands

1-2-3 includes several important commands that manipulate the worksheet in various ways. You activate commands by pressing the slash (/) key. This action displays a menu of commands from which you can choose the command you want.

You use spreadsheet commands at every phase of building and using a model. Because a spreadsheet holds in the computer's memory a model while you build it, you are not bound by the physical limitations of the printed page. Are some of your formulas repeated in different sections of your model? Use the spreadsheet's copy feature to quickly project your assumptions from one cell to another. Did you forget a row or a column? Simply insert the row or column at the appropriate point. Is one of your assumptions or formulas incorrect, or is there a typographical error in one of your headings? Correct the error instantly with 1-2-3's editing capabilities.

1-2-3 has many commands that allow you to perform a number of tasks in the spreadsheet. Commands are available to format the worksheet, name ranges, erase and copy data, perform calculations, store files, protect worksheet cells, protect files with passwords, and print your spreadsheets. The following list gives you an overview of the capabilities available with 1-2-3's spreadsheet commands.

Formatting the worksheet: Choose to display or print numbers with embedded commas, dollar signs, parentheses, or percent signs, and to specify the exact number of digits that will be displayed to the right of the decimal. (Note: International formats are available with Release 2.) Chapter 4 explains formatting.

Naming ranges: Name a range (a specified group of cells) so that you can use the area in formulas or as the range for a command. See Chapter 4 for more on ranges.

Copying cell entries: Use the /Copy command to make replicas of values, labels, or formulas in other cells, saving yourself time and typing trouble. Copy is discussed in Chapter 4.

Recalculating the worksheet: 1-2-3 offers a natural order of recalculation or iterative calculations. Natural recalculation discerns and evaluates first the most fundamental cell in the worksheet (that is, the cell on which most other cells are based); then natural recalculation progresses to the second most basic cell in the worksheet and evaluates that one, and so on, continuing until the entire worksheet is recalculated. Iterative calculation allows you to control the number of times a particular worksheet is recalculated. Recalculation is explained in Chapter 4.

1-2-3 file commands: Choose from basic loading and saving commands, load a text file from another program, import files from leading database and spreadsheet programs, and read Release 1A and Symphony® worksheets. (Note: Release 2 can translate to the file formats of those two programs as well.) You can create three types of files in 1-2-3: normal spreadsheet files (.WK1); text files (.PRN); and graph files (.PIC). 1-2-3's file commands are discussed in Chapter 3.

Protecting cells and files: Protect cells in a worksheet so that changes cannot be made, for example, in cells that contain important formulas. Hide ranges of cells and use passwords to protect worksheets when they are saved to disk. 1-2-3 also lets you password protect your worksheet files when you save them. A password-protected file is encrypted and cannot be examined or retrieved without the password. Your confidential or sensitive data is protected from use by anyone who does not have the correct password. Chapter 4 deals with cell and file protection.

Printing the worksheet: 1-2-3 has more printing flexibility than any other spreadsheet. Print the entire worksheet or any part of the worksheet. In addition, you can alter the left, right, top, and bottom margins on the page; change the page length and width; insert page headers and footers, which can even contain the date and page number; and send setup codes to the printer to alter the size and style of type used to print. Printing is covered in Chapter 5.

25

Spreadsheet Commands

When you are working with the 1-2-3 worksheet, you are actually seeing only a portion of the entire spreadsheet. Similarly, although you see only the values in the cells, 1-2-3 stores all the data, formulas, and formats in memory.

| What Is 1-2-3? | The 1-2-3 Electronic Spreadsheet | 1-2-3 Basic Concepts | 1-2-3 Formulas and Functions | **Spreadsheet Commands** | 1-2-3 Graphics | 1-2-3 Database Management | Keyboard Macros and the Lotus Command Language |

Introduction

An Overview of 1-2-3

Getting Started

1-2-3 Basics

Creating a Worksheet

Printing Reports

Creating and Printing Graphs

Managing Data

Understanding Macros

Appendix

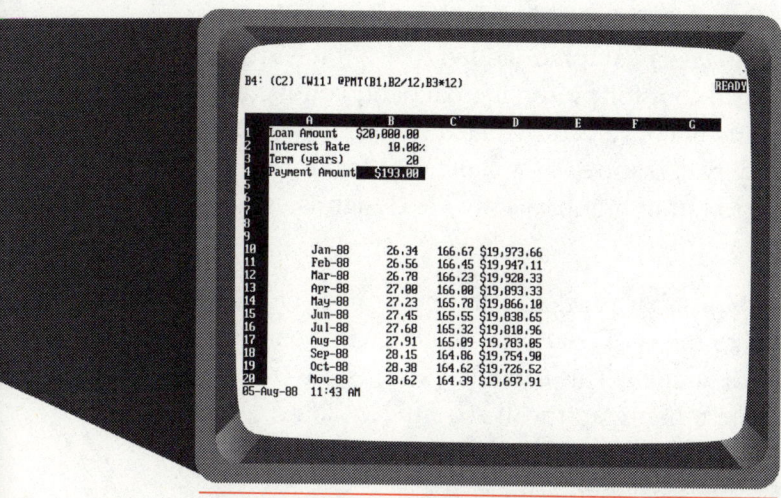

Here's what you see when you are working on a simple 1-2-3 spreadsheet. The values are displayed, not the formulas "behind" them. As you can see, the cell pointer is positioned on B4, and the formula for B4 is displayed in the control panel at the top of the screen.

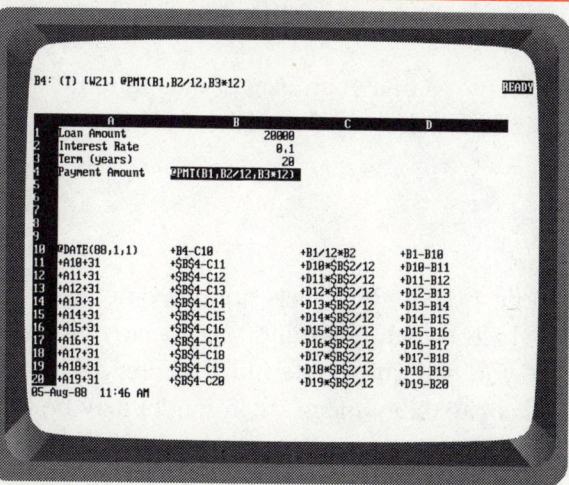

1-2-3 stores all the formulas with the worksheet. The formula in B4 is the same formula that is displayed in the control panel when cell B4 is highlighted.

27

1-2-3 Graphics

The spreadsheet alone makes 1-2-3 a powerful program with all the capabilities needed by many users. Graphics added to 1-2-3's spreadsheet extend 1-2-3 as a tool for presenting data and conducting "what if" analyses. As originally conceived by Mitch Kapor, the creator of 1-2-3, graphics capability was planned as a significant feature of 1-2-3. Mitch Kapor's background in graphics software design is evident in 1-2-3's graphics portion.

1-2-3 has five basic graph types: bar, stacked bar, line, scatter, and pie. You can represent up to six ranges of data on a single graph (except for pie graphs and scatter diagrams). This capability means, for example, that you can create a line graph with six different lines.

Create graphs with 1-2-3's **/G**raph command. Although the program has a number of options, the user need specify only a graph type and a single data range. After providing the required information, the user simply types **V**, for **V**iew. This command will plot the graph to the screen. If the computer has both a graphics and a text display, the graph will appear on the graphics screen while the spreadsheet remains on the text monitor. If you have only a graphics monitor, the graph will replace the spreadsheet on the display until you press a key.

With 1-2-3's graphing capability, you have an exceptional amount of flexibility in choosing the format, color, shading, labels, titles, and subtitles for graphs.

"What If" with Graphics

The most exciting thing about 1-2-3's graphics is not the variety of graphs, but the degree to which the graphics and spreadsheet elements are interrelated. With 1-2-3, you can quickly design and alter graphs as worksheet data changes. This capability means that graphs may be changed almost as fast as 1-2-3 recalculates the data.

You can perform true graphics "what if" analyses with 1-2-3. In fact, you can use the F10 function key on the IBM PC and PS/2 computers to replot a graph after making changes to the worksheet, without having to redefine the graph with the **/G** command. This replotting immediately shows the effects of changes on the current graph.

Printing Graphics

Because the basic 1-2-3 program is not capable of producing printed graphics, the program is accompanied by a second program, called PrintGraph, which you use to create printed or plotted copies of graphs. After you create a graph in 1-2-3, you can save the graph in a file on a disk. Create these files, called .PIC files, with the **/GS** (for **/G**raph **S**ave) command. The graph files can then be read into the PrintGraph program for additional formatting and printing.

The PrintGraph program offers a number of options for further formatting before the graphs are printed. The Color option allows parts of the graph to be assigned different colors. The Font option allows the labels and titles in the graph to be printed in one or several of eight different fonts, including a script face and a block face. The Size option allows the user to specify the size of the printed graph. A graph can be printed full size to occupy an entire printed page, or half size to fill half a page; or a manual option can be chosen. After the options have been selected, the PrintGraph program will print the graph to the specified graphics device.

With previous graphics software, the time and trouble involved in creating and changing graphs often outweighed the benefits. 1-2-3 graphs, however, can be quickly and easily created and changed. With 1-2-3, managers will use graphs more frequently, both to increase their own understanding and to communicate their analyses to others.

1-2-3 Graphics

With 1-2-3's **/G**raph command, you can easily create five different types of graphs directly from the worksheet. Each graph you create can then be printed with 1-2-3's PrintGraph program.

| What Is 1-2-3? | The 1-2-3 Electronic Spreadsheet | 1-2-3 Basic Concepts | 1-2-3 Formulas and Functions | Spreadsheet Commands | **1-2-3 Graphics** | 1-2-3 Database Management | Keyboard Macros and the Lotus Command Language |

1-2-3's PrintGraph program provides options for printing labels and titles in one of eight different fonts. PrintGraph also lets you change the size of the graph.

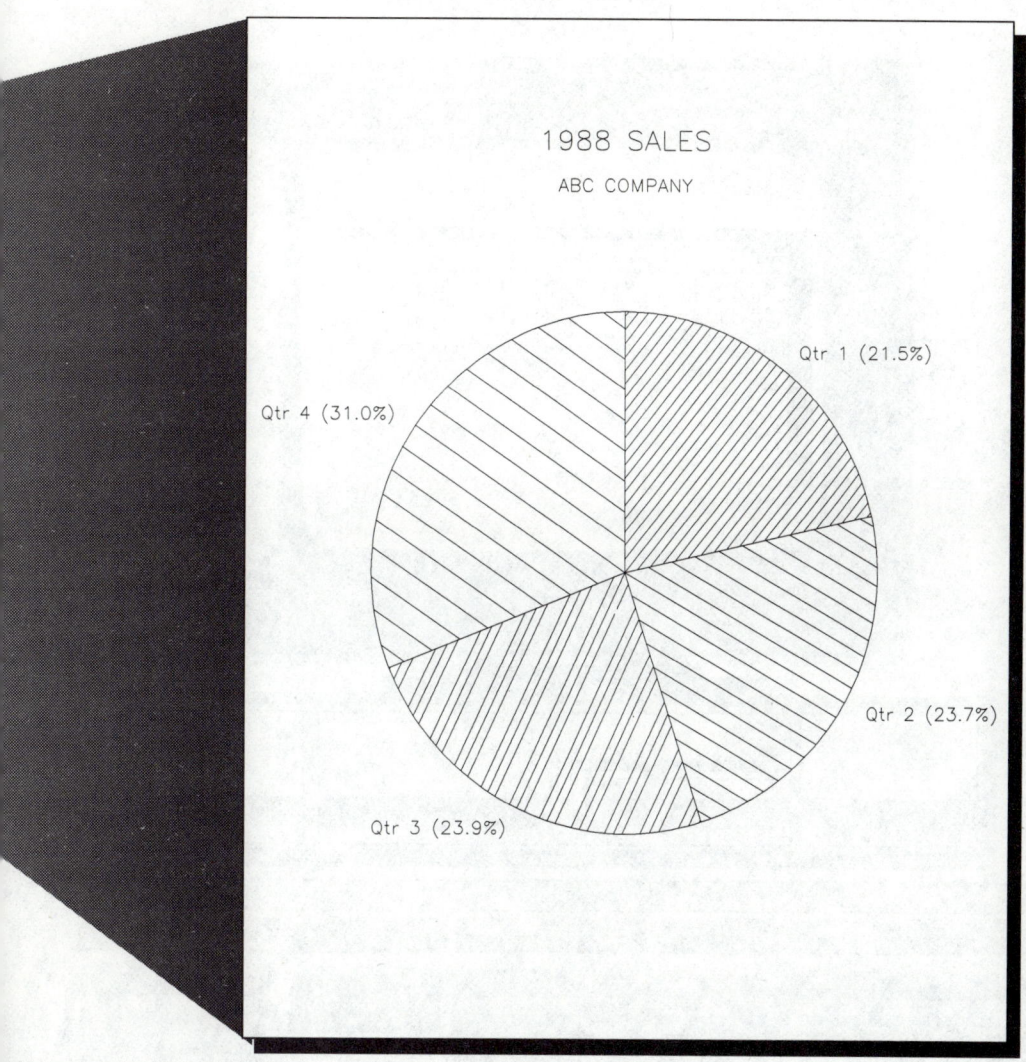

1988 SALES
ABC COMPANY

- Qtr 1 (21.5%)
- Qtr 2 (23.7%)
- Qtr 3 (23.9%)
- Qtr 4 (31.0%)

Introduction

An Overview of 1-2-3

Getting Started

1-2-3 Basics

Creating a Worksheet

Printing Reports

Creating and Printing Graphs

Managing Data

Understanding Macros

Appendix

31

1-2-3 Graphics

1-2-3's Graphic Capabilities

1-2-3's graphic capabilities give you a powerful way to present your data. In addition to 1-2-3's five basic graph types, you can choose the format, color, shading, labels, titles, and subtitles for graphs.

| What Is 1-2-3? | The 1-2-3 Electronic Spreadsheet | 1-2-3 Basic Concepts | 1-2-3 Formulas and Functions | Spreadsheet Commands | **1-2-3 Graphics** | 1-2-3 Database Management | Keyboard Macros and the Lotus Command Language |

Introduction

An Overview of 1-2-3

Getting Started

1-2-3 Basics

Creating a Worksheet

Printing Reports

Creating and Printing Graphs

Managing Data

Understanding Macros

Appendix

The line graph is the default graph for 1-2-3, meaning that if you do not specify a particular type, 1-2-3 will display the data as a line graph.

The bar graph is typically used to show the trend of numeric data across time, often comparing two or more data items.

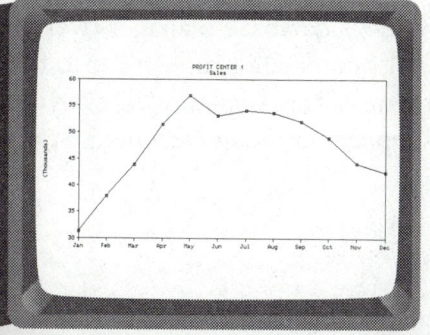

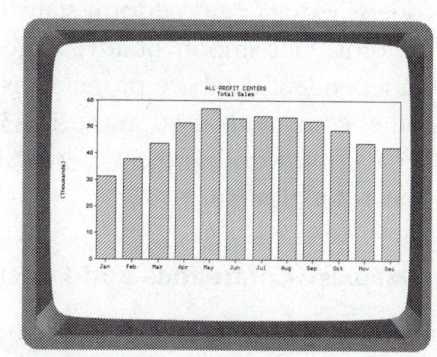

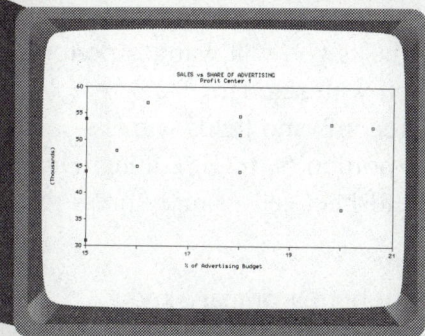

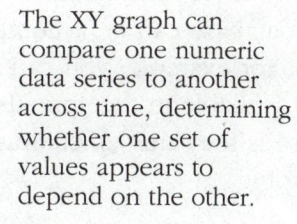

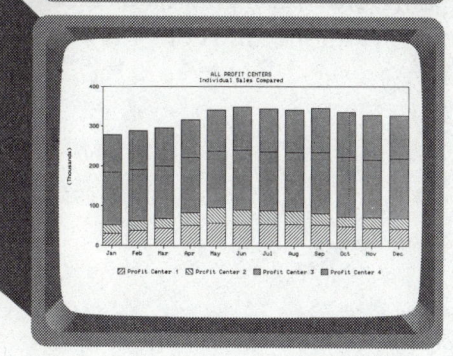

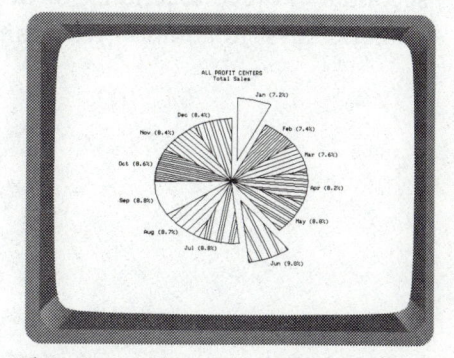

The XY graph can compare one numeric data series to another across time, determining whether one set of values appears to depend on the other.

The stacked bar type graphs two or more data series that total 100 percent of a specific category.

The pie graphs graph only one data series, the components of which total 100 percent of a specific numeric category.

33

1-2-3 Database Management

The column-row structure used to store data in a spreadsheet program is similar to the structure of a relational database. 1-2-3 provides true database-management commands and functions so that you can sort, query, extract, and perform statistical analyses on data in up to 8,192 records. One important advantage of 1-2-3's database manager over independent database programs is that its commands are similar to the other commands used in the 1-2-3 program. This similarity allows you to learn how to use the 1-2-3 database manager along with the rest of the 1-2-3 program.

Database Commands and Functions

Once you have built a database in 1-2-3 (which is no different from building any other spreadsheet table), you can perform a variety of functions on the database. Some of the tasks you will want to perform on a 1-2-3 database can be accomplished with standard 1-2-3 commands. For example, you can add records and fields with commands available in the spreadsheet portion of 1-2-3. Editing data in the database is the same as editing spreadsheet cells; simply press F2 and start typing.

You can also sort data. You can sort with both a primary and a secondary key, in ascending or descending order, using alphabetic or numeric keys. In addition, you can perform various kinds of mathematical analyses on a field of data over a specified range of records. For example, you can count the number of items in a database that match a set of criteria; compute a mean, variance, or standard deviation; and find the maximum or minimum value in the range. The capacity to perform statistical analysis on a database is an advanced feature for database management systems on any microcomputer.

Other database operations require database commands, such as **/DQU** (**/D**ata **Q**uery **U**nique) and **/DQF** (**/D**ata **Q**uery **F**ind). Several commands help the user make inquiries and clean the data of duplications. All of these commands are subcommands of the **/DQ** (**/D**ata **Q**uery) command.

You have several options for defining criteria with 1-2-3. The criteria range can contain up to 32 cells across the worksheet, with each cell containing multiple criteria. You can use numbers, text, and complex formulas as criteria.

1-2-3 also has a special set of statistical functions that operate only on information stored in the database. Like the query commands, the statistical functions use criteria to determine on which records they will operate. The database functions include @DCOUNT, @DSUM, @DAVG, @DVAR, @DSTD, @DMAX, and @DMIN.

35

1-2-3 Database Management

1-2-3's Database Capabilities

As you know, 1-2-3 is more than just a sophisticated number cruncher. In addition to the program's financial and graphical features, 1-2-3 offers a data management capability that uses many of the spreadsheet's powerful tools.

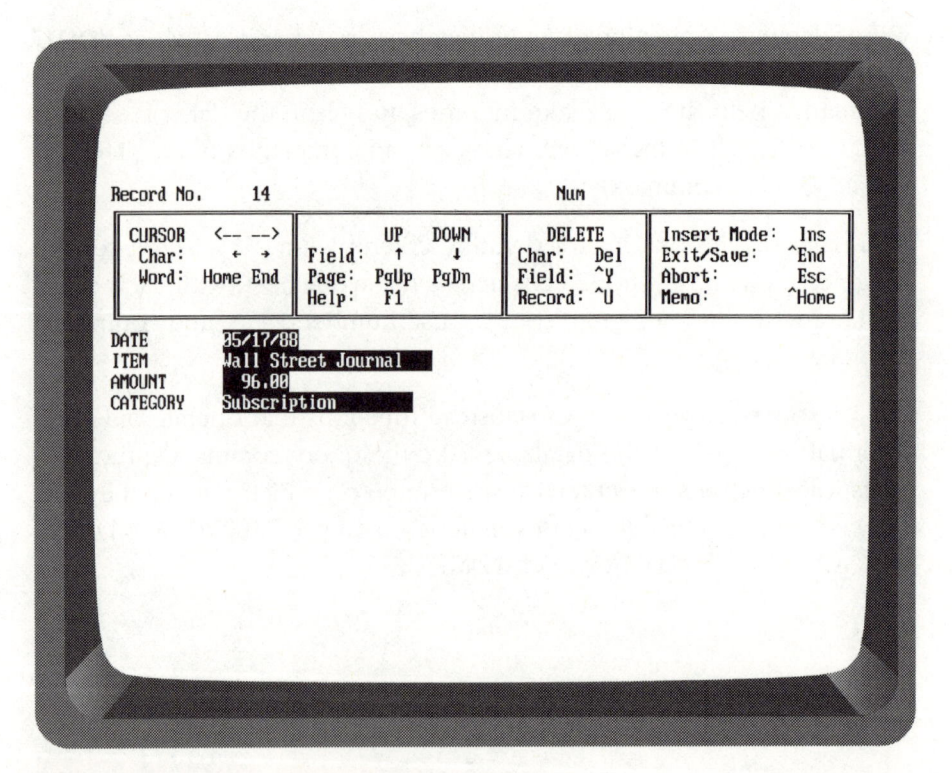

```
Record No.     14                              Num

CURSOR    <-- -->              UP    DOWN    DELETE          Insert Mode:  Ins
  Char:    ←   →      Field:    ↑     ↓       Char:  Del     Exit/Save:    ^End
  Word:   Home End    Page:   PgUp   PgDn     Field: ^Y      Abort:        Esc
                      Help:    F1             Record: ^U     Memo:         ^Home

DATE       05/17/88
ITEM       Wall Street Journal
AMOUNT         96.00
CATEGORY   Subscription
```

With dBASE III Plus, you can create a form screen for entering each record into your database.

| What Is 1-2-3? | The 1-2-3 Electronic Spreadsheet | 1-2-3 Basic Concepts | 1-2-3 Formulas and Functions | Spreadsheet Commands | 1-2-3 Graphics | **1-2-3 Database Management** | Keyboard Macros and the Lotus Command Language |

Introduction

An Overview of 1-2-3

Getting Started

1-2-3 Basics

Creating a Worksheet

Printing Reports

Creating and Printing Graphs

Managing Data

Understanding Macros

Appendix

A row in 1-2-3 is equal to a record in a conventional database. In that record, you might store a client's name, address, and phone number.

1-2-3 has sophisticated facilities for performing sort and search operations. You can order the database on any number of items and by a number of criterion, and you can locate a particular record with a few simple keystrokes.

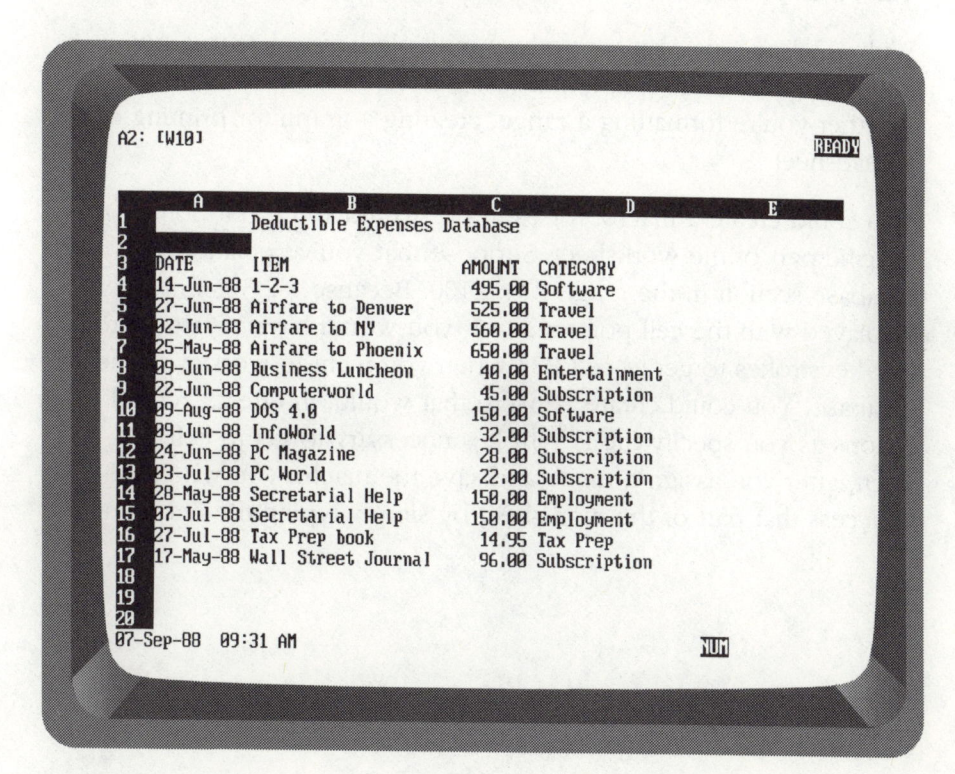

```
A2: [W10]                                                    READY

        A           B              C          D         E
 1              Deductible Expenses Database
 2
 3   DATE       ITEM                AMOUNT  CATEGORY
 4   14-Jun-88  1-2-3                495.00 Software
 5   27-Jun-88  Airfare to Denver    525.00 Travel
 6   02-Jun-88  Airfare to NY        560.00 Travel
 7   25-May-88  Airfare to Phoenix   650.00 Travel
 8   09-Jun-88  Business Luncheon     40.00 Entertainment
 9   22-Jun-88  Computerworld         45.00 Subscription
10   09-Aug-88  DOS 4.0              150.00 Software
11   09-Jun-88  InfoWorld             32.00 Subscription
12   24-Jun-88  PC Magazine           28.00 Subscription
13   03-Jul-88  PC World              22.00 Subscription
14   28-May-88  Secretarial Help     150.00 Employment
15   07-Jul-88  Secretarial Help     150.00 Employment
16   27-Jul-88  Tax Prep book         14.95 Tax Prep
17   17-May-88  Wall Street Journal   96.00 Subscription
18
19
20
07-Sep-88  09:31 AM                                         NUM
```

Using 1-2-3, you enter records across a single row.

37

Keyboard Macros and the Command Language

In addition to all of the capabilities available from the commands in 1-2-3's main menu, two other features make 1-2-3 the most powerful and popular integrated spreadsheet, graphics, and database program available today. Using 1-2-3's macros and Command Language, you can automate and customize 1-2-3 for your particular applications.

1-2-3's Keyboard Macros

With 1-2-3 macros, you can reduce multiple keystrokes to a two-keystroke operation: simply press two keys, and 1-2-3 does the rest, whether you're formatting a range, creating a graph, or printing a spreadsheet.

You could create a macro, for example, to move the cell pointer to a specific part of the worksheet. Suppose that you've positioned a database section in the range R23..Z100. Because 1-2-3 is first displayed with the cell pointer at A1, you would have to use quite a few keystrokes to get to cell R23 when you want to work with the database. You could create a macro that would, in effect, "record" your actions as you specify the keystrokes necessary to get to cell R23. Then, after you assign a name and save the macro, you would be able to access that part of the worksheet by simply typing the macro name.

The Lotus Command Language

You can best think of macros as the building blocks for Command Language programs. When you begin to add commands from the Command Language to simple keystroke macros, you can control and automate many of the actions required to build, modify, and update 1-2-3 models. At its most sophisticated level, 1-2-3's Command Language can be used as a full-fledged programming language for developing custom business applications.

When you use 1-2-3's Command Language, you'll see what kind of power is available for your 1-2-3 applications. For the application developer, the Command Language is much like a programming language (such as BASIC), but the programming process is simplified significantly by all the powerful features of 1-2-3's spreadsheet, database, and graphics commands.

The Command Language includes over 40 "invisible" commands that are not available from the keyboard to give you a greater range of control over your 1-2-3 applications.

Keyboard Macros and the Command Language

What Is a Macro?

A macro is a short program that reduces the number of keystrokes you must type to carry out a particular operation. 1-2-3 macros can save you time by automatically performing command sequences you use frequently.

Consider the following macro:

'/rfc0~~

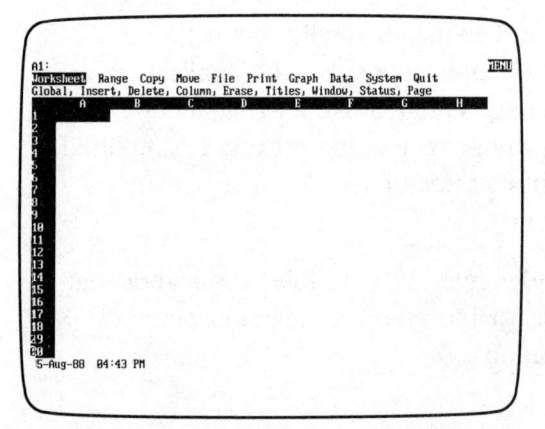

Except for the ' character, this macro is actually a shortcut that condenses the following steps:

/ signals 1-2-3 to display the main menu.

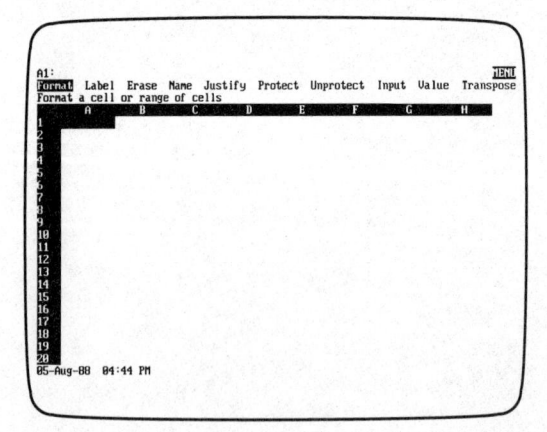

r selects **R**ange

f selects **F**ormat

40

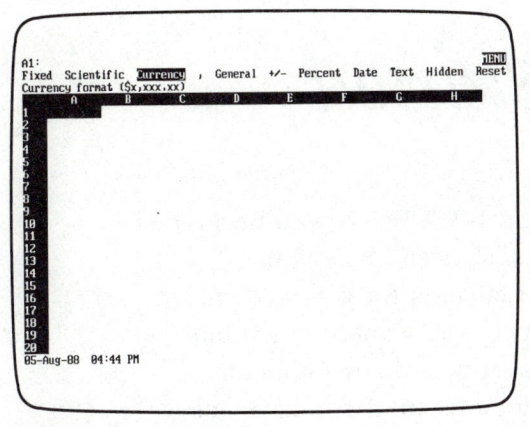

C selects **C**urrency

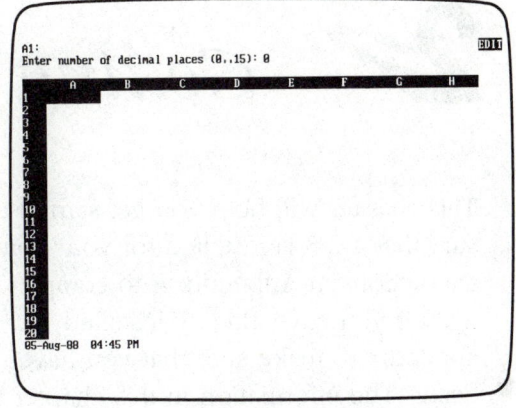

0 tells 1-2-3 to suppress the display of digits to the right of the decimal.

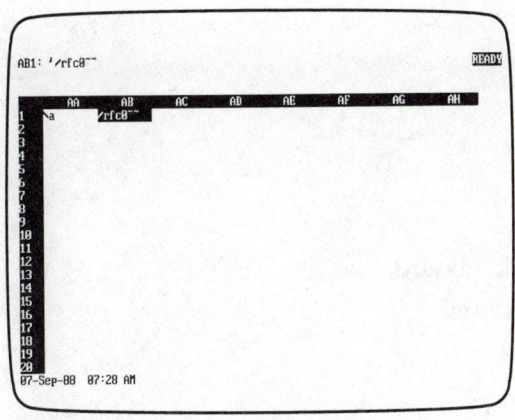

~ ~ are two tildes that, when used in a macro, represent the ⏎Enter key to 1-2-3.

What Is the Command Language?

The Command Language uses over 40 "invisible" commands that are not available from the keyboard to give you a greater range of control over your 1-2-3 applications.

41

2 *Getting Started*

This chapter will help you get started using 1-2-3. Before you begin, be sure that 1-2-3 is installed for your computer system. Follow the instructions in Appendix A to complete installation for your system. Even if you have already installed 1-2-3, you may want to check the appendix to make sure that you haven't overlooked any important details. The information in this chapter will be useful if you have little familiarity with computers or with 1-2-3. If you find this introductory material too basic and want to begin using the 1-2-3 spreadsheet immediately, skip to Chapter 3.

What is Covered in This Chapter?

In this chapter, you will learn about

- Starting 1-2-3
- Exiting 1-2-3
- Saving a 1-2-3 worksheet file
- Using the keys on your computer keyboard
- Using the 1-2-3 help system and tutorial

Key Terms Used in This Chapter

1-2-3 Access System	The 1-2-3 menu system that links all of 1-2-3's different functions, including the main 1-2-3 program and programs for printing graphs, translating non-1-2-3 files, installing 1-2-3, and accessing the 1-2-3 tutorial.
alphanumeric keys	The keys in the center section of your computer keyboard. Many of these keys function the same as those on a typewriter.
numeric keypad	The keys on the right side of the IBM PC, AT, and enhanced keyboards. This keypad is used for entering and calculating numbers and can also be used for moving the cursor on your computer screen.
function keys	The 10 keys on the left side of the PC and AT keyboards and the 12 keys at the top of the enhanced keyboard. These keys are used for special functions, such as accessing help, editing cells, and recalculating the worksheet.
control panel	The area above the reverse-video border of the 1-2-3 worksheet, containing three lines that display important information about the contents of a cell, command options and explanations, or special prompts and messages.

Starting 1-2-3

Starting 1-2-3 from DOS

Starting 1-2-3 from DOS requires several steps. (We're assuming that the 1-2-3 program is on your hard disk in a subdirectory named 123.)

Start 1-2-3 on a hard disk system as follows:

1. With the C> system prompt displayed on your screen, change to the 123 directory by typing *CD\123* and pressing Enter.
2. Start 1-2-3 by typing *123* and pressing Enter.

If you have a two floppy or a microfloppy disk system, the startup procedure is slightly different. (Note that in this book we use the term *microfloppy* to refer to the 3 1/2-inch disks that are used by the IBM PC Convertible and PS/2 computers.)

Start 1-2-3 on a floppy system as follows:

1. After booting your computer with your DOS disk, remove the DOS disk and place the 1-2-3 System disk into drive A.
2. If the A> prompt is not displayed, type *A:* and press Enter.
3. Start 1-2-3 by typing *123* at the A> system prompt, and press Enter.

After a few seconds, the 1-2-3 logo appears. The logo remains on-screen for a few seconds; then the worksheet is displayed, and you're ready to use 1-2-3.

Starting 1-2-3 from the 1-2-3 Access System

Lotus devised the 1-2-3 Access System as a way to link all of 1-2-3's different functions. This system is useful for moving quickly between the programs in the 1-2-3 package. Additionally, the Access System provides a series of menus that enable you to translate between 1-2-3 and other programs, such as dBASE®, Symphony®, and VisiCalc®.

To start the 1-2-3 Access System on a hard disk system,

1. Type *CD \123* and press Enter.
2. Type *lotus* at the C> prompt and press Enter.

To start the 1-2-3 Access System on a floppy system,

1. Place the 1-2-3 System disk into drive A.
2. Type *A:* and press Enter.
3. Type *lotus* and press Enter.

The 1-2-3 Access System then appears. The following paragraphs explain each of the options in the Access System's menu bar.

1-2-3, logically enough, starts 1-2-3. Be sure that you have the System disk in drive A if you are using a two-drive system.

PrintGraph initiates the PrintGraph program for printing graphs. For more about this topic, see Chapter 6.

Translate accesses the Translate utility. This utility provides a link between Release 1A and 2 of 1-2-3, and between 1-2-3 and outside programs like dBASE, Symphony, Jazz®, and VisiCalc. For more about the Translate utility, see *Using 1-2-3,* Special Edition.

Install accesses the Install program, which you use to change the options set during installation. For more information and complete installation instructions, see Appendix A.

View takes you though the 1-2-3 tutorial, "A View of 1-2-3."

Starting 1-2-3

You can start 1-2-3 in two different ways: from within the 1-2-3 Access System, or directly from DOS. Most users start directly from DOS because this method is easier, faster, and uses less memory.

| Introduction | **Starting 1-2-3** | Exiting 1-2-3 | Learning the Keyboard | Learning the Screen Display | Using 1-2-3's Help Feature |

Starting 1-2-3 Directly From DOS

```
C>CD\123
C>123
```

```
A>123
```

On a hard disk system, change directories by typing `CD\123` and press `Enter`. Next type `123` and press `Enter`.

On a two floppy drive system, put the System disk in drive A, then type `123` and press `Enter`.

Starting Access System From DOS

```
C>CD\123
C>lotus
```

```
A>lotus
```

On a hard disk system, type `CD\123` and press `Enter`, then type `LOTUS` and press `Enter`.

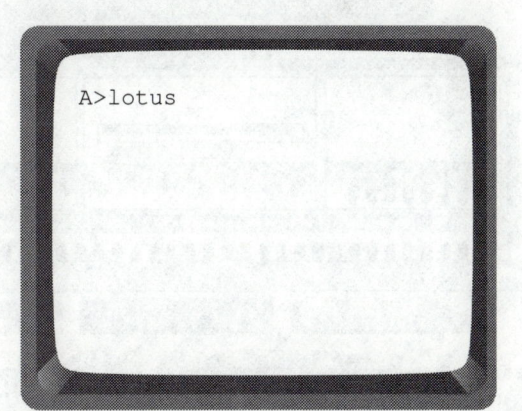

On a two floppy drive system, put the System disk in drive A. Now type `LOTUS` and press `Enter`.

Introduction

An Overview of 1-2-3

Getting Started

1-2-3 Basics

Creating a Worksheet

Printing Reports

Creating and Printing Graphs

Managing Data

Understanding Macros

Appendix

47

Starting 1-2-3

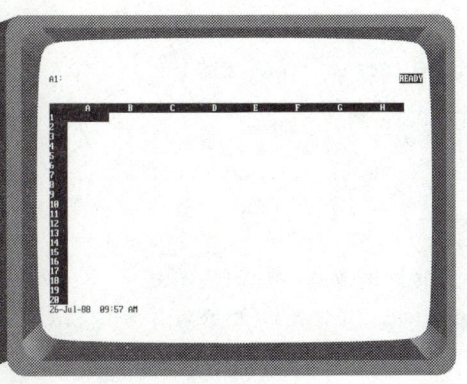

| Introduction | **Starting 1-2-3** | Exiting 1-2-3 | Learning the Keyboard | Learning the Screen Display | Using 1-2-3's Help Feature |

1-2-3 starts 1-2-3.

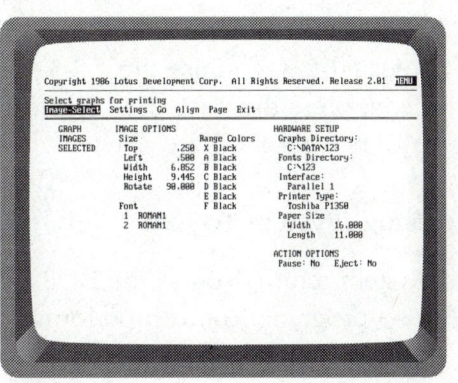

PrintGraph accesses the PrintGraph program, used for printing graphs from 1-2-3.

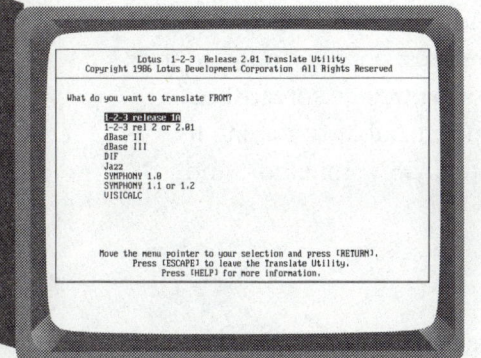

Translate allows you to translate files between 1-2-3 and other popular programs.

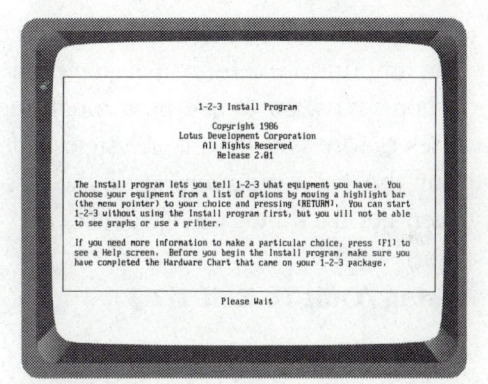

Install activates the installation procedure for 1-2-3.

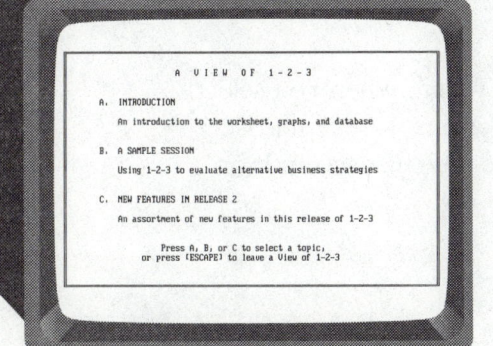

View takes you through the 1-2-3 tutorial, called A View of 1-2-3.

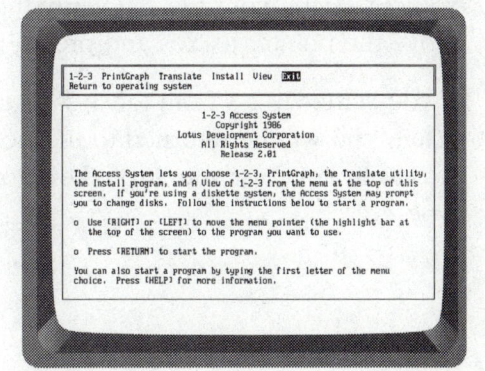

Exit quits the 1-2-3 program and takes you to DOS.

Introduction

An Overview of 1-2-3

Getting Started

1-2-3 Basics

Creating a Worksheet

Printing Reports

Creating and Printing Graphs

Managing Data

Understanding Macros

Appendix

49

Exiting 1-2-3

To exit 1-2-3, you use the 1-2-3 main command menu. To access the menu, press the slash (/) key. The two commands you'll use to return to DOS from 1-2-3 are **/S**ystem and **/Q**uit.

Using /System To Exit 1-2-3

/System returns you to the DOS system prompt but does not exit the 1-2-3 program. You can perform system operations at the DOS level, including changing directories and drives, and then return to the 1-2-3 spreadsheet by typing *exit*. To select the **S**ystem option, type *s* or use the pointer to highlight the selection.

You'll find that **/S**ystem is a useful command when you need to check the amount of memory you have on disk before you copy a file to it or when you want to see how much memory a particular spreadsheet uses before you load it. **/S**ystem saves you the trouble of having to quit the 1-2-3 program, issue the appropriate DOS commands, and then get back into the spreadsheet.

Using /Quit To Exit 1-2-3

/Quit, also available on the 1-2-3 main menu, allows you to exit the worksheet and the 1-2-3 program. You are asked to verify this choice before you exit 1-2-3 because your data will be lost if you quit 1-2-3 without saving your file. To verify that you want to exit, type *y* or move the pointer to **Y**es and press Enter.

If you started 1-2-3 from the 1-2-3 Access System, when you select **/Q**uit, you will be returned to the Access System. To exit the 1-2-3 Access System, use the arrow keys to move the cursor to **exit** or type *e*.

Before You Quit, /File Save

There is one danger with computerized spreadsheeting that does not exist in the paper-and-pencil world. If you keep track of your business accounts on an accountant's pad, using pencil, paper, and pocket calculator, when you decide to quit working, you simply get up from your desk and walk away. There's nothing to "exit," nothing to turn off (except, perhaps, the calculator), and nothing that might cause your work to vanish from your desk. The accountant's pad, with its hand-written numbers, remains on the desk until morning, when you are ready to start again.

With electronic spreadsheets—and with computer files in general—the risk of a power outage or unavoidable human error can be costly in terms of data and time. If you select **/Q**uit without having saved your file, and then—not thinking—select **Y**es at the verification prompt, you're out of luck as far as your data is concerned. Any work you'd done since the last time you saved the file is lost; you can only recover the data by typing it back in.

To use **/F**ile **S**ave,

1. Display the 1-2-3 main menu by typing /
2. Select **F**ile by positioning the cursor on that item or by typing *f* (Press enter if you have selected the command by moving the cursor.)
3. Choose **S**ave or press *s*.
4. Enter a file name that you haven't used before; one that in some way identifies the file so that you will be able to find it later.
5. Press Enter, and the file is saved to disk.

51

Exiting 1-2-3

Using /System To Exit 1-2-3

/System returns you to the DOS system prompt but does not exit the 1-2-3 program. You can perform system operations at the DOS level, including changing directories and drives, and then return to the 1-2-3 spreadsheet by typing ⒺⓍⒾⓉ.

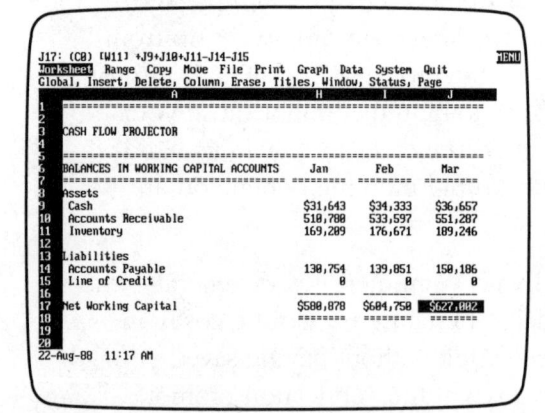

Access the **/S**ystem command by first pressing ⑦.

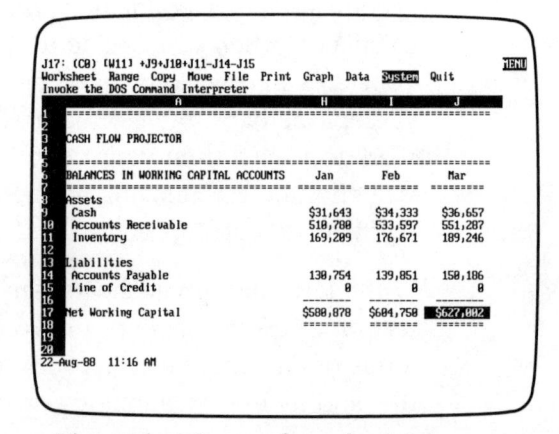

Then select **S**ystem from the 1-2-3 menu bar.

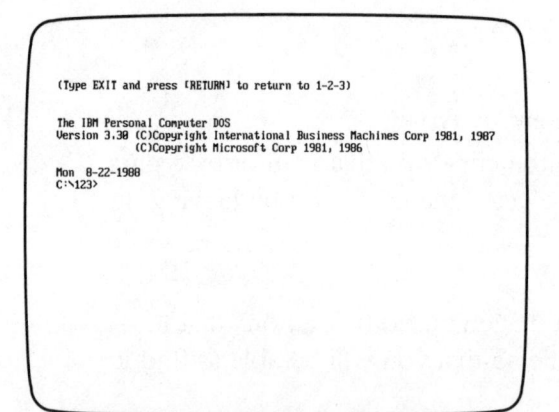

When the DOS prompt is displayed, you can perform various DOS operations or access another program.

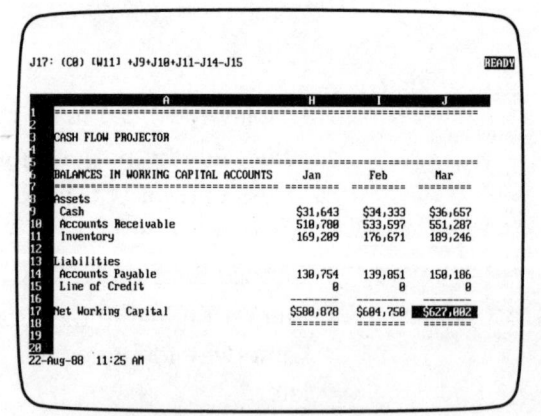

When you are ready to return to 1-2-3, type ⒺⓍⒾⓉ and you are returned to the current worksheet, in the exact place you issued the **/S**ystem command.

52

Using /Quit To Exit 1-2-3

/Quit exits the worksheet and the 1-2-3 program. You are asked to verify this choice before you exit 1-2-3 because your data will be lost if you quit 1-2-3 without saving your file. To verify that you want to exit, type **Y** or move the pointer to Yes and press ⏎Enter.

Call up the 1-2-3 menu by pressing /.

Remember to use **F**ile **S**ave first, if you haven't already done so.

Select **/Q**uit.

Verify that you want to leave 1-2-3 by selecting **Y**es.

53

Learning the Keyboard

Before you begin learning 1-2-3, you need to get to know your keyboard. The three most popular keyboards, which are shown in the graphics on the next pages, are divided into three sections: the alphanumeric keys on the center, the numeric keypad on the right, and the function key section on the left or across the top. The IBM enhanced keyboard, used on PS/2 computers, also has a separate grouping of cursor-movement keys.

The Alphanumeric Keys

Although most alphanumeric keys are the same as those on a typewriter, in 1-2-3, several of the keys have special functions. For example, you'll use the slash (/) key to access the 1-2-3 menu and the period (.) key to separate all addresses when a range of cells is defined. The graphic on page 59 highlights each of these important keys.

The Numeric Keypad and Cursor-Movement Keys

The keys in the numeric keypad and on the right side of the IBM PC and AT keyboards are used mainly for cursor movement. The PS/2 enhanced keyboard has separate keys for cursor movement.

When you want to use the numeric keypad to enter numbers rather than to position the cursor (on the PC or AT keyboards), you can either press Num Lock before and after you enter the numbers or press Shift when you press the number keys.

Neither way is ideal because you have to worry about switching between functions. PS/2 owners don't have this problem. If you don't have a PS/2, you can create a simple macro to handle the problem for you.

The Function Keys

The function keys F1 through F10 are used for special tasks, such as accessing Help, editing cells, and recalculating the worksheet. A plastic function-key template that reminds you of each key's function on the IBM-PC is provided by Lotus. Another version of the template is available for COMPAQ® owners. The graphics on the next pages provide illustrations of each of the keyboards. On page 59, you will find a table that explains each key's function.

Learning the Keyboard

The keyboard of the IBM PC.

Function Keys   Alpha-Numeric   Numeric
                          Keys   Keypad /
                                             Cursor Keys

56

| | Starting | Exiting | **Learning the Keyboard** | Learning the Screen | Using 1-2-3's Help |
| Introduction | 1-2-3 | 1-2-3 | | Display | Feature |

The keyboard of the IBM Personal Computer AT.

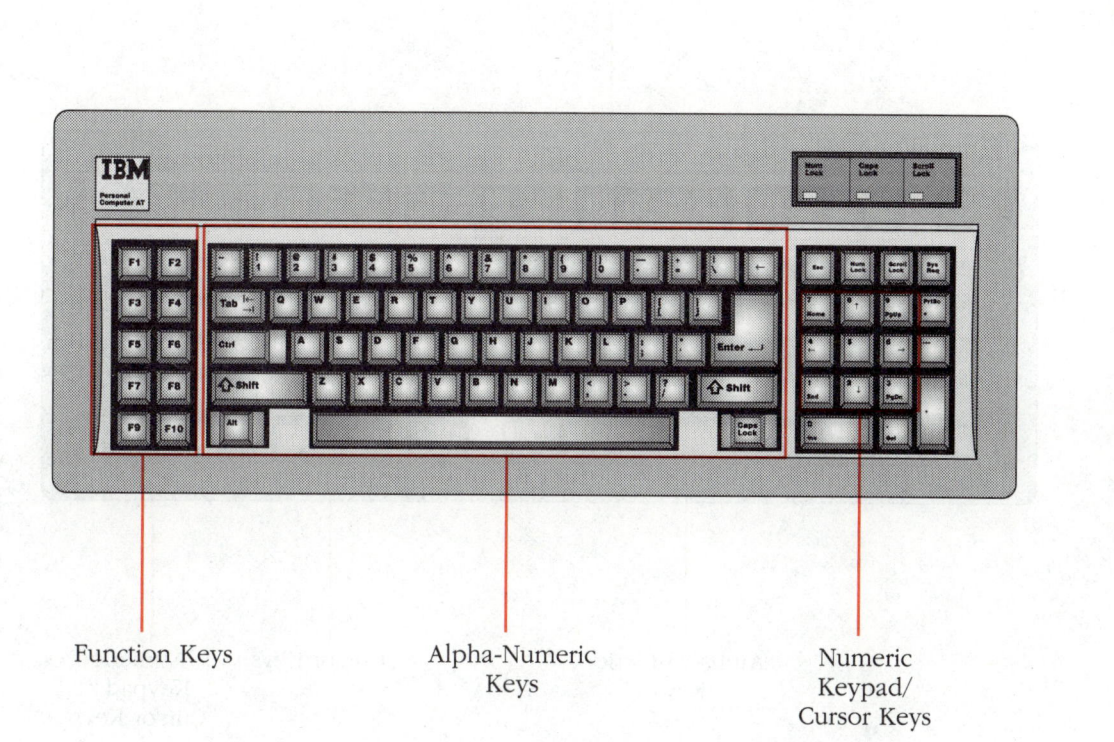

Function Keys   Alpha-Numeric Keys   Numeric Keypad/ Cursor Keys

Introduction

An Overview of 1-2-3

Getting Started

1-2-3 Basics

Creating a Worksheet

Printing Reports

Creating and Printing Graphs

Managing Data

Understanding Macros

Appendix

57

Learning the Keyboard

The IBM Extended Keyboard.

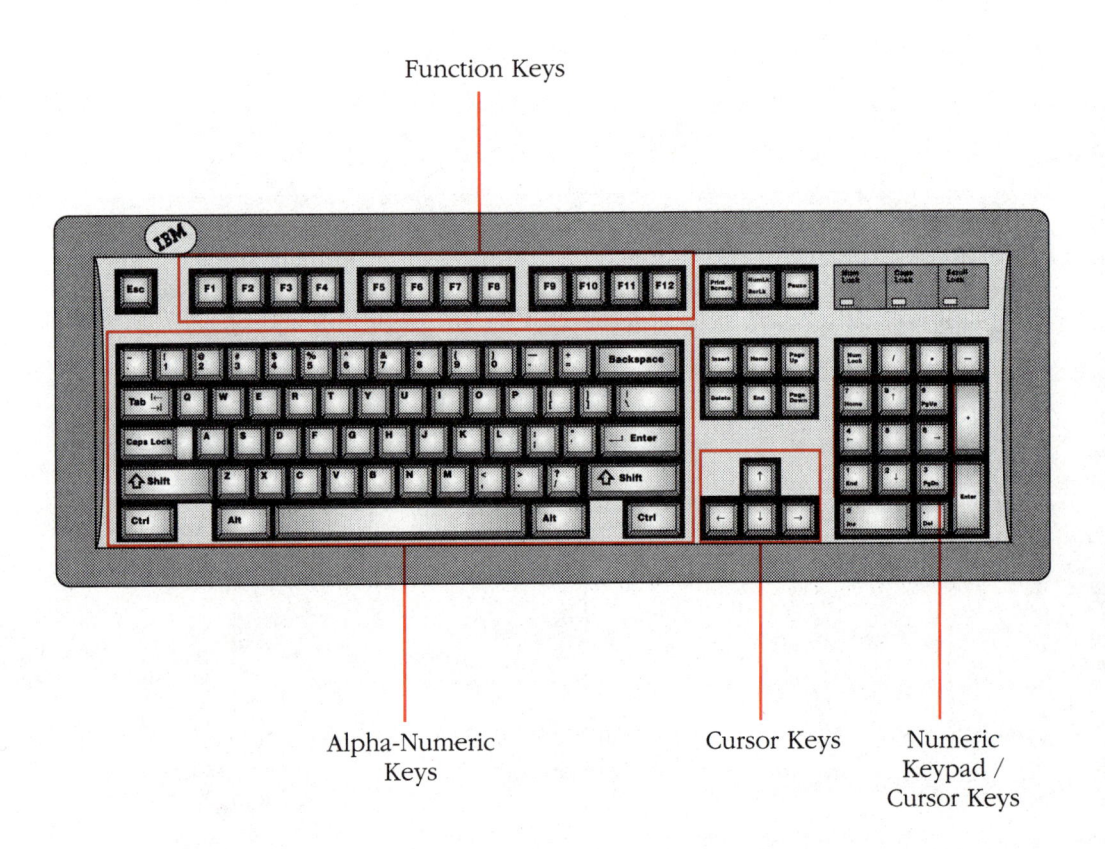

Function Keys

Alpha-Numeric Keys

Cursor Keys

Numeric Keypad / Cursor Keys

Tab — Moves cursor one screen right. **Shift Tab** moves cursor one screen left.

Alt — When used with other keystrokes, invokes macros and Command Language programs.

Shift — Changes lowercase to uppercase letters and characters. When not in Num Lock mode, allows you to type numbers on the numeric keypad.

Backspace — During cell definition, erases the previous character in a cell.

?/ — Calls up the 1-2-3 main menu and can function as a division sign.

>. — Separates cell addresses and anchors cell addresses during pointing. Also used as a decimal point.

Num Lock — Activates the numeric character of keys in the numeric keypad.

Esc — Escapes from command menu and moves to previous menu; erases current entry during range of command specification, returns from a help screen.

Del — Deletes character above cursor during editing process.

NumLk ScrLk — In Scroll Lock position, scrolls entire screen one row or column when pointer is moved; in Break position, is used with **Ctrl** to return 1-2-3 to READY mode or to halt execution of macro.

Function Keys

F1 (Help) Accesses 1-2-3's on-line help facility.

F2 (Edit) Shifts 1-2-3 to EDIT mode.

F3 (Name) In POINT mode, displays a list of range names in worksheet. Pressing **F3** a second time switches to a full screen display of range names.

F4 (Abs) During cell definition, changes a relative cell address into an absolute or mixed address.

F5 (GoTo) Moves cursor to cell coordinates (or range name) provided.

F6 (Window) Moves cursor to the other side of a split screen.

F7 (Query) Repeats the most recent Data Query operation.

F8 (Table) Repeats the most recent Data Table operation.

F9 (Calc) Recalculates the worksheet.

F10 (Graph) Redraws graph defined by the current graph settings.

Learning the Screen Display

The main 1-2-3 display is divided into two parts: the control panel at the top of the screen and the worksheet area. A reverse border separates the two areas. This border contains the letters and numbers that mark the columns and rows.

Other important areas of the screen are the mode indicators (upper right corner), the lock key indicators (lower right corner), and the message area (lower left corner). The message area normally shows the date and time, but will show an error message when certain kinds of errors are made.

The Control Panel

The control panel is the area above the reverse-video border. This area has three lines, each with a special purpose. The first line, F7:(C2)[W11]CPMT@PMT(F4,F6/12,F5), contains information about the *current cell* (the cell where the pointer is located). This line shows the address of the cell, the display format chosen, and the content of the cell. This line may also show the protection status and column width of the cell. The second line contains the characters that are being entered or edited. The third line explains the command currently highlighted.

The Mode Indicators

One of 1-2-3's different modes is always in effect, depending on what you are doing. The mode indicator is shown in the upper right corner of the screen.

Lock Key Indicators

1-2-3 lets you know when you have turned on one of the lock keys—Num Lock, Caps Lock, or Scroll Lock. These indicators appear in reverse-video in the lower right corner of the screen.

Status Indicators

Other indicators that report the status of the worksheet include general message indicators such as CALC or OVR, and warnings such as CIRC and MEM. When an error occurs, 1-2-3 displays a message in the lower left corner of the screen. To clear the error and get back to READY mode, press Esc or Enter.

Learning the Screen Display

The control panel displays information about the current cell.

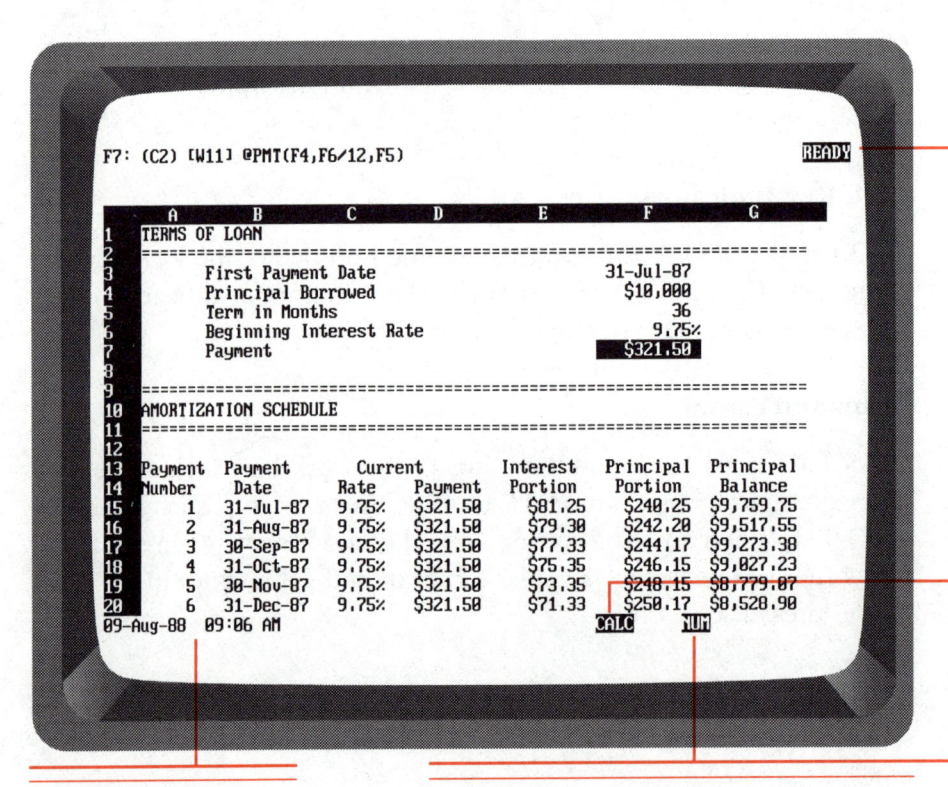

```
F7: (C2) [W11] @PMT(F4,F6/12,F5)                              READY

        A         B          C          D         E         F         G
   1  TERMS OF LOAN
   2  ==================================================================
   3         First Payment Date                        31-Jul-87
   4         Principal Borrowed                        $10,000
   5         Term in Months                                 36
   6         Beginning Interest Rate                     9.75%
   7         Payment                                   $321.50
   8
   9  ==================================================================
  10  AMORTIZATION SCHEDULE
  11  ==================================================================
  12
  13  Payment  Payment    Current            Interest  Principal  Principal
  14  Number   Date       Rate    Payment    Portion   Portion    Balance
  15     1     31-Jul-87  9.75%   $321.50    $81.25    $240.25    $9,759.75
  16     2     31-Aug-87  9.75%   $321.50    $79.30    $242.20    $9,517.55
  17     3     30-Sep-87  9.75%   $321.50    $77.33    $244.17    $9,273.38
  18     4     31-Oct-87  9.75%   $321.50    $75.35    $246.15    $9,027.23
  19     5     30-Nov-87  9.75%   $321.50    $73.35    $248.15    $8,779.07
  20     6     31-Dec-87  9.75%   $321.50    $71.33    $250.17    $8,528.90
  09-Aug-88  09:06 AM                                  CALC   NUM
```

Error Messages

When an error occurs in 1-2-3, a message is displayed in the lower left corner of the screen. To clear the error and return to READY mode, press [Esc] or [↵Enter].

Lock Key Indicators

IBM personal computers have three "lock" keys that work as toggles: Num Lock, Caps Lock, and Scroll Lock. These keys are known as lock keys because they lock the keyboard into a certain function. To turn off the lock feature on each of these keys, you must press the key a second time. When a lock key is active, 1-2-3 displays in the lower right corner a symbol in reverse-video indicating which lock key is in use.

62

Indicator	Meaning	Indicator	Meaning
READY	1-2-3 is waiting for a command or cell entry.	**MENU**	A menu item is being selected.
VALUE	A number or formula is being entered.	**HELP**	1-2-3 is displaying a help screen.
LABEL	A label is being entered.	**ERROR**	An error has occurred, and 1-2-3 is waiting for you to press Esc or ↵Enter to acknowledge the error.
EDIT	A cell entry is being edited.		
POINT	A range is being pointed to.	**WAIT**	1-2-3 is in the middle of a command and cannot respond to commands. Wait flashes on and off.
FILES	1-2-3 is waiting for you to select a file name from the list of file names.		
NAMES	1-2-3 is waiting for you to select a range from the list of range names.	**FIND**	1-2-3 is in the middle of a Data Query operation and cannot respond to commands.

Indicator	Meaning	Indicator	Meaning
STAT	1-2-3 is displaying the status of your worksheet.	**HAL**	HAL, a Lotus add-in that provides a natural-language interface for 1-2-3, is active and can be accessed by pressing the backslash (\) key.
CALC	The worksheet has not been recalculated since the last change to cell contents.		
CIRC	A circular reference has been found.	**CMD**	A keyboard macro or Command Language program is executing.
MEM	Random-access memory is almost exhausted. MEM flashes on and off.	**STEP**	Alt 2 has been pressed, and you are currently stepping through a macro or Command Language program one cell at a time.
SST	A keyboard macro or Command Language program is in single-step execution.		

Indicator	Meaning	Indicator	Meaning
OVR	The Ins key has been pressed, and 1-2-3 is in typeover mode.	**CAPS**	Caps Lock has been pressed.
		SCROLL	Scroll Lock has been pressed.
NUM	Num Lock has been pressed.	**END**	The End key has been pressed.

Using 1-2-3's Help Features

One of the biggest selling points of 1-2-3 is its user-friendliness. Lotus obviously went to a great deal of trouble to ensure that the spreadsheet is easy to learn and use.

Getting Help

1-2-3 does have a context-sensitive help system. When you need clarification on a particular topic, you can press **F1** and select the topic you need from the list that is displayed.

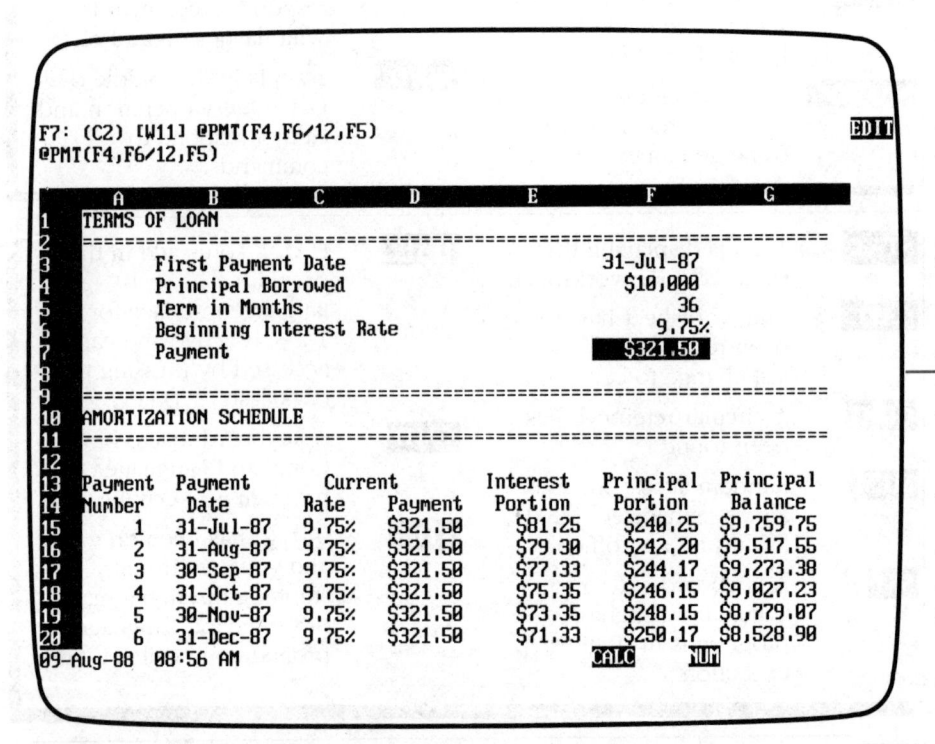

```
F7: (C2) [W11] @PMT(F4,F6/12,F5)                                    EDIT
@PMT(F4,F6/12,F5)
          A          B          C         D          E          F          G
   1  TERMS OF LOAN
   2  ==========================================================================
   3         First Payment Date                            31-Jul-87
   4         Principal Borrowed                            $10,000
   5         Term in Months                                     36
   6         Beginning Interest Rate                         9.75%
   7         Payment                                       $321.50
   8
   9  ==========================================================================
  10  AMORTIZATION SCHEDULE
  11  ==========================================================================
  12
  13  Payment   Payment     Current          Interest   Principal  Principal
  14  Number    Date       Rate   Payment    Portion    Portion    Balance
  15     1      31-Jul-87  9.75%  $321.50    $81.25     $240.25    $9,759.75
  16     2      31-Aug-87  9.75%  $321.50    $79.30     $242.20    $9,517.55
  17     3      30-Sep-87  9.75%  $321.50    $77.33     $244.17    $9,273.38
  18     4      31-Oct-87  9.75%  $321.50    $75.35     $246.15    $9,027.23
  19     5      30-Nov-87  9.75%  $321.50    $73.35     $248.15    $8,779.07
  20     6      31-Dec-87  9.75%  $321.50    $71.33     $250.17    $8,528.90
  09-Aug-88  08:56 AM                                   CALC       NUM
```

If you need to access the help screen for financial functions, for example, you can display the help screen directly from your worksheet.

					Using
	Starting	Exiting	Learning the	Learning the Screen	**1-2-3's Help**
Introduction	1-2-3	1-2-3	Keyboard	Display	**Feature**

To access the Help Index, move the cursor to the `Help Index` option at the bottom of your screen.

When the Help Index is displayed, you can choose from 25 topics. To access the help screens for functions, select `@Functions`.

From the @Functions screen, you can select a help screen for any one of the eight categories of functions.

When you select `Financial` from the @Functions screen, 1-2-3 displays the description and syntax of the financial functions.

Introduction

An Overview of 1-2-3

Getting Started

1-2-3 Basics

Creating a Worksheet

Printing Reports

Creating and Printing Graphs

Managing Data

Understanding Macros

Appendix

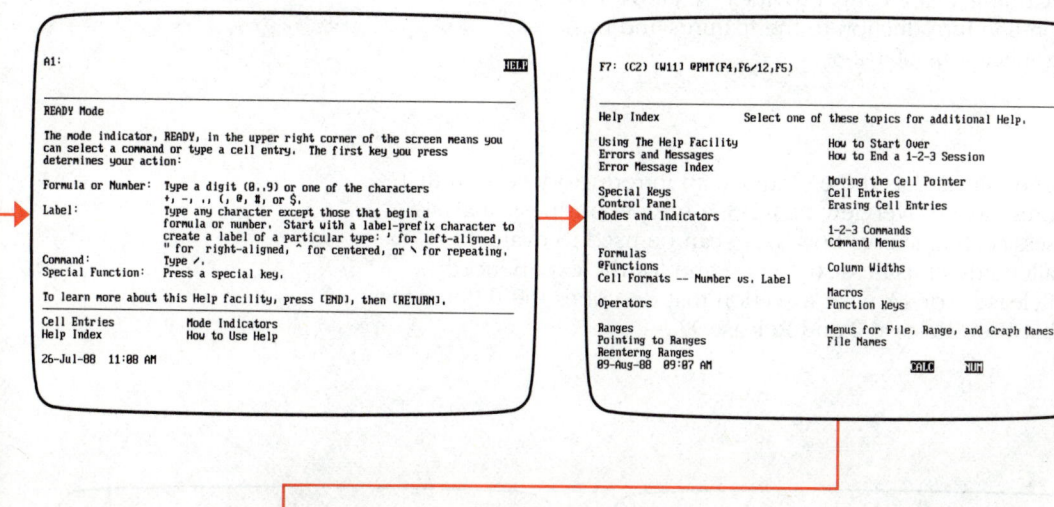

65

Using 1-2-3's Help Features

The 1-2-3 Tutorial

The most conspicuous user-friendly feature of 1-2-3 is the support Lotus provides for new users who are learning 1-2-3. Lotus provides "A View of 1-2-3," an on-line introduction to the features and business applications of 1-2-3.

The tutorial has three sections: an introductory section that presents an overview of 1-2-3; a sample business analysis session that shows how 1-2-3 can be used to evaluate alternative business strategies; and for the experienced Release 1 or 1A user, a section that describes the differences between Release 2 and Release 1A.

1-2-3 Access Screen.

Tutorial screen.

| Introduction | Starting 1-2-3 | Exiting 1-2-3 | Learning the Keyboard | Learning the Screen Display | **Using 1-2-3's Help Feature** |

Introduction

An Overview of 1-2-3

Getting Started

1-2-3 Basics

Creating a Worksheet

Printing Reports

Creating and Printing Graphs

Managing Data

Understanding Macros

Appendix

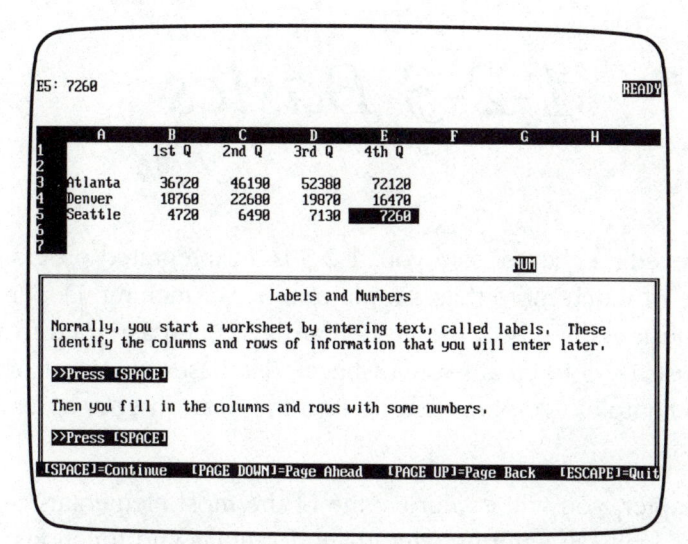

This tutorial screen explains how to enter labels and numbers in a worksheet.

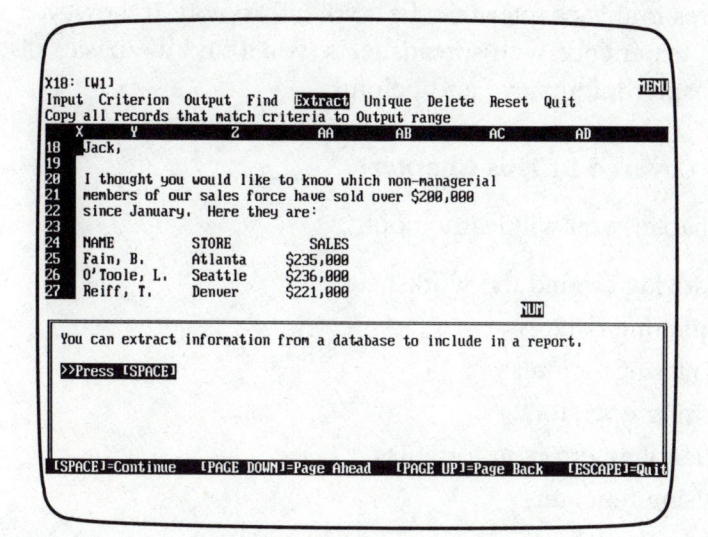

This tutorial screen introduces the steps for extracting information from a 1-2-3 database.

67

3   *1-2-3 Basics*

As the preceding chapter told you, 1-2-3 is an integrated program that is capable of much more than simple number crunching. Depending on your business needs or the tasks that have been assigned to you, you can use 1-2-3 to create spreadsheets, databases ranging from simple to complex, graphics that tie into the data on your spreadsheet, and reports.

In this chapter, you will explore some of the most elementary operations in 1-2-3: entering data, using formulas and functions, and moving around the spreadsheet, among other tasks. If you have used other spreadsheet programs and are new only to 1-2-3, some of the procedures in this chapter may be "old hat" to you. If, however, this is your first experience with spreadsheets, you'll find the basics discussed in this chapter informative and helpful.

What Is Covered in This Chapter?

In this chapter, you will learn about

- Moving around the worksheet
- Entering data
- Entering formulas
- Using operators
- Handling errors in formulas
- Using functions
- Entering labels
- Editing data

Key Terms Used in This Chapter

cursor-movement keys	The keys on the right side of the IBM PC and AT keyboard that also function as a numeric keypad when the Num Lock key is pressed. On the PS/2 enhanced keyboard, a separate cursor-movement keypad is positioned between the alphanumeric keys and the numeric keypad.
function keys	The keys on the left side of the keyboard (or across the top of the alphanumeric keys on the PS/2 enhanced keyboard) that are used for special functions.
cell pointer	The highlighted block that allows you to enter data into a cell on the spreadsheet.
values	Values can be numbers or formulas. (Note: Formulas can include 1-2-3's built-in functions, as well.)
data	The term to describe any information entered in a cell on the spreadsheet.
operators	Mathematical or logical operators that specify actions to be performed on data.
order of precedence	The order in which an equation or formula is executed, determining which operators are acted on first.

Moving Around the Spreadsheet

Soon after you start entering data in your worksheet, you will find that you need some easy ways to move the cell pointer quickly and accurately. Remember that the 1-2-3 spreadsheet is immense—8,192 rows and 256 columns, or more than 2,000,000 cells. As your use of 1-2-3 becomes more extensive, you may have blocks of data of various sizes in widely separated parts of the worksheet. The program provides several ways to move the cell pointer quickly anywhere in the worksheet.

Remember that the cell pointer is not the same as the cursor. The cell pointer is the bright rectangle that highlights an entire cell. The cursor is the blinking line that is sometimes inside the cell pointer and sometimes in the control panel. The cursor indicates the position on the screen where your keyboard activity takes effect; the cell pointer indicates the cell that is affected. Whenever you move the cell pointer, the cursor is inside the pointer and moves also. That is why we sometimes talk about cursor-movement keys when we really mean keys that move the cell pointer.

When 1-2-3 is in READY mode, the cursor-movement keys are used to move the cell pointer; when 1-2-3 is in POINT mode, these keys are used to point out a range. The cursor-movement keys either cannot be used at all or have a different action when you are in EDIT mode, making a cell entry, or in the process of entering a 1-2-3 command.

Using the Basic Cursor-Movement Keys

The arrow keys on the numeric keypad, or on a separate pad of the enhanced keyboard, are the basic keys for moving the cell pointer. The cell pointer moves in the direction of the arrow on the key as long as you hold down the key. When you reach the edge of the screen, the worksheet scrolls in the direction of the arrow.

If you press the Scroll Lock key to activate the scroll function, the worksheet scrolls in the direction of whatever arrow key you press no matter where the cell pointer is positioned on the screen. Leaving the scroll function off is usually easier and less confusing.

You can scroll the worksheet one screenful at a time to the left or right by holding down the Ctrl key and pressing the left- or right-arrow key. You also can scroll the worksheet to the right with the Tab key, and to the left with Shift-Tab (hold down the Shift key while you press Tab). These four keys and key combinations provide quick ways of "paging through" the worksheet. To get the same effect up or down, don't use the up- and down-arrow keys—use the PgUp and PgDn keys.

The Home key provides a quick way to return to the beginning of the worksheet. From anywhere in the worksheet, pressing Home causes the cell pointer to return to cell A1. (Note: As you'll learn later in this chapter, some keys, such as Home and End, have different actions in EDIT mode.)

Using the End Key for Cursor Movement

1-2-3 uses the End key in a unique way. When you press an arrow key after you have pressed and released the End key, the cell pointer moves in the direction of the arrow key to the next boundary between a blank cell and a cell that contains data. Remember, however, that if there are gaps in the blocks of data, the End key procedure will probably be less useful because the cell pointer will go to the boundaries of each gap.

You can also use the End key, followed by the Home key, to move the cell pointer from any position on the spreadsheet to the lower right corner of your active worksheet. In a sense, the End-Home combination has the opposite effect of the Home key used alone, because the Home key always moves the cell pointer to cell A1, the upper left corner of every spreadsheet.

Jumping to a Cell

The F5 (GoTo) key gives you a way to jump directly to a cell location. To move the cell pointer to any cell on the spreadsheet, just press the F5 function key. When 1-2-3 asks you for the address to go to, type in the cell address you want.

Moving Around the Spreadsheet

Using the Basic Cursor-Movement Keys

The arrow keys on the numeric keypad, or on a separate pad of the enhanced keyboard, are the basic keys for moving the cell pointer. The cell pointer moves in the direction of the arrow on the key as long as you hold down the key. When you reach the edge of the screen, the worksheet scrolls in the direction of the arrow.

The PS/2 ENHANCED KEYBOARD

Key Action in Edit Mode

[←] Moves the cursor one column left

[→] Moves the cursor one column right

[↑] Moves the cursor one row up

[↓] Moves the cursor one row down

[Tab⇥] or [Ctrl][→] Moves the cursor on screen to the right

[⇧Shift][Tab⇥] or [Ctrl][←] Moves the cursor on screen to the left

[PgUp] Moves the cell pointer up an entire screen

[PgDn] Moves the cell pointer down an entire screen

[Home] Returns the cell pointer to cell A1 from any location in the worksheet. Also used after the [End] key to position the pointer at the end of the active worksheet

[End] When entered prior to any of the arrow keys, positions the cell pointer in the direction of the arrow key to the cell boundary of an empty and filled space

[F5] (GoTo) Moves the cell pointer to the cell coordinates (or range name) provided

| Introduction | **Moving Around the Spreadsheet** | Entering Data and Formulas | Using Mathematical Operators in Formulas | Using Functions | Entering Labels | Editing Data in the Worksheet | Managing Files |

When you begin to enter data, READY changes to LABEL, indicating that you are entering text.

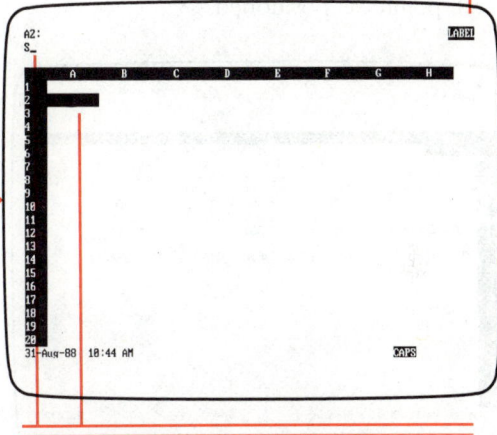

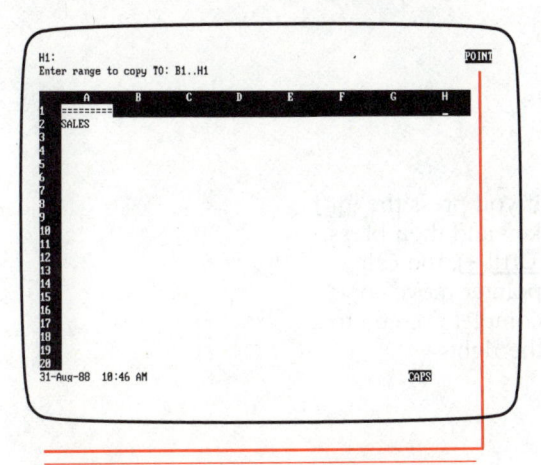

The cell pointer is positioned ready for you to enter data in cell A1.

The single character cursor appears in the cell pointer and in the control panel.

POINT indicates that the cell pointer can be positioned and/or expanded to highlight a range in your worksheet.

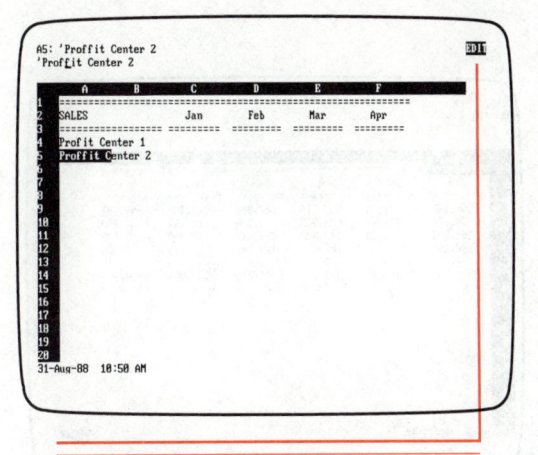

In EDIT mode, the cell pointer cannot be moved. You can, however, move the cursor in the control panel to edit a label or value.

Introduction

An Overview of 1-2-3

Getting Started

1-2-3 Basics

Creating a Worksheet

Printing Reports

Creating and Printing Graphs

Managing Data

Understanding Macros

Appendix

73

Moving Around the Spreadsheet

Using the Scroll Lock Key

When you press the [Scroll Lock] key, the worksheet scrolls in the direction of whatever arrow key you press, no matter where the cell pointer is positioned.

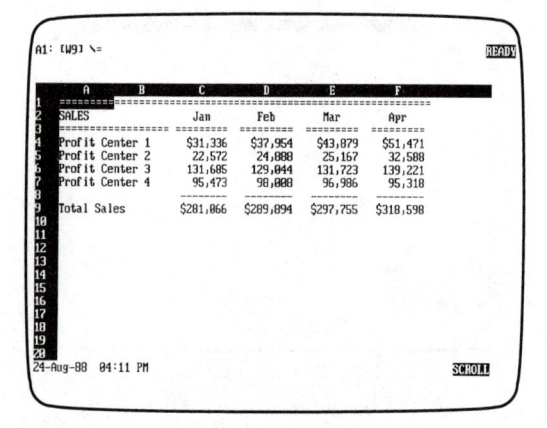

With the cell pointer positioned in A1, press the [Scroll Lock] key.

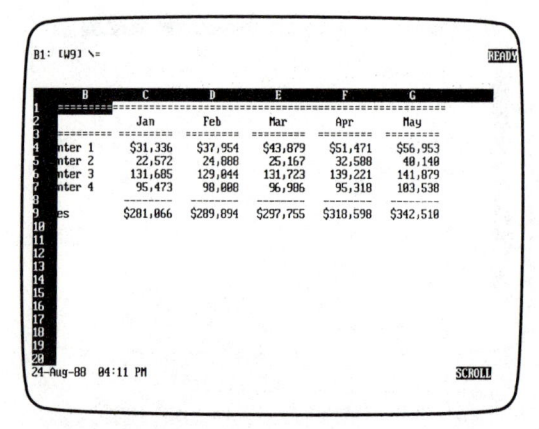

When you press [→], notice the screen scrolls to the right.

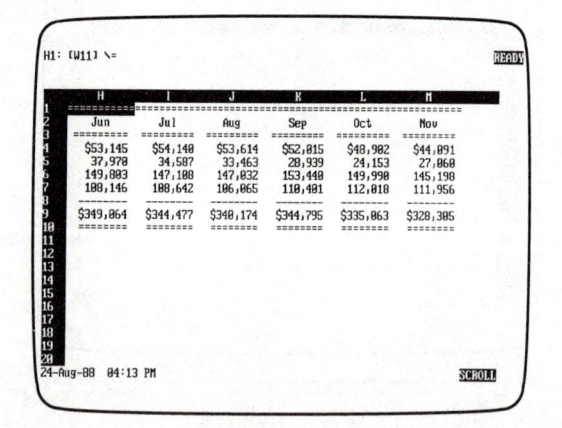

If you press the [Scroll Lock] key and then press [Ctrl][→], the cell pointer moves one complete screen to the right.

Using the Home Key

You can use the [Home] key to move the cell pointer in your worksheet when 1-2-3 is in READY or POINT mode. The [Home] key also moves the cursor in the control panel when 1-2-3 is in EDIT mode.

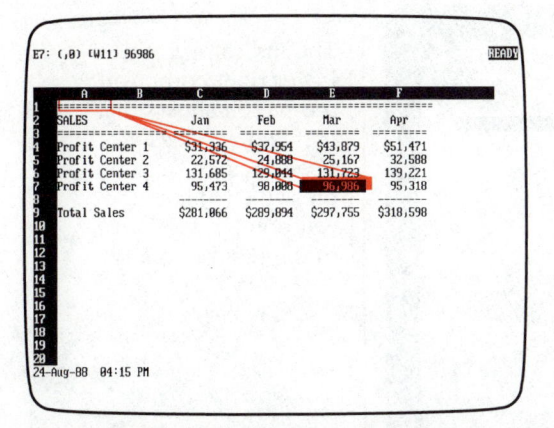

Press [Home] in READY mode, and the cell pointer moves to A1.

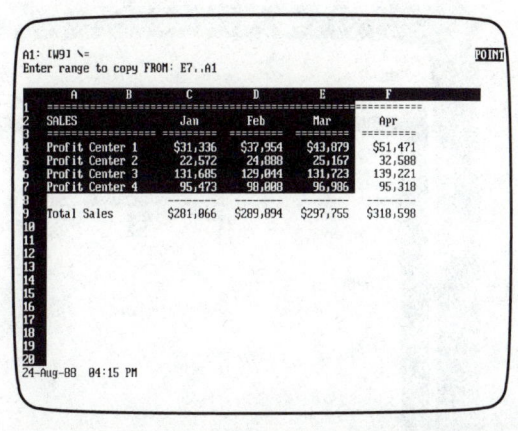

When you press [Home] in POINT mode, the cell pointer highlights a rectangle with one corner being in A1 and the opposite corner located where the cell pointer was originally positioned.

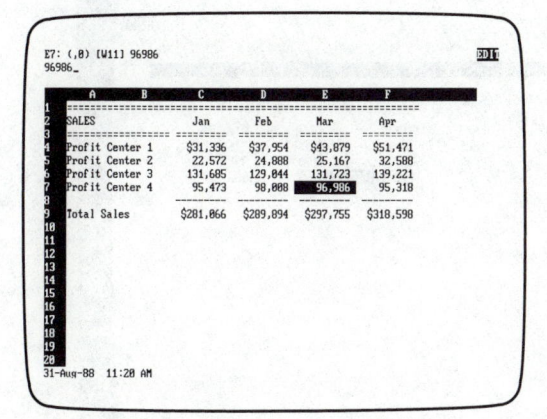

Press [F2] (EDIT) and notice that the cursor is positioned after the last character of your cell entry.

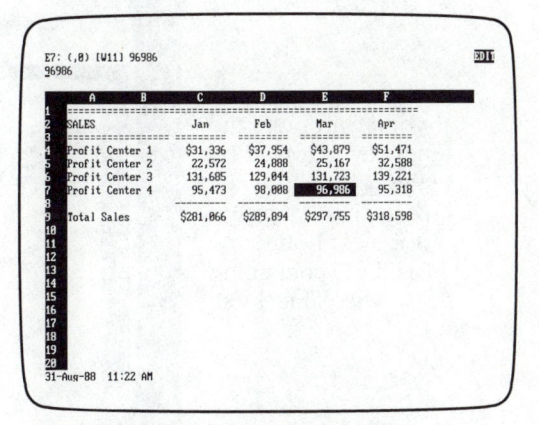

When you press [Home] in EDIT mode, the cursor moves to the first character in the cell entry.

75

Moving Around the Spreadsheet

Using the End Key for Moving the Cell Pointer

In addition to using the cursor keys to move the cell pointer around the screen, you can use the [End] key.

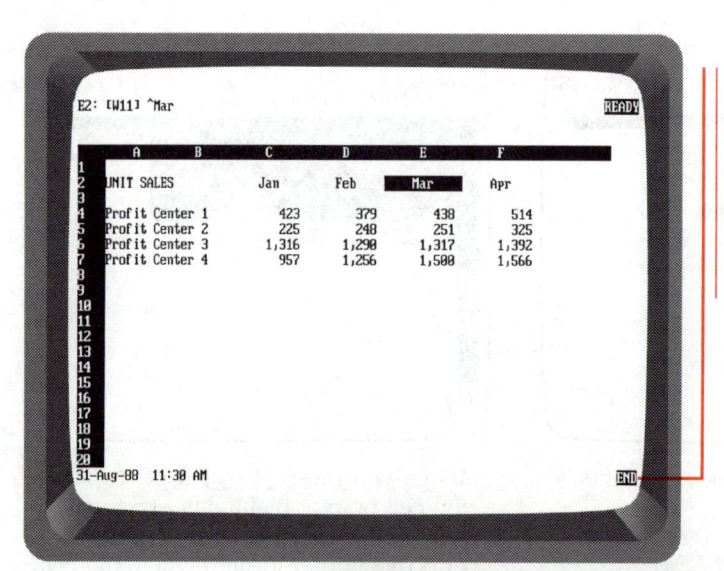

The indicator in the lower right corner of the screen shows that the [End] key has been pressed. If you press the [↓] key, the cell pointer will jump to the first boundary.

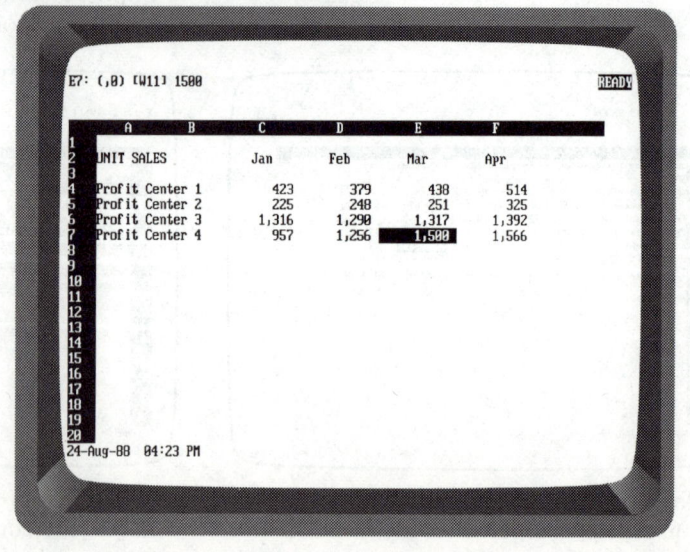

If you again press the [End] key followed by the [↓] key, the cell pointer will jump to the next boundary, cell E7, containing the value 1500.

| Introduction | **Moving Around the Spreadsheet** | Entering Data and Formulas | Using Mathematical Operators in Formulas | Using Functions | Entering Labels | Editing Data in the Worksheet | Managing Files |

If you repeat the process one more time, the cell pointer will jump all the way to the bottom boundary of the spreadsheet, cell E8192.

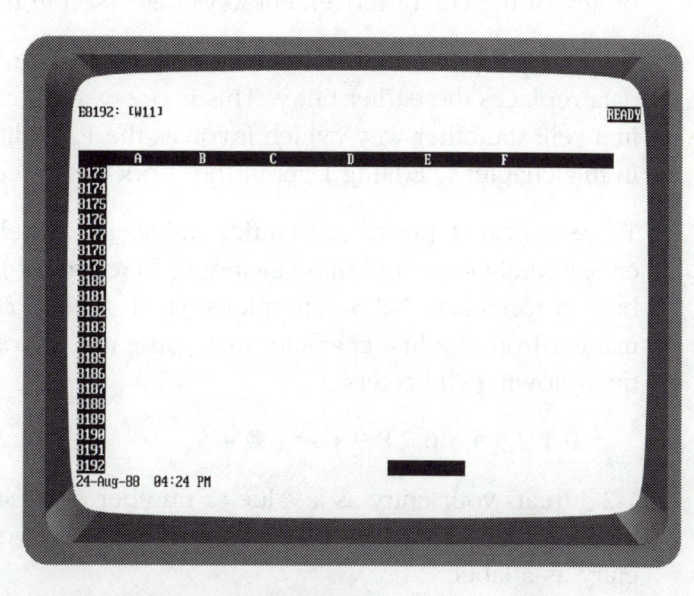

The **End** key works in similar fashion for the other arrow keys. Pressing **End** ↑ moves the pointer to the lower row of the active worksheet. Here, the corner is cell E7, which contains the value 1500.

Introduction

An Overview of 1-2-3

Getting Started

1-2-3 Basics

Creating a Worksheet

Printing Reports

Creating and Printing Graphs

Managing Data

Understanding Macros

Appendix

77

Entering Data and Formulas

You enter data into a cell simply by highlighting the cell with the cell pointer and then typing the entry. To complete the entry, press Enter or any of the cursor-movement keys discussed in this chapter.

If you enter data into a cell that already contains information, the new data replaces the earlier entry. This is one way to change information in a cell; the other way, which involves the F2 (Edit) key, is explained in this chapter's "Editing Data in the Worksheet" section.

There are two types of cell entries: values and labels. Values can be either numbers or formulas (including functions, which 1-2-3 treats as built-in formulas). 1-2-3 determines which type of cell entry you are making from the first character that you enter. If you start with one of the following characters,

 0 1 2 3 4 5 6 7 8 9 + - . (@ # $

1-2-3 treats your entry as a value (a number or a formula). If you begin by entering a character other than one of the above, 1-2-3 treats your entry as a label.

Entering Numbers

The rules for entering numbers are simple.

1. A number cannot begin with any character except 0 through 9, a decimal point, a minus sign (-), or a dollar sign ($). Numbers can also begin with a plus sign (+), or be entered in parentheses, but the + and the ( ) will not appear in the cell.

2. You can end a number with a percent sign (%), which tells 1-2-3 to divide by 100 the number that precedes the sign.

3. A number cannot have more than one decimal point.

4. You can enter a number in scientific notation—what 1-2-3 calls the Scientific format (for example, 1.234E+06).

If you do not follow these rules, 1-2-3 will beep when you press Enter, and 1-2-3 will automatically shift to EDIT mode just as though you had pressed F2.

Entering Data and Formulas

Entering Formulas

In addition to simple numbers, formulas also can be entered into cells. You can enter formulas either by typing the formula into the cell or by typing and moving the cell pointer so that 1-2-3 enters the cell addresses for you.

Suppose that you want to create a formula that adds a row of numbers. For example, suppose that you want to add the amounts in cells B1, C1, D1, and E1, and place the result in cell F1. To do this, you can type the +B1+C1+D1+E1 into cell F1. The + sign at the beginning of the formula causes 1-2-3 to recognize that the formula is a formula and not a label.

Because we started with +, 1-2-3 recognizes our entry as a formula and switches to VALUE mode, the appropriate mode for entering numbers and formulas.

Remember that two methods can be used to enter a formula that contains a cell address: typing and pointing. Both methods accomplish the same result, and you can mix and match the two techniques within the same formula.

For example, to enter the formula +B1+C1+D1+E1 by pointing, you begin with the cell pointer highlighting cell F1, and you enter the first plus sign into F1; then you move the cell pointer to B1. The mode indicator in the upper right corner of the screen shifts from VALUE to POINT mode as you move the cell pointer to cell B1. Notice that the address for the cell appears after the plus sign in the second line of the control panel—that is, +B1.

To continue to the next address in the formula, keep the cell pointer in cell B1 and type another plus sign. The cursor moves immediately from cell B1 to the cell at which it was located when you began entering the formula—in this case, cell F1. Also, the mode indicator shifts back to VALUE. Now move the cell pointer to cell C1 and type another plus sign. Continue this sequence of pointing and entering plus signs until you have the formula you want. Then press Enter to complete the operation.

Remember that you may use a combination of pointing and typing. Use whatever works best for you. Usually, the easiest method is to point at cells that are close to the cell you are defining, and type references to distant cells.

Entering Data and Formulas

Entering Data

Entering data is one of the easiest techniques you'll learn as you explore 1-2-3. You enter data into a cell simply by highlighting the cell with the cell pointer and then typing the entry. To complete the entry, press ↵Enter or any cursor-movement key.

If you enter data into a cell that already contains information, the new data replaces the earlier entry. This is one way to change information in a cell.

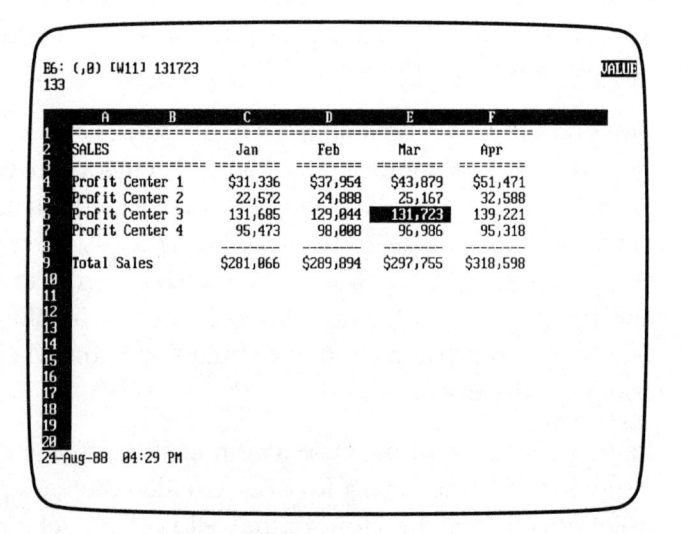

The other way, which involves the F2 (Edit) key, is explained in this chapter's "Editing Data in the Worksheet" section.

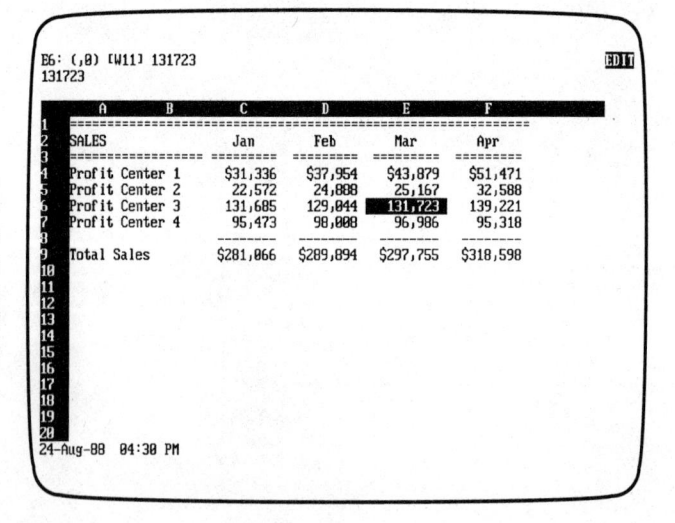

82

Entering Formulas

In addition to simple numbers, formulas also can be entered into cells. You can enter formulas either by typing the formula into the cell or by typing and moving the cell pointer so that 1-2-3 enters the cell addresses for you.

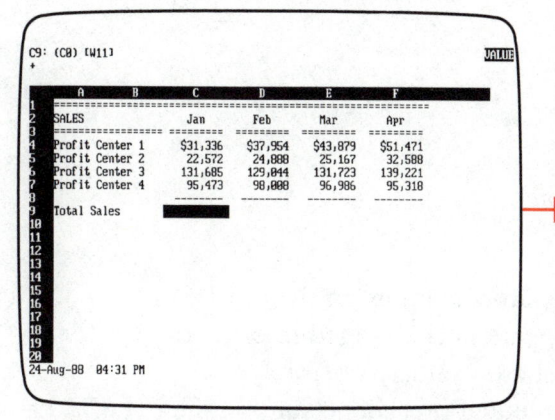

To enter a formula by pointing, begin on the cell that will hold the resulting value, and type [+].

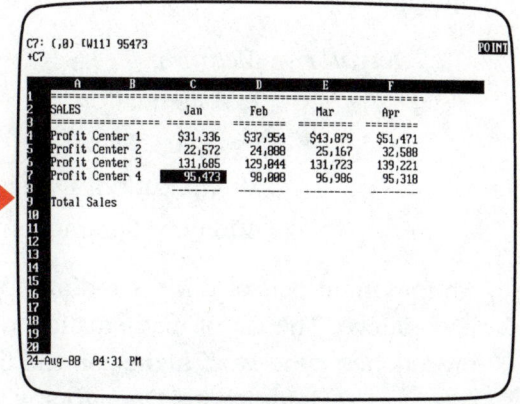

Move to the first cell address used in the formula, and type [+].

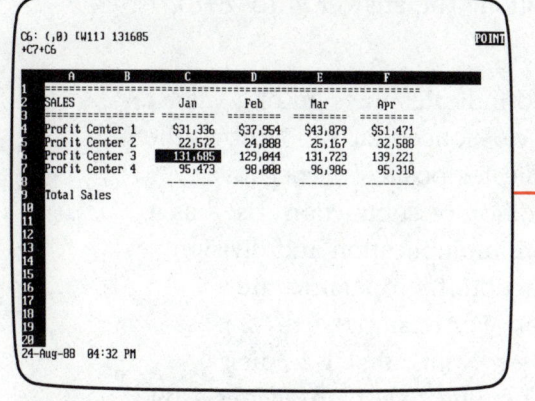

Move to the next cell address used in the formula, and type [+].

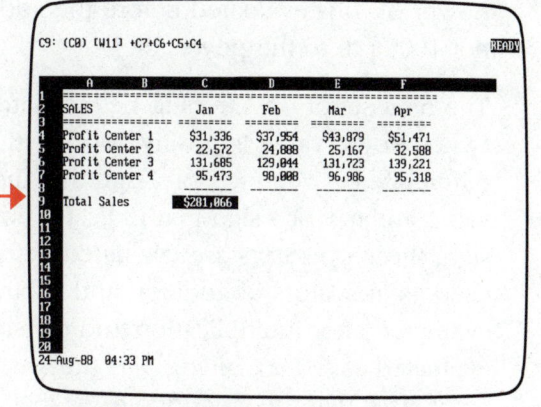

Repeat this procedure until all the necessary cell addresses are entered. Then press [↵Enter].

Using Mathematical Operators in Formulas

Using Mathematical Operators in Formulas

Operators indicate arithmetic operations in formulas. Operators can be separated into two types: mathematical and logical. The mathematical operators are

Operator	Meaning
^	Exponentiation
+, -	Positive, Negative
*, /	Multiplication, Division
+, -	Addition, Subtraction

An important part of understanding operators is knowing their order of precedence. The list of mathematical operators is arranged in order of precedence. Operators higher on the list are evaluated before operators that are lower. Operators with equal precedence are on the same line; in these cases, the operators are evaluated from left to right.

The first operator that is evaluated in a formula is exponentiation—the power of a number. In the formula 8+2^3, for example, 2^3 (2 to the power of 3) is evaluated before the addition. The answer is 16 (8+8), not 1000 (10 to the power of 3).

The next set of operators to be evaluated indicates the sign of a value (whether the value is positive or negative). Notice that 1-2-3 knows the difference between a + or - sign that indicates positive or negative value and a + or - sign that indicates addition or subtraction. Used as a sign, these operators are evaluated before multiplication and division; used as indicators of addition and subtraction, the operators are evaluated after multiplication and division. For example, 5+4/-2 is evaluated as 5+(-2), giving 3 as the answer. Notice that 1-2-3 first recognizes that the - sign indicates that 2 is negative, then divides 4 by -2, and finally adds 5 to -2, giving the answer of 3.

Correcting Errors in Formulas

It is easy to make errors entering formulas. The more complex the formula you are trying to use, the more likely you are to confirm the saying "Whatever can go wrong, will." 1-2-3 provides ways to help you discover and correct the inevitable errors.

If you attempt to enter a formula that contains a logical or mathematical error, the program will beep, change to EDIT mode, and move the cursor to the section of the formula where the problem most likely exists. You can then correct the problem and continue.

If you don't know what the problem is, you can buy yourself some think time by converting the formula to a label. Do this by pressing the Home key and then entering an apostrophe (') at the beginning of the formula. Then use the **/C**opy command to copy the label-formula to another section of the worksheet for debugging and testing. When you have discovered the problem, correct the original formula and remove the apostrophe.

If your formula is long and complex, try breaking it into logical segments and testing each segment separately. Using smaller segments is not only an aid in debugging, but may also be necessary in order for the program to accept the formula. 1-2-3 limits cell entries to 240 characters.

Some common errors are open parentheses and commas missing from built-in formulas (functions). What appears to be a logical error may be only a missing punctuation mark. When 1-2-3 beeps to indicate a formula error, check the formula for a missing parenthesis or comma at the place where the cursor is positioned.

The program also provides two commands, discussed extensively in the next chapter, to help you examine and analyze your formulas. The **/P**rint **P**rinter **O**ptions **O**ther **C**ell-Formulas command will print a list of all the formulas in your worksheet. The **/W**orksheet **G**lobal **F**ormat **T**ext command produces a screen display that shows all your formulas in their spreadsheet locations.

Using Mathematical Operators in Formulas

Operators in Formulas

Operators indicate arithmetic operations in formulas. Operators can be separated into two types: mathematical and logical. Actually, formulas wouldn't be formulas without operators. Consider the following formula:

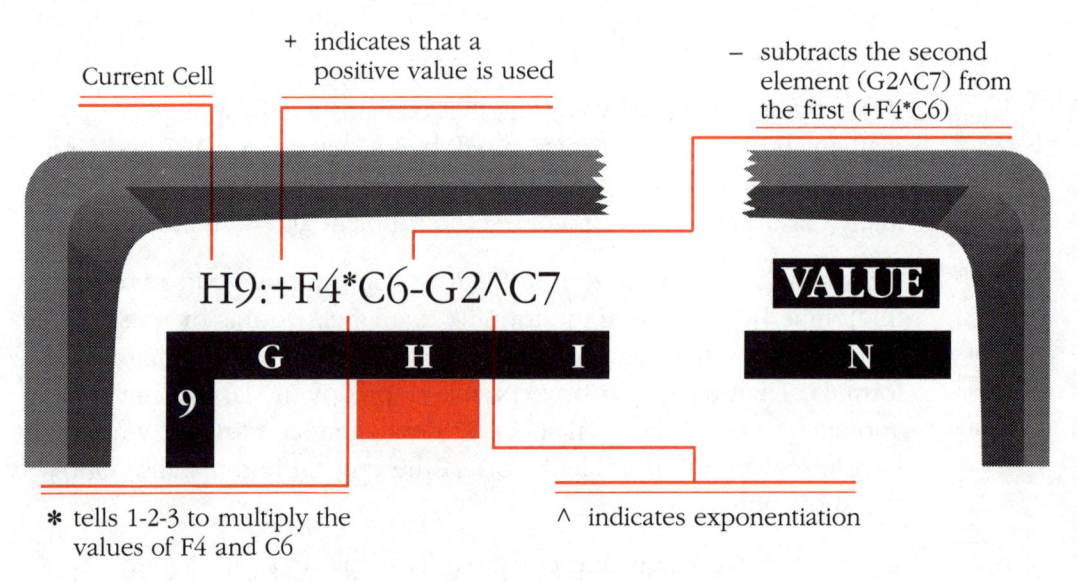

Current Cell

+ indicates that a positive value is used

− subtracts the second element (G2^C7) from the first (+F4*C6)

H9: +F4*C6-G2^C7   VALUE

* tells 1-2-3 to multiply the values of F4 and C6

^ indicates exponentiation

You can always use parentheses to override the order of precedence. Consider the order of precedence in the following formulas, where B3=2, C3=3, and D3=4, and see whether you get the same answers. In the first two formulas, notice particularly how parentheses affect the order of precedence and, ultimately, the answer.

Formula	Evaluation	Answer
+C3-D3/B3	3-(4/2)	1
(C3-D3)/B3	(3-4)/2	− 0.5
+D3*C3-B3^C3	(4*3)-(2^3)	4
+D3*C3*B3/B3^C3-25/5	((4*3*2)/(2^3)-(25/5))	−2

Correcting Errors in Formulas

If you attempt to enter a formula and 1-2-3 does not accept your entry, you can debug the formula by converting it to a label.

1-2-3 will beep and change from VALUE to EDIT mode if a formula you are attempting to enter contains an error.

If you can't correct the problem while 1-2-3 is in EDIT mode, you can convert the formula to a label by pressing [Home], ['] (apostrophe), and [↵Enter].

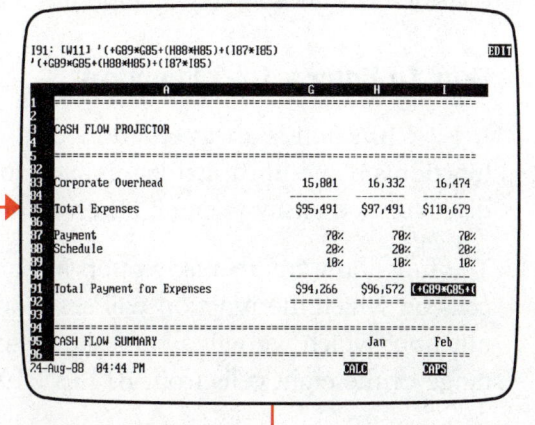

Copy the formula to another section of the worksheet.

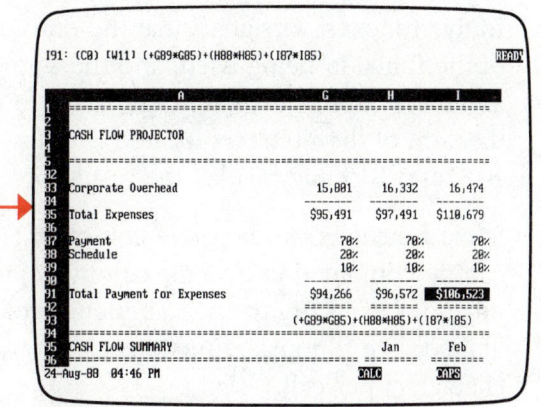

Debug the formula, and then copy it back as a label to the original cell, delete the prefix, and press [↵Enter].

87

Using Functions

Like most electronic spreadsheets, 1-2-3 includes built-in functions. These functions are of three basic types: (1) simple abbreviations for long or complex mathematical formulas—these functions are considered formulas by 1-2-3; (2) non-mathematical, "string" functions that work with alphanumeric data—these functions manipulate labels; and (3) special functions that provide information or perform other specialized spreadsheet tasks. All three types of functions are considered values by 1-2-3, and all three are entered in the same way.

How To Enter a 1-2-3 Function

A 1-2-3 function is always identified by the @ symbol preceding the function's name in capital letters. So identified, functions can be distinguished easily from all other entries.

The function's arguments, written in parentheses, specify the cell or cells on which the function will act. For example, the following function, which we will assume lies in cell B21, computes the total of a range of the eight cells from B12 to B19:

    B21: @SUM(B12..B19)

In this function, @ signals that the entry is a function, SUM is the name of the function being used, and the statement (B12..B19) is the argument (in this case, a range). This function tells 1-2-3 to compute the sum of the numbers located in cells B12, B13, B14, B15, B16, B17, B18, and B19 and display the result in cell B21.

Some functions can be quite complex. For example, several functions can be combined in a single cell by having one function use other functions as its arguments. The length of an argument, however, is limited; like formulas, functions can contain a maximum of 240 characters per cell.

1-2-3's Function Library

Mathematical functions	@ABS, @INT, @MOD, @ROUND, @SQRT, @RAND
Trigonometric functions	@PI, @SIN, @COS, @TAN, @ASIN, @ACOS, @ATAN, @ATAN2
Logarithmic functions	@LOG, @EXP, @LN
Statistical functions	@SUM, @MAX, @MIN, @COUNT, @AVG
Investments and Depreciation Analysis functions	@NPV, @IRR, @PV, @FV, @PMT, @RATE, @TERM, @CTERM, @SLN, @DDB, @SYD
Data Management functions	@CHOOSE, @HLOOKUP, @VLOOKUP, @INDEX
Database Statistical functions	@DAVG, @DCOUNT, @DMAX, @DMIN, @DSTD, @DSUM, @DVAR
Logical functions	@IF, @ISERR, @ISNA, @TRUE, @FALSE, @ISSTRING, @ISNUMBER
Special functions	@CELL, @CELLPOINTER, @NA, @ERR, @ROWS, @COLS, @@
Date and Time functions	@DATE, @DATEVALUE, @DAY, @MONTH, @YEAR, @NOW, @TIME, @TIMEVALUE, @SECOND, @MINUTE, @HOUR, @TODAY
String functions	@FIND, @MID, @LEFT, @RIGHT, @REPLACE, @LENGTH, @EXACT, @LOWER, @UPPER, @PROPER, @REPEAT, @TRIM, @N, @S, @STRING, @VALUE, @CLEAN
LICS functions	@CHAR, @CODE

Using Functions

Understanding Functions

Functions consist of three parts: the @ sign, a function name, and an argument or range. (Note: *Range* refers to the range of cells that will be used by the function.)

The @ Symbol

The @ symbol tells 1-2-3 to read the information that follows it as a function.

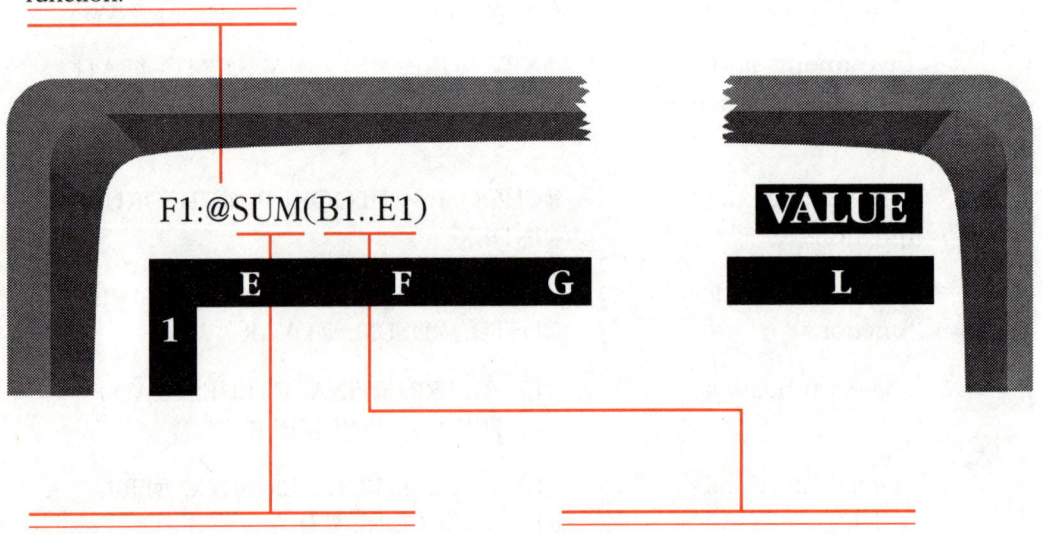

F1:@SUM(B1..E1)

The Function Name

In this instance, the function name is SUM. 1-2-3 has a wide variety of functions that are capable of performing various tasks—from simple addition and division to complex statistical analysis and depreciation functions.

Range

The range in this function is B1 to E1, meaning that all values in the cells in the rectangular area starting at and including B1 through E1 will be added by the SUM function.

Entering Formulas Containing Functions

When you enter a formula containing a function that requires a cell address, you can enter the cell address by typing or pointing.

To enter the formula @SUM(C7..C4), for example, follow this procedure.

Move the cell pointer to the cell where you want to locate the formula, and type @ S U M (

Move the cell pointer to C7, and press . to anchor the cell pointer.

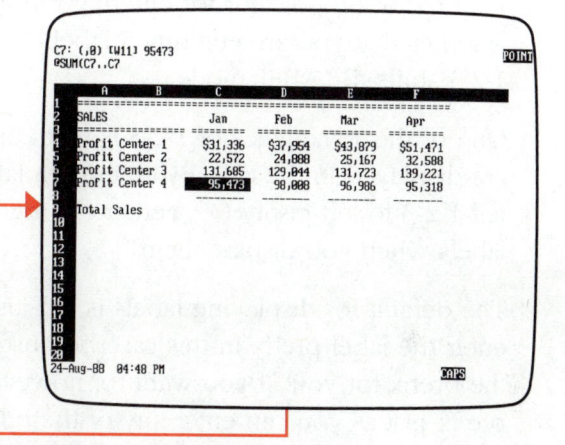

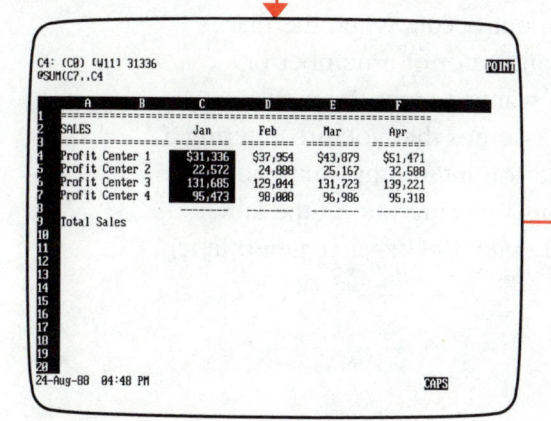

Press the ↑ key to highlight the range of cells between C7 and C4

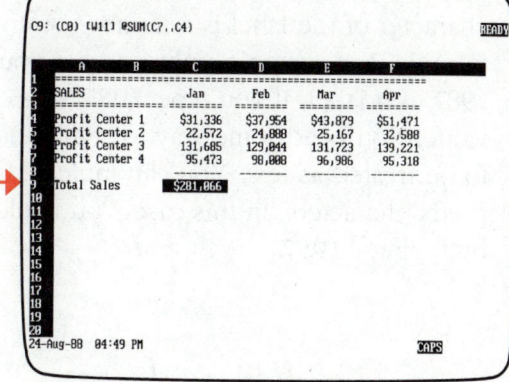

Finally type the closing) and press ←Enter. 1-2-3 will enter the sum of C7..C4.

91

Entering Labels

You can enter labels, which are commonly used for row and column headings and a variety of other purposes, that are up to 240 characters long and may contain any string of characters and numbers. A label that is too long for the width of a cell continues (for display purposes) across the cells to the right, as long as the neighboring cells contain no other entries.

When you make an entry into a cell and the first character is not a number or an indicator for entering numbers and formulas, 1-2-3 assumes that you are entering a label. As you type the first character, 1-2-3 shifts to LABEL mode.

One of the advantages of 1-2-3 is that you can control how the labels are displayed in the cell. By entering a label prefix character, you can tell 1-2-3 to left-justify ('), center (^), right-justify ("), or repeat (\) labels when you display them.

The default for displaying labels is left-justification. You don't have to enter the label prefix in this case because 1-2-3 automatically supplies the prefix for you. If you want to, however, you can enter the ' label prefix just as you can enter any of the other label prefixes.

The one exception for all types of alignment occurs when the first character of the label is a number or an indicator of a number or formula. For example, suppose that you want to enter the number 1987 as a label. If you type *1987*, 1-2-3 assumes that you are entering a value. You need some way to signal that you intend this numeric entry to be treated as text. You can indicate this by using one of the label-prefix characters. In this case, you could enter 1987 as a centered label by typing *^1987*.

Aligning Labels

The label-prefix characters that you use to align a label as you type it in are

- ' Left-justifies
- " Right-justifies
- ^ Centers
- \ Repeats

In addition, you can use the **/R**ange **L**abel command (available by selecting **/R**ange from the main menu bar) or the **/W**orksheet **G**lobal Label-Prefix command (available by selecting **/W**orksheet from the main menu bar) to change or set the alignment of labels.

Controlling Label Prefixes

You can control label prefixes in several ways. For example, suppose that you enter labels and then you decide that you want the labels to be centered. You could change all the label prefixes manually or, using the **/R**ange **L**abel command, you could change the prefixes all at once. When you select this command, you are given the following choices:

    Left   Right   Center

Each choice gives you the appropriate label prefix. If you select **C**enter, 1-2-3 asks you to designate a range of cells to change. When you specify a range and press Enter, the cells are displayed as centered.

Another option for changing label prefixes modifies the default setting for text justification. The command to do this is **/W**orksheet **G**lobal **L**abel-Prefix. This command gives you the same options as the **/R**ange **L**abel command. Previously entered cells, however, are not affected by the **/W**orksheet **G**lobal **L**abel-Prefix command. Only subsequent entries will show the change. In addition, cells that have been previously set, using **/R**ange **L**abel, will maintain the alignment set by that command.

93

Entering Labels

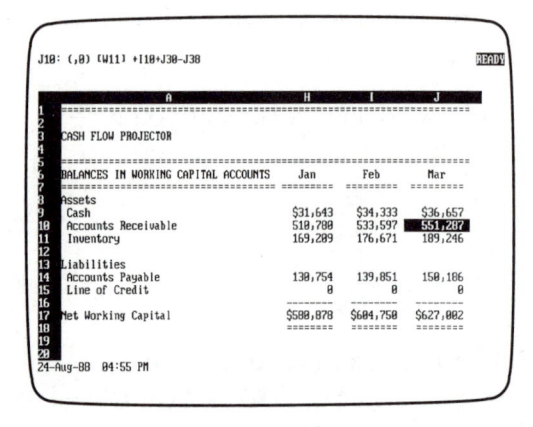

Entering Labels

Labels play an important role in spreadsheet development. Without labels on a spreadsheet, *you* might know that column H is January data and row 11 is Inventory Assets, but how would someone else who is not familiar with the spreadsheet know? Labels make our work clearer, help people find information quickly, and help set off the values in the spreadsheet.

Label Length

A label that is too long for the width of a cell continues (for display purposes) across the cells to the right, as long as the neighboring cells contain no other entries.

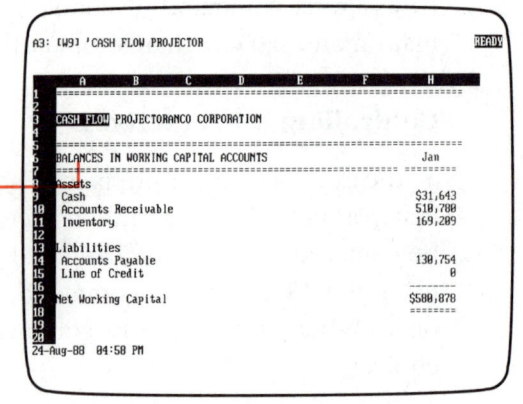

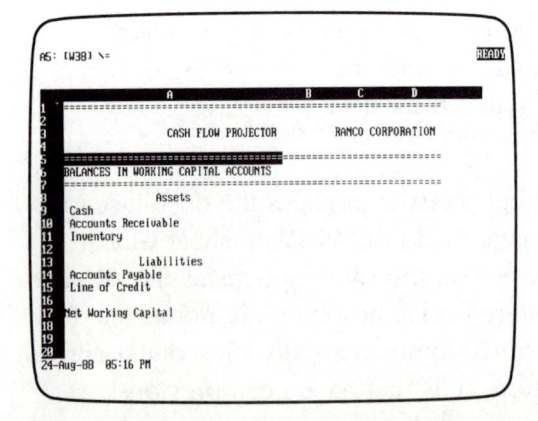

Label Justification

Labels can be left-justified, centered, or right-justified.

Repeating Label Characters

To use the repeat character and create a separator line, place the pointer on the first cell of the line on which you want the separator line to appear. Type `\` `=` and then press `↵Enter`. The cell is then filled with equal signs.

Controlling Label Prefixes

1-2-3 gives you three methods for controlling the alignment of labels in your worksheet. You can align labels manually by typing at the beginning of your label the prefix for aligning a label to the right (") or for centering a label (^). Remember that left alignment is the default alignment, so 1-2-3 automatically enters the prefix for left alignment as soon as you type a character that 1-2-3 recognizes as a label character. You can also align labels by using the **/R**ange **L**abels or **/W**orksheet **G**lobal **L**abel-Prefix command.

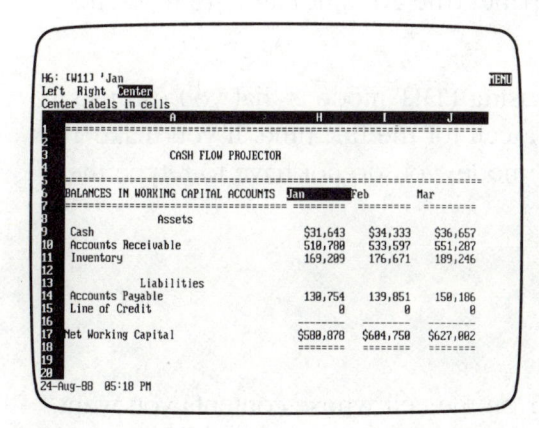

You can change the alignment of a range of labels by using the **/R**ange **L**abel command.

You can also change the alignment from left to right or center for the whole worksheet by using the **/W**orksheet **G**lobal **L**abel-Prefix command.

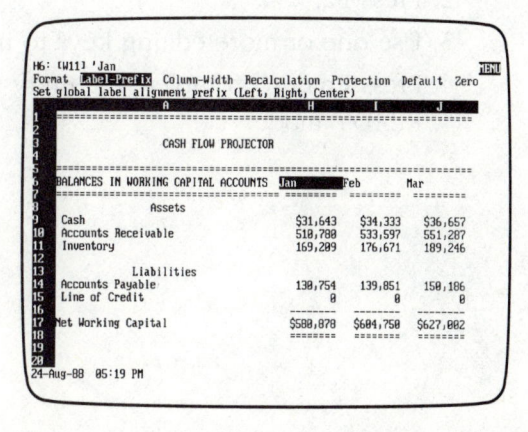

Editing Data in the Worksheet

When you start using 1-2-3, one of the first things you will want to do is modify the contents of cells without retyping the complete entry. This modification is quite easy to do in 1-2-3. You begin by moving the cursor to the appropriate cell and pressing the F2 (Edit) key. An alternative to "typing over" an existing entry is to press F2 when you are entering cell contents.

After you press F2, the mode indicator in the upper right corner of the screen changes to EDIT. The contents of the cell are then duplicated in the second line of the control panel (the edit line) and are ready for editing.

One thing to remember about using EDIT mode is that you can use it also when you enter data into a cell for the first time. If you make a mistake when you are in EDIT mode, you do not have to retype the entire entry.

How To Edit a Cell Entry

To edit the contents of a cell,

1. Position the cell pointer on the cell whose contents you want to change.
2. Press F2.
3. Use one or more editing keys to modify the cell's contents.
4. Press Enter to complete the entry and return the worksheet to READY mode.

Key Action in Edit Mode

Key	Action
←	Moves the cursor one position to the left
→	Moves the cursor one position to the right
Tab or Ctrl →	Moves the cursor five characters to the right
Shift Tab or Ctrl ←	Moves the cursor five characters to the left
Home	Moves the cursor to the first character in the entry
End	Moves the cursor to the last character in the entry
Backspace	Deletes the character just to the left of the cursor
Ins	Toggles between INSERT and OVERTYPE modes
Del	Deletes the character above the cursor
Esc	Clears the edit line but does not take you out of EDIT mode

Editing Data in the Worksheet

To edit data in a cell, move the cell pointer to the cell containing the data you want to edit, and press [F2] (Edit).

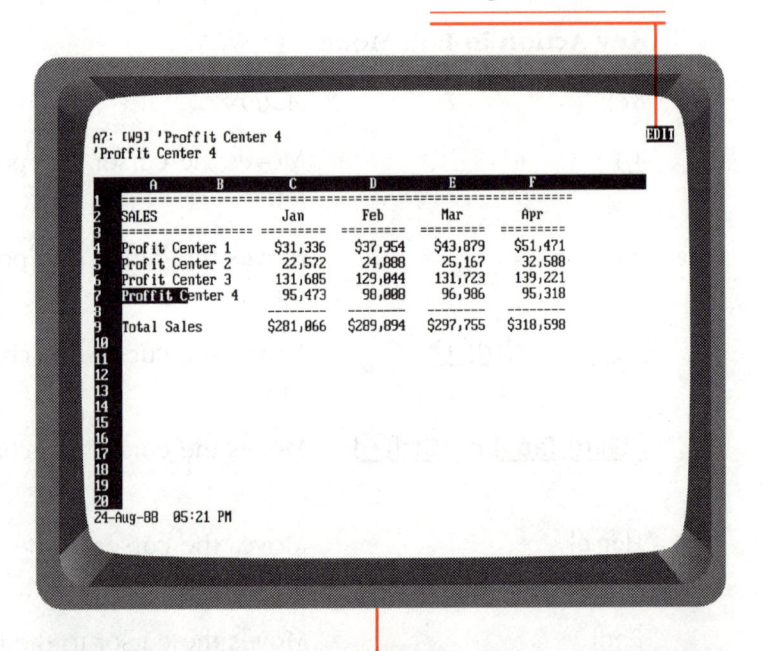

Notice that the mode changes to EDIT.

With the contents of the cell displayed in the second line of the control panel, move the cursor to the part of the entry you want to edit.

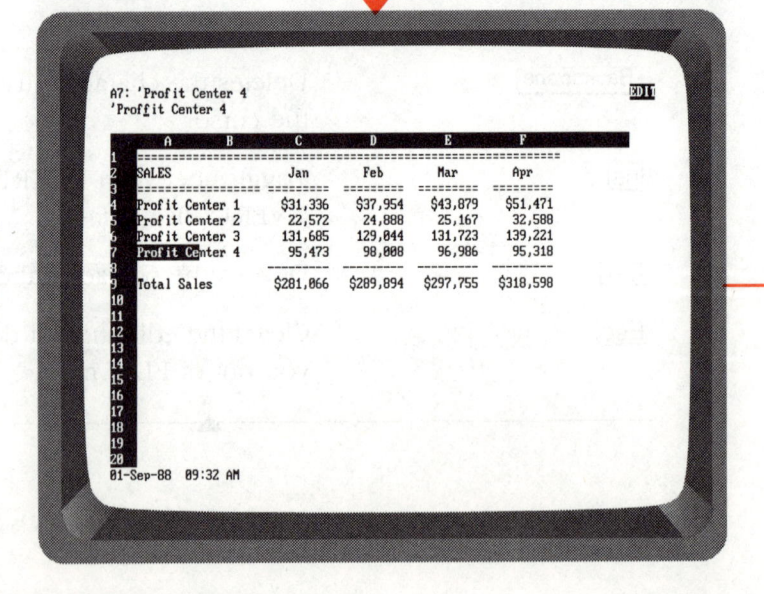

| Introduction | Moving Around the Spreadsheet | Entering Data and Formulas | Using Mathematical Operators in Formulas | Using Functions | Entering Labels | **Editing Data in the Worksheet** | Managing Files |

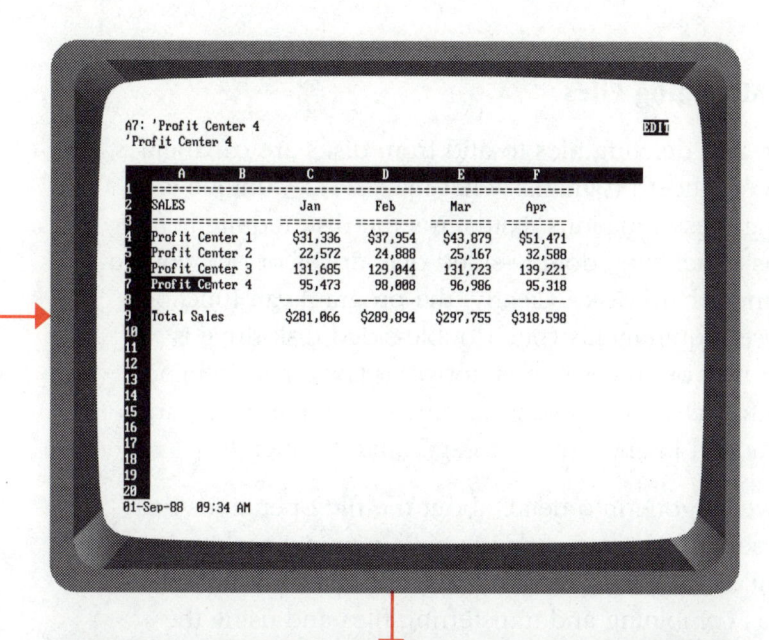

Press the [Del] key to delete the character above the cursor.

Press [←Enter] or type a new character and then press [←Enter] to complete your edit.

Introduction

An Overview of 1-2-3

Getting Started

1-2-3 Basics

Creating a Worksheet

Printing Reports

Creating and Printing Graphs

Managing Data

Understanding Macros

Appendix

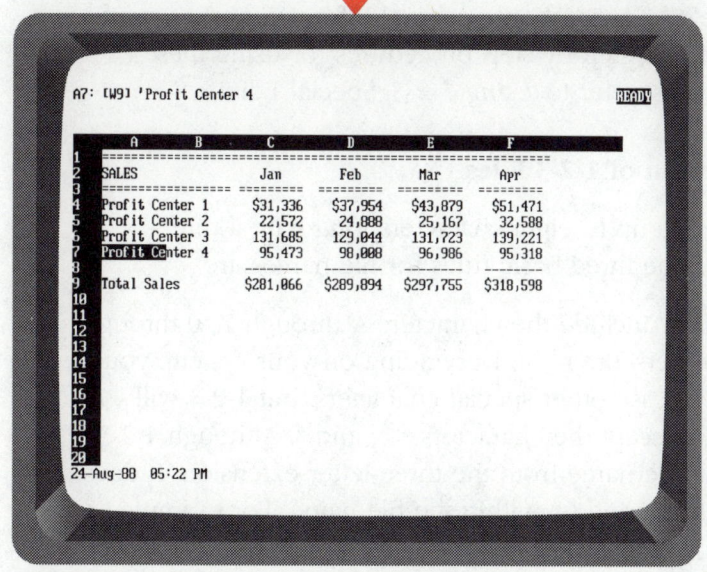

A Note About INSERT and OVERTYPE Modes:

When 1-2-3 is in INSERT mode, new characters are inserted to the left of the cursor. If you activate OVERTYPE mode by pressing [Ins] on your numeric keypad, a new character replaces the character positioned directly above the cursor.

Managing Files

Introduction to Managing Files

Storing, retrieving, and deleting files to and from disks are capabilities common to all spreadsheet programs. What makes 1-2-3 unique is its scale in performing these functions. Lotus lists the disk requirements for the program as either "two double-sided disk drives or one double-sided disk drive and a hard disk." Clearly, the program can function with less than these requirements (one double-sided disk drive is enough to squeak by), but this setup is not what Lotus had in mind. Lotus wrote 1-2-3 for users who intend to mix and match many large files that will be moved in and out of storage quite frequently.

For this section, we've gone into detail about the file operations that beginning 1-2-3 users need most often; namely, naming, saving, retrieving, deleting, and listing files. For more specialized file operations, such as combining and transferring files and using the Translate Utility, we've provided only general information. For more detailed information and step-by-step procedures for using these advanced 1-2-3 features, refer to *Using 1-2-3,* Special Edition.

A General Description of 1-2-3 Files

1-2-3 file names can be up to eight characters long with a three-character extension. The three basic rules for file names are

1. File names may include the characters A through Z, 0 through 9, and the underscore (_). Depending on your system, you may be able to use other special characters, but 1-2-3 will definitely not accept the characters <>, and *. Although 1-2-3 separates the file name from the three-letter extension, it does not accept the period (.) within the file name. For example, 1-2-3 will not accept the file name SALES1.1.TXT

2. File names may not contain blanks.

3. 1-2-3 automatically converts lowercase letters to uppercase letters in file names.

File Extensions in 1-2-3

Although you determine the eight-character name, 1-2-3 creates the extension automatically according to the type of file you are handling. The three possible file extensions are

- .WK1 For worksheet files (with Release 2; WKS with previous releases)
- .PRN For print files
- .PIC For graph files

Note: Release 2 easily reads older 1-2-3 worksheets with .WKS extensions and Symphony worksheets with .WRK and .WR1 extensions, but Release 2 writes the new files with .WK1 extensions when you save the worksheet. If you want to run .WK1 files with earlier versions of 1-2-3, you will need to use the Translate Utility, discussed later in this section.

In addition to creating files with the .WK1, .PRN, and .PIC extensions, 1-2-3 Release 2 lets you supply your own extension. To create a file name with your extension, enter the file name according to the rules listed above, enter a period, and then add an extension of one to three characters. Note that 1-2-3 will not display in the lists of .WK1, .PIC, or .PRN files any file name with your own extension. The /**F**ile **R**etrieve command, for example, will retrieve all .WK1 files but not files with your special extensions. To retrieve your special file, type the file name after the `Name of file to retrieve: C:\` prompt.

Managing Files

1-2-3 File Names

1-2-3 file names can be up to eight characters long with a three-character extension.

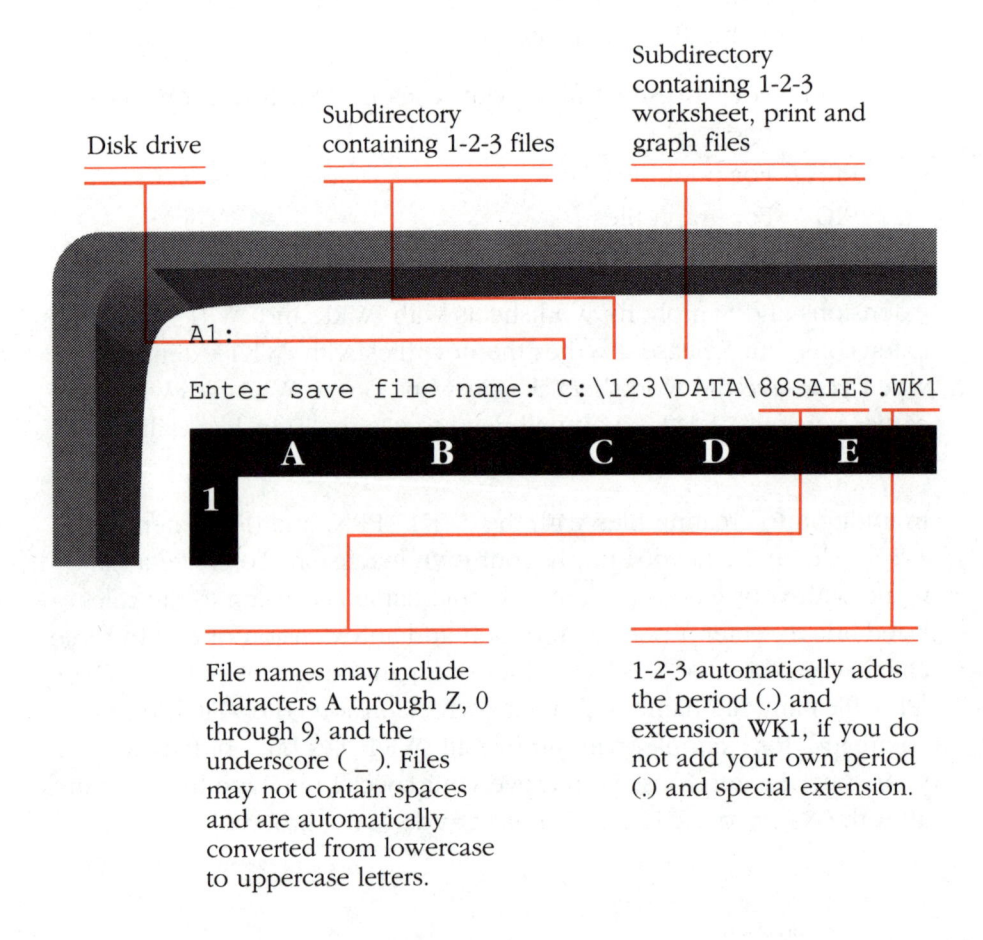

Disk drive

Subdirectory containing 1-2-3 files

Subdirectory containing 1-2-3 worksheet, print and graph files

```
A1:
Enter save file name: C:\123\DATA\88SALES.WK1
```

	A	B	C	D	E
1					

File names may include characters A through Z, 0 through 9, and the underscore (_). Files may not contain spaces and are automatically converted from lowercase to uppercase letters.

1-2-3 automatically adds the period (.) and extension WK1, if you do not add your own period (.) and special extension.

File Extensions in 1-2-3

1-2-3 creates automatically the file extension for your file names, if you do not add the period (.) and extension yourself. 1-2-3 uses three types of extensions, depending on the type of file format:

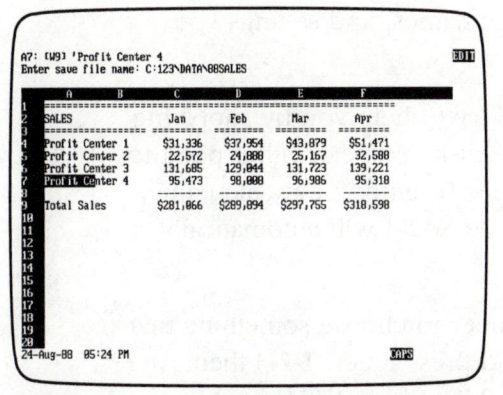

.WK1 is the extension automatically added to all names of worksheet files.

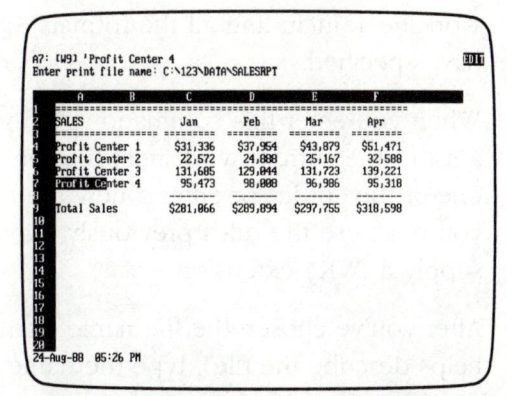

.PRN is the extension automatically added to names of 1-2-3 files that you save in print (ASCII) format. PRN files can be printed or imported.

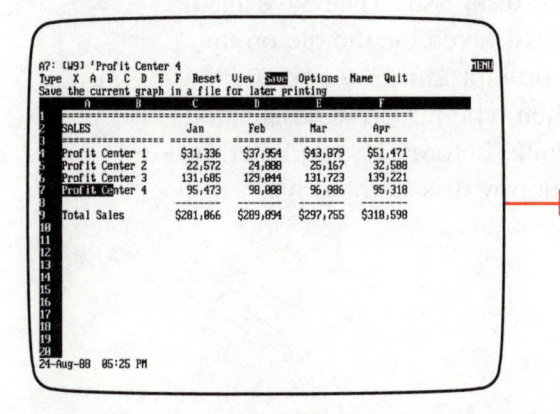

To print a graph you create in 1-2-3 from 1-2-3's PrintGraph program, you must save the file by using the **/G**raph **S**ave command. 1-2-3 automatically adds the extension .PIC to these files.

Managing Files

Saving and Naming Files

1-2-3's basic file function of storing files is easy to perform. The /**F**ile **S**ave command allows you to save an entire worksheet in a file on disk. The /**F**ile **S**ave command makes an exact copy of the current worksheet, including all the formats, range names, and settings you have specified.

When you enter this command, 1-2-3 will try to help you by supplying a list of the current worksheet files on the disk. You can either point to one of the entries or enter a new file name. To enter a new file name, you must use the rules previously explained. 1-2-3 will automatically supply a .WK1 extension.

After you've chosen the file name (remember to choose something that helps describe the file), type the name and press Enter. 1-2-3 then saves the file with the name given, and 1-2-3 assigns .WK1 as an extension.

If you use a hard disk system, you may want to save your worksheets on floppy disks as well as on the hard disk. To do this process, after you've saved the worksheet on the hard disk, issue /**F**ile **S**ave again. When you see the file name you have just saved (as the file on the hard disk), press the Esc key until the prompt `Enter save file name:` is the only thing remaining. Then type the drive designation for the floppy disk and the new file name. Before pressing Enter, make sure that you have placed the correct floppy disk in the drive.

Checking Disk Space before Saving

As you use 1-2-3, you'll notice that before long you have several worksheet files that take up significant disk space. Hard disk users have less to worry about than floppy disk users in this respect. No matter what type of system you are using, however, you need to keep track of the amount of disk space that your files use. Nothing is worse than getting the message `Disk full` after you have worked on an important worksheet and are attempting to save it.

You can get around this problem by using 1-2-3's **/S**ystem command. Whenever you type */s* from READY mode, 1-2-3 "steps aside" and displays the DOS prompt. (Even though the DOS prompt is displayed, 1-2-3 and your worksheet are still in memory.) From the DOS prompt, you can enter the DOS CHKDSK command to see how much space is available on your disk. You can also use the FORMAT command to format a new disk if you need one.

Hard disk users also can use **/S**ystem to exit to DOS so that they can check and format disks. If your hard disk is almost full, you may want to erase old files after you ensure that you have made a proper backup.

When you are finished with the DOS operations, type *exit* to return to the 1-2-3 worksheet. Now you can save the model on which you were working.

One point to remember: When you use **/S**ystem to exit to DOS, *do not* start any program from DOS that will alter memory, such as a memory-resident program. If you do, you won't be able to return to the 1-2-3 worksheet, and you will lose any work that you had not saved.

Managing Files

Saving Files

The **/F**ile **S**ave command allows you to save an entire worksheet in a file on disk. The **/F**ile **S**ave command makes an exact copy of the current worksheet, including all the formats, range names, and settings you have specified.

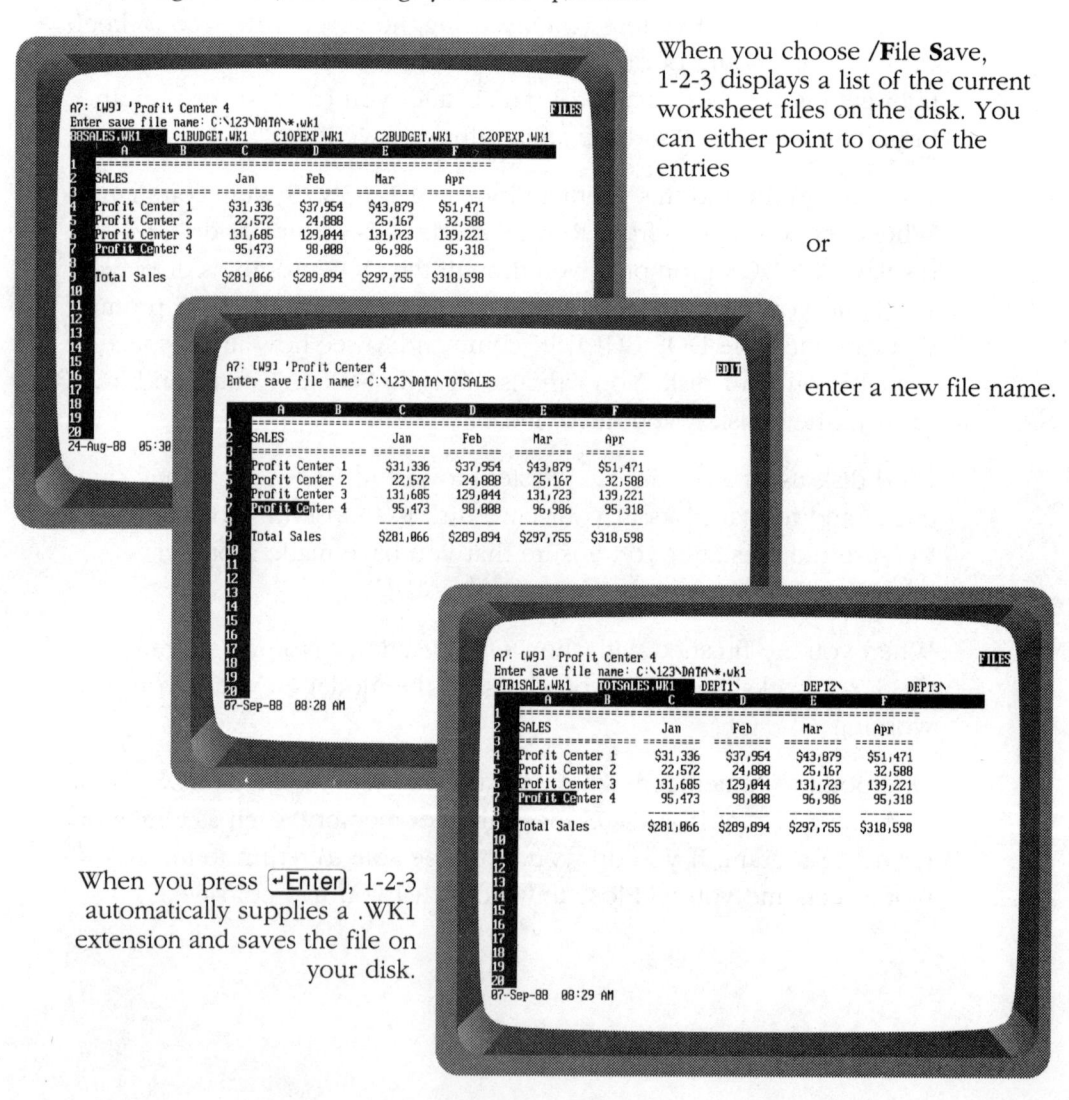

When you choose **/F**ile **S**ave, 1-2-3 displays a list of the current worksheet files on the disk. You can either point to one of the entries

or

enter a new file name.

When you press ⏎Enter, 1-2-3 automatically supplies a .WK1 extension and saves the file on your disk.

106

Naming Files

Remember to be expressive when you are thinking of a file name for the new file. Choose a file name that relates something about the file's contents. The following list provides some good examples of file names:

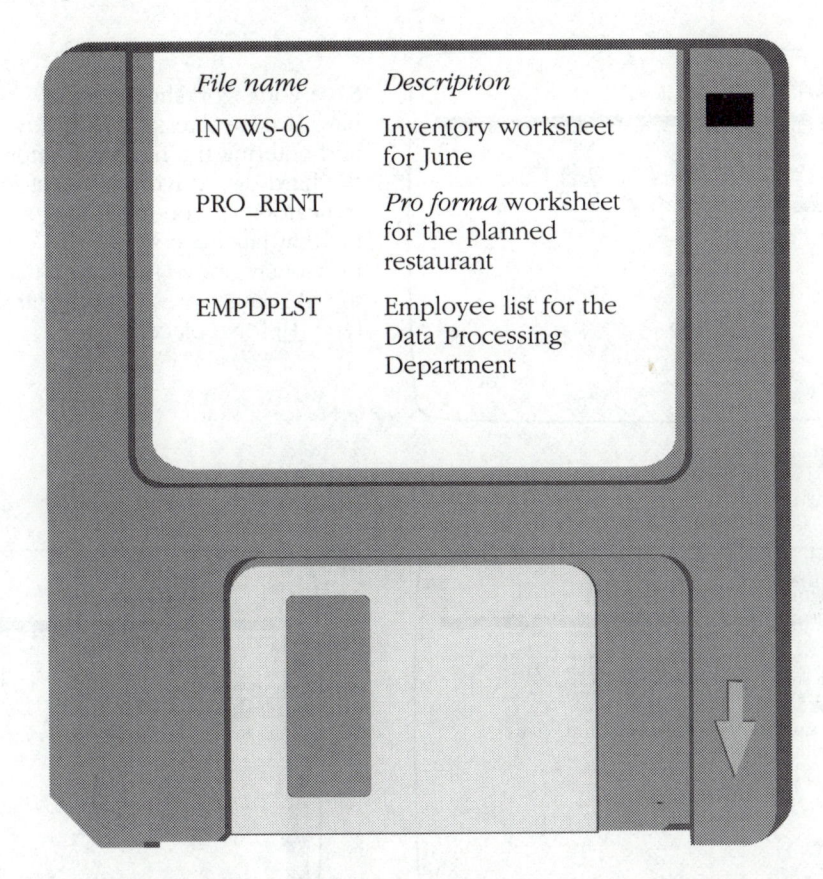

File name	Description
INVWS-06	Inventory worksheet for June
PRO_RRNT	*Pro forma* worksheet for the planned restaurant
EMPDPLST	Employee list for the Data Processing Department

If you work with many different worksheets that contain basically the same information, you'll need to make the names similar without, of course, using the same name. In the previous examples, the name INVWS-06 was given to an inventory worksheet for the month of June. Following this naming scheme, you would name the inventory worksheets for July and August INVWS-07 and INVWS-08, respectively. This naming technique will help you recall file names later.

Managing Files

Saving your Worksheet on the Hard Disk and also on a Floppy Disk

If 1-2-3 automatically saves your worksheet files on your computer's hard disk, you can also save a backup file of your worksheet on a floppy disk.

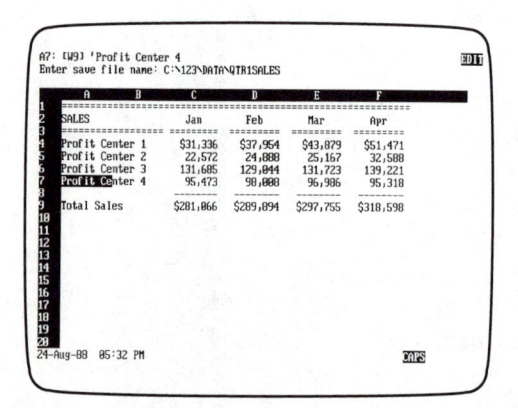

Save your worksheet on the hard disk by pressing /**F**ile **S**ave and entering the file name after the hard disk drive and directory indicators. (If you are saving a file that has been saved previously, move the cursor to the file name, press [↵Enter], and type [R] for replace.)

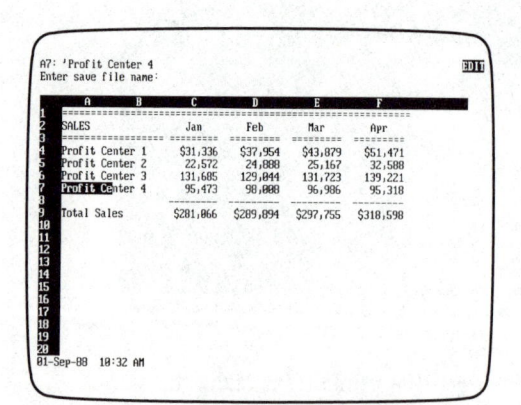

After you have saved your worksheet on the hard disk, issue /**F**ile **S**ave again, and press the [Esc] key until the prompt `Enter save file name:` is the only thing remaining.

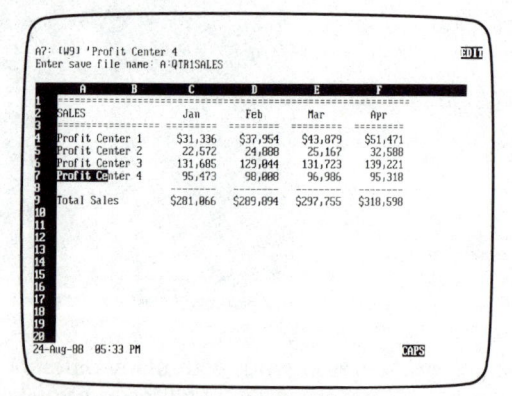

Finally type the disk drive designation (for example A:), enter the file name, and press [↵Enter].

108

Checking Disk Space before Saving

Before issuing the /**F**ile **S**ave command, you should check the amount of disk space available on your disk.

To check the amount of disk space before you issue /**F**ile **S**ave, use the /**S**ystem command to temporarily leave 1-2-3 and return to DOS. (/**S**ystem allows you to keep your worksheet in memory while having access to DOS.)

When your screen displays the amount of memory available, and you are certain enough space is available on the disk, type [E][X][I][T]. If you need to format a floppy disk, use the DOS FORMAT command.

At the DOS prompt, type [C][H][K][D][S][K] and the drive containing the disk you want to check.

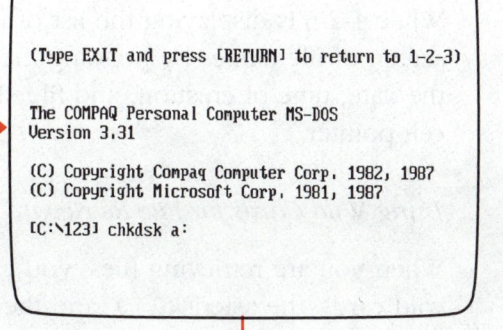

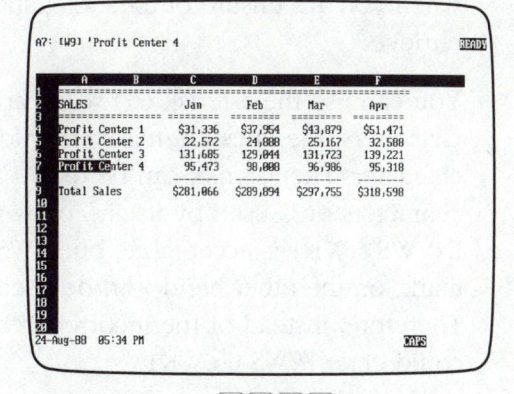

After you type [E][X][I][T], the worksheet will be displayed again exactly as it appeared when you issued /**S**ystem.

Managing Files

Retrieving Files

To call a file back into memory from disk, use the **/F**ile **R**etrieve command. Again, 1-2-3 displays a list of all files currently on disk with the extensions .WK1 or .WKS.

Whenever you need to choose a file name, 1-2-3 helps you by displaying a list of the files on the current drive and directory. If the file name you want is in the list, you can select it by moving the cursor to that name and pressing Enter. Otherwise, you can type in the file name you want.

While 1-2-3 is displaying the list of file names, you can show a full screen of file names by pressing the F3 (Name) key. You will also see the date, time of creation, and file size of each file highlighted by the cell pointer.

Using Wild Cards for File Retrieval

When you are retrieving files, you can use *wild cards* with 1-2-3. These wild cards, the asterisk (✶) and the question mark (?), are helpful when you need to limit the number of files displayed on-screen or when you are unsure of the exact spelling of a file you want to retrieve.

You can use the asterisk (✶) wild card in place of any combination of characters; the question mark (?) wild card stands for any one character. The asterisk can be used only when it follows other characters or is used by itself. Following these rules, the name INVWS✶.WK1 is acceptable, but ✶WS-06.WK1 is not. The question mark, on the other hand, can be used in any character position. Therefore, instead of the incorrect retrieval name ✶WS-06.WK1, you could enter ???WS-06.WK1.

Retrieving Files from Subdirectories

1-2-3 keeps track of subdirectory names as well as file names. These names are displayed in the current directory, with the subdirectories distinguished from files by the backslash (\) that appears after the subdirectory name.

If you point to a subdirectory name and press Enter during a 1-2-3 file command, 1-2-3 switches to that subdirectory and displays a list of its files. The list includes any subdirectories of this subdirectory. You then can specify a file name in that subdirectory.

If you want to access a file on a different drive or in a directory that is not a subdirectory of the current directory, use the Esc key or the Backspace key. Pressing the Esc key once while the default path name shows on the control panel changes 1-2-3 to EDIT mode; you can then edit the file specification just as you would any label entry. Pressing the Esc key a second time erases the current drive and directory specification; you can then enter the specification for the drive and directory you want. (The **/W**orksheet **G**lobal **D**efault **D**irectory command is a small exception: for this command, the default path name appears on the control panel in EDIT mode; pressing the Esc key once erases the path name.)

You can use the Backspace key to erase the path name, one directory at a time. To reverse the process, select a subdirectory name from the list of files and then press Enter.

If you want to find out more about DOS path names and subdirectories, you can consult *Using PC DOS,* 2nd Edition or *MS-DOS User's Guide,* 2nd Edition, both by Chris DeVoney, and *Managing Your Hard Disk,* by Don Berliner with Chris DeVoney. All three books are published by Que Corporation.

Managing Files

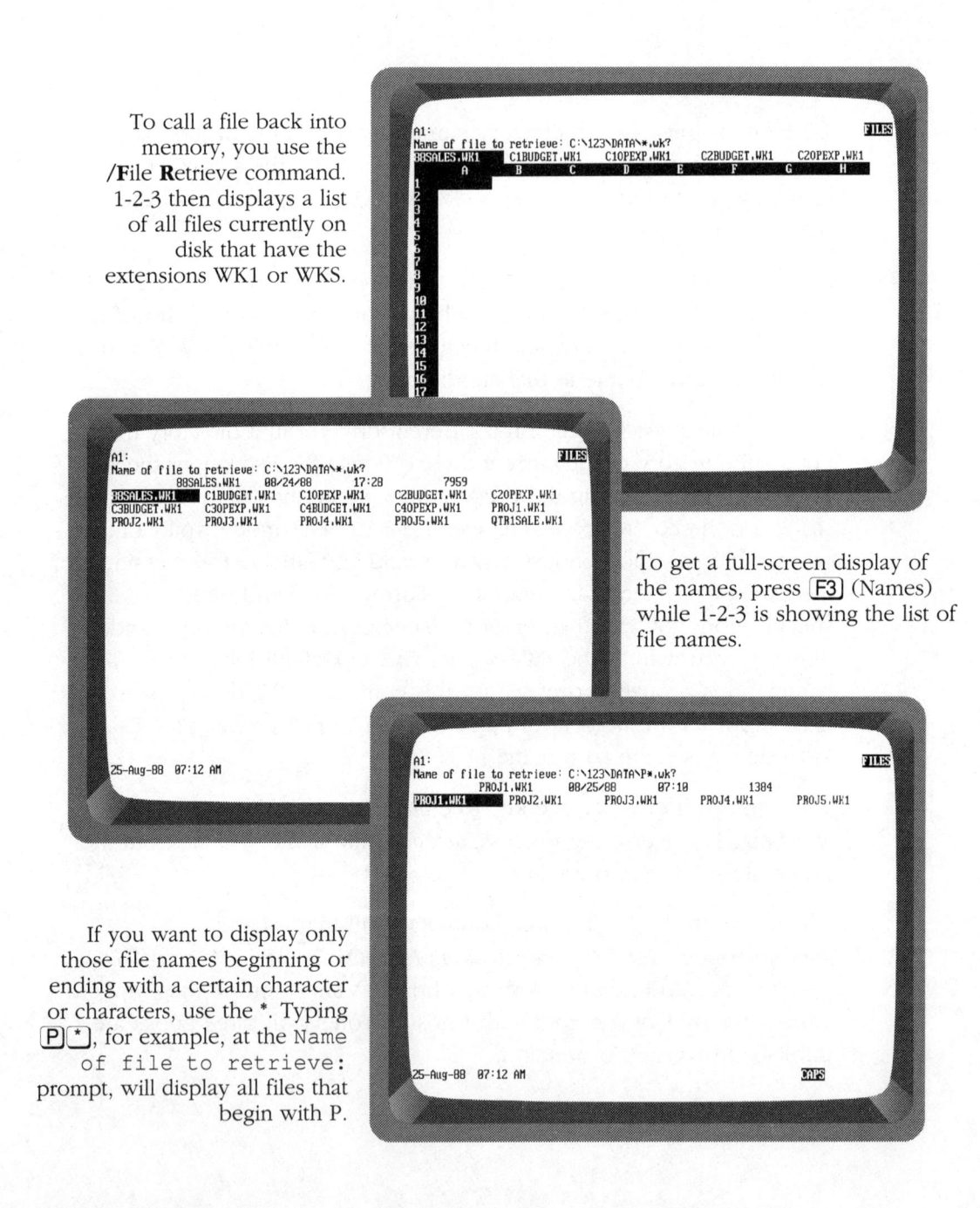

To call a file back into memory, you use the **/F**ile **R**etrieve command. 1-2-3 then displays a list of all files currently on disk that have the extensions WK1 or WKS.

To get a full-screen display of the names, press [F3] (Names) while 1-2-3 is showing the list of file names.

If you want to display only those file names beginning or ending with a certain character or characters, use the *. Typing [P][*], for example, at the `Name of file to retrieve:` prompt, will display all files that begin with P.

112

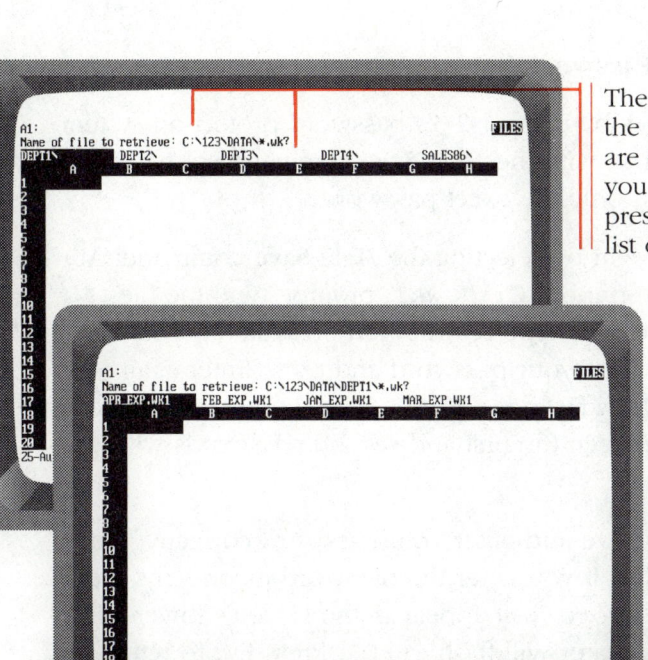

| Introduction | Moving Around the Spreadsheet | Entering Data and Formulas | Using Mathematical Operators in Formulas | Using Functions | Entering Labels | Editing Data in the Worksheet | **Managing Files** |

The \ (backslash) key after the name indicates that these are subdirectory names. When you point to a subdirectory and press Enter, 1-2-3 displays the list of files in that subdirectory.

This screen shows the files in the DEPT1 department. After the `Name of file to retrieve:` prompt, you can see the path that 1-2-3 followed to retrieve the specified files.

Introduction

An Overview of 1-2-3

Getting Started

1-2-3 Basics

Creating a Worksheet

Printing Reports

Creating and Printing Graphs

Managing Data

Understanding Macros

Appendix

Some valid file names, drive, and directory specifications are

B:\SAMPLE1.WK1	Worksheet file on drive B
C:\123\SAMPLE1.WK1	Worksheet file in subdirectory 123 on drive C
C:\123\DATA*.PIC	List of all .PIC files in subdirectory DATA of subdirectory 123 on drive C. 1-2-3 displays the list and waits for you to select a specific file name.
A:*.*	List of all files on drive A. 1-2-3 displays all file names and waits for you to select a specific file name.

113

Managing Files

Protecting Files with Passwords

You can protect your files by using 1-2-3's password protection system. You can create a password with the **/F**ile **S**ave command so that your file can be retrieved with only the exact password.

To create a password, begin by selecting the **/F**ile **S**ave command. At the `Enter save file name: C:\*.wk1` prompt, type the file name, leave a space, and then type *p*. After you press Enter, you will see a password prompt; type your password and press Enter again. 1-2-3 then asks you to `Verify password;` type the password once more. Any difference between the first and second passwords will result in nonacceptance.

After you issue **/F**ile **R**etrieve and enter your password correctly, the worksheet will appear. But if you enter the password incorrectly, the words `Incorrect password` will appear in the screen's lower-left corner, and the mode indicator will flash `ERROR`. Press Esc to return to a blank worksheet.

1-2-3 will accept any LICS character in a password, which can be as many as 15 characters long. You need to be careful, however, because 1-2-3 will accept the password only in the exact uppercase or lowercase letters you entered. For example, if you entered *pdfund* as your password, 1-2-3 would not retrieve the file if you typed *PDFUND* or *PDfund* or any other combination of uppercase and lowercase letters. Be sure not to forget your password.

Steps for Password Protecting a Worksheet

When you want to password protect a worksheet, follow these steps:

1. Type / to bring up the 1-2-3 menu.
2. Issue the **F**ile **S**ave command.
3. Enter the file name, leave a space, type *p*, and press Enter.
4. Type the password.
5. Press Enter.
6. Verify the password by typing it again.
7. Press Enter.

You can delete a password by retrieving the file with the password you want to delete. Then, when you are ready to save the file, select the **/F**ile **S**ave command. When the prompt appears, erase `[PASSWORD PROTECTED]` by pressing the Backspace or Esc key. Proceed with the **/F**ile **S**ave operation, and 1-2-3 will save the file without the password.

To change a password, complete the first two steps for deleting the password name. After you have deleted `[PASSWORD PROTECTED]`, press the space bar, type *p*, and press Enter. At this point, 1-2-3 will prompt you for a new password and ask you to verify it. Once you have completed these steps and saved the file, the new password will be stored.

Managing Files

Password Protecting a Worksheet

You may find that you want to protect your worksheet by using 1-2-3's password protection features.

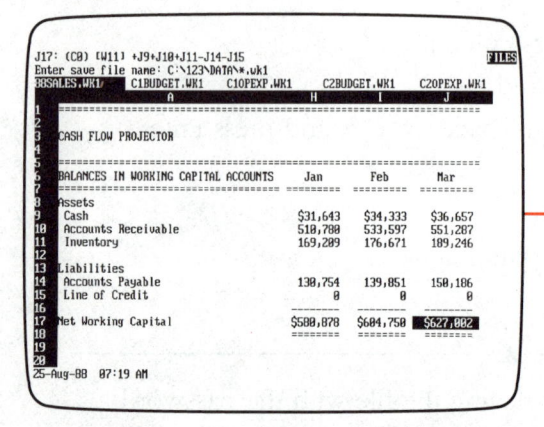

To create a password, start with selecting **/F**ile **S**ave.

Then, at the `Enter save file name:` prompt, type the file name, leave a space, and type [P].

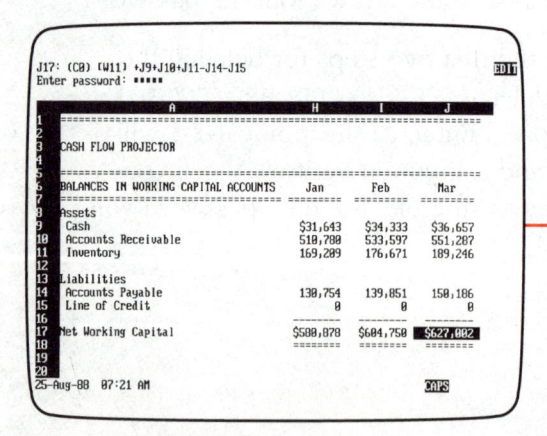

You will then see the password prompt. Type your password and press [↵Enter].

1-2-3 then asks you to verify the password by typing it in. The password is never displayed on-screen; it is always "hidden" by boxes that appear as you type.

Retrieving a Password Protected File

When you use /File Retrieve to open the protected file, you must enter the password exactly as you entered it when you created the password; otherwise, you won't be able to open the file.

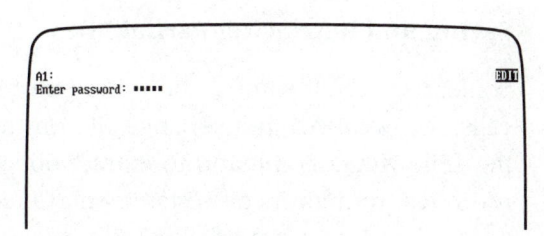

Deleting a Password

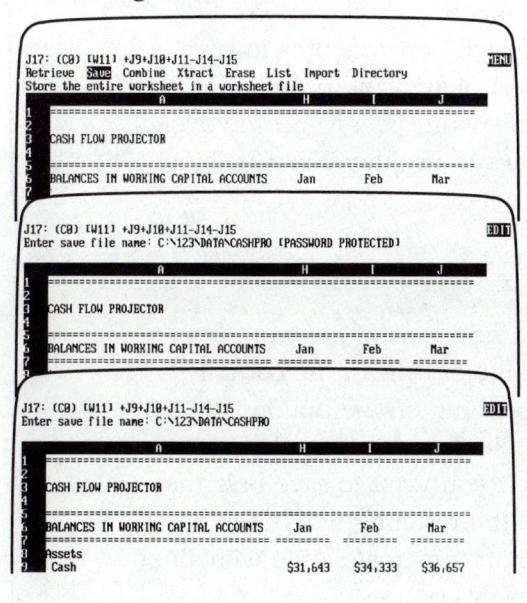

Delete a password by selecting /File Save.

When the prompt appears, erase [PASSWORD PROTECTED], and press the ⬅Backspace or Esc key.

Press ⏎Enter to finally save the file without the password.

Changing a Password

Change a password by completing the first two steps in deleting a password. After you have deleted [PASSWORD PROTECTED], press the space bar, type P, press ⏎Enter, and type a new password when prompted.

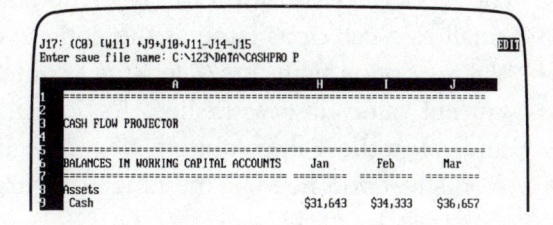

Introduction

An Overview of 1-2-3

Getting Started

1-2-3 Basics

Creating a Worksheet

Printing Reports

Creating and Printing Graphs

Managing Data

Understanding Macros

Appendix

Managing Files

Saving and Retrieving Partial Files

Sometimes you'll want to store only part of a worksheet (a range of cells, for instance) in a separate file on disk. For example, you can use the /**F**ile **X**tract command to extract outlays from an expense report or revenues from an income statement. One of the best uses for a partial save is breaking up worksheet files that are too large to be stored on a single disk.

Conversely, you may have several worksheets with like information. Suppose that you own a store in which each department is its own profit center. At the end of the month, you may want to use a partial file retrieve to combine each department's worksheet to get the overall picture of the store's profit and loss. You can use the /**F**ile **C**ombine command to perform these operations.

Extracting Information

With the /**F**ile **X**tract command, you can save part of the worksheet file—either the formulas existing in a range of cells or the current values of the formulas in the range, depending on the option you select. Both options create a worksheet file that you can reload into 1-2-3 with the /**F**ile **R**etrieve command. If you want to save only the current values, however, remember that the resulting worksheet file will contain numbers but no formulas. You can create a file with all of the formulas intact by selecting the **F**ormulas option.

The /**F**ile **X**tract command requires also that you specify the portion of the worksheet you want to save. The range to be saved can be as small as a cell or as large as the entire worksheet. When you use the **V**alues option with the /**F**ile **X**tract command, you can "lock" the current values in a worksheet. To lock the values, issue the command and select the **V**alues option. Next, specify the portion of the worksheet you need as the range to extract. You can select the entire worksheet as your range, if necessary. This selection will save the current values stored in the worksheet. You can think of this process as taking a snapshot of the current worksheet. You can then reload the new, values-only file into the worksheet and print or graph it.

/File Xtract Formulas preserves any formulas that are in the extract range. This option can be particularly useful if your worksheet is too large to fit on one disk, because you can split the file across two disks and still preserve the formulas you need.

Combining Files

Another function you will want to perform is that of making copies of certain ranges of cells from other worksheets and placing them into strategic spots in the current worksheet. For example, if you work for a large firm, you may want to combine several divisions' balance sheets and income statements in one consolidated worksheet.

A simple technique for accomplishing this kind of consolidation is to start with and keep a copy of an "empty master." You will always have an empty master ready when the time to perform a consolidation occurs. When you start with an empty master, you can copy the first divisional worksheet onto the master, leaving the original copy of the divisional worksheet untouched.

Copying a range of cells can be helpful also when you want to combine quarterly data into a yearly statement. Again, the formats must be compatible, and you will benefit by keeping an empty master.

The command used to combine data in the preceding examples is **/File Combine**. The **C**opy option copies the new worksheet or range over the existing worksheet or range; **A**dd sums the values in both areas; and **S**ubtract decreases the values in the existing worksheet or range by the values in the incoming worksheet or range.

Managing Files

Using /File Xtract

The /**F**ile **X**tract command lets you copy a part of your worksheet to a separate file.

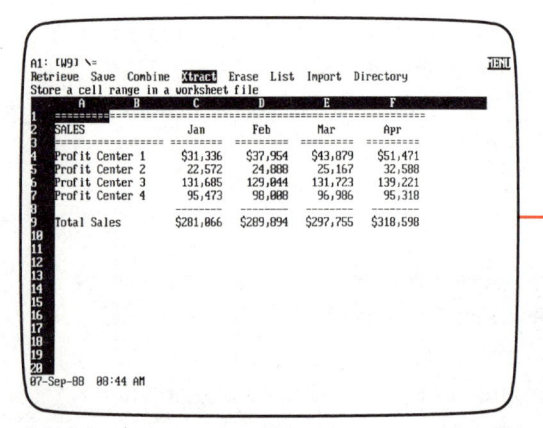

Select /**F**ile **X**tract.

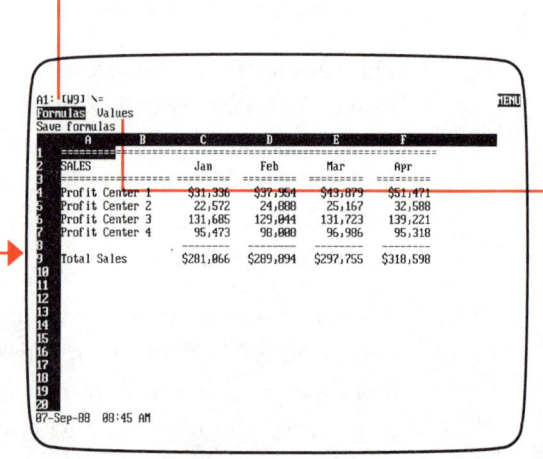

Choose either **F**ormulas or **V**alues.

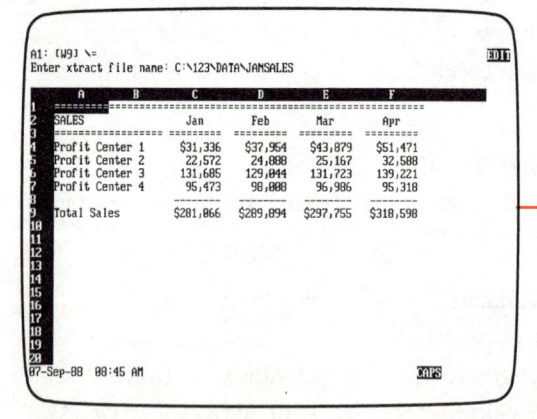

Enter a file name for the file where the data will be extracted.

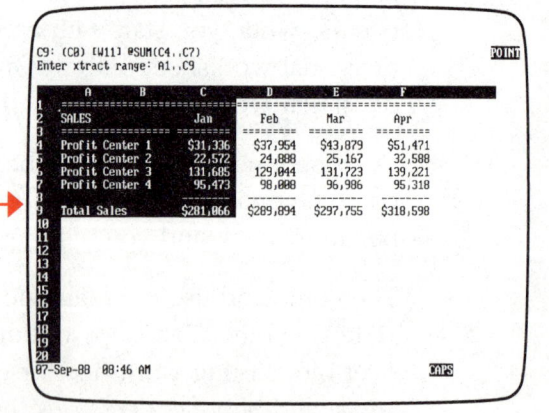

Highlight the range you want to extract, and press ⏎Enter.

/**F**ile **E**xtract gives you the option of extracting formulas as they are.

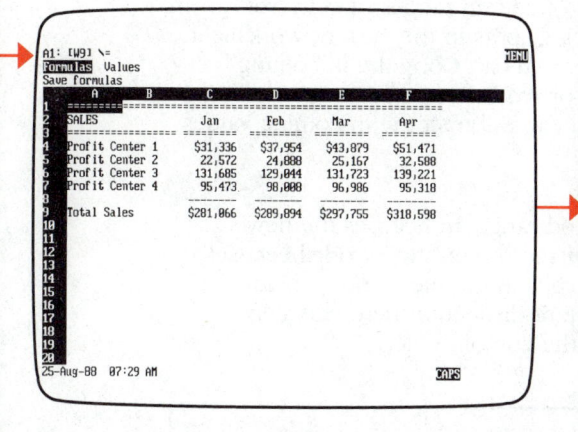

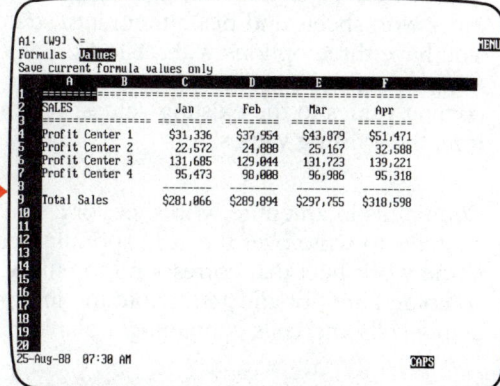

The formula in C9 is retained in the new file.

/**F**ile **X**tract gives you the option of extracting data and converting formulas to values.

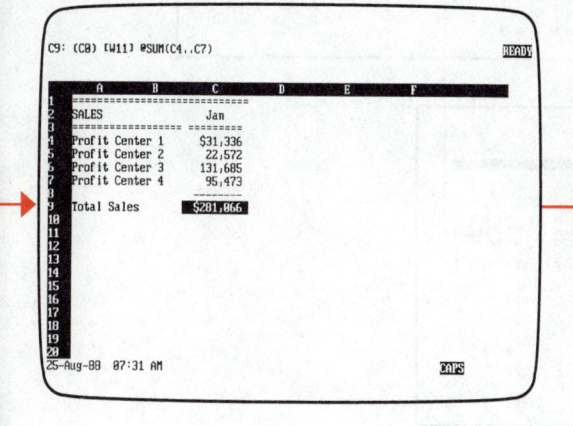

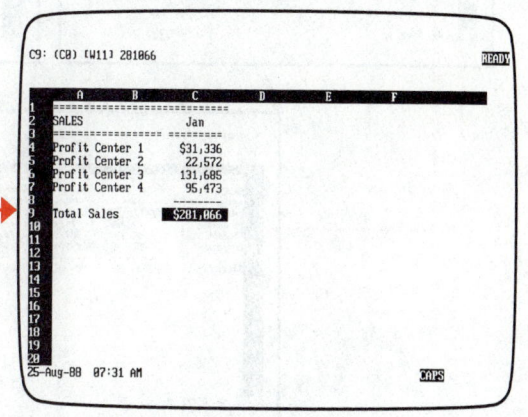

The formula in C9 is converted to a value.

121

Managing Files

Combining Files

You can use **/F**ile **C**ombine to make copies of certain ranges of cells from other worksheets and place them into strategic spots in the current worksheet. You have three options with **/F**ile **C**ombine: you can **C**opy the in-coming range or worksheet over the existing range or worksheet; you can **A**dd the in-coming values to the existing values; or you can **S**ubtract the in-coming values from the existing values.

Copy pulls in an entire worksheet or a named range and causes the new contents to write over the corresponding cells in the existing worksheet. Cells in the worksheet that correspond to empty cells in the file or range being combined are not affected. (Note the important distinction here between empty cells and cells containing a blank in the combine file.)

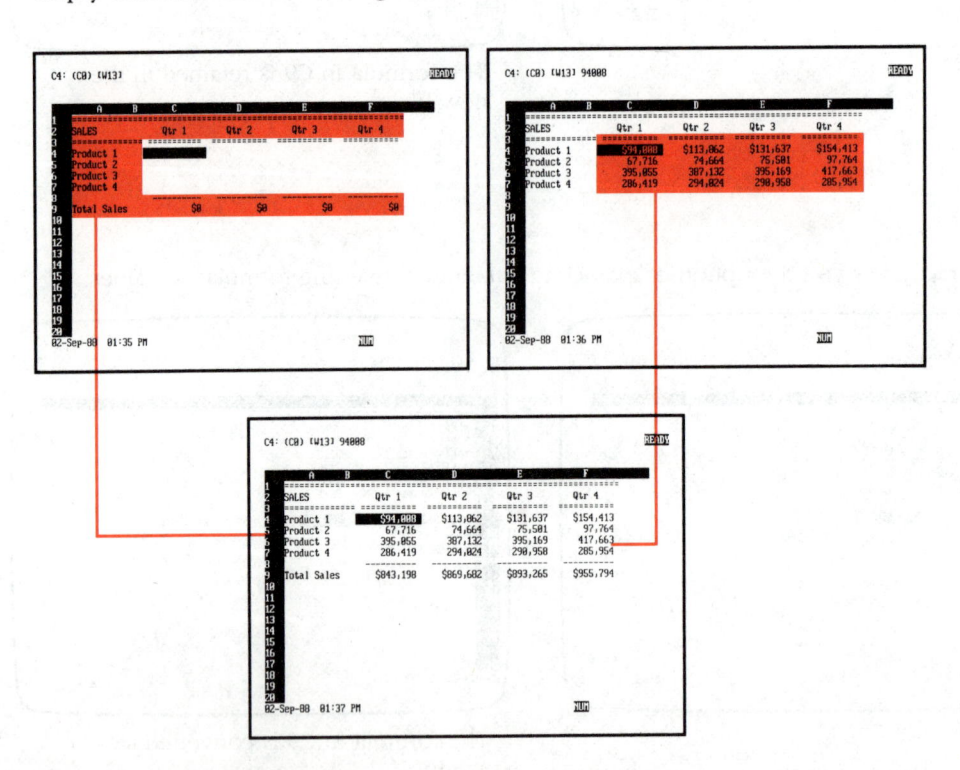

122

| Introduction | Moving Around the Spreadsheet | Entering Data and Formulas | Using Mathematical Operators in Formulas | Using Functions | Entering Labels | Editing Data in the Worksheet | **Managing Files** |

Add pulls in the values from an entire worksheet or a named range and adds these values to the corresponding cells in the current worksheet. The **A**dd command affects only cells in the worksheet that are blank or contain numeric values. Cells containing formulas or labels are unchanged. Cells in the file being combined that contain labels or string formulas are not added.

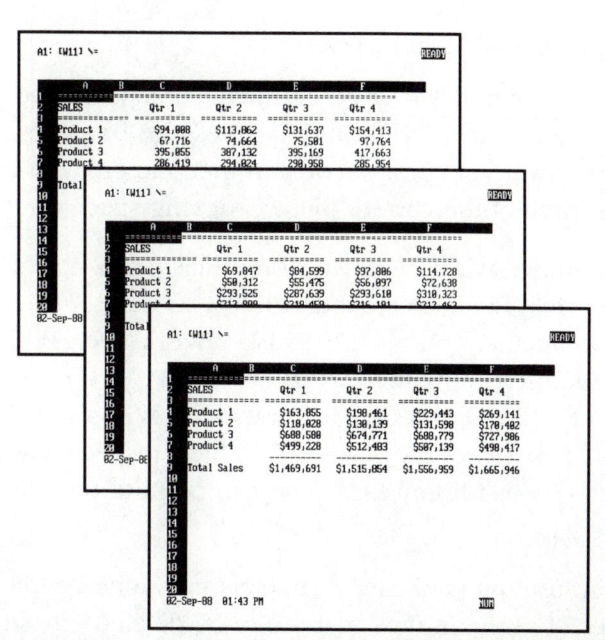

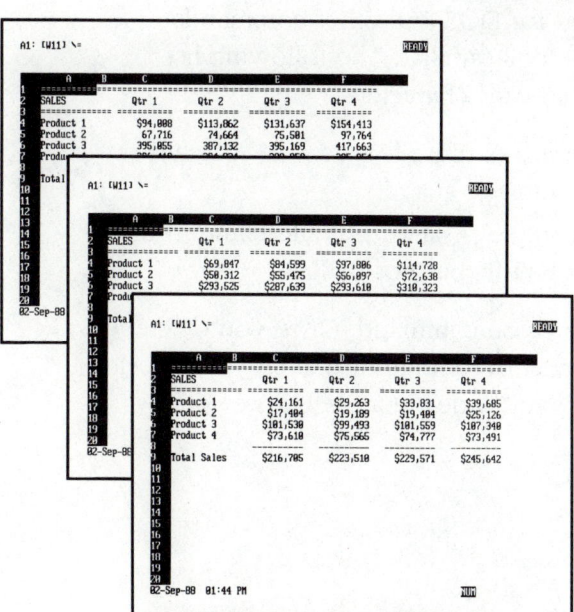

Subtract pulls in an entire worksheet or a named range and subtracts the values from the corresponding cells in the current worksheet. When an existing cell is empty, the incoming value is subtracted from zero. Like **A**dd, **S**ubtract affects only cells in the worksheet that are blank or contain numeric values. Cells containing formulas or labels in the current worksheet are unaffected, and cells from the worksheet being combined that contain labels or string formulas are not subtracted.

Introduction

An Overview of 1-2-3

Getting Started

1-2-3 Basics

Creating a Worksheet

Printing Reports

Creating and Printing Graphs

Managing Data

Understanding Macros

Appendix

123

Managing Files

Deleting Files and Listing Files

When you save files to disk, you may sometimes find that the disk is full. To alert you, 1-2-3 flashes the message `Disk full` in the screen's lower left corner. You can then either swap disks or delete one or more of the current files occupying space on the disk.

You have two ways to delete stored files in 1-2-3. The first way is to use the **/F**ile **E**rase command. When you issue */FE*, a menu prompt will ask whether you want to erase a **W**orksheet, **P**rint, **G**raph, or **O**ther file. According to your choice (**W**, **P**, or **G**), 1-2-3 will show you only .WK1 files (created in Release 2) or .WKS files (if created in Release 1 or 1A), .PRN files, or .PIC files, respectively. If you choose **O**ther, 1-2-3 will list all files. You can point to the file you want erased, or type its name and press Enter.

You can use the wild-card characters mentioned earlier to display all the files of a certain type that are to be deleted. These characters are the same wild-card characters used for DOS and other commands throughout 1-2-3, and they should look familiar. The following list shows some examples of using wild-card characters:

- * Matches the remaining characters of a file name. B* matches BOB, BARNEY, BOQUIST, etc.
- ? Matches all characters in a single position in a file name. B?RD matches BARD, BIRD, and BYRD, but not BURT.

Be careful when you use the **/F**ile **E**rase command. Once you delete a file, you cannot recover that file by conventional means. Always check and double-check that you really want to delete a file before you do so.

Listing Different Types of Files

1-2-3 can list all the names of a certain type of file on the active drive and directory with the /**F**ile **L**ist command. The choices for file types are

    Worksheet Print Graph Other

Worksheet, **P**rint, and **G**raph list the three types of 1-2-3 data files. The fourth choice, **O**ther, lists all files of all types on the current drive and directory.

Which drive is the active drive depends on the /**W**orksheet **G**lobal **D**efault **D**irectory setting and whether that setting has been overridden by the /**F**ile **D**irectory command.

Specifying a Drive

You use the /**W**orksheet **G**lobal **D**efault **D**irectory or the /**F**ile **D**irectory commands to change the drive and directory. /**W**orksheet **G**lobal **D**efault **D**irectory can change the default drive and directory. /**F**ile **D**irectory, on the other hand, changes the drive and directory temporarily for only the current worksheet session. Hard disk users can use the default directory setting to their advantage. For example, you could set the default directory to C:\DATA. When you want to retrieve a file, you'll see that 1-2-3 displays the subdirectories \DATA\DEPT1, \DATA\DEPT2, and \DATA\COMPANY. After you've chosen the proper directory, 1-2-3 again displays the files stored in that directory so that you can make a choice. Setting the default directory this way will save time if you use worksheets in different subdirectories.

Managing Files

Deleting Files

You can delete a file two ways with 1-2-3: by using /**F**ile **E**rase or by accessing DOS by issuing the /**S**ystem command and erasing the file at DOS level.

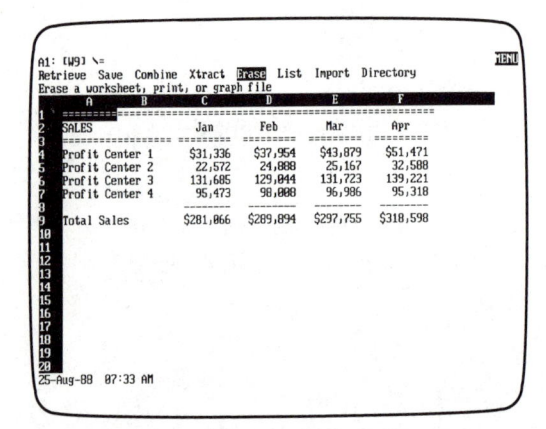

To use /**F**ile **E**rase, you call up the 1-2-3 main menu by pressing / and then select **F**ile **E**rase.

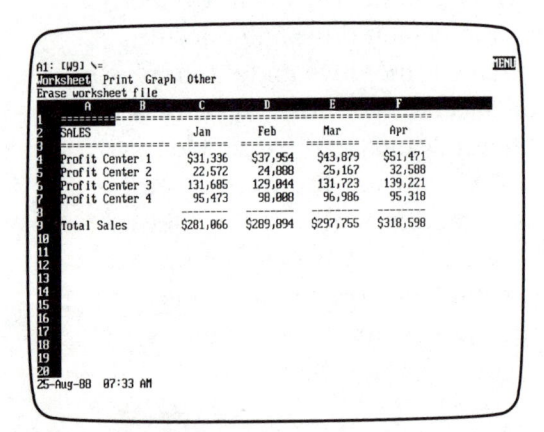

A prompt then asks whether you want to erase a worksheet, print, graph, or other file. Depending on your choice of file, 1-2-3 then displays the files with the appropriate extensions.

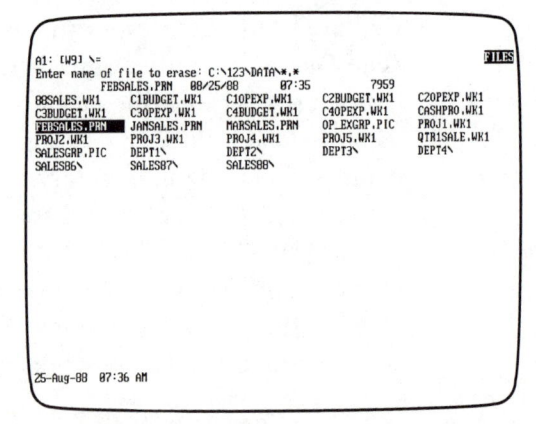

If you choose **O**ther, 1-2-3 displays all files. Simply point to the file you want erased, or type the file name and press ↵Enter.

Listing Files

Use **/File List** to display the files on the current drive and directory.

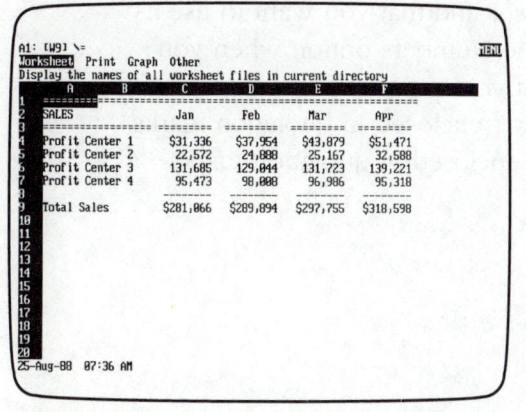

When you select the command, you are asked to choose to display worksheet, print, graph, or other files.

After you choose one of these options and press ⏎Enter, the list of files is displayed.

Introduction

An Overview of 1-2-3

Getting Started

1-2-3 Basics

Creating a Worksheet

Printing Reports

Creating and Printing Graphs

Managing Data

Understanding Macros

Appendix

127

Managing Files

Transferring Files

A powerful 1-2-3 feature is its capacity to interface with outside programs. To do this interface, you use the **/F**ile **I**mport, **/P**rint **F**ile **O**ptions **O**ther **U**nformatted commands, and the Translate Utility. In this section, we'll give you an overview of these features. For more specific information, including step-by-step instructions on translating dBASE files to 1-2-3 and vice versa, see *Using 1-2-3,* Special Edition.

Transferring Files with /File Import

Use the **/F**ile **I**mport command to copy standard ASCII files to specific locations in the current worksheet. For example, .PRN (print) files are standard ASCII text files. Other standard ASCII files include those produced by different word processing and BASIC programs. Many programs, for example database programs, have the capability of producing ASCII files as 1-2-3 does.

Generally, you should use the **T**ext option for importing an ASCII file that was created with your word processor and that you want to use as documentation to create a report. Use the **N**umbers option when you import a delimited file. Remember that if you import a file with **N**umbers, any column headings that aren't enclosed in quotation marks will not be imported. Headings that are enclosed in quotation marks will be imported as labels.

Transferring Files with the Translate Utility

The Translate Utility is used to import files from dBASE II, dBASE III, dBASE III Plus, and VisiCalc into 1-2-3, and to export 1-2-3 files in dBASE II, dBASE III, dBASE III Plus, and DIF formats. This feature provides good communication with dBASE, including dBASE III Plus (which is not listed on the menu but can be accessed by selecting dBASE III). The Translate Utility also provides translation capabilities between all of Lotus's products, allowing free interchange of worksheets between 1-2-3 Release 2.01 and Symphony, Jazz, and earlier releases of 1-2-3.

Basically, the Translate Utility involves the following steps:

1. Choose the format (program) from which to translate.
2. Choose the format (program) to translate to.
3. Choose the file from which to translate.
4. Type the name of the file to be created.

When you choose a file name, Translate gives you a list of files from which to choose, based on your choice of format. (As a format choice, for example, you may have chosen *.WK1 for 1-2-3 Release 2.0 or 2.01 or *.DBF for a dBASE file.) You can then choose one of the displayed file names or you can press Esc to edit the subdirectory or file name.

As you begin the translation process, an indicator appears on the screen, informing you of the progress of the translation.

129

Managing Files

Transferring Files Using /File Import

Use the **/F**ile **I**mport command to copy standard ASCII files to specific locations in the current worksheet. .PRN (print) files are one example of standard ASCII text files created to print after the current 1-2-3 session. Other standard ASCII files include those produced by different word processing, database and BASIC programs.

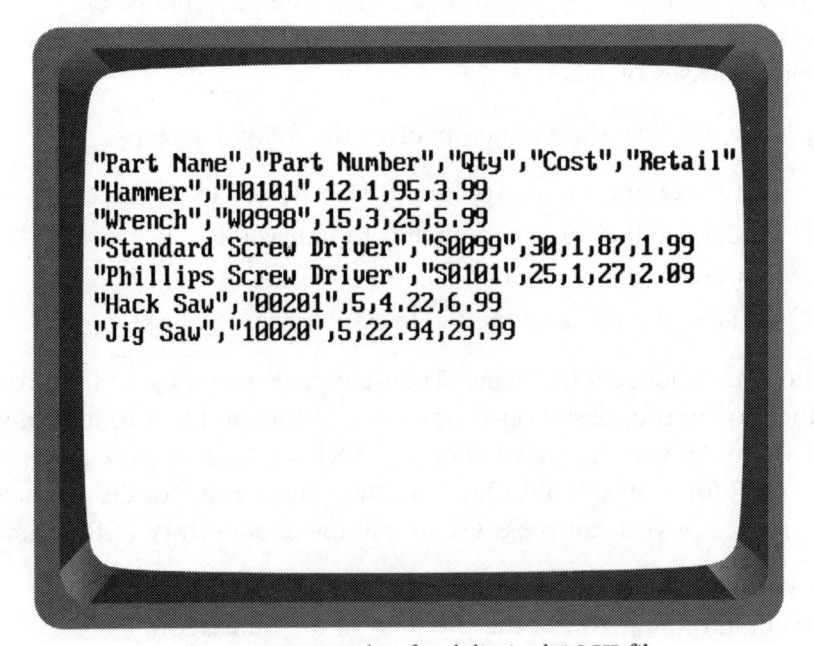

```
"Part Name","Part Number","Qty","Cost","Retail"
"Hammer","H0101",12,1.95,3.99
"Wrench","W0998",15,3.25,5.99
"Standard Screw Driver","S0099",30,1.87,1.99
"Phillips Screw Driver","S0101",25,1.27,2.09
"Hack Saw","00201",5,4.22,6.99
"Jig Saw","10020",5,22.94,29.99
```

This screen shows an example of a delimited ASCII file. Notice that the text is enclosed in quotation marks, but the values are not. Note also that each data item is separated—or *delimited*—by commas.

Using the Translate Utility

You'll use the Translate Utility to import files from dBASE and VisiCalc and to export 1-2-3 files to dBASE and DIF formats. For more specific instruction about these procedures, see *Using 1-2-3, Special Edition*.

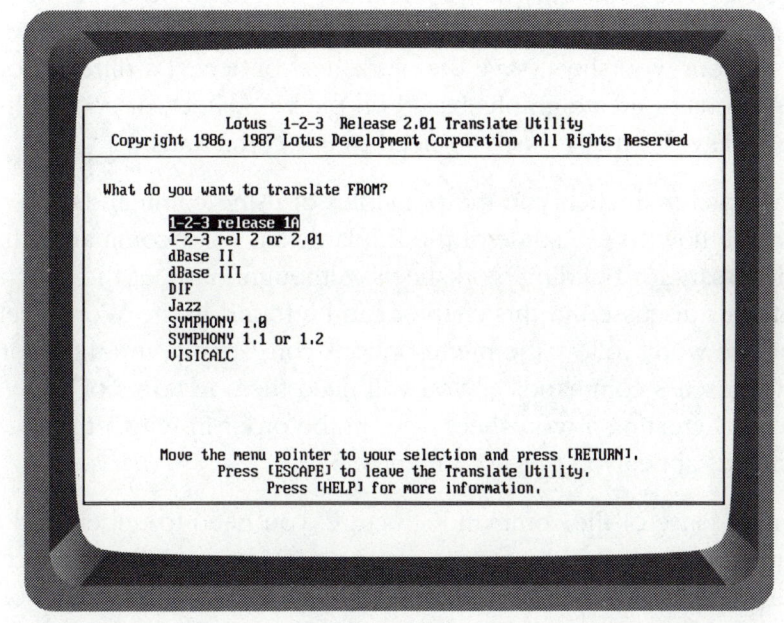

```
        Lotus  1-2-3  Release 2.01 Translate Utility
    Copyright 1986, 1987 Lotus Development Corporation  All Rights Reserved

What do you want to translate FROM?

        1-2-3 release 1A
        1-2-3 rel 2 or 2.01
        dBase II
        dBase III
        DIF
        Jazz
        SYMPHONY 1.0
        SYMPHONY 1.1 or 1.2
        VISICALC


        Move the menu pointer to your selection and press [RETURN].
              Press [ESCAPE] to leave the Translate Utility.
                   Press [HELP] for more information.
```

This screen shows the opening menu of the Translate Utility.

4 *Creating a Worksheet*

Using 1-2-3 means using 1-2-3 commands. Commands are the tools the program provides for performing its tasks. If you want to rearrange the data on your worksheet, save the worksheet or access a different one, print reports or create graphs based on the worksheet, or accomplish a wide variety of other tasks, you need to use commands.

This chapter will teach you the principles of using commands and show you how to use some of the fundamental 1-2-3 commands that are necessary for building worksheets. Although many of the commands discussed in this chapter can be found in the **W**orksheet menu, we won't follow the menu options consistently; in other words, we will discuss commands as you will need them in terms of the process of creating a worksheet—not in the order in which the commands appear on the 1-2-3 menus.

To make sense of the command structure, you need to understand one preliminary concept: the concept of ranges. Some commands affect the entire worksheet, but others affect only certain cells or groups of cells. 1-2-3 uses the term *range* for a rectangular block of cells, and 1-2-3 builds many highly useful actions around the concept of ranges. This chapter explains ranges and the group of commands you use to manipulate ranges.

Key Terms Used in This Chapter

range	A range is a rectangular group of cells that is used in a worksheet operation. For example, the rectangular area A10..D10 is a range.
/Range	These commands are used to manipulate cells in specified ranges. The **/R**ange command is found on the 1-2-3 main menu.
/Worksheet commands	These commands affect the entire worksheet or predefined areas of the worksheet. The **/W**orksheet command is available on the main menu.
absolute cell addressing	When you copy or move a formula and do not want a cell address to change, you can create an absolute address, meaning that the address will not change.
relative cell addressing	When you copy or move a formula, the addresses of the cells in that formula are changed to fit the new location.

What Does This Chapter Cover?

In this chapter, you learn how to

- Use ranges in a worksheet
- Use **/R**ange commands
- Name, list, and erase ranges
- Use **/W**orksheet commands
- Manipulate cell contents
- Copy cell contents
- Move cell contents
- Save your worksheet
- Access DOS by using **/S**ystem

133

Selecting Commands from Command Menus

If commands are the tools for performing 1-2-3 tasks, command menus are the toolboxes. The menus display the commands that are available for use. In 1-2-3, the command menus are especially helpful for several reasons. First, 1-2-3 lists the full command words.

To display the main command menu, press the slash (/) key. Remember to press the slash key while 1-2-3 is in READY mode whenever you want to activate a command.

A second feature of the command menu is illustrated on the display's third line. This line contains an explanation of the **W**orksheet menu item on which the command cursor is positioned. In fact, as you point to the different items in the command menu by moving the cursor across the list, a new explanation appears in the third line for each command-menu item. This action occurs with every command menu.

A third friendly aspect of command menus relates to how a command is initiated. You can either point to the option you want, or you can enter the first letter of the command name.

To point to the command-menu item, use the left- and right-arrow keys on the right side of the keyboard. When you have positioned the cursor on the proper item, press Enter. If you move the cursor to the last item in the list and then press the right-arrow key again, the cursor will "round the horn" and reappear on the first item in the list. Similarly, if the cursor is on the first item in the menu, press the left-arrow key to move the cursor to the last option. Note that you can move the cursor to the end of the command line also by pressing the End key, and you can move the cursor to the beginning of the line by pressing the Home key.

Entering the first letter of the command-menu item is the other way to select a command. For example, to select the **/W**orksheet **S**tatus command, which informs you of the status of several of 1-2-3's global parameters, you type / to select the main command menu, followed by *w* to select **W**orksheet. At this point, another menu appears.

▼

To select a command,

1. Type / to bring up the 1-2-3 command menu.
2. Move the cell pointer to the command you want by using the arrow keys and press enter or type the first letter of the command.

▲

If you make the wrong command selection, you can press Esc at any time to return to the previous command menu. For instance, if you realize that you should have entered **D**elete, not **I**nsert, press Esc to return to the **W**orksheet menu. You can press Esc as many times as necessary to return to whatever point you want in the series of command menus, even to return you out of MENU mode altogether. One alternative to pressing Esc repeatedly is to hold down the Ctrl (Control) key and then press the Break key. Doing so cancels the entire command and returns 1-2-3 to READY mode.

Setting up two alternatives for command selection is just one of the ways that 1-2-3 has oriented itself successfully to both the novice and the experienced user. The novice can point to the different commands and get a full explanation of each one, and the experienced user can enter at high speed a long series of commands, using the first-letter convention without reading the explanations.

In this chapter, you'll learn about the commands you need to use to create a worksheet. Other commands, such as /**D**ata and /**G**raph commands, are discussed in their appropriate chapters.

135

Selecting Commands from Command Menus

Selecting Commands from Command Menus

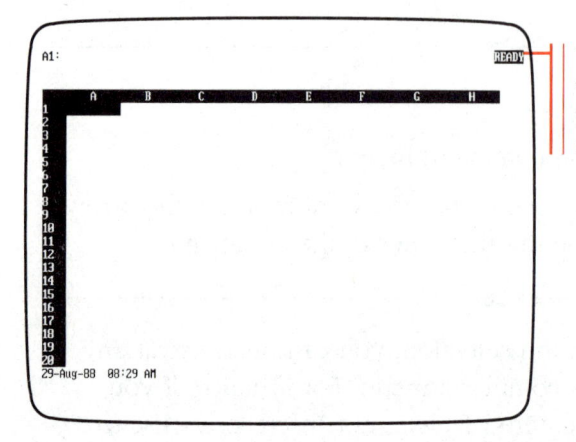

You can activate a command when you press the / key while 1-2-3 is in READY mode.

The main 1-2-3 menu appears on the second line of the control panel.

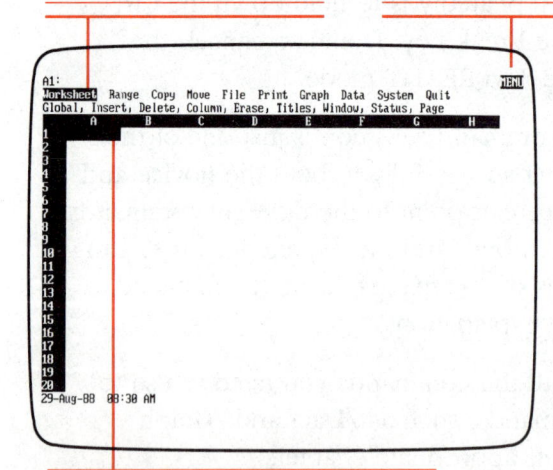

As soon as you press /, 1-2-3 changes to MENU mode.

The third line of the control panel displays the command options that are available for the command highlighted in the second line.

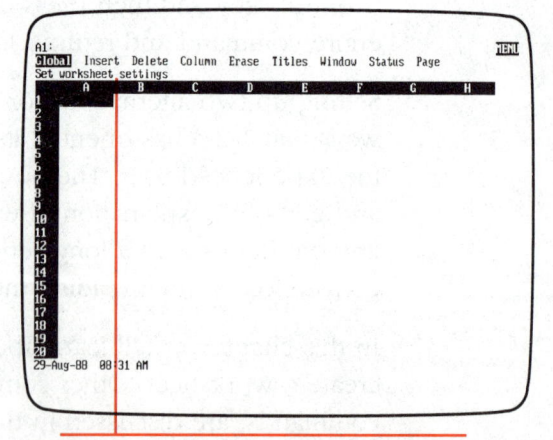

As soon as you select a command from one of the submenus, the third line of the control panel displays an explanation of the command.

136

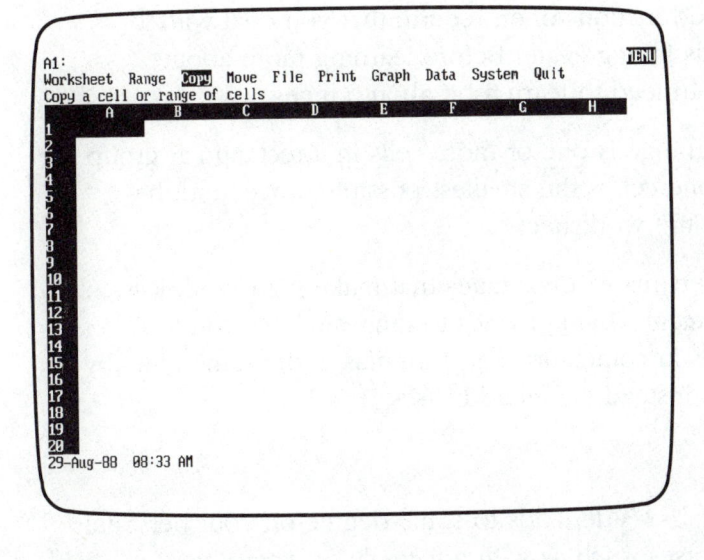

| Introduction | **Selecting Commands from Command Menus** | Using Ranges in the Worksheet | Using Worksheet Commands | Moving the Contents of Cells | Copying the Contents of Cells | Saving Your Files before You Quit (/Quit) | Accessing DOS from 1-2-3 |

```
A1:                                                        MENU
Worksheet Range Copy Move File Print Graph Data System Quit
Copy a cell or range of cells
     A       B       C       D       E       F       G       H
 1
 2
 3
 4
 5
 6
 7
 8
 9
10
11
12
13
14
15
16
17
18
19
20
29-Aug-88  08:33 AM
```

Pointing Method:

Type ⌐/⌐ to bring up the 1-2-3 command menu.

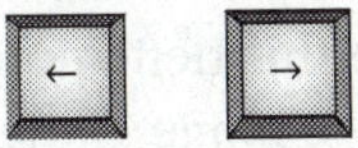

← →

Move the cell pointer to the command you want by using the arrow keys.

Press ⌐Enter⌐.

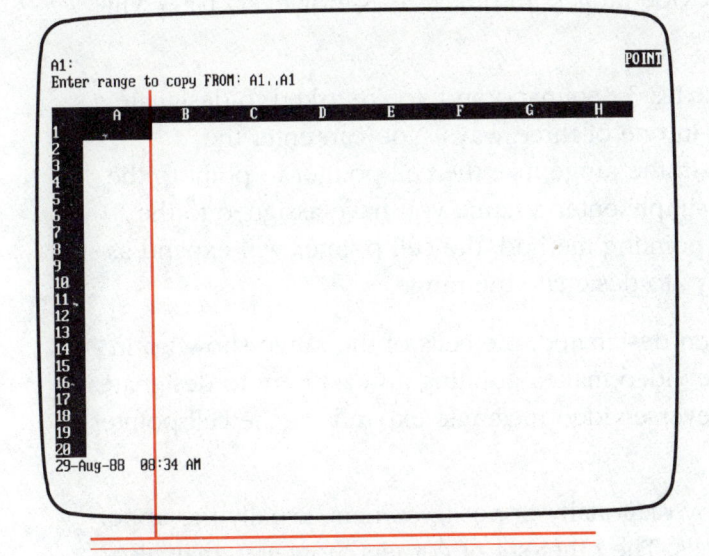

```
A1:                                                       POINT
Enter range to copy FROM: A1..A1
     A       B       C       D       E       F       G       H
 1
 2
 3
 4
 5
 6
 7
 8
 9
10
11
12
13
14
15
16
17
18
19
20
29-Aug-88  08:34 AM
```

Typing Method:

Type ⌐/⌐ to bring up the 1-2-3 command menu.

Move the cell pointer to the command you want by typing the first letter of the command.

Typing ⌐C⌐, for example, will select the **C**opy command from 1-2-3's main menu and take you directly to the Enter Range to Copy From: prompt.

Introduction

An Overview of 1-2-3

Getting Started

1-2-3 Basics

Creating a Worksheet

Printing Reports

Creating and Printing Graphs

Managing Data

Understanding Macros

Appendix

137

Using Ranges in the Worksheet

1-2-3's commands and functions often require that you deal with a *range*, a group of cells in aggregate. Before learning more about 1-2-3's commands, you need to learn a bit about ranges.

1-2-3's definition of a range is one or more cells in a rectangular group. With this definition, one cell is the smallest possible range, and the largest range is the entire worksheet.

The use of ranges offers many advantages that make your work less tedious and more efficient. Giving names to ranges allows you to process blocks of cells in commands and formulas at the same time, by using the range name instead of cell addresses.

Entering a Range

When to use ranges in 1-2-3 depends to some degree on your personal preference. In many cases, such as with a formula or macro, you decide whether to provide ranges. In other cases, however, 1-2-3 will prompt you for ranges.

When you are using a 1-2-3 command and you're asked to designate a range, you can do so in one of three ways. You can enter the addresses of the cells in the range, use the cell pointer to point to the cells in the range, or simply enter a name you have assigned to the range. If you use the pointing method, the cell pointer will expand as you use the arrow keys to designate the range.

When a range has been designated, the cells of the range show up in reverse video. Reverse video makes pointing an easy way to designate ranges, because the reverse-video rectangle expands as the cell pointer moves.

Ranges are specified by diagonally opposite corners, usually the upper-left and lower-right cells. The other set of corners, however, may also be used to identify the range. The usual custom is to separate the two cell addresses that specify the corners by one or two periods (such as A7..D10). If you choose a single period to separate the cell addresses, however, 1-2-3 will automatically change the number of periods to two.

Naming Ranges

You can assign a name to a range of cells. Range names can be up to 15 characters long and should be descriptive. The advantage of naming ranges is that range names are easier to understand than cell addresses, and they allow you to work more naturally. For example, the phrase SALES_MODEL25 is a more understandable way of describing the sales for Model #25 than using the cell coordinates A7..D10.

You create range names with the **/R**ange **N**ame **C**reate and **/R**ange **N**ame **L**abels commands. These commands do not have quite the same effect, however. When you **C**reate a name, you assign a name to a group of cells, perhaps as few as one cell but probably more. When you assign a **L**abel, you pick up a label from the spreadsheet and make that label the range name of a one-cell range above, below, to the left, or to the right of the label. You can assign more than one label at a time, but each label applies only to one adjacent cell.

/Range **N**ame **C**reate is ideal when you need to give a name to a multi-cell range. If you have a series of one-cell entries with adjacent labels, or a series of columns or rows with headings, using the **/R**ange **N**ame **L**abels command is best.

To use **/R**ange **N**ame **C**reate to specify a name for any range, even one cell, first type a slash (/) from READY mode. At the main command menu, type an *r* to access the **R**ange command menu. Select **N**ame and then **C**reate. You can then enter any name you want, but be careful to use a unique name that cannot be confused with a cell address.

The **/R**ange **N**ame **L**abels command is similar to **/R**ange **N**ame **C**reate except that the names for ranges are taken directly from adjacent label entries. The adjacent entry must be a label; numeric entries and blank cells are ignored. If you use the **/R**ange **N**ame **L**abels command and specify that the appropriate name for cell B1 is to the left in cell A1, you can assign the name CASH to the range B1. In this example, place the cell pointer on cell A1, type */rnlr*, and press Enter; the name CASH will be assigned to the one-cell range to the right—cell B1.

139

Using Ranges in the Worksheet

What Is a Range?

1-2-3's definition of a range is one or more cells in a rectangular group. One cell is the smallest possible range, and the largest range is the entire worksheet.

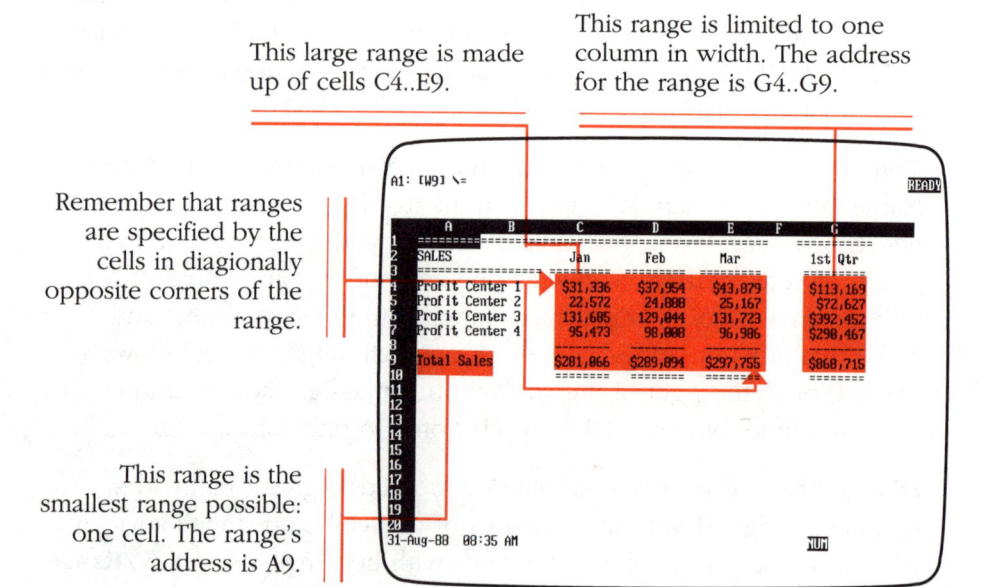

This large range is made up of cells C4..E9.

This range is limited to one column in width. The address for the range is G4..G9.

Remember that ranges are specified by the cells in diagonally opposite corners of the range.

This range is the smallest range possible: one cell. The range's address is A9.

How do You Enter a Range?

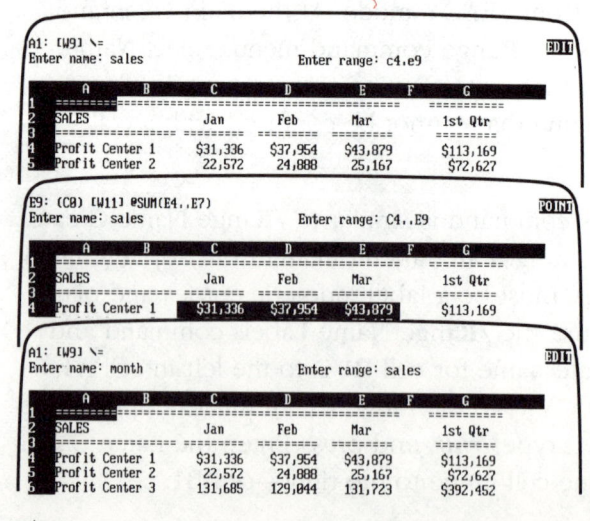

1. You can type the cell addresses of the beginning and ending cells of the range.

2. You can point to cells with the cell pointer.

3. You can name a range and enter the name.

140

Naming Ranges

1-2-3's **/R**ange **N**ame command lets you tag a specific range of the worksheet with a name you give it. After naming a range, you can then enter the name rather than the cell addresses indicating the range's boundaries.

The **/R**ange **N**ame command, for example, lets you give the name SALES to the cells C4 to E4.

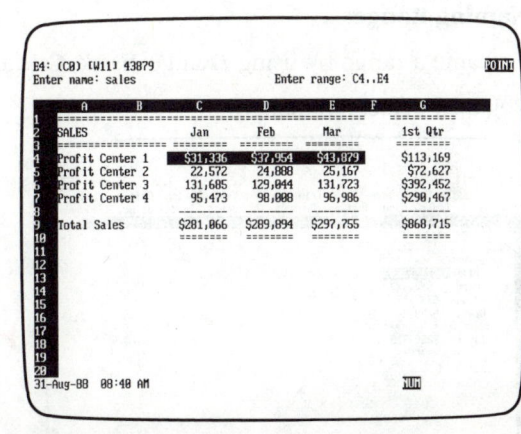

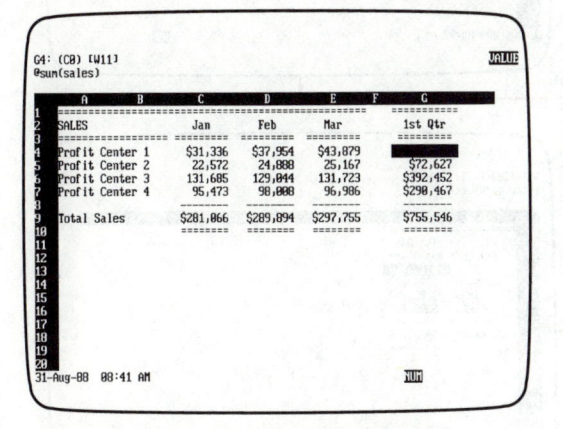

Once you have named the range, you can use it in a formula or in response to a command prompt that asks for a range.

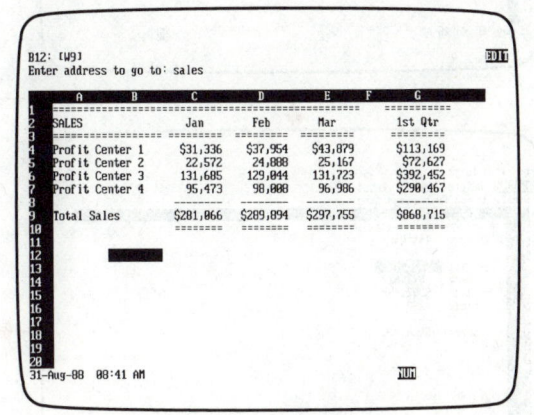

You can also use a range name to jump from one part of the worksheet to another. Typing SALES after pressing the `F5` GoTo key moves the cell pointer to the first cell of the range SALES.

141

Using Ranges in the Worksheet

Using /Range Name Create or /Range Name Labels

You can name ranges in one of two ways: by issuing the **/R**ange **N**ame **C**reate command to create a new range name or by using **/R**ange **N**ame **L**abels to use a label already on the worksheet as a name for a range.

Naming Ranges

To name a range by using **/R**ange **N**ame **C**reate,

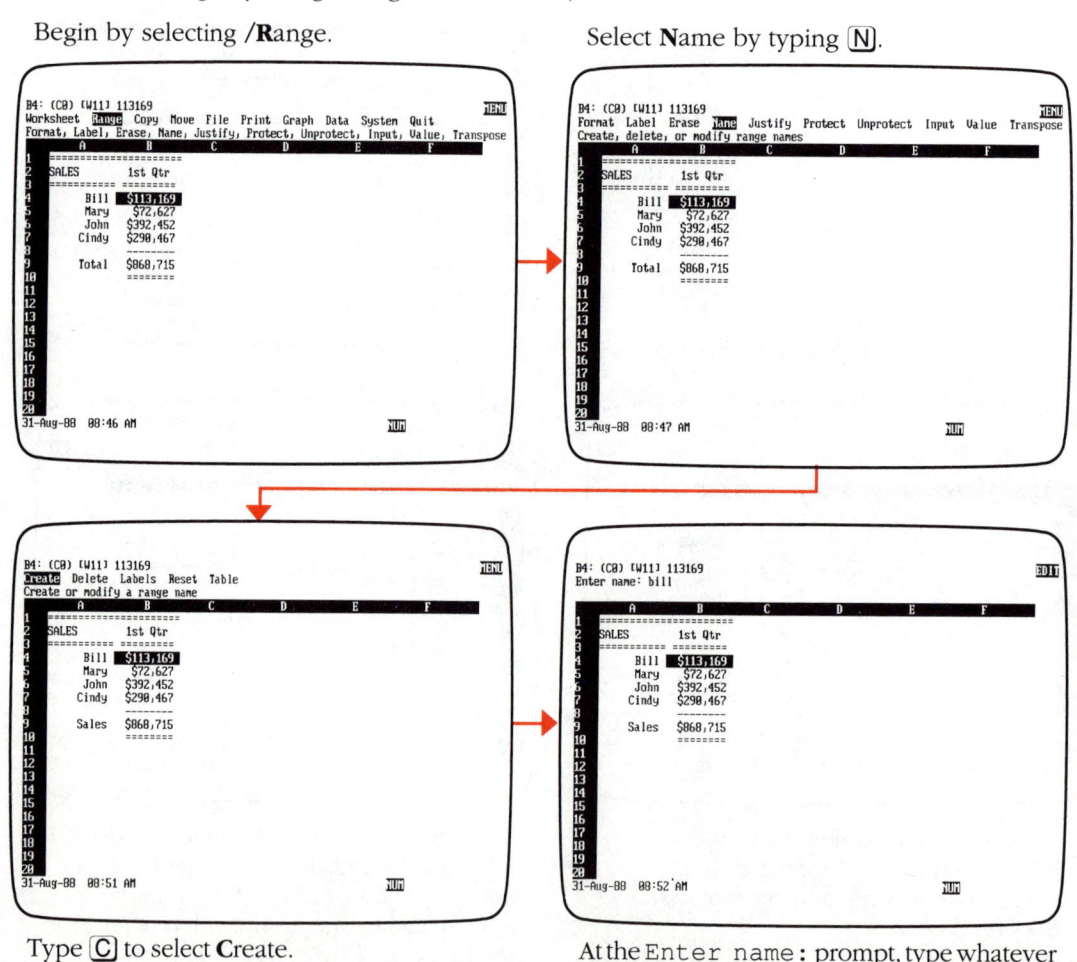

Begin by selecting **/R**ange.

Select **N**ame by typing [N].

Type [C] to select **C**reate.

At the Enter name: prompt, type whatever range name you want and then press [↵Enter]. Don't use a name, however, that could be confused with a cell address.

142

/Range Name Labels

To name a range by using **/R**ange **N**ame **L**abels, follow these steps:

Position the cell pointer on the label you want to use as the range name. Remember that you can use this command only on adjacent cells.

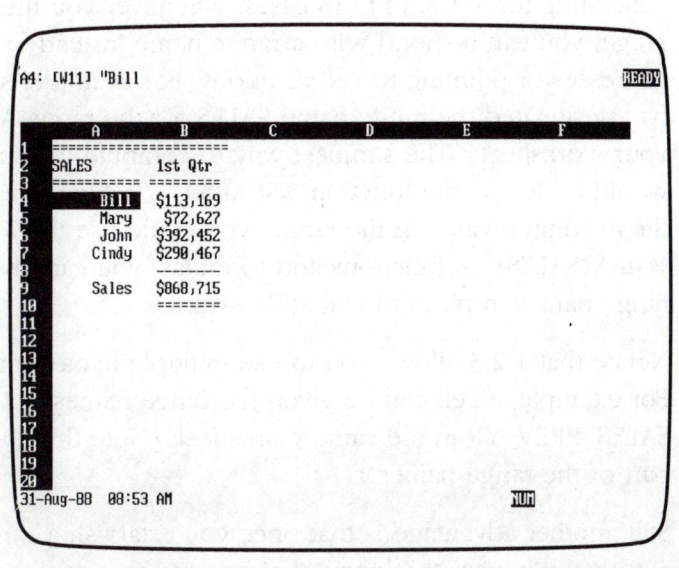

```
A4: [W11] "Bill                                          READY

       A            B         C         D         E         F
 1  ====================
 2  SALES       1st Qtr
 3  ====================
 4      Bill    $113,169
 5      Mary     $72,627
 6      John    $392,452
 7      Cindy   $290,467
 8              --------
 9      Sales   $868,715
10              ========
11
12
13
14
15
16
17
18
19
20
31-Aug-88  08:53 AM                                        NUM
```

Type **/ R N L R** (if the range you want to name is to the right of the current cell).

Press **↵Enter**.

```
A4: [W11] "Bill                                           MENU
Right Down Left Up
Each label in range names cell to its right
       A            B         C         D         E         F
 1  ====================
 2  SALES       1st Qtr
 3  ====================
 4      Bill    $113,169
 5      Mary     $72,627
 6      John    $392,452
 7      Cindy   $290,467
 8              --------
 9      Sales   $868,715
10              ========
11
12
13
14
15
16
17
18
19
20
31-Aug-88  08:53 AM                                        NUM
```

143

Using Ranges in the Worksheet

Using Range Names To Streamline Your Work

Range names can be useful tools for processing commands and generating formulas. In both cases, whenever you must designate a range, you can respond with a range name instead of entering cell addresses or pointing to cell locations. For example, suppose that you had designated the range name SALES for the range A5..J5 in one of your worksheets. The simplest way to compute the sum of this range would be to use the function @SUM(SALES). Similarly, to determine the maximum value in the range, you could use the function @MAX(SALES). In functions and formulas, you can always use range names in place of cell addresses.

Notice that 1-2-3 allows you to use multiple names for the same range. For example, a cell can be given the range names SALES_1987 and SALES_PREV_YR in the same worksheet. (Note that the underlines are part of the range names.)

Still another advantage is that once you establish a range name, 1-2-3 automatically uses that name throughout the worksheet in place of cell addresses.

You can also designate the ranges of cells to be printed or extracted and saved to another worksheet. Suppose that you set up special names corresponding to different areas, and then you want to print, or extract and save to another worksheet, the corresponding portions of the current worksheet. When 1-2-3 prompts you for a range, you can enter a predefined range name rather than actual cell addresses. For example, suppose that you were using the /**P**rint **P**rinter **R**ange command to print a portion of a worksheet. In response to the `Enter Print range:` prompt, you could enter the range name PAGE_1 or the name PAGE_5.

A third example using range names involves the F5 (GoTo) key. Instead of specifying the cell address you want to move to, enter the range name, and 1-2-3 takes you there.

Deleting Range Names

You can delete range names individually or all at once. The **/R**ange **N**ame **D**elete command allows you to delete a single range name, and the **/R**ange **N**ame **R**eset command causes all range names to be deleted. Because of the latter command's power, you should use the command with caution.

If you delete a range name, 1-2-3 no longer uses that name and reverts to cell addresses. For example, @SUM(REVENUES) returns to @SUM(A5..J5). The contents of the cells within the range, however, remain intact. To erase the contents of ranges, you use the **/R**ange **E**rase command, which is explained next.

Erasing Ranges

With the **/R**ange **E**rase command, you can erase sections of the worksheet. You can use this command on a range as small as a single cell or as large as the entire worksheet.

To remove a range, issue the **/R**ange **E**rase command. 1-2-3 prompts you to supply a range to delete. Either by pointing or by entering the coordinates from the keyboard, you instruct 1-2-3 to erase the range. After you press Enter, 1-2-3 immediately erases the range.

After you erase a range, you cannot recover it. If you want to restore the range, you will have to re-enter all the data.

You can erase ranges more easily if you have already assigned names to them. For example, if you assign the name CGS to a range and decide you want to erase this portion of the worksheet, type **/R**ange **E**rase and enter the range name CGS rather than the cell coordinates.

Using Ranges in the Worksheet

Deleting Range Names

The **/R**ange **N**ame command provides two options for deleting range names. You can delete a single range name with the **/R**ange **N**ame **D**elete command, or you can delete all range names in the worksheet with the **/R**ange **N**ame **R**eset command.

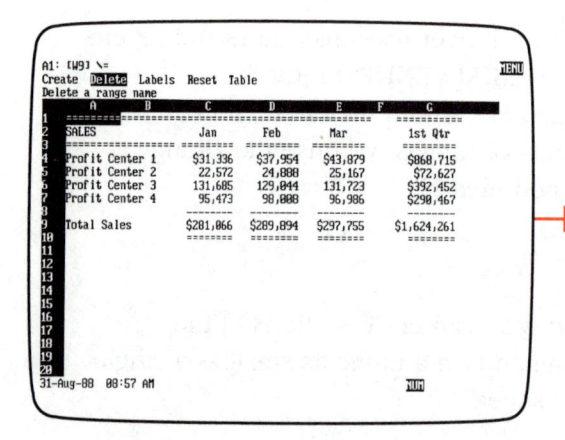

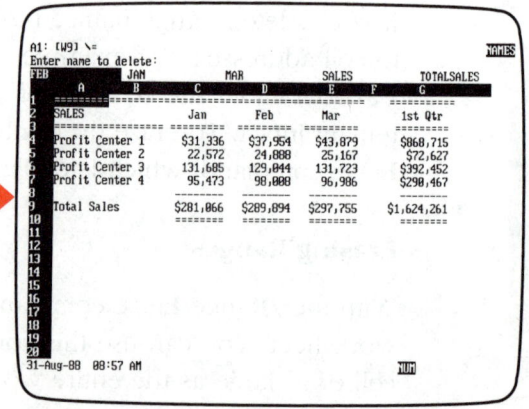

To delete one range name, press [/][R][N][D].

When 1-2-3 displays a list of range names, either type the range name or move the cursor to the range name you want to delete and press [↵Enter].

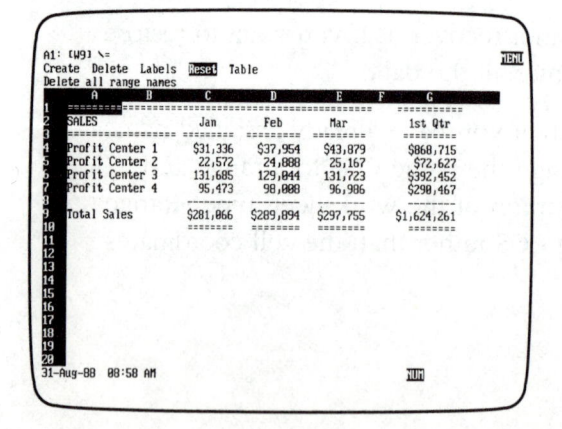

To delete all range names in your worksheet, press [/][R][N][R]. Use the command with caution. 1-2-3 does not give you a chance to verify your selection and will delete all range names as soon as you enter the command.

146

Erasing Ranges

With the **/R**ange **E**rase command, you can erase a single cell or erase a range as large as the entire worksheet.

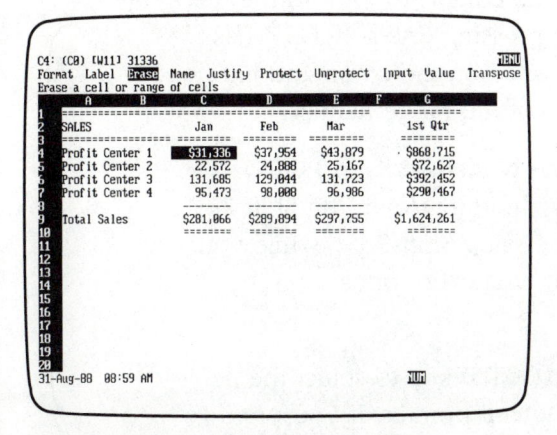

Select **/R**ange **E**rase to begin the command.

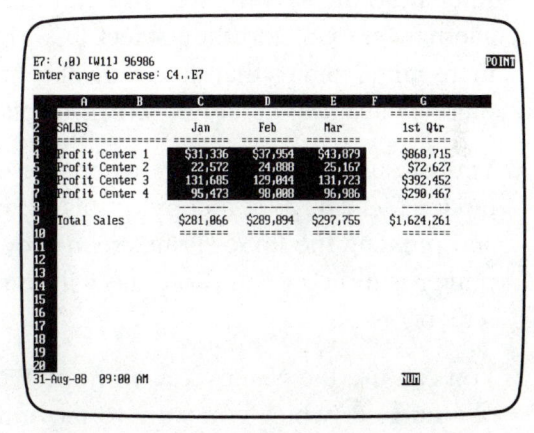

When 1-2-3 prompts you for a range, point to the range you want to erase.

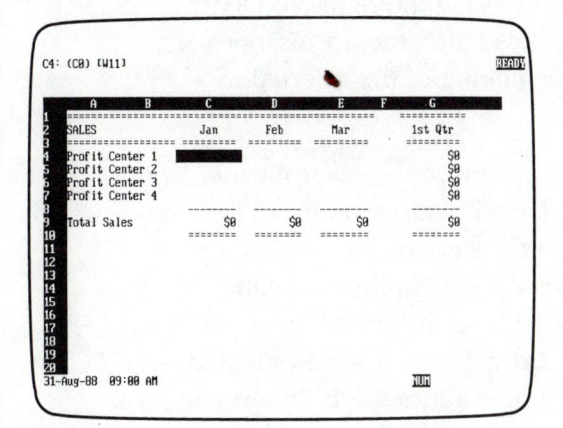

Finally, press ↵Enter to erase the range.

TIP: Although you can denote a range to be erased by typing the cell addresses of the range or by entering a range name, pointing to the range allows you to see the boundaries of the range you want to erase before 1-2-3 erases the range.

147

Using Ranges in the Worksheet

Getting a List of Range Names

Suppose that you type the **/R**ange **E**rase command and then can't remember the name of the range you want to erase. You could press the F3 (Names) key to produce a list of the range names in the current worksheet.

After 1-2-3 displays the list, you can use the cursor to point to the first alternative, CGS, and then select CGS by pressing Enter. If 1-2-3 has more range names than it can display at once on the command line, press F3 again to get a full screen display of the range names.

You can use the Names key whenever the worksheet is in POINT mode. You can print a copy of this list by holding down the Shift key and pressing the PrtSc (PrintScreen) key. (Using Shift-PrtSc while your printer is turned on and on-line will print whatever appears on the screen.)

You can use the Names key with the F5 (GoTo) key to select the name of a range to which you want to move the cell pointer. If you press F5 and then press F3, 1-2-3 displays in the control panel an alphabetical list of your spreadsheet's range names. To designate the range you want to go to, select a name from the list by using the right- and left-arrow keys or the space bar. When you press Enter, the list disappears, and the cell pointer is positioned at the beginning of the selected range.

If you have more range names than 1-2-3 can fit on the control panel, you can use the arrow keys or the space bar to "wrap around" to the rest of the names, or you can press F3 again. After you press F3 a second time, the worksheet disappears, and 1-2-3 displays the entire list (or as much of it as the screen can hold). Use the space bar or the arrow keys, including the up- and down-arrow keys, or the Home and End keys to select the name of the range you want to go to. When you press Enter, the list disappears and the worksheet reappears with the cell pointer at the beginning of the selected range.

Creating a Table of Range Names

If you are using range names in a worksheet and have created several range names, you may want to document the names in a table in the worksheet. To perform this task, 1-2-3 provides the **/R**ange **N**ame **T**able command. Creating a range name table is simple, but you must exercise care in your placement of the table. Make certain that your placement will not write the table over an important part of the worksheet.

To create the range name table, you select the **/R**ange **N**ame **T**able command. When 1-2-3 asks for the location for the table, indicate the cell where you want the upper-left corner of the table to appear, and then press Enter.

1-2-3 writes a table that consists of all your range names in a column, with the referenced ranges in the cells to the immediate right of each range name.

A Review of Ranges

Action	Command or Function Key
Naming ranges	**/R**ange **N**ame **C**reate **/R**ange **N**ame **L**abels
Delete ranges	**/R**ange **N**ame **D**elete **/R**ange **N**ame **R**eset
Erase ranges	**/R**ange **E**rase
List ranges	Names (F3) GoTo (F5)
Create range name table	**/R**ange **N**ame **T**able

149

Using Ranges in the Worksheet

Listing Range Names

After you've specified several range names, you may forget which ranges you've named on the worksheet. Fortunately, 1-2-3's prepared for that. By pressing [F3] (Names), you can display a list of all range names that have been specified on the worksheet.

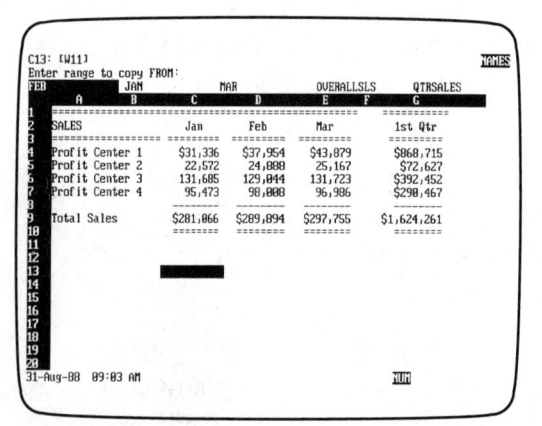

To get a list of range names, simply make sure that the worksheet is in POINT mode and press [F3] (Names).

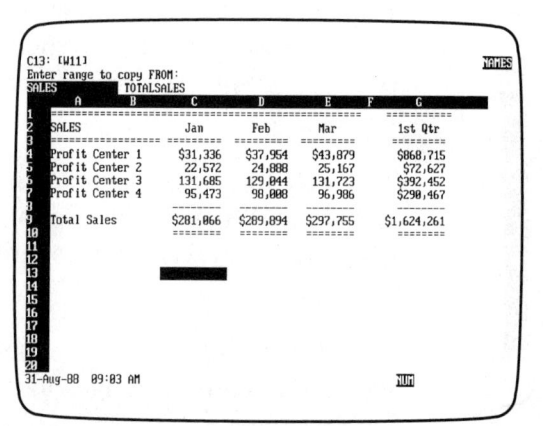

If the range names extend beyond the right edge of the control panel, you can use the arrow keys to display the additional names.

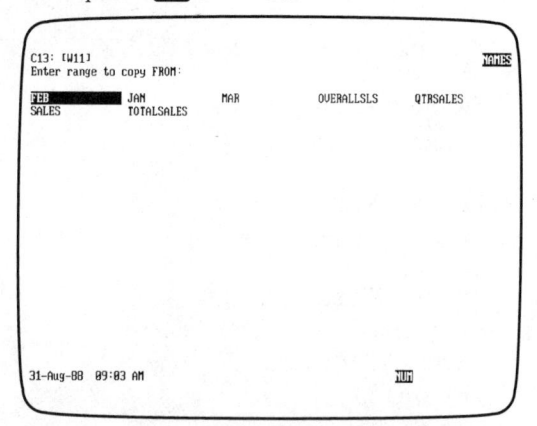

You can also press [F3] a second time to display the entire list of range names.

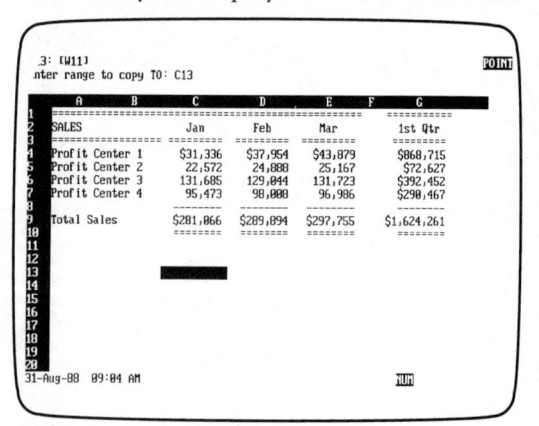

When you move the cursor to the name you want to use and press [↵Enter], 1-2-3 returns you to the worksheet.

> NOTE: You can also print the list of range names by pressing the [PrtSc] (PrintScreen) key.

150

Creating a Table of Range Names

If you are using range names in a worksheet and have created several large names, you may want to document the names in a table in the worksheet by using the **/R**ange **N**ame **T**able command.

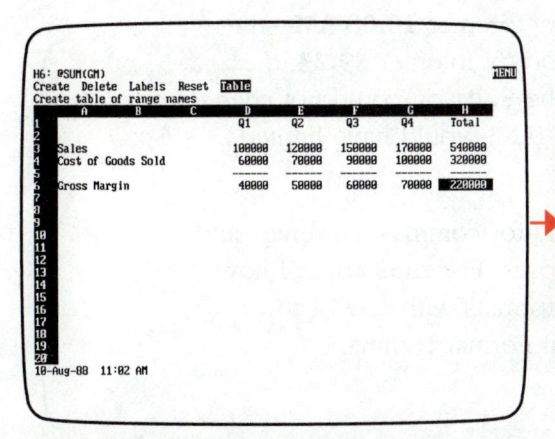

To create the range name table, select **/R**ange **N**ame **T**able.

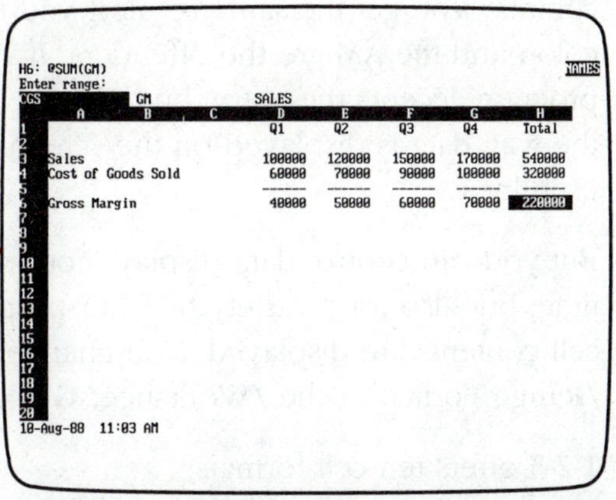

When 1-2-3 asks for the location for the table, indicate the cell where you want the upper left corner of the table to appear. Then press ⏎Enter.

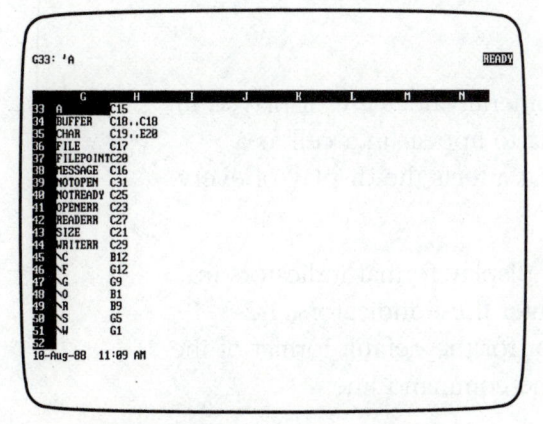

NOTE: Creating a range name table is simple, but you must exercise care in your placement of the table. Make certain that your placement will not write the table over an important part of the worksheet.

1-2-3 then produces a table of range names with their cell addresses on the worksheet.

151

Using Ranges in the Worksheet

Formatting Cell Contents with /Range Format

You may have already discovered that 1-2-3 expects you to enter data in a certain way. If, for example, you try to enter **1,234**, the program beeps, switches to EDIT mode, and waits for you to remove the comma. You get the same result if you try to enter **10:08 AM**—the colon and the AM are the offenders. If you try to enter **$9.23**, the program accepts the entry, but without the **$**. If you could not change the way data is displayed on the screen, 1-2-3 would have limited usefulness.

But you can control data display, not only for commas, currency, and time, but also for a variety of other purposes. **Formats** control how cell contents are displayed. You change formats with one of the **/R**ange **F**ormat or the **/W**orksheet **G**lobal **F**ormat commands.

1-2-3 offers ten cell formats:

Fixed	**+/-** (Horizontal Bar Graph)
Scientific	**P**ercent
Currency	**D**ate (includes Time format)
, (Comma)	**T**ext
General	**H**idden

These formats primarily affect the way numeric values are displayed in a worksheet. **T**ext format causes a formula to appear in a cell as a formula rather than a value. **H**idden format affects the display of every kind of entry.

All formats specified with **/R**ange **F**ormat display format indicators in the command line. You do not have to enter these indicators; 1-2-3 automatically provides them. The indicator for the default format of the worksheet, however, will not appear in the command line.

Setting Range and Worksheet Global Formats

Although you will probably use the /**R**ange **F**ormat command frequently to format individual ranges in your worksheet, you can also change the default format for the whole worksheet. The /**W**orksheet **G**lobal **F**ormat command controls the format of all the cells in the worksheet, and the /**R**ange **F**ormat command controls specific ranges within the worksheet.

Generally, you use the /**W**orksheet **G**lobal **F**ormat command when you are just starting to enter data in a worksheet. You will want to choose a format that the majority of cells will take. Once you have set all the cells to that format, you can use the /**R**ange **F**ormat command to override the global format setting for specific cell ranges.

The /**R**ange **F**ormat command takes precedence over the /**W**orksheet **G**lobal **F**ormat command. This means that whenever you change the global format, all the numbers and formulas affected will change automatically unless they were previously formatted with the /**R**ange **F**ormat command. In turn, when you format a range, the format for that range will override any already set by /**W**orksheet **G**lobal **F**ormat.

General Format

General format is the default format for all new worksheets. When numbers are displayed in **G**eneral format, insignificant zeros to the right of the decimal point are suppressed. If numbers are too large or too small to be displayed normally, scientific notation is used.

Using Ranges in the Worksheet

Fixed Format

1-2-3's **F**ixed format is similar to **G**eneral format in that it does not display commas or dollar signs. The difference is that **F**ixed format lets you control the number of places to the right of the decimal point.

Scientific Format

Scientific format causes 1-2-3 to display numbers in exponential scientific notation. Unlike **G**eneral format, however, **S**cientific format lets you control the number of decimal places and so determine the amount of precision that will be displayed.

Currency Format

Currency format displays numbers in cells with a currency indicator before each entry, and with commas separating hundreds from thousands, hundreds of thousands from millions, etc. Negative values appear in parentheses ( ). The dollar sign is the default for the currency indicator. **C**urrency format also gives you the option of controlling the number of places to the right of the decimal point.

Comma Format

The **,** (Comma) format resembles **C**urrency format, except that no dollar signs appear when the numbers are displayed. Commas separate hundreds from thousands, hundreds of thousands from millions, etc. Parentheses ( ) identify negative numbers. After the **,** (Comma) format has been chosen, you can specify the number of decimal places you want.

The +/- Format

The **+/-** format creates a horizontal bar graph of plus or minus signs, depending on the value of the number you enter in the cell. Asterisks are displayed if the size of the bar graph exceeds the column width. If zero is entered in a cell, a period (.) is displayed on the graph and left-justified in the cell.

Some applications use this format to mark a value in a long column of numbers. As you scan the column, the +'s and -'s stand out and are easy to locate.

Percent Format

The **P**ercent format is used to display percentages; when you select this format you also select the number of decimal places. The values displayed in the worksheet are the values you enter, multiplied by 100 and followed by a percent sign. When you use the **P**ercent format, remember to enter numbers with the correct decimal point. To display 12%, for example, you must enter .12, not 12.

Date and Time Formats

1-2-3 represents any given date internally as an integer equal to the number of days from December 31, 1899, to the given date. For example, January 1, 1900, is represented by the number 1; December 31, 2099 (which is the last date in 1-2-3's calendar), is represented by 73050. To enter a date into the worksheet, you use one of the date functions: @DATE, @DATEVALUE, or @NOW.

1-2-3 calculates a period of hours as a fraction expressed in decimals. The calculations are based on a 24-hour clock, so-called military time. Use one of the time functions: @TIME, @TIMEVALUE, or @NOW to enter a time into the worksheet.

You can specify nine date and time formats with the **/R**ange **F**ormat **D**ate and **/W**orksheet **G**lobal **F**ormat **D**ate commands.

Using Ranges in the Worksheet

Text Format

Text format displays formulas as they are entered in the command line, not the computed values that 1-2-3 normally displays. Numbers entered using this format are displayed in the same manner used in General format.

Probably the most important application of this format is setting up table ranges for **/D**ata **T**able commands, but another important application is debugging. Because you can display all the formulas on the screen with the **T**ext format, finding and correcting problems is a relatively easy task. When you use this technique for debugging your model, you may have to widen the cell width to see your complete formulas.

Hidden Format

Hidden format will suppress the display of cell contents for any range that you indicate after you invoke the **/R**ange **F**ormat **H**idden command. If, instead, you want to hide all the cells in a column or range of columns, use the **/W**orksheet **C**olumn **H**idden command, discussed in this chapter.

Although a cell with **H**idden format will appear as a blank cell on the screen, its contents will be displayed in the control panel when you place the cursor over the cell. The hidden cell will be a part of calculations as if it weren't hidden. All formulas and values can be calculated and readjusted when values are changed.

Reset Format

The **/R**ange **F**ormat **R**eset command resets the format of the indicated range to the global default setting. When the format of a range is reset, the format indicator for any cell within the range disappears from the control panel.

Controlling the International Formats

1-2-3 allows you to control the punctuation and currency sign displayed by **,** (Comma) and **C**urrency formats, and to control the way the date and time are displayed when you use the special international **D**ate and **T**ime formats. To control these settings globally for the worksheet, use the **/W**orksheet **G**lobal **D**efault **O**ther **I**nternational command.

Using Ranges in the Worksheet

Using /Range Format

The control panel indicates all formats, except the default format, of the cells highlighted by the cell pointer.

You can set the format for the whole worksheet with the /**W**orksheet **G**lobal **F**ormat command.

To set the format for a range, use /**R**ange **F**ormat. /**R**ange **F**ormat overrides /**W**orksheet **G**lobal **F**ormat.

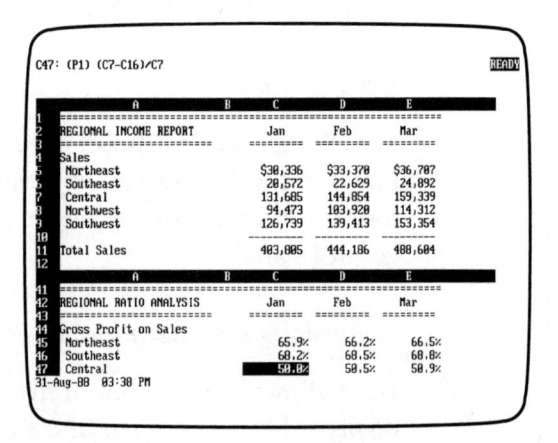

Follow these steps to change the format of a cell or of a range of cells:

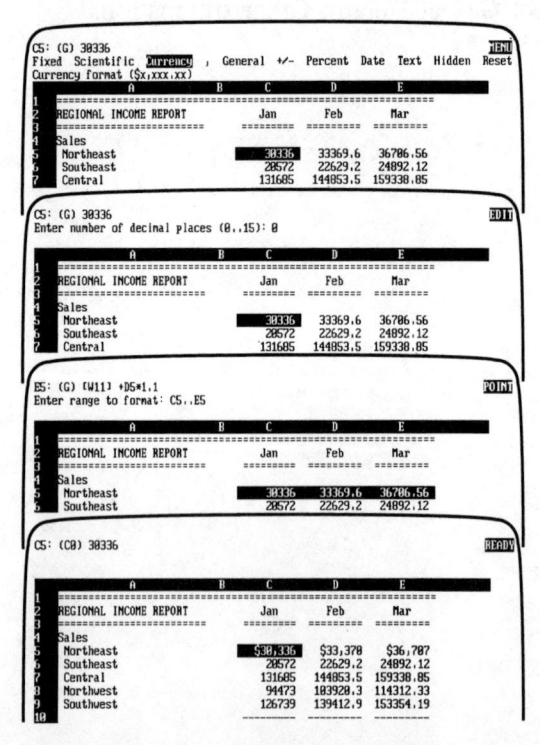

Select /**R**ange **F**ormat. When the format menu is displayed, select the type of format you want to set.

If the format you want to use prompts you to enter the number of decimal places, enter a new number or press ⏎Enter to accept the default number.

Highlight the range you want to format.

Press ⏎Enter to complete the command.

158

	Format	*Examples* *Value (or Formula)* *Entered*	*Value as Displayed* *(when formatted* *with no decimal* *places)*
Fixed	Fixes the number of decimal places displayed.	15.56	16
Scientific	Displays large or small numbers, using scientific notation.	-21	-2E+01
Currency	Displays currency symbols (e.g. $) and commas.	234567.75	$234,568
, (Comma)	Inserts commas to mark thousands and multiples of thousands.	234567	234,567
General	Displays values with up to 10 decimals or in scientific notation.	26.003	26.003
+/-	Creates horizontal bar graphs or time duration graphs on computers that do not have graphs.	3 -3	+++ ---
Percent	Displays a decimal number as a whole number with a % sign.	0.25	25%
Date	Displays serial-date numbers /**R**ange **F**ormat **D**ate **T**ime sets time formats.	@DATE(88,9,1) @NOW	01-Sep-88 03:27 PM
Text	Displays formulas as text, but continues to evaluate formulas as numbers.	+B5+B6 @SUM(C4..C8)	+B5+B6 @SUM(C4..C8)
Hidden	Hides contents from the display and does not print contents, but continues to evaluate contents.	289	
Reset	Returns the format to the current /**W**orksheet **G**lobal format.		

159

Using Worksheet Commands

1-2-3 offers a group of commands that are similar to the **R**ange commands but affect the entire worksheet or preset segments of it. With **R**ange commands, you define the range of cells that is affected by the commands; you do not have the same liberty with **W**orksheet commands—they affect the entire worksheet or entire rows or columns.

| Introduction | Selecting Commands from Command Menus | Using Ranges in the Worksheet | **Using Worksheet Commands** | Moving the Contents of Cells | Copying the Contents of Cells | Saving Your Files before You Quit (/Quit) | Accessing DOS from 1-2-3 |

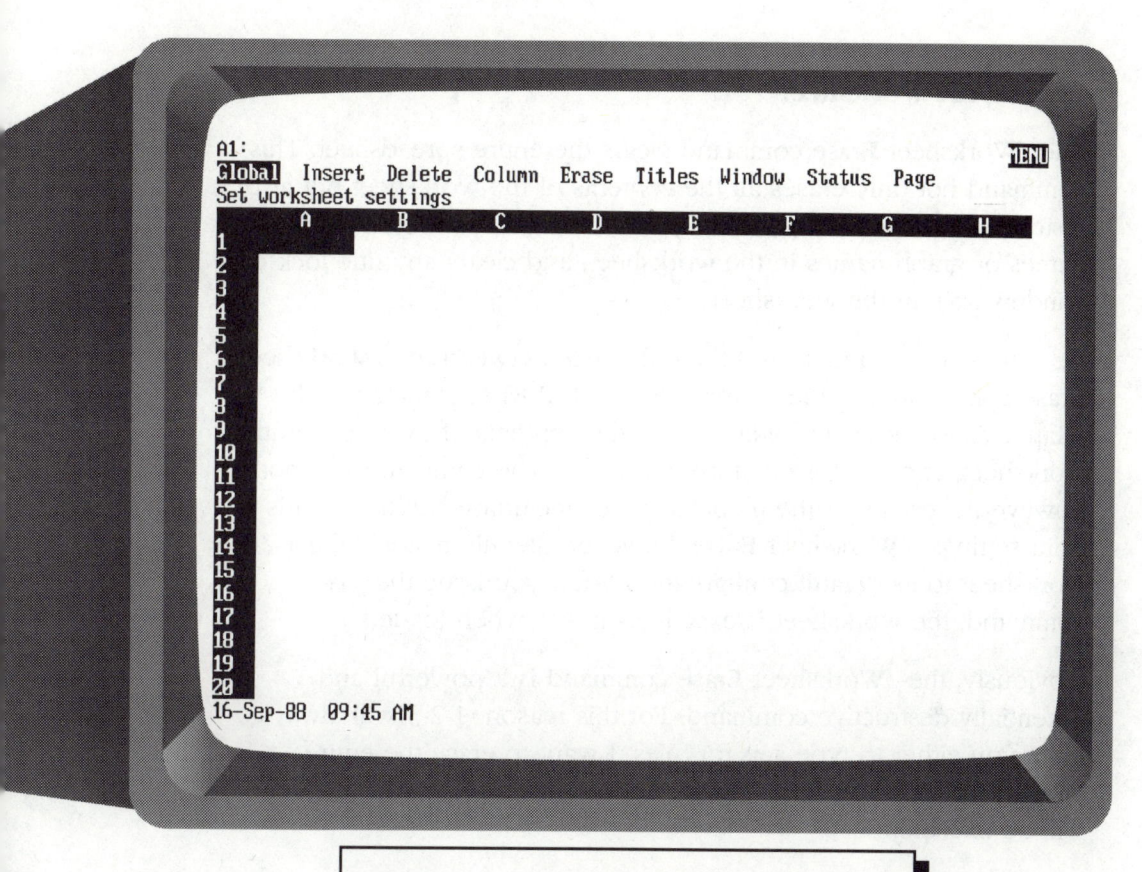

```
A1:                                                                MENU
Global Insert Delete Column Erase Titles Window Status Page
Set worksheet settings
   A          B          C          D          E       F       G       H
 1
 2
 3
 4
 5
 6
 7
 8
 9
10
11
12
13
14
15
16
17
18
19
20
16-Sep-88  09:45 AM
```

Global	Affects the entire worksheet.
Insert	Inserts columns and rows.
Delete	Deletes rows and columns.
Column	Sets column width and display.
Erase	Clears the entire spreadsheet.
Titles	Freezes display of titles.
Window	Splits the screen.
Status	Checks status of global settings.
Page	Inserts page-break character.

Introduction

An Overview of 1-2-3

Getting Started

1-2-3 Basics

Creating a Worksheet

Printing Reports

Creating and Printing Graphs

Managing Data

Understanding Macros

Appendix

161

Using Worksheet Commands

Erasing the Worksheet

The **/W**orksheet **E**rase command clears the entire spreadsheet. This command not only erases all the contents of the worksheet but also restores all global settings to their default condition, destroys any range names or graph names in the worksheet, and clears any title lock or window split in the worksheet.

Be sure that you understand the difference between the **/W**orksheet **E**rase command and the **/R**ange **E**rase A1..IV8192 command. The **/R**ange **E**rase command will remove the contents of every cell in the worksheet, except those that are protected. The command will not, however, alter any of the global settings, including column widths or print settings. **/W**orksheet **E**rase, however, literally restores the 1-2-3 worksheet to its default configuration. After you issue the */we* command, the worksheet is exactly as it was when loaded.

Obviously, the **/W**orksheet **E**rase command is a powerful and potentially destructive command. For this reason, 1-2-3 will always force you either to type a *y*, for "Yes, I want to erase the entire worksheet," or to point to **Yes** and press Enter, before this command will be executed.

Warning: Once a worksheet has been erased in this way, you cannot recover it. Always save your worksheets before you erase them.

Setting Column Widths

You can control the width of columns in the worksheet to accommodate data entries that are too wide for the default column width of 9 characters. You also can reduce column widths, perhaps to give the worksheet a better appearance when a column contains narrow entries. In 1-2-3, you can set the width of all the columns in the worksheet at once or separately control the width of each column.

Suppose that you are setting up a projection of expenses for the next five years and want to display the full descriptions of the expense items (some of them 20 characters wide). You can set the first column of your projection of expenses to be 20 characters wide (to accommodate the descriptions) and then set the other columns to whatever width you want.

The command used to set individual column widths is /**W**orksheet **C**olumn **S**et-Width. You can set one column width at a time either by entering a number or by using the left- and right-arrow keys followed by Enter. The advantage of the left- and right-arrow keys is that the column width expands and contracts each time you press a key. To get a good idea of what the width requirements are, experiment when you enter the command.

Remember two things about this command. First, you must position the pointer in the proper column before you initiate the command. Otherwise, you will have to start over. Second, to reset the column width to the standard setting, you must use the /**W**orksheet **C**olumn **R**eset-Width command.

You can also control all the column widths in the worksheet at once. 1-2-3's command to do this process is /**W**orksheet **G**lobal **C**olumn-Width. This command is one of the **G**lobal commands—commands that affect the entire worksheet. Many of the **G**lobal commands have corresponding **R**ange commands to affect only certain areas of the worksheet, although in this case the corresponding command is the /**W**orksheet **C**olumn **S**et-Width command, as explained previously.

163

Using Worksheet Commands

/Range Erase versus /Worksheet Erase

Before using **/W**orksheet **E**rase, keep in mind the differences between this command and **/R**ange **E**rase

Using /Range Erase

/Range **E**rase removes data in unprotected cells in the specified range but does not change any global settings, such as column widths or print settings.

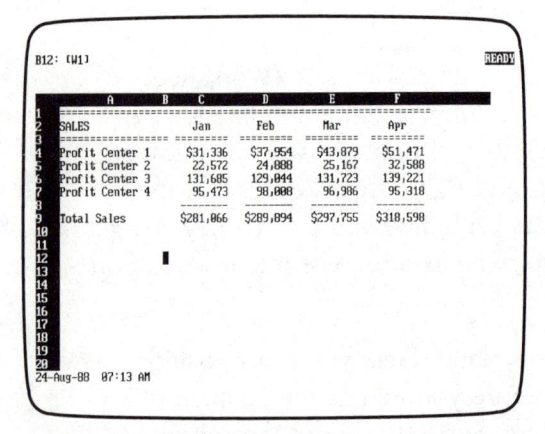

Notice that this sales worksheet varies in column width and format. (Two rows are formatted in currency; three rows are formatted in comma ⟨,⟩ format.)

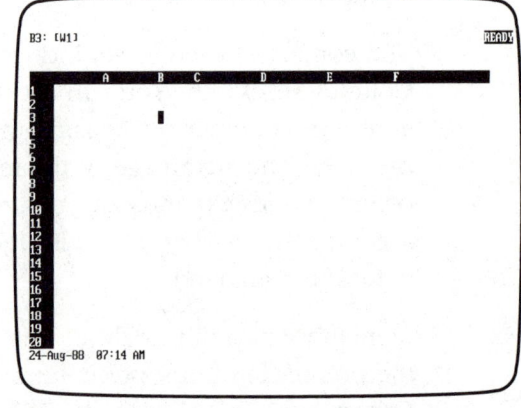

After you erase a range with **/R**ange **E**rase, 1-2-3 redisplays the worksheet. The original settings, however, remain. Notice for example, that the column width of column B is still 1.

If you reenter values, notice that the worksheet retains the original format settings.

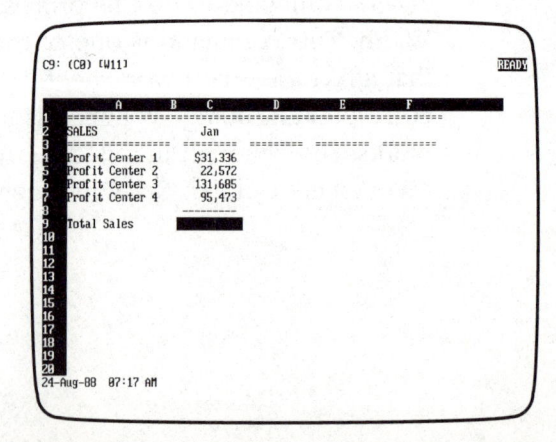

| Introduction | Selecting Commands from Command Menus | Using Ranges in the Worksheet | **Using Worksheet Commands** | Moving the Contents of Cells | Copying the Contents of Cells | Saving Your Files before You Quit (/Quit) | Accessing DOS from 1-2-3 |

Using /Worksheet Erase

/Worksheet **E**rase deletes the active worksheet from your computer's memory, erasing not only all data but also all settings that are not default settings. After you use the **/W**orksheet **E**rase, 1-2-3 displays a new worksheet with all default settings restored.

Original Worksheet

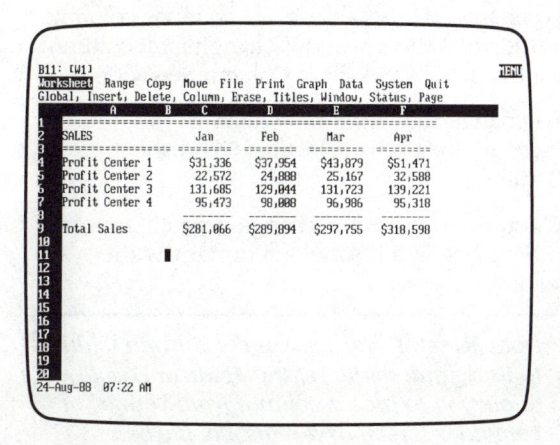

New Worksheet

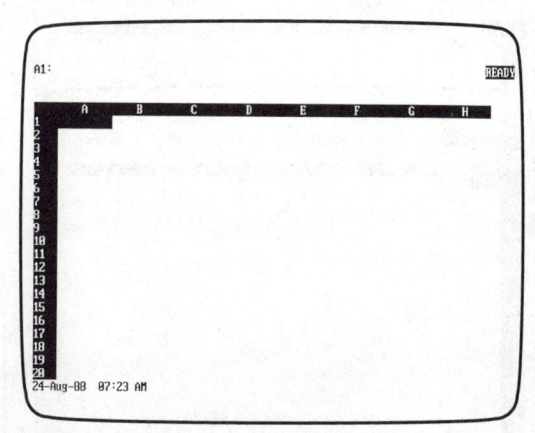

Notice that the new worksheet contains different column widths from those that were set in the original worksheet.

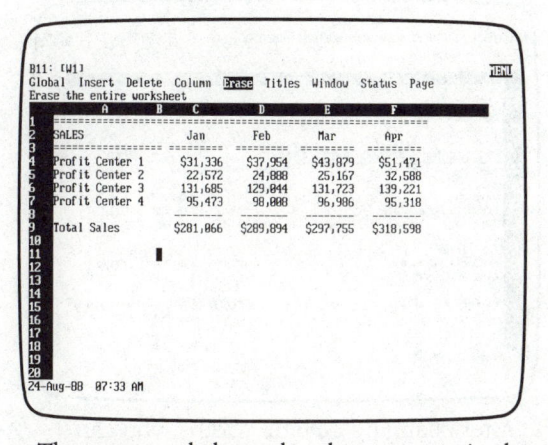

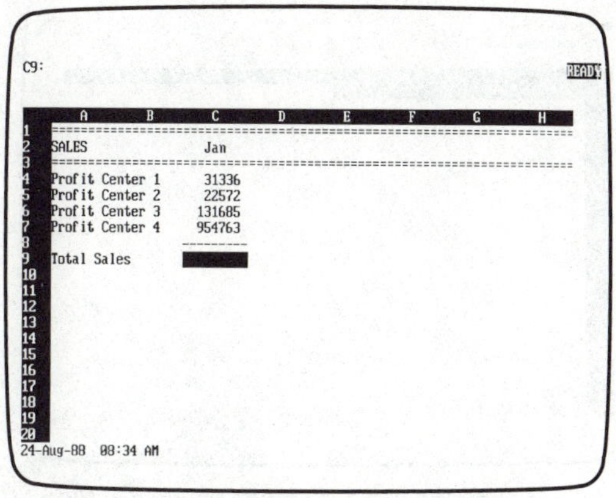

The new worksheet also does not retain the special format settings that were set in the original worksheet.

Introduction

An Overview of 1-2-3

Getting Started

1-2-3 Basics

Creating a Worksheet

Printing Reports

Creating and Printing Graphs

Managing Data

Understanding Macros

Appendix

165

Using Worksheet Commands

Setting Column Widths

You can change the width of the columns in the worksheet to accommodate data entries that are longer than the default column width of 9 characters. You can also reduce column widths. Two commands, **/W**orksheet **C**olumn **S**et-Width and **/W**orksheet **G**lobal **C**olumn-Width, let you change column widths in the worksheet.

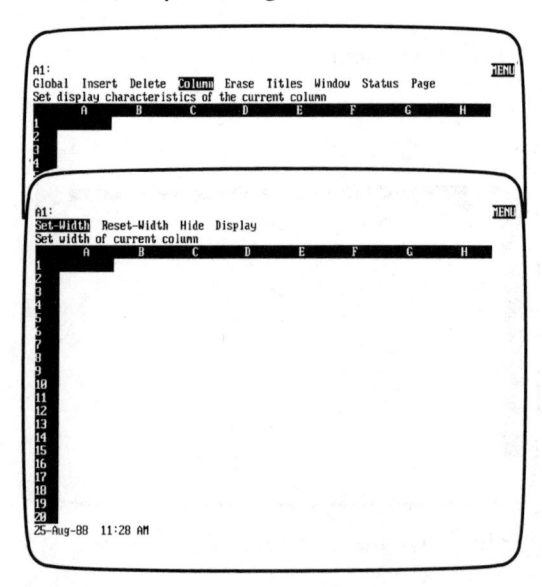

Using /Worksheet Column

To change the widths of one or more columns in the worksheet without changing all column widths, use **/W**orksheet **C**olumn **S**et-Width.

To change the width of column A, for example, begin by selecting **/W**orksheet **C**olumn.

When the options for changing width appear, choose **S**et-Width to widen or narrow the column.

> Note: **R**eset-**W**idth returns the column width to its default width setting. **H**ide or **D**isplay allow you to hide a column from your computer screen and redisplay it when needed. (See "Hiding Columns" in this chapter.)

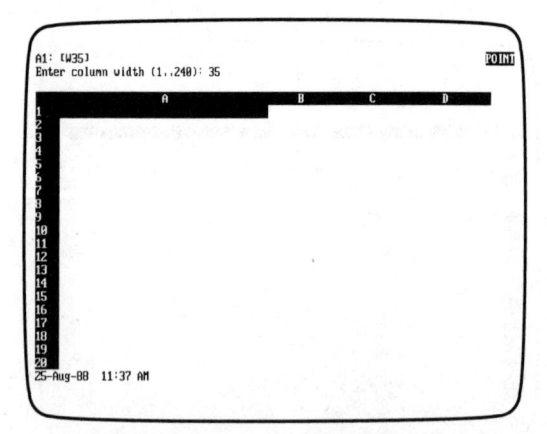

When the `Enter Column Width:` prompt appears, either type a width between 1 and 240 or move the cursor until it highlights the width you want.

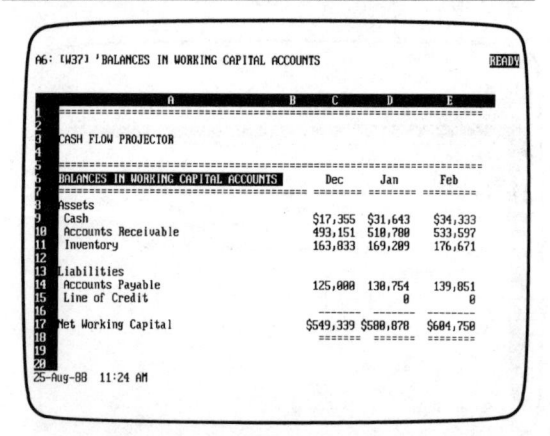

After changing column widths, you can continue entering data into your worksheet.

166

Using /Worksheet Global Column-Width

To change the widths of all columns in the worksheet at once, use **/W**orksheet **G**lobal **C**olumn-Width.

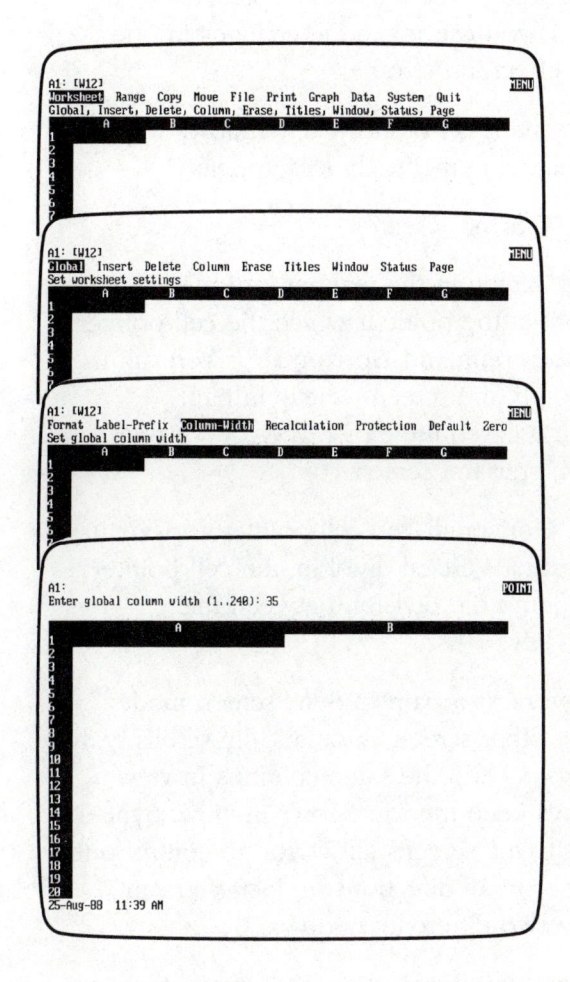

Select **W**orksheet from the main command menu.

Choose **G**lobal from the Worksheet Menu.

Choose **C**olumn-Width

When the `Enter Global Column Width:` prompt appears, either type a width between 1 and 240 or move the cursor until it highlights the width you want. Finally press ⏎Enter.

167

Using Worksheet Commands

Splitting the Screen

You can split the 1-2-3 screen display into two parts, either horizontally or vertically. This feature helps you to overcome some of the inconvenience of not being able to see the entire spreadsheet at one time. By splitting the screen, you can make the changes in one area and immediately see their effect in the other.

The command for splitting the screen is **/W**orksheet **W**indow. When you enter this command, the following menu choices appear:

>   **H**orizontal   **V**ertical   **S**ync   **U**nsync   **C**lear

Horizontal and **V**ertical split the screen in the manner indicated by their names. The screen will split at the point at which the cell pointer is positioned when you select the command **H**orizontal or **V**ertical. In other words, you don't have to split the screen exactly in half. Remember that the dividing line will require either one row or one column, depending on how you split the screen.

After you split the screen using **H**orizontal, the cell pointer appears in the top window. When you create a **V**ertical division, the cell pointer appears in the left window. To jump the division between the windows, use the F6 (Window) key.

The **S**ync and **U**nsync options work as a pair. In **S**ync screen mode, when you scroll one screen, the other screen automatically scrolls with it. Horizontally split screens always keep the same columns in view, and vertically split screens always keep the same rows in view. **S**ync is the standard default for 1-2-3. **U**nsync screens allow you to control one screen independently of the other in all directions. In fact, you can even show the same cells in the two different windows.

The **C**lear option removes the split-window option and reverts the screen to a single window. When you use this option, the single window takes on the settings of the top or left-hand window, depending on how the screen was split.

Freezing Titles on the Screen

The **/W**orksheet **T**itles command is similar to the **/W**orksheet **W**indow command. With both commands, you can see one area of a worksheet while you work on another area. The unique function of the **/W**orksheet **T**itles command, however, is that it freezes all the cells to the left or above (or both to the left and above) the cell pointer's current position so that those cells cannot move off the screen.

Because the normal screen, without any special column widths, shows 20 rows by 7 columns, you undoubtedly will have to shift the screen if your data is outside of this screen area. In fact, you may have to scroll the screen several different times in order to enter or view all the items.

To keep the headings in view, even when you scroll the screen, enter /wt when the cell pointer is highlighting the desired location. The following options then are displayed:

> **B**oth **H**orizontal **V**ertical **C**lear

If you select **H**orizontal, the rows on the screen above the cell pointer become frozen. That is, they don't move off the screen when you scroll up and down. If you select **V**ertical, the columns to the left of the cell pointer are frozen and move only when you scroll up and down (but not when you move left and right). The **B**oth option freezes the rows above and the columns to the left of the cell pointer. Remember to move the cell pointer to the desired location before executing the /WT command. **C**lear unlocks the worksheet titles.

When you freeze rows or columns, you cannot move the cell pointer into the frozen area. If you try to move the cell pointer into the frozen area, 1-2-3 will beep and not allow the cell pointer to move into the protected area. Similarly, using the Home key will move the cell pointer only to the upper-left cell in the unlocked area. Normally, the Home key moves the cell pointer to cell A1. You can, however, get past this restriction by using the F5 (GoTo) key.

169

Using Worksheet Commands

Splitting the Screen

At times, the size of a 1-2-3 spreadsheet can be unwieldy. For example, if you want to compare data in column F with data in column N you need to be able to "fold" the worksheet so that you can see both parts at the same time.

The **/W**orksheet **W**indow command lets you split the screen

        horizontally   or   vertically.

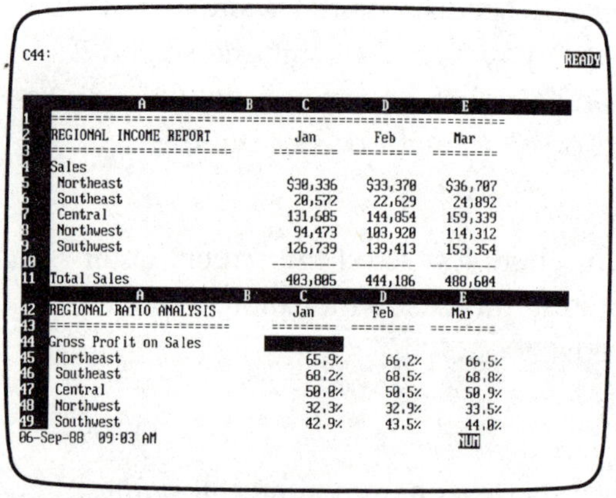

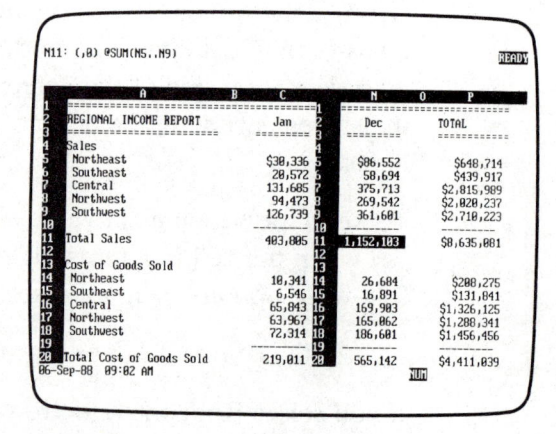

/Worksheet **W**indow also gives you the option of having the windows scroll

        independently   or   together.

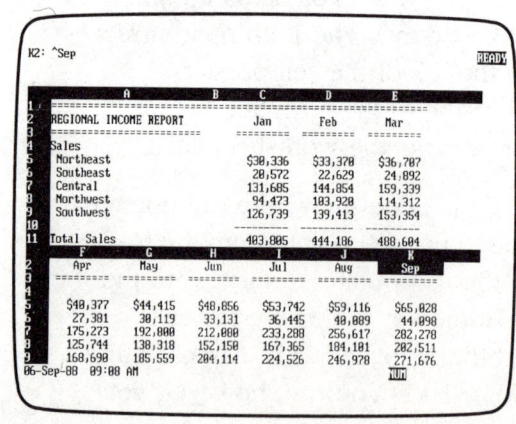

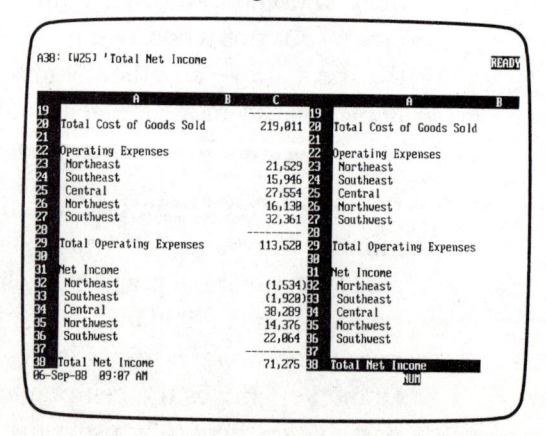

| Introduction | Selecting Commands from Command Menus | Using Ranges in the Worksheet | **Using Worksheet Commands** | Moving the Contents of Cells | Copying the Contents of Cells | Saving Your Files before You Quit (/Quit) | Accessing DOS from 1-2-3 |

Using /Worksheet Window

To split your screen into two horizontal or two vertical windows, use **/W**orksheet **W**indow. Select **W**orksheet from the main command menu.

Choose **W**indow from the **W**orksheet menu.

Choose either **H**orizontal or **V**ertical. For example, if you want to compare two columns that cannot be seen together on the default 1-2-3 display, choose **V**ertical.

To split the screen, press ⏎Enter after highlighting **V**ertical or simply press Ⓥ.

After the screen is split, you can change the screen from scrolling together or scrolling independently (or vice versa). To change the method of scrolling, select **/W**orksheet **W**indow and choose **S**ync or **U**nsync.

*Note: To return to the normal, single-window screen, type **/WWC** (for **/W**orksheet **W**indow **C**lear) and press ⏎Enter.*

Introduction

An Overview of 1-2-3

Getting Started

1-2-3 Basics

Creating a Worksheet

Printing Reports

Creating and Printing Graphs

Managing Data

Understanding Macros

Appendix

171

Using Worksheet Commands

Freezing Titles

If you need to freeze a column or row so that it remains in view as you scroll to different parts of the worksheet, use the **/W**orksheet **T**itles command. This command freezes all the cells to the left and/or above the cell pointer's current position so that those cells cannot move off the screen.

To keep the headings in rows 18 and 19 and/or the data in column A on the screen, use the **/W**orksheet **T**itles.

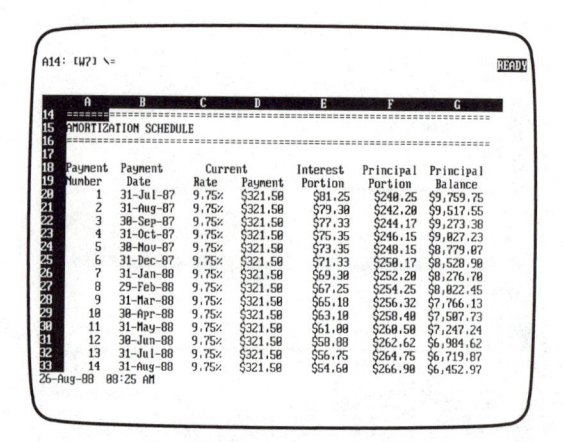

To keep the headings in rows 18 and 19 and/or the payment numbers in column A on the screen, follow these steps:

Select **/W**orksheet.

Choose **T**itles from the **W**orksheet menu.

Select **B**oth or **H**orizontal or **V**ertical.

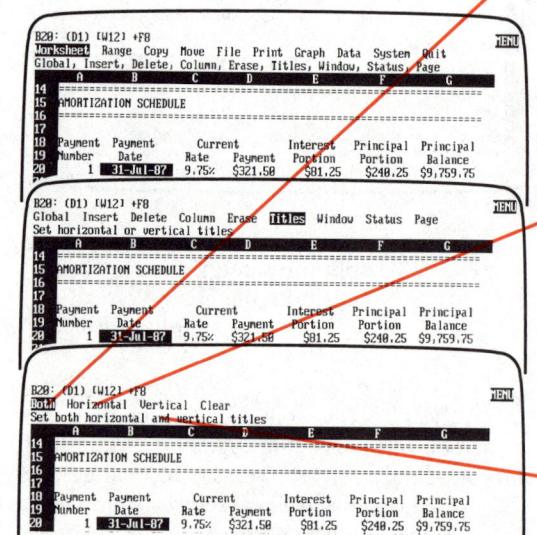

When 1-2-3 is in READY mode, you cannot move the cell pointer to the titles row(s) or column(s). To move the cell pointer to the titles area, use the [F5] (GoTo) key.

172

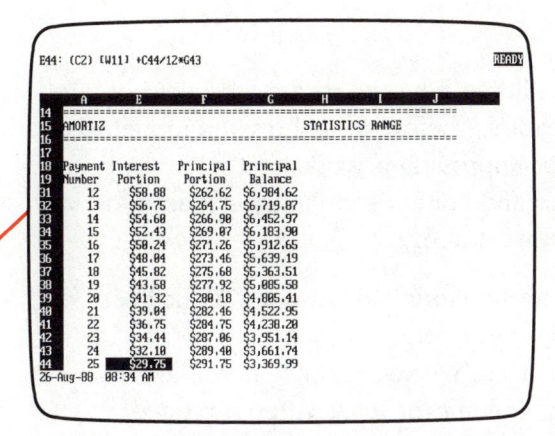

/**W**orksheet **T**itle **B**oth keeps the row(s) above the cell pointer and the column(s) to the left of the cell pointer displayed on the screen.

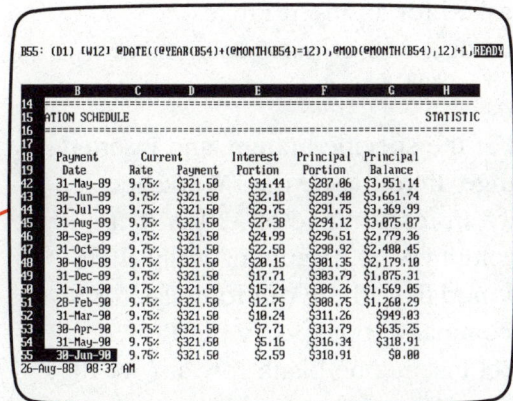

/**W**orksheet **T**itle **H**orizontal keeps the row(s) above the cell pointer displayed on the screen.

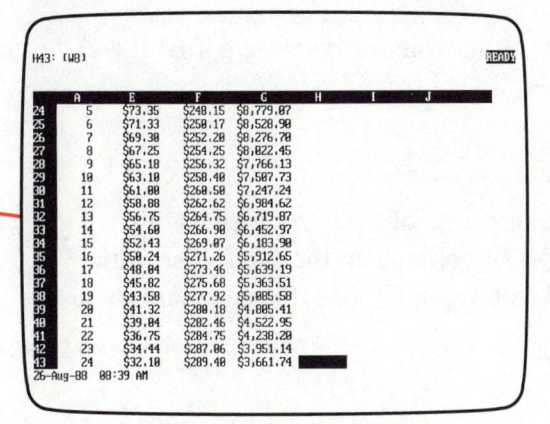

/**W**orksheet **T**itle **V**ertical keeps the column(s) to the left of the cell pointer displayed on the screen.

To unlock /**W**orksheet **T**itles, select **C**lear from the **T**itles menu.

173

Using Worksheet Commands

Inserting Rows and Columns

Suppose that you have finished building a model in a worksheet but want to dress up its general appearance before you show the model to anyone. One of the techniques for improving a worksheet's appearance is to insert blank rows and columns in strategic places to highlight headings and other important items.

The command for inserting rows and columns in 1-2-3 is **/W**orksheet **I**nsert. You can insert multiple rows and columns each time you invoke this command. After you select **/W**orksheet **I**nsert, you are asked for the method of insertion, **C**olumn or **R**ow. After you have selected one or the other, you are asked for an insert range. Depending on how you set up this range, one or more columns or rows will be inserted.

Inserted columns appear to the left of the specified range, and inserted rows appear above the specified range. If you issue the **/W**orksheet **I**nsert **C**olumn command and specify an insert range of A10..A10, a single blank column is inserted at column A. 1-2-3 automatically shifts all the values over one column and modifies all the cell formulas for the change. If you then repeat the command, but specify the **R**ow option and a range of A10..A10, 1-2-3 inserts one blank row at row 10. The values that were contained in row 10 move to row 11.

1-2-3 does not have the capability of inserting or deleting partial rows and columns.

Deleting Rows and Columns

Deleting rows and columns is the opposite of inserting them. With 1-2-3, you can delete multiple rows or columns at the same time with the **/W**orksheet **D**elete command. After you choose this command, you then choose **C**olumn or **R**ow from the submenu that appears on the screen. If you choose **R**ow, 1-2-3 asks you to specify a range of cells to be deleted. Just as for the **/W**orksheet **I**nsert command, the range you specify includes one cell from a given row.

For example, to delete rows 2 and 3 in the worksheet, you should specify A2..A3. Other acceptable range designations are B2..B3, C2..C3, C2..G3, etc.

The easiest way to designate the range to be deleted is to point to the appropriate cells. You also can enter the cell addresses from the keyboard. Pointing to cells, however, helps you to avoid inadvertently choosing the wrong range.

Remember that when you use the **/W**orksheet **D**elete command, the rows or columns you delete are gone forever. This action includes all the cells in the rows or columns, not just the range of cells you specify. You may be able to get the values back if you have previously saved a copy of the model on disk. But if you don't have a copy of the model, the rows and columns are lost.

The **/W**orksheet **D**elete command is different from the **/R**ange **E**rase command. The difference is best explained by using the analogy of a paper spreadsheet. The manual equivalent of the **/W**orksheet **D**elete command is to cut apart the columnar sheet (using a pair of scissors), remove the unwanted columns and/or rows, and then paste the pieces of the sheet back together. The **/R**ange **E**rase command, on the other hand, is like using an eraser to erase ranges of cells from the sheet.

There are two differences between **/W**orksheet **D**elete and **/R**ange **E**rase. First, **/W**orksheet **D**elete deletes entire columns and rows and readjusts the worksheet to fill the gaps, whereas **/R**ange **E**rase erases particular ranges, and the cells are merely blanked.

Using Worksheet Commands

Inserting Columns and Rows

Whether you want to add data to your worksheet or you want to add blank rows to separate sections of your worksheet, you can use the /**W**orksheet **I**nsert command to insert columns or rows.

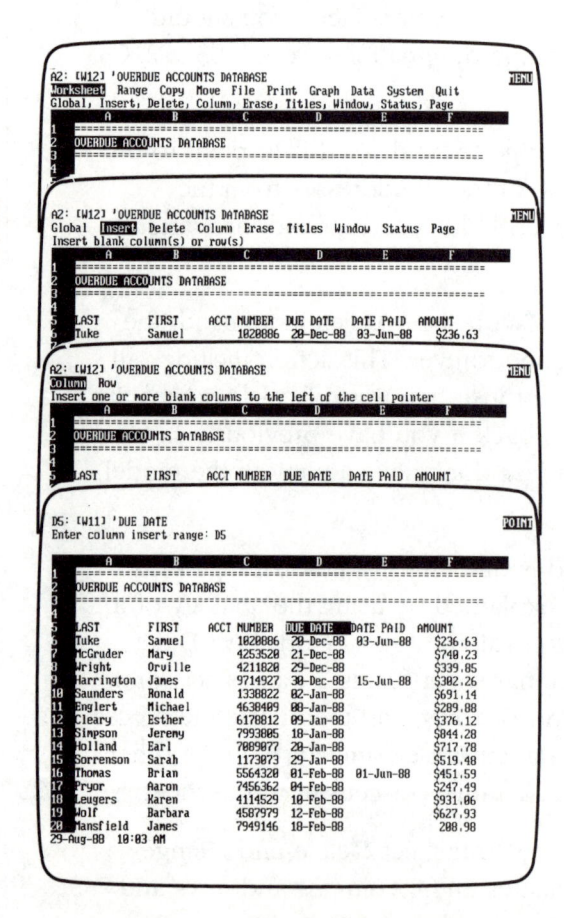

To add a new column of data to this database, use /**W**orksheet **I**nsert **C**olumn. Begin by choosing **W**orksheet from the 1-2-3 main menu.

Next, select **I**nsert.

Choose **C**olumn. (If you want to insert a new, blank row, choose **R**ow.)

When the `Enter Column Insert Range:` prompt appears, move the cell pointer to the column where you want the new column inserted. (You may need to press [Esc] once to free the cell pointer.) Existing data will be moved to the right of the cursor.

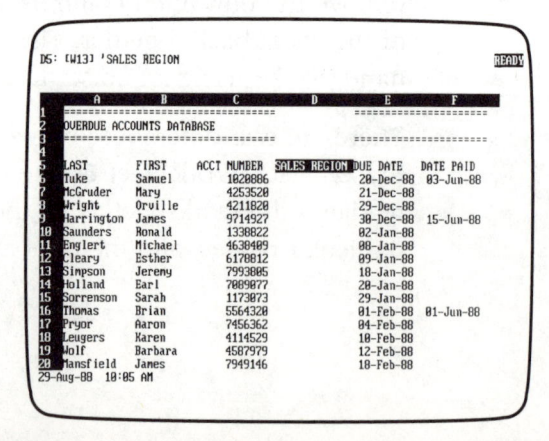

When you press [↵Enter], a blank column will be displayed, ready for you to enter new data to the database.

176

| Introduction | Selecting Commands from Command Menus | Using Ranges in the Worksheet | **Using Worksheet Commands** | Moving the Contents of Cells | Copying the Contents of Cells | Saving Your Files before You Quit (/Quit) | Accessing DOS from 1-2-3 |

Deleting Columns and Rows

To delete a column or row, you complete steps similar to the steps for inserting a column or row. After you select **/W**orksheet, choose **D**elete.

Select either **C**olumn or **R**ow.

Designate the range where you want the column(s) or row(s) deleted.

And press ⏎Enter.

Remember that **/W**orksheet **D**elete is different from **/R**ange **E**rase.

/Worksheet **D**elete "cuts" apart the columnar sheet, removing the unwanted columns or rows, and then pastes the pieces of the sheet back together. **/R**ange **E**rase simply erases data from a cell or range of cells.

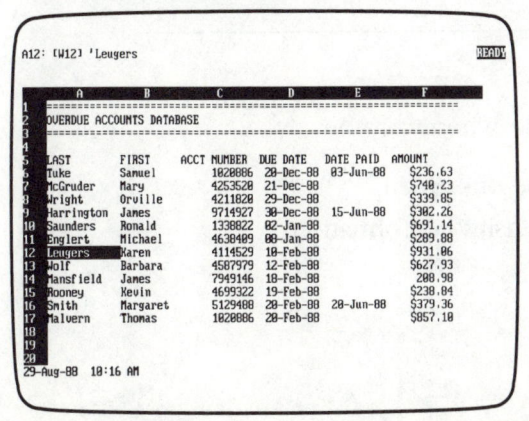

Introduction

An Overview of 1-2-3

Getting Started

1-2-3 Basics

Creating a Worksheet

Printing Reports

Creating and Printing Graphs

Managing Data

Understanding Macros

Appendix

177

Using Worksheet Commands

Hiding Columns

With the **/W**orksheet **C**olumn **H**ide command, you can suppress the display of any column in the worksheet. One important use for this command is to suppress display of unwanted columns when you are printing reports. When you hide intervening columns, a report can display on a single page data from two or more separated columns.

Numbers and formulas in hidden columns are still present and cell references to cells in hidden columns continue to work properly. But the hidden columns do not appear on the display. You can tell which columns are missing only by noting the break in column letters at the top of the display. The hidden columns are temporarily redisplayed, however, when you use certain commands, such as **/C**opy or **/M**ove; the hidden columns are marked with an asterisk (such as H*) during this temporary display. To redisplay hidden columns, use **/W**orksheet **C**olumn **D**isplay.

When you select the **/W**orksheet **C**olumn **H**ide command, 1-2-3 prompts you for the range of column to hide. You must invoke the command once for each range of adjacent columns that you hide.

If the screen has been split, certain 1-2-3 commands affect only the current window. For example, the **/W**orksheet **C**olumn **H**ide command can be used to hide a column in the current window without affecting the display in the other window.

▼

When To Hide Columns

You can use the **/W**orksheet **C**olumn **H**ide whenever you

- Want to fit noncontiguous columns on-screen
- Want to suppress the display of sensitive information

- Need to print a report that does not include all columns
- Want to hide the display of all cells that have a numeric value of zero

▲

Suppressing the Display of Zeros

The **/W**orksheet **G**lobal **Z**ero command allows you to suppress the display of all the cells in the worksheet that have a numeric value of zero. This technique is often useful for preparing reports for presentation. You can enter formulas and values for all the items in the report, including the zero items, and then display the results with all the zeros removed. The **/W**orksheet **G**lobal **Z**ero command also has an option to reinstate the display of zero values. If you use /*wgz*, save the file, and then retrieve the file, /*wgz* will be disabled and the display of zeros will no longer be suppressed.

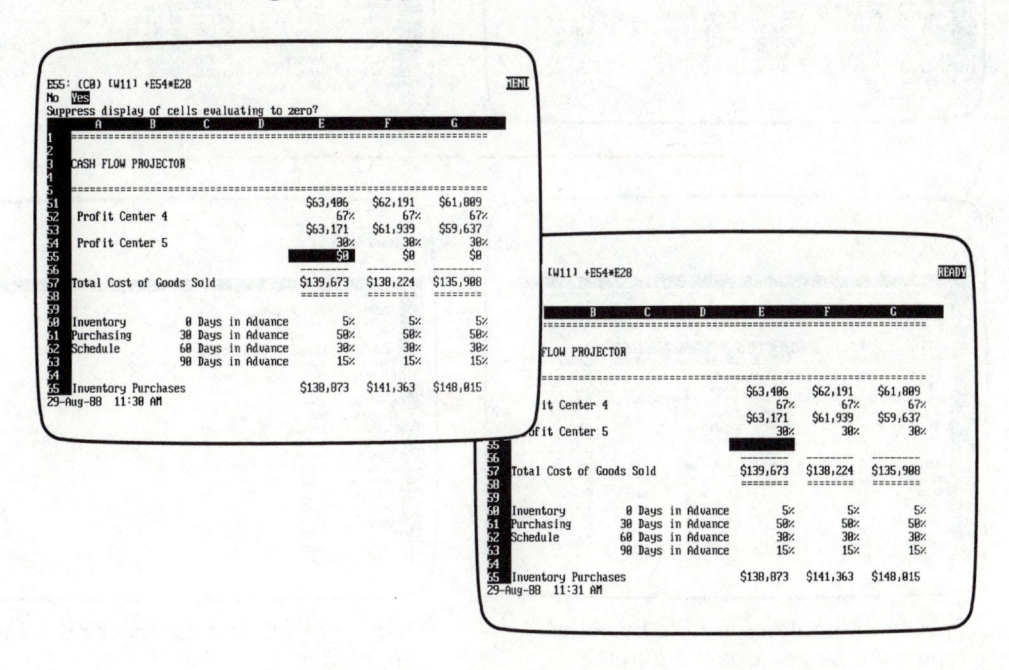

179

Using Worksheet Commands

Hiding Columns

At times, you will want to suppress the display of columns on your worksheet. Whether you want to hide sensitive information or simply want to create more room for the more important columns on your report, use /**W**orksheet **C**olumn **H**ide to hide the specified information.

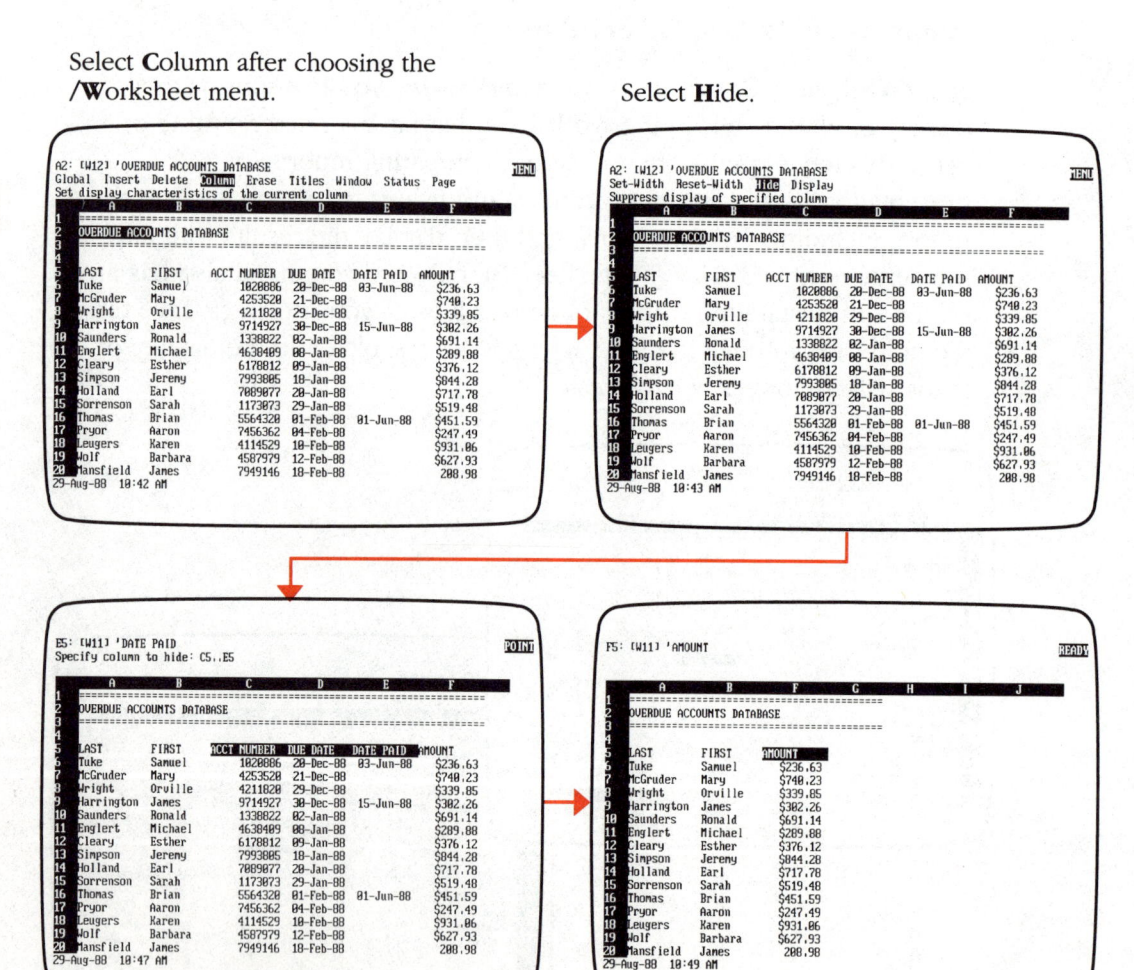

Select **C**olumn after choosing the /**W**orksheet menu.

Select **H**ide.

Specify the columns to hide by either typing the range or pointing to the range.

Press ⏎**Enter**, and the specified columns are hidden from view.

180

| Introduction | Selecting Commands from Command Menus | Using Ranges in the Worksheet | **Using Worksheet Commands** | Moving the Contents of Cells | Copying the Contents of Cells | Saving Your Files before You Quit (/Quit) | Accessing DOS from 1-2-3 |

```
F5: [W11] 'AMOUNT                                          POINT
Enter range to copy FROM: F5..F5
       A          B         C*       D*        E*       F
  1  ============================================================
  2  OVERDUE ACCOUNTS DATABASE
  3  ============================================================
  4
  5  LAST       FIRST     ACCT NUMBER DUE DATE  DATE PAID  AMOUNT
  6  Tuke       Samuel      1020886   20-Dec-88 03-Jun-88  $236.63
  7  McGruder   Mary        4253520   21-Dec-88            $740.23
  8  Wright     Orville     4211820   29-Dec-88            $339.85
  9  Harrington James       9714927   30-Dec-88 15-Jun-88  $302.26
 10  Saunders   Ronald      1338822   02-Jan-88            $691.14
 11  Englert    Michael     4638409   08-Jan-88            $289.88
 12  Cleary     Esther      6178812   09-Jan-88            $376.12
 13  Simpson    Jeremy      7993805   18-Jan-88            $844.28
 14  Holland    Earl        7089077   20-Jan-88            $717.78
 15  Sorrenson  Sarah       1173073   29-Jan-88            $519.48
 16  Thomas     Brian       5564320   01-Feb-88 01-Jun-88  $451.59
 17  Pryor      Aaron       7456362   04-Feb-88            $247.49
 18  Leugers    Karen       4114529   10-Feb-88            $931.06
 19  Wolf       Barbara     4587979   12-Feb-88            $627.93
 20  Mansfield  James       7949146   18-Feb-88             208.98
29-Aug-88  10:50 AM
```

This screen shows how hidden columns are temporarily displayed when using /**C**opy.

```
F2: [W11]                                                  READY
       A          B         F          C        D         E
  1  ===========================   1 =============================
  2  OVERDUE ACCOUNTS DATABASE     2 ASE
  3  ===========================   3 =============================
  4                                4
  5  LAST       FIRST     AMOUNT   5 ACCT NUMBER DUE DATE DATE PAID
  6  Tuke       Samuel    $236.63  6    1020886  20-Dec-88 03-Jun-88
  7  McGruder   Mary      $740.23  7    4253520  21-Dec-88
  8  Wright     Orville   $339.85  8    4211820  29-Dec-88
  9  Harrington James     $302.26  9    9714927  30-Dec-88 15-Jun-88
 10  Saunders   Ronald    $691.14 10    1338822  02-Jan-88
 11  Englert    Michael   $289.88 11    4638409  08-Jan-88
 12  Cleary     Esther    $376.12 12    6178812  09-Jan-88
 13  Simpson    Jeremy    $844.28 13    7993805  18-Jan-88
 14  Holland    Earl      $717.78 14    7089077  20-Jan-88
 15  Sorrenson  Sarah     $519.48 15    1173073  29-Jan-88
 16  Thomas     Brian     $451.59 16    5564320  01-Feb-88 01-Jun-88
 17  Pryor      Aaron     $247.49 17    7456362  04-Feb-88
 18  Leugers    Karen     $931.06 18    4114529  10-Feb-88
 19  Wolf       Barbara   $627.93 19    4587979  12-Feb-88
 20  Mansfield  James      208.98 20    7949146  18-Feb-88
06-Sep-88  10:19 AM                                          NUM
```

As you can see, even though columns C through E are hidden in the first window, they are not hidden in the adjacent window.

Introduction

An Overview of 1-2-3

Getting Started

1-2-3 Basics

Creating a Worksheet

Printing Reports

Creating and Printing Graphs

Managing Data

Understanding Macros

Appendix

181

Using Worksheet Commands

Recalculating the Worksheet

One of the primary functions of a spreadsheet program is to recalculate all the cells in a worksheet when a value or a formula in one of the cells changes. 1-2-3 provides two basic recalculation methods: *automatic recalculation* and *manual recalculation*. Using automatic recalculation, which is the default, 1-2-3 recalculates the worksheet whenever any cell in the worksheet changes. In manual recalculation, the worksheet is recalculated only when the user requests it, either from the keyboard or from a macro.

1-2-3 also provides three orders of recalculation: the *natural order* and two linear orders, either *column-wise* or *row-wise*. Natural order is the default, but you can choose any of the three orders.

You also can choose the number of times the spreadsheet is recalculated; because of circular references, the spreadsheet may need to be recalculated several times whenever you request recalculation.

You select all the recalculation options by using the **/W**orksheet **G**lobal **R**ecalculation command.

As a beginning 1-2-3 user, you may not need to change the recalculation settings at all. 1-2-3's default settings are **A**utomatic recalculation (meaning the program recalculates cells each time a cell's content changes) and **N**atural order (meaning that 1-2-3 does not recalculate any given cell until after the cells that it depends on have been recalculated). To save processing time, you may want to switch to **M**anual recalculation so that 1-2-3 recalculates the worksheet only when you press F9 (Calc).

For more specialized applications, the **C**olumn-wise and **R**ow-wise calculation method may be used. Be extremely careful when you use these orders of recalculation, however: if they are used improperly, they can cause forward and circular reference errors or may result in producing erroneous values on the worksheet.

Key Terms To Remember

Automatic recalculation	Worksheet is recalculated whenever a cell changes.
Manual recalculation	Worksheet is recalculated only when you press F9 (Calc).
Natural order of recalculation	1-2-3 does not recalculate any given cell until after the cells that it depends on have been recalculated.
Column-wise recalculation	Recalculation begins at A1 and continues down column A; then goes to B1 and down column B, etc.
Row-wise recalculation	Recalculation begins at cell A1 and proceeds across row 1; then goes to row 2, etc.
Iterative recalculation	Recalculates the worksheet a specified number of times whenever you change cell contents (in automatic recalculation) or press F9 (in manual recalculation).

For more information on automatic, manual, and iterative recalculation and on the natural, column-wise, and row-wise orders of recalculation, refer to *Using 1-2-3,* Special Edition. In that book, you'll find in-depth discussions and step-by-step examples on using each of these recalculation features.

Using Worksheet Commands

Recalculation Methods

One of the primary functions of a spreadsheet program is to recalculate all the cells in a worksheet when a value or a formula in one of the cells changes. 1-2-3 provides two basic recalculation methods: *automatic recalculation* and *manual recalculation*.

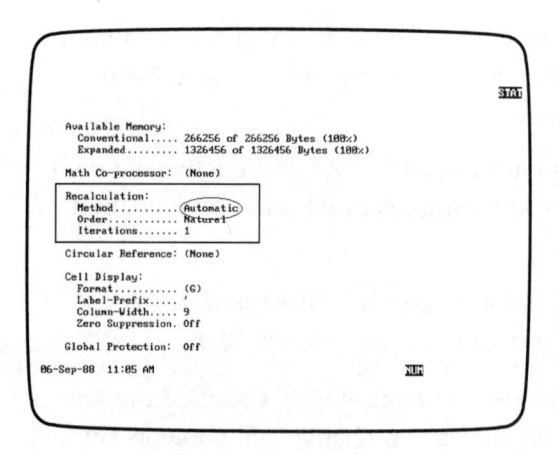

Automatic

Using automatic recalculation, which is the default, 1-2-3 recalculates the worksheet whenever any cell in the worksheet changes. In manual recalculation, the worksheet is recalculated only when the user requests it, either from the keyboard or from a macro.

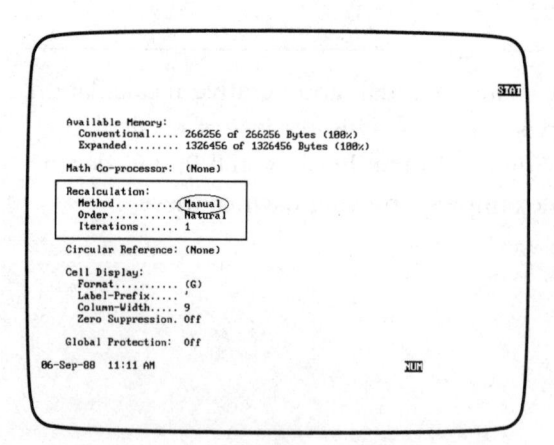

Manual

The Worksheet is recalculated only when you press F9 (Calc).

| Introduction | Selecting Commands from Command Menus | Using Ranges in the Worksheet | **Using Worksheet Commands** | Moving the Contents of Cells | Copying the Contents of Cells | Saving Your Files before You Quit (/Quit) | Accessing DOS from 1-2-3 |

Natural

1-2-3 does not recalculate any given cell until after the cells that it depends on have been recalculated.

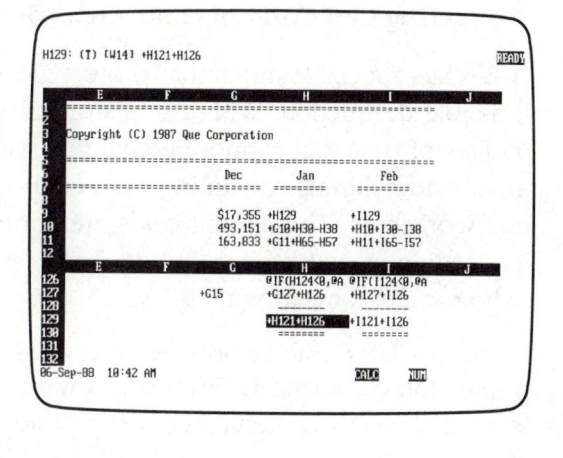

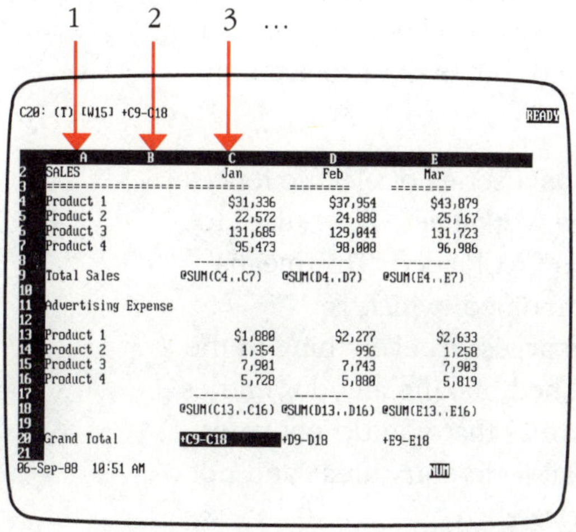

Column-wise

Recalculation begins at A1 and continues down column A; then goes to B1 and down column B, etc.

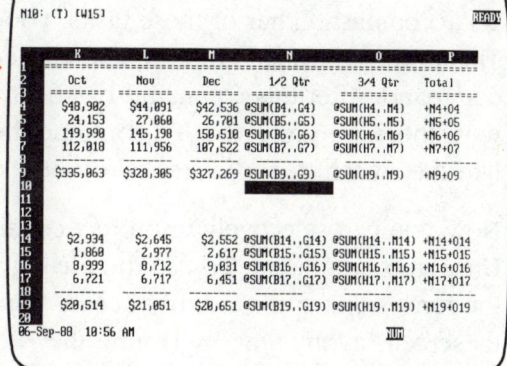

Row-wise

Recalculation begins at cell A1 and proceeds across row 1; then goes to row 2, etc.

Introduction

An Overview of 1-2-3

Getting Started

1-2-3 Basics

Creating a Worksheet

Printing Reports

Creating and Printing Graphs

Managing Data

Understanding Macros

Appendix

185

Using Worksheet Commands

Protecting Cell Contents and Areas of the Worksheet

1-2-3 has special features that protect areas of a worksheet from possible destruction. With a series of commands, you can set up ranges of cells that cannot be changed without special effort. In fact, rows and columns containing protected cells cannot be deleted from the worksheet. These commands are particularly beneficial when you are setting up worksheets in which data will be entered by people who are not familiar with 1-2-3.

When you first create a worksheet, every cell is protected. The global protection command is disabled, however. This condition means that each cell has the potential of being protected, but is not protected at the moment.

This protection system may be thought of as a series of electric fences that are set up around all of the cells in the worksheet. The "juice" to these fences is turned off when the sheet is first loaded. This means that all the cells in the worksheet can be modified, which is appropriate because you will want to have access to everything in the worksheet at this time. After you have finished making all your entries in the worksheet, however, there may be areas that you do not want modified, or you may want to set up special form-entry areas and not allow the cell pointer to move anywhere else.

To accomplish either of these tasks, you must first enable protection. This is accomplished with the **/W**orksheet **G**lobal **P**rotection **E**nable command. After this command has been issued, all of the cells in the worksheet are protected. To continue the analogy, this command is like the switch that activates all of the electric fences in the worksheet.

Now you can selectively unprotect certain ranges with the **/R**ange **U**nprotect command. To use the analogy once again, you tear down the fences that surround these cells. You can, of course, reprotect these cells at any time by issuing the **/R**ange **P**rotect command.

Suppose that you create a worksheet that includes a number of long and important formulas. You may want to protect these formulas against accidental deletion by using 1-2-3's protection capability. But what if you need to make a change in several of these formulas? You could move around the worksheet, unprotecting cells, changing the formulas, and then protecting the cells again. Or you could use the **/W**orksheet **G**lobal **P**rotection **D**isable command to lower the fences around all the cells. After making the necessary changes, you could restore protection to all of the cells by using the **/W**orksheet **G**lobal **P**rotection **E**nable command.

For even more protection, you can limit the movement of the cell pointer by using the **/R**ange **I**nput command. You must use this command, which allows movement to only **/R**ange **U**nprotected cells, when you set up the special form-entry areas mentioned previously.

For example, suppose that you create a simple worksheet. Every cell in the worksheet is protected except E5, E7, and E9. Note that unprotected cells are indicated in the control panel by the **U** prefix.

Now suppose that you issue the **/R**ange **I**nput command. 1-2-3 will prompt you to supply a data input range. In our example, this could be the range A1..F20 or the range E1..E9. The exact size of the range doesn't matter, as long as the range includes all of the unprotected cells. After the range has been specified, the cell pointer will jump immediately to cell E5 and wait for you to enter a number or label. Also, the upper-left corner of the input range is positioned at the upper-left corner of the screen. Don't press Enter to terminate the input; use one of the arrow keys. Once again, you will want to make a cell entry and use an arrow key to move on.

The /RI command remains in effect until you press either the Enter key or the Esc key. Then the cell pointer returns to the upper-left corner of the input range, and the worksheet returns to the same position on the screen as before the /RI command was issued.

Using Worksheet Commands

Protecting the Worksheet

With a series of commands, you can protect the whole worksheet or ranges of cells that cannot be changed without special effort. To turn protection on and off, you need to learn three commands: /**W**orksheet **G**lobal **P**rotection, /**R**ange **U**nprotect, and /**R**ange **P**rotect.

Protecting the Whole Worksheet with /Worksheet Global Protection

When a new worksheet is first loaded, protection is turned off so that you can make changes and add data. The /**W**orksheet **G**lobal **P**rotection **E**nable command turns on the worksheet's protection system.

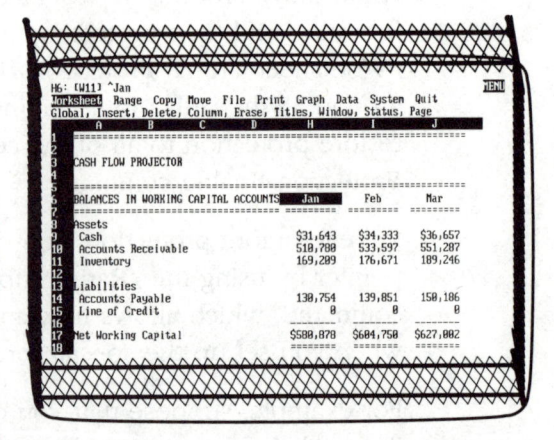

To protect a worksheet, begin by selecting /**W**orksheet **G**lobal.

Choose **P**rotection.

Choose **E**nable to turn protection on.

All cells in the worksheet are protected as indicated by the PR in the first line of the control panel.

188

| Introduction | Selecting Commands from Command Menus | Using Ranges in the Worksheet | **Using Worksheet Commands** | Moving the Contents of Cells | Copying the Contents of Cells | Saving Your Files before You Quit (/Quit) | Accessing DOS from 1-2-3 |

Turning Off Protection in a Range

After selecting the **/W**orksheet **G**lobal **P**rotection **E**nable command, you are unable to make changes to the cells in your worksheet. If you want to turn off protection for a range in your worksheet, use **/R**ange **U**nprotect.

After selecting **/R**ange, choose **U**nprotect.

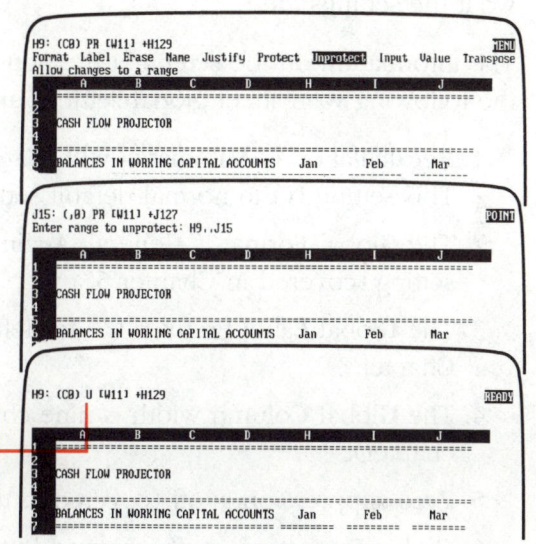

Enter the range of cells where you want to add or change data.

After you indicate the range and press ⏎Enter, unprotected cells are identified by a U in the control panel.

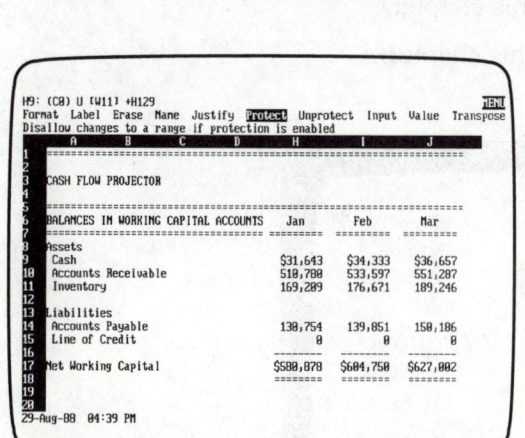

*Tip: If you want to restrict the movement of the cursor to those cells that are unprotected, use the /**R**ange **I**nput command. Entering the range H9..J17, for example, locks the cursor movement within that area of the worksheet.*

Use **/R**ange **P**rotect to turn on protection once again.

Introduction

An Overview of 1-2-3

Getting Started

1-2-3 Basics

Creating a Worksheet

Printing Reports

Creating and Printing Graphs

Managing Data

Understanding Macros

Appendix

Using Worksheet Commands

Checking the Status of Global Settings

Use the **/W**orksheet **S**tatus command to check the status of all the global settings for the worksheet. This command gives you an easy way to check the settings without having to experiment to find out what the settings are.

The information on the screen at the bottom of the page indicates that the following worksheet global settings are active:

1. **R**ecalculation is **A**utomatic, with **N**atural order and **1** iteration. This setting is the normal default setting (covered in this chapter).
2. The **G**lobal **F**ormat is **G**eneral. Again, this setting is the default setting (covered in Chapter 5).
3. The **G**lobal **L**abel-Prefix is (') for left-justification (covered in Chapter 3).
4. The **G**lobal **C**olumn width is nine characters (covered in this chapter).
5. **Z**ero suppression is off (covered in this chapter).
6. **G**lobal **P**rotection is off (covered in this chapter).

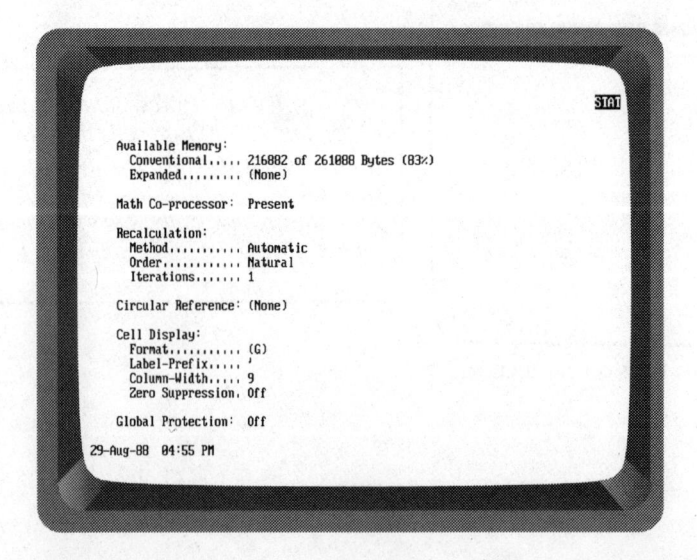

```
                                                              STAT

   Available Memory:
      Conventional...... 216882 of 261888 Bytes (83%)
      Expanded.......... (None)

   Math Co-processor:  Present

   Recalculation:
      Method............ Automatic
      Order............. Natural
      Iterations........ 1

   Circular Reference: (None)

   Cell Display:
      Format............ (G)
      Label-Prefix...... '
      Column-Width...... 9
      Zero Suppression. Off

   Global Protection:  Off

   29-Aug-88  04:55 PM
```

190

Entering a Page-Break Character

The **/W**orksheet **P**age command inserts a blank row, and then a page-break character in the cell at which the cursor was originally positioned. This command is similar to the **/W**orksheet **I**nsert **R**ow command that inserts a row at the row(s) specified by the cell pointer. **/W**orksheet **P**age inserts a new row into the worksheet at the current location of the cell pointer. The command then places the page-break character in the cell directly above the cursor.

The page-break character is used when printing a range from the worksheet. Printing is covered in detail in Chapter 5, but you should realize now that the best time to insert page-break characters is while you are building the worksheet. As you become more experienced in building worksheets and printing reports based on those worksheets, you will learn to think in terms of printed pages as you build. Thinking ahead will save time and minimize confusion when you're ready to print.

The page break is effective only when positioned at the left edge of the range being printed. When the page break is in effect, the contents of the other cells in that row within the print range are not printed.

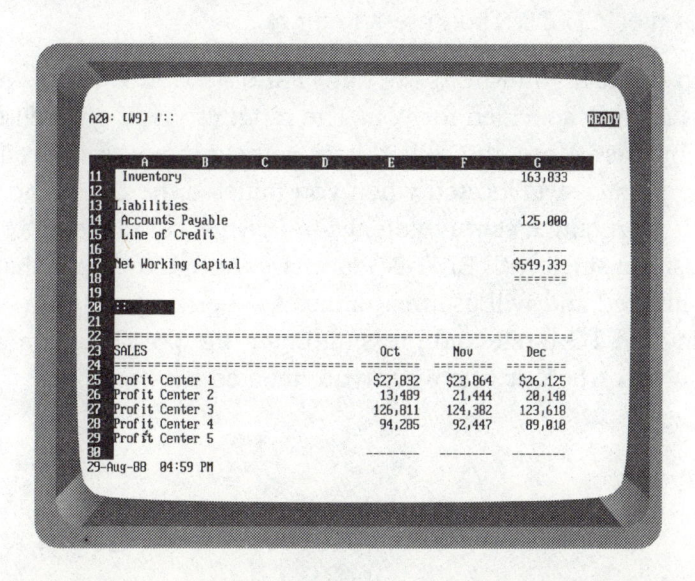

191

Moving the Contents of Cells

In the days of manual spreadsheets, the process of moving data around on the page was called *cutting and pasting* because scissors and glue were used to move sections of the spreadsheet. 1-2-3 lets you cut sections of the worksheet and paste them automatically.

With the **/M**ove and **/C**opy commands, you can move and copy the contents of cells and ranges of cells from one part of the worksheet to another. The difference between moving and copying is that data that is *moved* from one cell to another disappears from the first cell; data that is *copied* appears in both cells.

Suppose that on your worksheet, you want to move the contents of range C1..D3 to the range E1..F3. After you enter **/M**ove, 1-2-3 responds with the message Enter range to move FROM. You will notice that a range is already specified after this message. If the cell pointer was at cell D7 when you started, the range specified would be D7..D7. 1-2-3 always tries to stay one step ahead in helping you designate ranges.

Next, you need to enter the appropriate range. As soon as you begin typing, the D7..D7 disappears. As you type, the characters appear where the D7..D7 was. To designate the proper FROM range for this example, enter *C1..D3*. Then press Enter.

1-2-3 then will ask you to Enter the range to move TO. Again, a range is already specified for you. The range is just a one-cell range this time but, as before, the cell address is the address of the cell at which the pointer was located when you initiated the command. To enter your own range, start typing again. For the TO range, you can specify just the single cell E1. 1-2-3 is smart enough to know that E1..F3 is implied and will use that range. As soon as you finish designating the TO range and pressing Enter, the pointer will return immediately to where it was when you initiated the command.

Note that the cell pointer does not have to be positioned at the beginning of the TO or FROM ranges when you initiate the /Move command.

Also, remember that when you move a range of cells, the TO range is completely overwritten by the FROM range, and the previous contents of those cells are lost forever. If there are other cells whose formulas depend on the cell addresses of the lost cells, the other cells will be given the value ERR instead of the cell address.

Use the expanding cursor for pointing to ranges. When you select /Move and are asked to enter a range, 1-2-3 automatically makes the current cell one corner of the range. If you do not want that cell to be a part of the FROM range, press Esc and move the cell pointer to the cell you want to appear as the upper-left corner of the FROM range and press the period (.) key. Use the arrow keys to move the cell pointer over and down. Notice that the cursor "expands" so that the entire range is highlighted. When the FROM range has been highlighted, press Enter.

Use the End key for pointing to large ranges. Suppose that you want to move the contents of the range A1..C5 to the range that begins at cell A7. When the range prompt A1..A1 appears, press the End key and then the down-arrow key. The cell pointer jumps to cell A5, and the prompt reads `A1..A5`. Now move the cell pointer by pressing the End key and then the right-arrow key. The prompt now reads `A1..C5`. This process would have taken seven keystrokes if we had used only the arrow keys; instead, the range was entered in only four keystrokes. The difference is even more dramatic when you work with larger ranges.

Moving the Contents of Cells

Using the /Move Command

Instead of cutting and pasting bits of a paper spreadsheet, the 1-2-3 **M**ove command allows you to electronically cut and paste ranges or cells to another part of your worksheet.

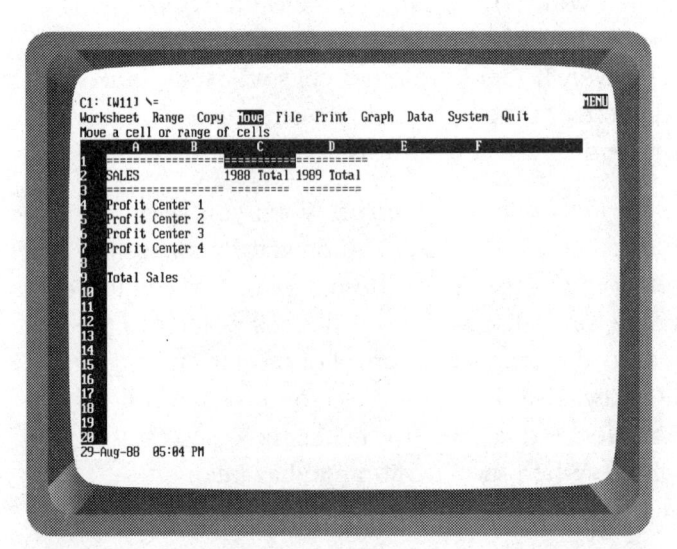

In this example, we want to move the range C1..D3 to E1..F3. To use the /**M**ove command, you select the command from 1-2-3's main menu.

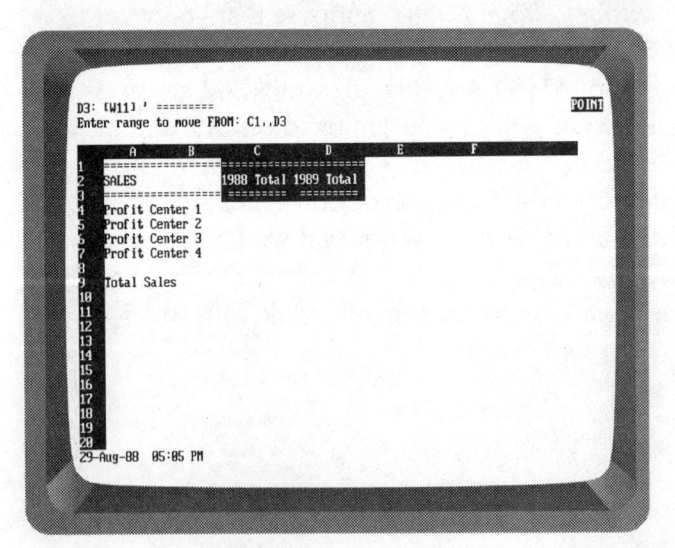

Specify the range of cells you want to move, enter the range to which you want to move the designated range, and press [↵Enter].

194

| Introduction | Selecting Commands from Command Menus | Using Ranges in the Worksheet | Using Worksheet Commands | **Moving the Contents of Cells** | Copying the Contents of Cells | Saving Your Files before You Quit (/Quit) | Accessing DOS from 1-2-3 |

Introduction

An Overview of 1-2-3

Getting Started

1-2-3 Basics

Creating a Worksheet

Printing Reports

Creating and Printing Graphs

Managing Data

Understanding Macros

Appendix

When the Enter Range to Move TO: prompt appears, move the cell pointer to (or type the cell address of) the upper left cell of the new location.

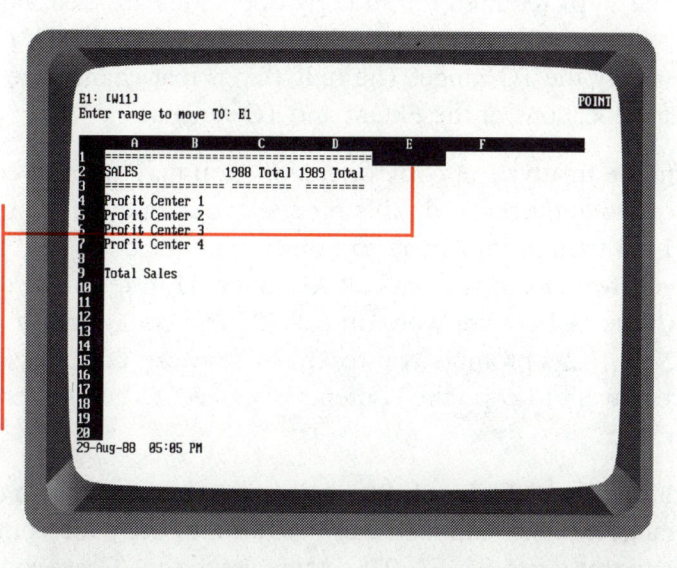

As soon as you press Enter, 1-2-3 moves the specified range to the new location.

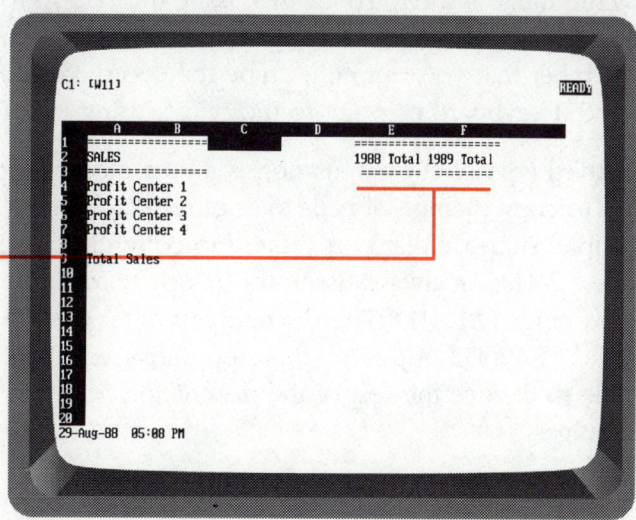

195

Copying the Contents of Cells

Many times you will want to copy the contents of cells to other locations in a worksheet. In this section, you'll look at the four different ways in which you can copy data in 1-2-3.

The steps required for all copy operations are basically the same: first, issue the /Copy command; second, specify the FROM range; third, specify the TO range. The only things that change are the size, shape, and locations of the FROM and TO ranges.

In the first type of copy operation, you may want to copy from one cell to another. To do this process, you issue the command /Copy. 1-2-3 then prompts you to Enter range to copy FROM. Because you want to copy from cell A1, enter *A1* in response to this message. (If the cell pointer were on cell A1, you could simply press Enter). Next, 1-2-3 prompts you to Enter range to copy TO. Because you want to copy the contents of cell A1 to cell A2, enter *A2* as the TO range.

In the second type of copy operation, you copy from one cell to a range of cells. Suppose that you want to copy the contents of cell A1 into the range B1..H1. To do this, issue the /Copy command, specify A1 as the FROM range, and then specify B1..H1 as the TO range. Remember that you can either type the coordinates of the TO range from the keyboard or point to the range, using POINT mode.

The third type of copy operation is a little more complicated. You may want to copy a range of cells to another place in the worksheet. For example, suppose that you wanted to copy the range A1..H1 to the range A2..H2. As always, issue the /Copy command, and enter the FROM range (A1..H1). Then, when you enter the TO range, specify A2 instead of A2..H2. Although this step may seem illogical, it's not: 1-2-3 is able to deduce the rest of the destination from the first cell of the TO range.

1-2-3 has four types of copy operations:

- Copy from one cell to another cell
- Copy from one cell to a range of cells
- Copy from a range to another range of equal size
- Copy from a range to a larger range

In the fourth type of copy operation, you may want to copy a range of cells to an even larger range of cells somewhere else in the worksheet. For example, suppose that you want to copy the range A1..H1 into the rectangular block A2..H20. As before, you issue the /Copy command and define the FROM range as A1..H1. The TO range is A2..H20.

You can think of this type of copy as an extension of the previous type. In essence, the results of this copy operation could have been reached by repeating the copy command 19 times and specifying 19 different single-row TO ranges. The first TO range would be A2, the second would be A3, the third A4, and so on. The results are the same for either method, but you can save a great deal of time by using the A2..H20 range as shown.

The concept of TO ranges is tricky. The best way to learn about the effects of using different TO and FROM ranges is to experiment on your own. After a while, the rules of copying will be second nature to you.

Copying the Contents of Cells

1-2-3 has four types of copy procedures, although they all are similar.

When you want to copy data, you can copy in one of four ways:

1. Copy from one cell to another cell

2. Copy from one cell to a range of cells

3. Copy from a range to another range of equal size

4. Copy from a range to a larger range

| Introduction | Selecting Commands from Command Menus | Using Ranges in the Worksheet | Using Worksheet Commands | Moving the Contents of Cells | **Copying the Contents of Cells** | Saving Your Files before You Quit (/Quit) | Accessing DOS from 1-2-3 |

1. In this copy operation, the cell A1 has been copied to cell A2.

2. Here, A1 has been copied to the range B2..H2.

3. This screen shows that the range A1..H1 has been copied to A2.

4. In this screen, the small range A1..H1 has been copied to the larger range A2..A20.

Introduction

An Overview of 1-2-3

Getting Started

1-2-3 Basics

Creating a Worksheet

Printing Reports

Creating and Printing Graphs

Managing Data

Understanding Macros

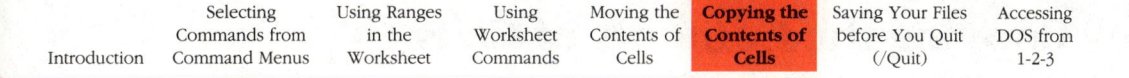

Appendix

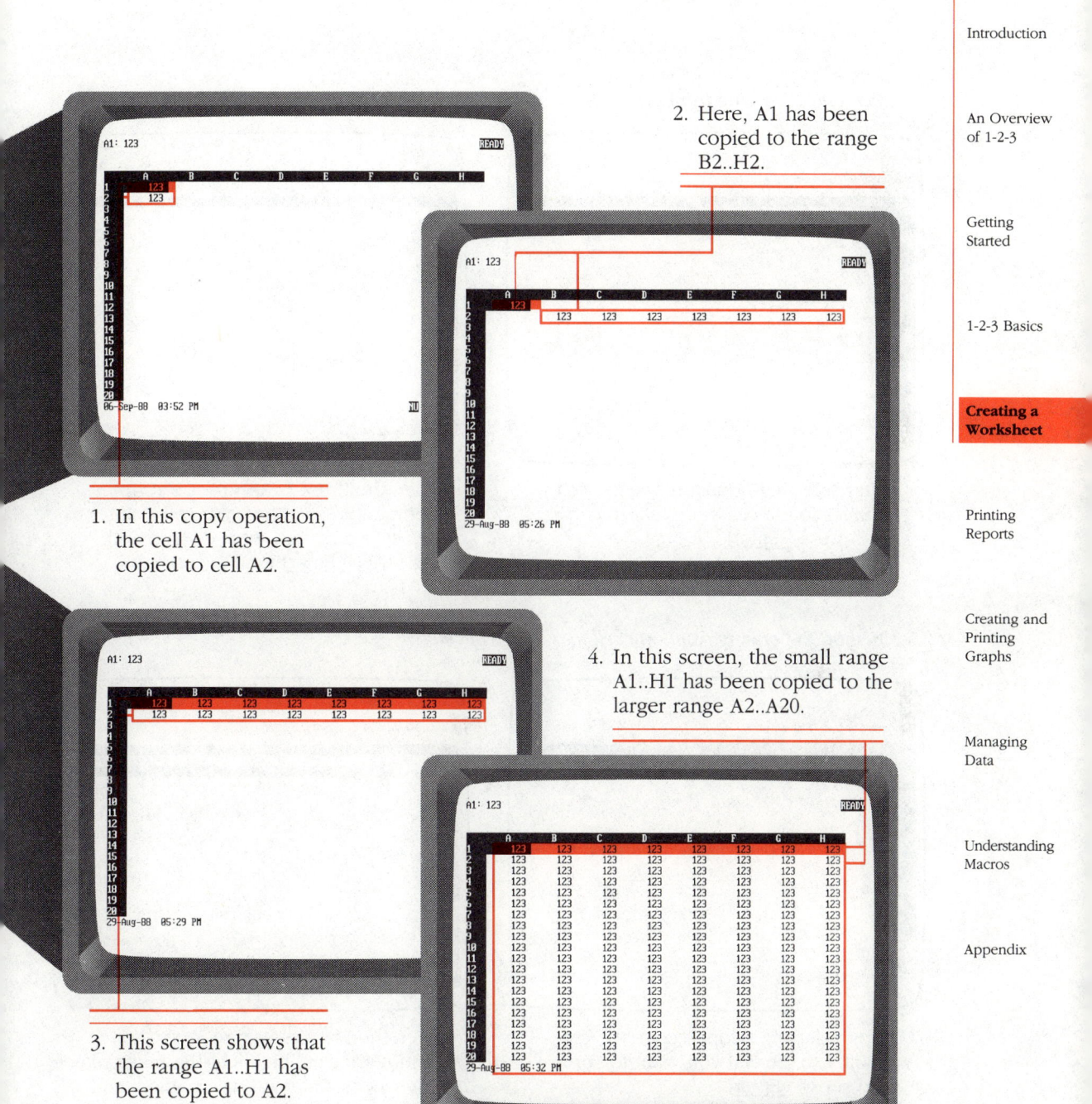

199

Copying the Contents of Cells

Method 1: Copying from one cell to another cell

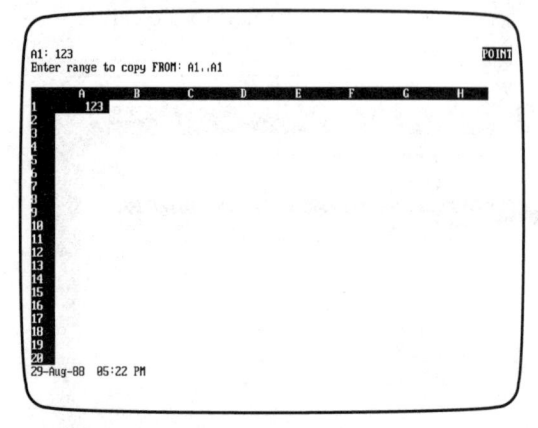

After selecting /Copy, move the cell pointer to the cell you want to copy, and press ↵Enter.

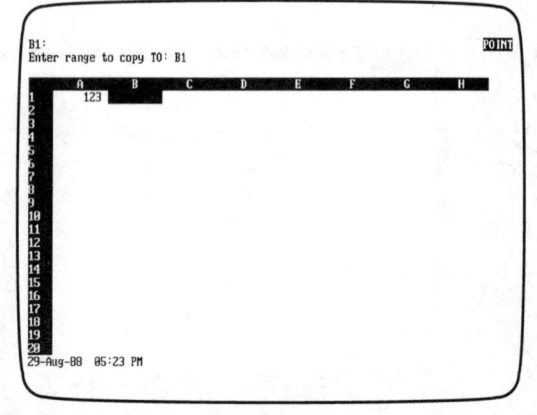

When the `Enter Range To Copy:` prompt appears, move the cell pointer to the cell where you want data copied, and press ↵Enter.

Method 2: Copying from one cell to a range of cells

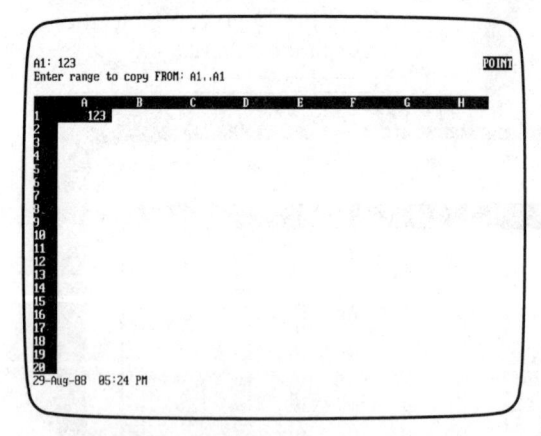

After selecting /Copy, move the cell pointer to the cell you want to copy, and press ↵Enter.

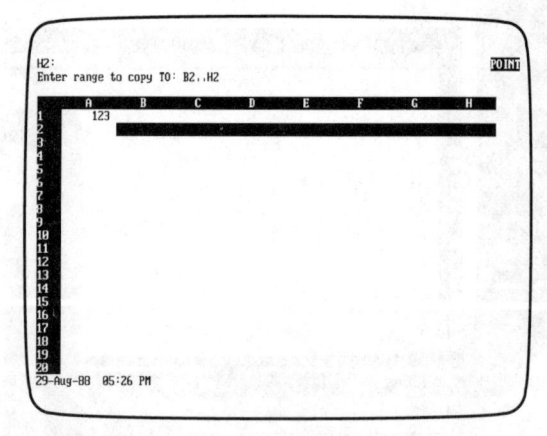

When the `Enter Range To Copy:` prompt appears, highlight the range of cells where you want data copied, and press ↵Enter.

Method 3: Copying from a range to another range of equal size

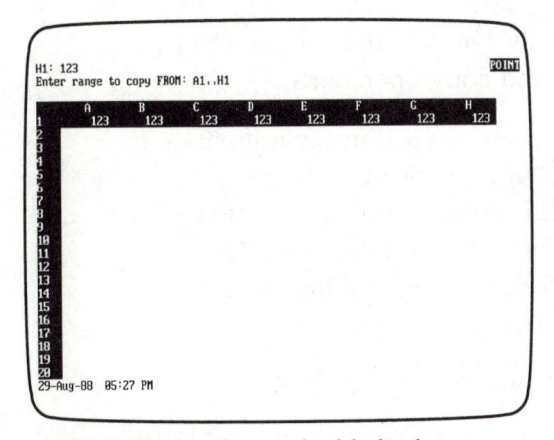

After selecting /Copy, highlight the range of cells you want to copy, and press ⏎Enter.

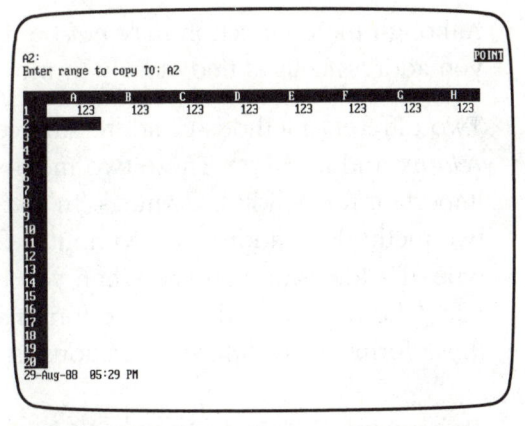

When the `Enter Range To Copy:` prompt appears, move the cell pointer to the first cell of the range where you want data copied, and press ⏎Enter.

Method 4: Copying from a range to a larger range

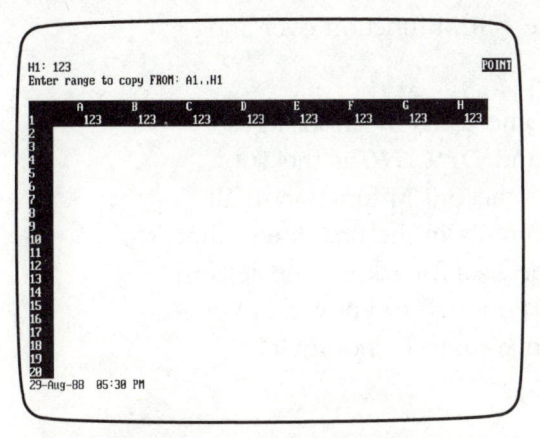

After selecting /Copy, highlight the range of cells you want to copy, and press ⏎Enter.

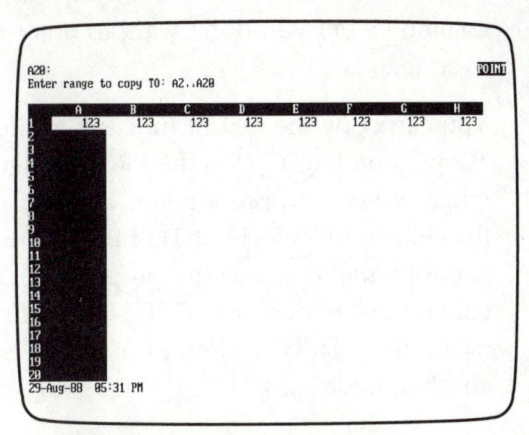

When the `Enter Range To Copy:` prompt appears, highlight either the rows across which you want data copied or the columns under which you want data copied, and press ⏎Enter.

201

Copying the Contents of Cells

Addressing Cells

Although the connection may not be readily obvious, the way in which you address cells is tied closely to move and copy operations.

Two different methods of addressing cells can be used in replication: *relative* and *absolute*. These two methods of referencing cells are important for building formulas. In fact, it is difficult to talk about the two methods of addressing without treating both topics at once. The type of addressing you use when you reference cells in formulas can affect the results yielded by the formulas when you copy or move those formulas to different positions in the worksheet.

Referencing Cells with Relative Addressing

1-2-3's default is relative addressing. Relative addressing means that when you copy or move a formula, unless you specify otherwise, the addresses of the cells in the formula will be adjusted automatically to fit the new location. For example, suppose that you want to sum the contents of several columns of cells, as you've already done for column C, but you don't want to enter the @SUM function over and over again.

You can copy the @SUM function to the other cells by choosing /Copy, entering *C10* as the FROM range and *D10..G10* as the TO range. When you press Enter, 1-2-3 copies the @SUM function to all the cells in the specified TO range. The formula in the first line of the control panel contains the proper cell addresses for adding the cells in column D—not column C. 1-2-3 was smart enough to know that you meant the relative addresses of the cells in column D, not their absolute addresses.

Key Terms in This Section

Relative addressing	When you move or copy a formula, the addresses of cells in that formula are adjusted.
Absolute addressing	When you move or copy a formula, the addresses of cells are not adjusted.
Mixed addressing	When you copy a formula, some cells may change, depending on the direction of the /Copy command.

Mixing Relative and Absolute Addressing

In some cases, a formula has an important address that cannot be changed as the formula is copied. In 1-2-3, you can create an *absolute address*, an address that will not change at all as the address is copied. You also can create a *mixed address*, an address that will sometimes change, depending on the direction of the /Copy. *Mixed cell-addressing* refers to a combination of relative and absolute addressing. Because a cell address has two components—a column and a row—it is possible to fix (make absolute) either portion while leaving the other unfixed (relative).

If you plan to copy cells that have absolute addressing, you must prepare the cell to be copied by entering dollar signs in the appropriate column and row designations. This symbol tells 1-2-3 that the cell has been changed to an absolute address. If you forget to prepare the cell, you may get results you neither expected nor wanted.

Use the F4 (Abs) key to set absolute and relative references. There are two ways to enter dollar signs in the formula for cell D10 in the example. You can type the dollar signs as you enter the formula, or you can use the F4 (Abs) key to have 1-2-3 automatically enter the dollar signs for you.

For more information and examples on using different addressing techniques, consult *Using 1-2-3,* Special Edition.

203

Copying the Contents of Cells

Relative versus Absolute Addressing

1-2-3's default is relative addressing. Relative addressing means that when you copy or move a formula, unless you specify otherwise, the addresses of the cells in the formula will be adjusted automatically to fit the new location.

Relative Addressing

The formulas in cells E65 and F65 illustrate relative addressing. Both formulas were created by copying the formula in D65 to cells E65 and F65.

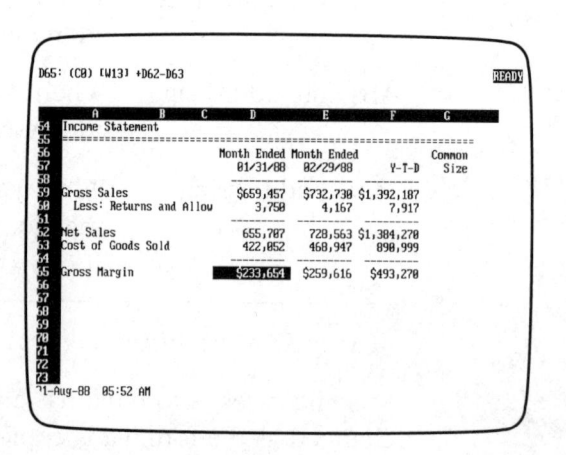

Enter the formula in D65.

Copy the contents of D65 to E65 and F65.

Notice that each formula is adjusted to its new location.

Absolute Addressing

In some cases, a formula has an important address that cannot be changed as the formula is copied. To keep an address enter a $ before the cell's column letter and before the cell's row number.

The formulas in G60, G62, G63, and G65 illustrate absolute addressing. All four formulas were created by copying the formula in G59 to G60, G62, G63 and G65.

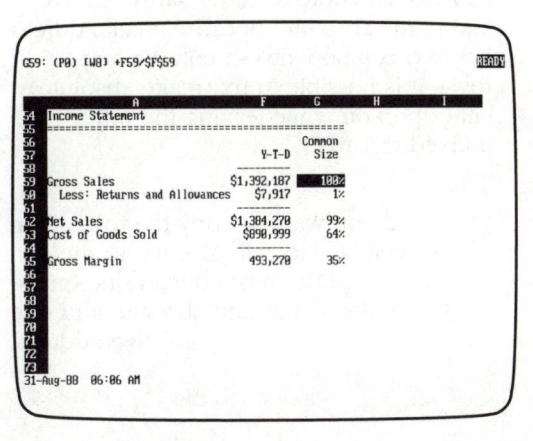

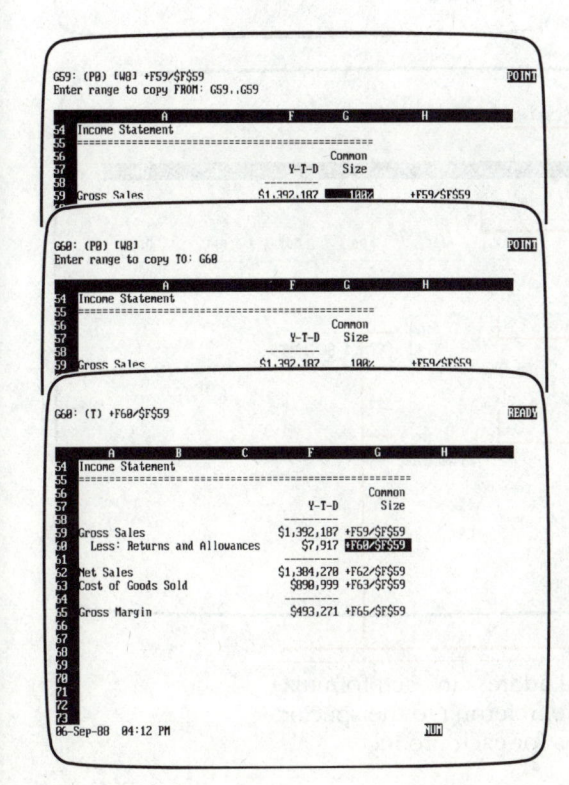

When you enter the formula in D65, enter $ before F and before 59 in the second part of the formula.

Copy the contents of G59 to G60, G62, G63 and G65.

Notice that the first address of each formula is adjusted to its new location, but the second address remains F59 in all four formulas.

205

Copying the Contents of Cells

Mixed Cell Addressing

In addition to creating relative and absolute cell addresses, you also can create a mixed address, an address that is partly relative and partly absolute. Because a cell address has two components—a column and a row—it is possible to fix (make absolute) either portion while leaving the other unfixed (relative).

If you want to copy the formula in cell D10 to cell D15, the formula in D10 must contain one mixed address, and one absolute and one relative address.

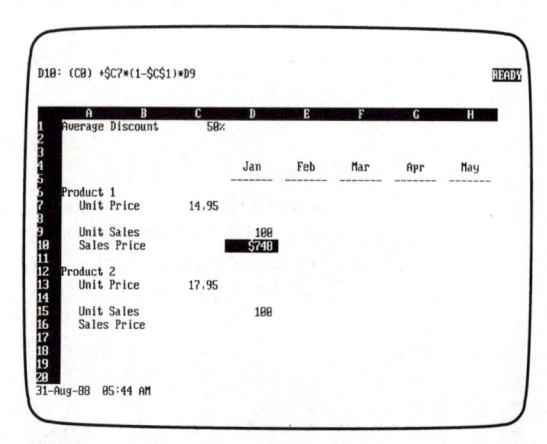

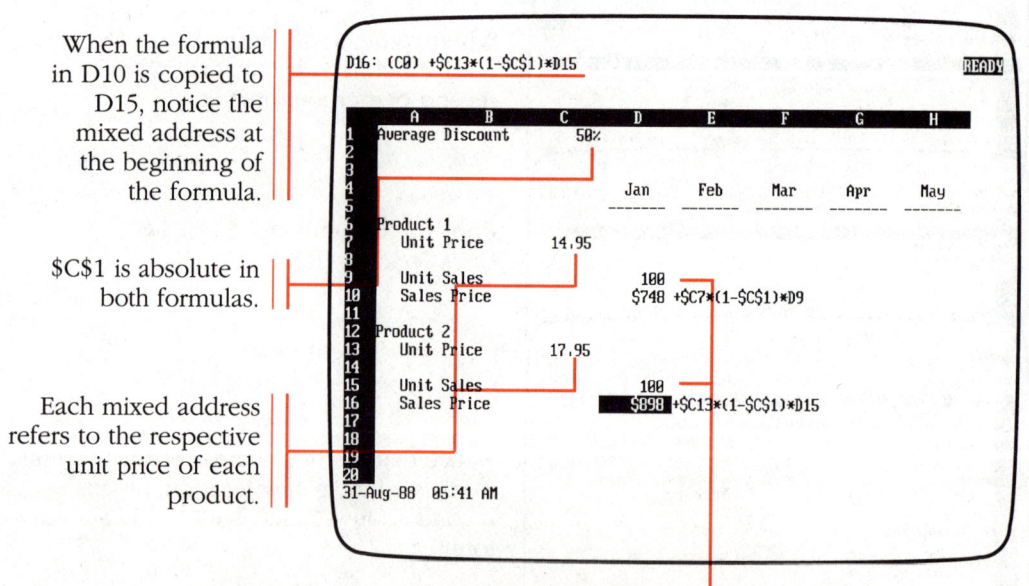

When the formula in D10 is copied to D15, notice the mixed address at the beginning of the formula.

C1 is absolute in both formulas.

Each mixed address refers to the respective unit price of each product.

The final address in each formula is relative, referring to the specific unit sales for each product.

206

Changing a Cell Address with F4

You can change a cell address from relative to absolute and vice versa by typing or deleting the $ when necessary. The F4 function key, however, lets you automatically change the cell address. To use F4, 1-2-3 must be in POINT or EDIT mode.

Move the cell pointer to the formula you want to change and press F2 (Edit).

With the cell address displayed in the control panel, press F4 once to change the address to absolute.

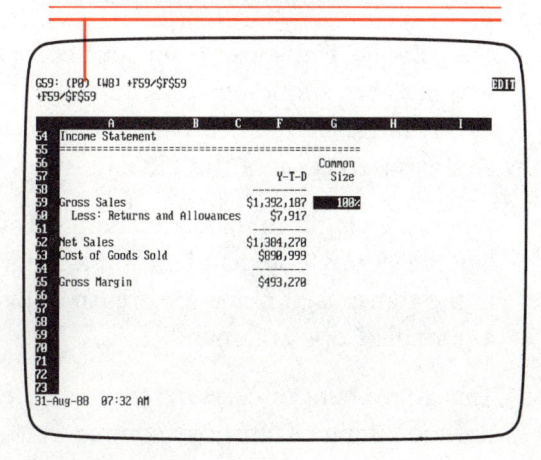

If you press F4 a second time, the address becomes mixed with the row absolute and column relative.

If you press F4 a third time, the address becomes mixed with the column absolute and the row relative.

Pressing F4 a fourth time changes the mixed address to relative.

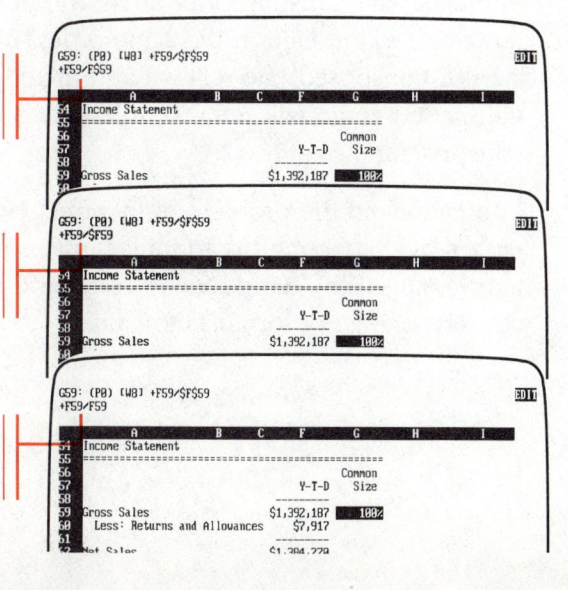

Copying the Contents of Cells

Transposing Rows and Columns with the /Range Transpose Command (/RT)

For copy operations that are difficult to perform with 1-2-3's normal copy commands, 1-2-3 has two specialized copy commands: **/R**ange **T**ranspose and **/R**ange **V**alue. The **/R**ange **T**ranspose command copies columns into rows and rows into columns. The **/R**ange **V**alue command, which is explained in the next section, copies the values (but not the formulas) from one range to another.

The **/R**ange **T**ranspose command copies each row of the FROM range into the corresponding column of the TO range, or each column of the FROM range into the corresponding row of the TO range. The result is a transposed copy of the FROM range.

When copying formulas, the **/R**ange **T**ranspose command behaves just like the **/C**opy command. When a range is transposed, cell references in the transposed range are adjusted, just as references are adjusted in a normal **/C**opy command.

This adjustment of cell references can lead to serious trouble when you use the **/R**ange **T**ranspose command to transpose a range containing formulas. The transposed formulas will be incorrect; the values, however, will remain in the same order. Because the cell references are not transposed, the relative and mixed cell references in the transposed range will refer to unintended locations after the transposition.

You can avoid the problem of incorrect cell references in transposed ranges by converting the formulas in the FROM range to values before transposing. The **/R**ange **V**alue command is a convenient way to convert a range of formulas to values.

Converting Formulas to Values with the /Range Value Command (/RV)

The **/R**ange **V**alue command lets you copy the values of the cells in one range to another range. This command is useful whenever you want to preserve the current values of a range of cells instead of having only the changed values after the worksheet has been updated. What is particularly important about the **/R**ange **V**alue command is that it converts formulas to values. You don't have to worry, therefore, about formulas that depend on cell references (when using **/R**ange **T**ranspose, for example).

Miscellaneous Comments on Copying

Remember the following points whenever you intend to copy data within the worksheet:

- When you copy a cell, 1-2-3 automatically copies the format of the cell with it. This automatic format-copying feature saves you from having to preset the format for an entire range of cells before copying to them.
- Sometimes the TO and FROM ranges will overlap when you copy. The general rule is that if you do not overlap the end points of the FROM and TO ranges, you will have no problems with the copy. If you do overlap them, however, you may get mixed results. You can overlap ranges legitimately when the FROM and TO ranges have the same upper-left boundary.
- Note particularly the finality of the **/C**opy command. If you copy over the contents of a cell, you have no way to retrieve the contents. Make sure that you have properly designated your ranges before you press Enter.

209

Copying the Contents of Cells

Transposing Rows and Columns

The **/R**ange **T**ranspose command, which is a specialized sort of copy command, is used to transpose data in rows to columns or data in columns to rows.

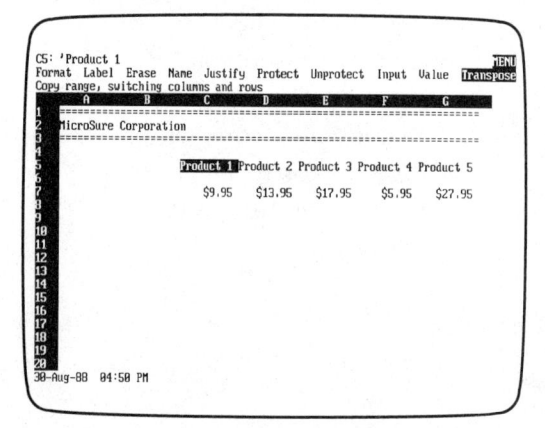

To transpose the data in C5..G7 to columnar format, begin by selecting **/R**ange **T**ranspose.

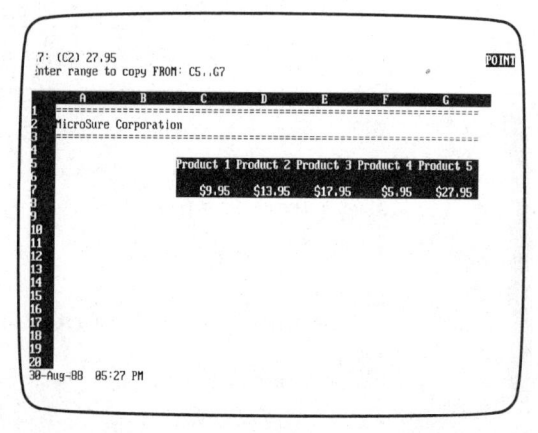

When the Enter range to copy FROM: prompt appears, highlight the range of cells you want transposed.

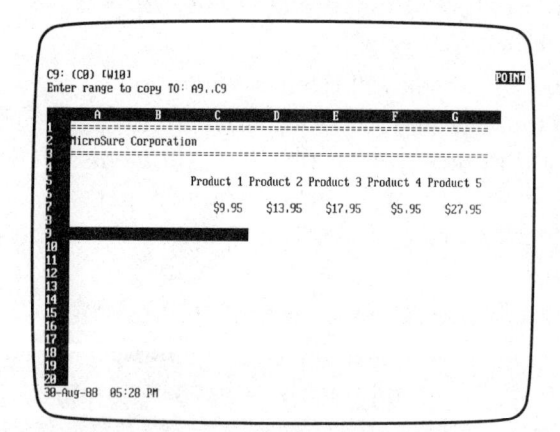

When the Enter range to copy TO: prompt appears, highlight the columns where you want the data copied. In this example, three columns (A, B, C) must be highlighted because the original data covers three rows.

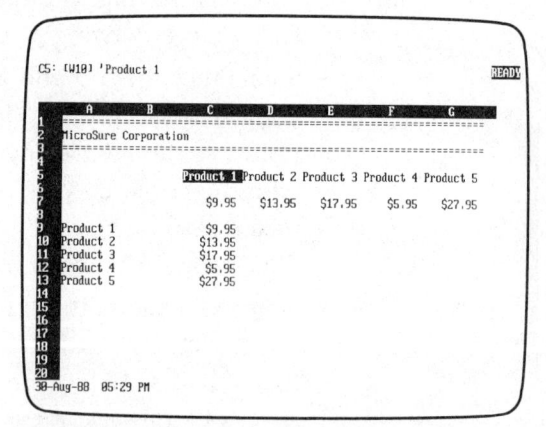

Notice that **/R**ange **T**ranspose copies data from row to column format and vice versa. The original data remains.

210

| Introduction | Selecting Commands from Command Menus | Using Ranges in the Worksheet | Using Worksheet Commands | Moving the Contents of Cells | **Copying the Contents of Cells** | Saving Your Files before You Quit (/Quit) | Accessing DOS from 1-2-3 |

Converting Formulas with /Range Value

The **/R**ange **V**alue command lets you copy the values—not the formulas—of cells in a range to another range.

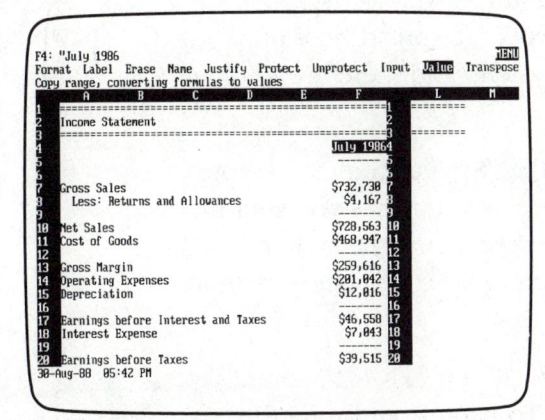

Use **/R**ange **V**alue, for example, to copy the data in column F to column L, converting all formulas in column F to values.

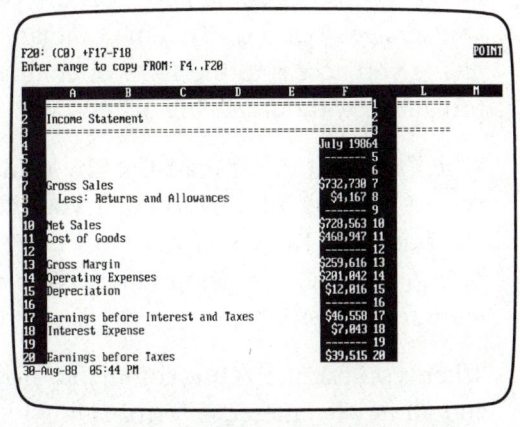

After selecting **/R**ange **V**alue, highlight the range you want copied and converted to values.

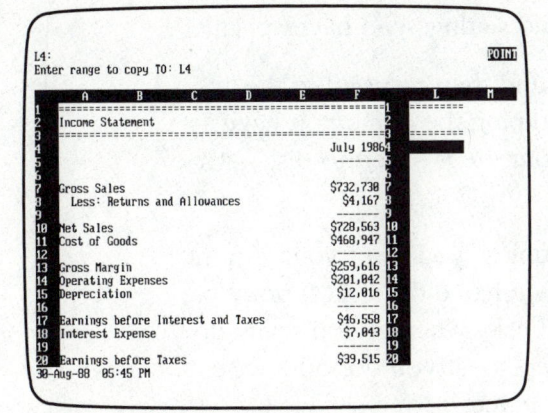

Move the cursor to the beginning cell where you want the data copied.

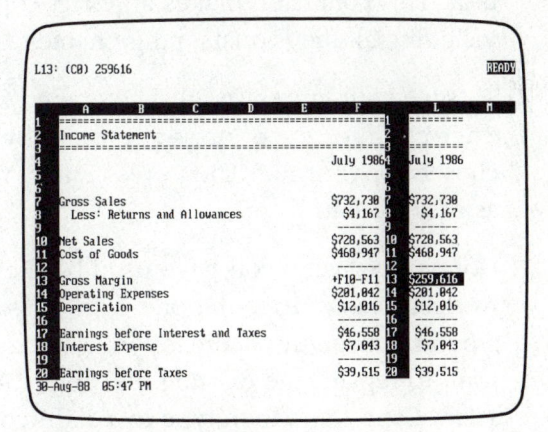

Notice that the formula in F13 has become a value in L13.

Introduction

An Overview of 1-2-3

Getting Started

1-2-3 Basics

Creating a Worksheet

Printing Reports

Creating and Printing Graphs

Managing Data

Understanding Macros

Appendix

211

Saving Your Files before You Quit (/Quit)

You already may have discovered on your own 1-2-3 provides two ways to exit the spreadsheet: the **/Q**uit command and the **/S**ystem command. Both commands are options on 1-2-3's main command menu. The **/Q**uit command exits the program as well as the spreadsheet, but the **/S**ystem command exits the spreadsheet only, giving you access to the DOS operating system, and therefore to other programs, without leaving 1-2-3.

When you exit the spreadsheet by using the **/S**ystem command, you do not lose the information that you have entered unless you shut the computer off. By typing *exit* (for "exit the system") at the system prompt and then pressing Enter, you return to your worksheet with all the information intact.

When you use the **/Q**uit command, however, you exit 1-2-3 entirely, and all newly entered information is lost. To keep from losing the information, you need to save your file before you **/Q**uit.

Use the **/F**ile **S**ave command to save an entire worksheet to a file on disk. This command makes an exact copy of the current worksheet, including all the formats, range names, and settings you have specified.

To save your current worksheet, type */fs* and then respond to the `Enter save file name:` prompt by typing the name you have chosen for your file. Then press Enter. Your file is saved to disk—it's as easy as that.

Don't use a name you have used before unless you want your current worksheet to replace the one with the same name on disk. If you do type in a name that's already in use, 1-2-3 asks whether you really do want to replace the existing file. Select **R**eplace if you do; otherwise, select **C**ancel and then type in a different name.

Legal File Names	Illegal File Names
SALESRPT.WK1	SALES RPT.WK1
MYSCHED.PRN	MY.SCHED.PRN
TOM_BBS.TXT	TOM*BBS.TXT
RRV1332.WK1	RRV<13>.WK1

Whenever you have to choose a file name for a file command, 1-2-3 helps you by displaying a list of the 1-2-3 files on the current drive and directory. If the file name you want is in the list, you can select it by pointing. If you want to replace an existing file, you can point to one of the entries on the list and then press Enter. Otherwise, you can type in the file name you want. 1-2-3 automatically supplies a .WK1 extension.

When a worksheet is saved, the date and time are saved with all other data. This addition can be helpful if you want to see the last time a file was accessed. If you want to see the date and time information, use the /**F**ile **L**ist command and highlight the name of the file you are interested in.

To be certain you have accurate dates and times, make sure that the date and time have been entered correctly with the DOS DATE and TIME commands. If your system has an internal clock, you won't have to worry about entering the time and date.

To call a file back into main memory from disk, use the /**F**ile **R**etrieve command. Again, 1-2-3 will display a list of all the file names currently on disk.

Saving Your Files before You Quit (/Quit)

Use the **/F**ile **S**ave command to save an entire worksheet to a file on disk. This command makes an exact copy of the current worksheet, including all the formats, range names, and settings you have specified.

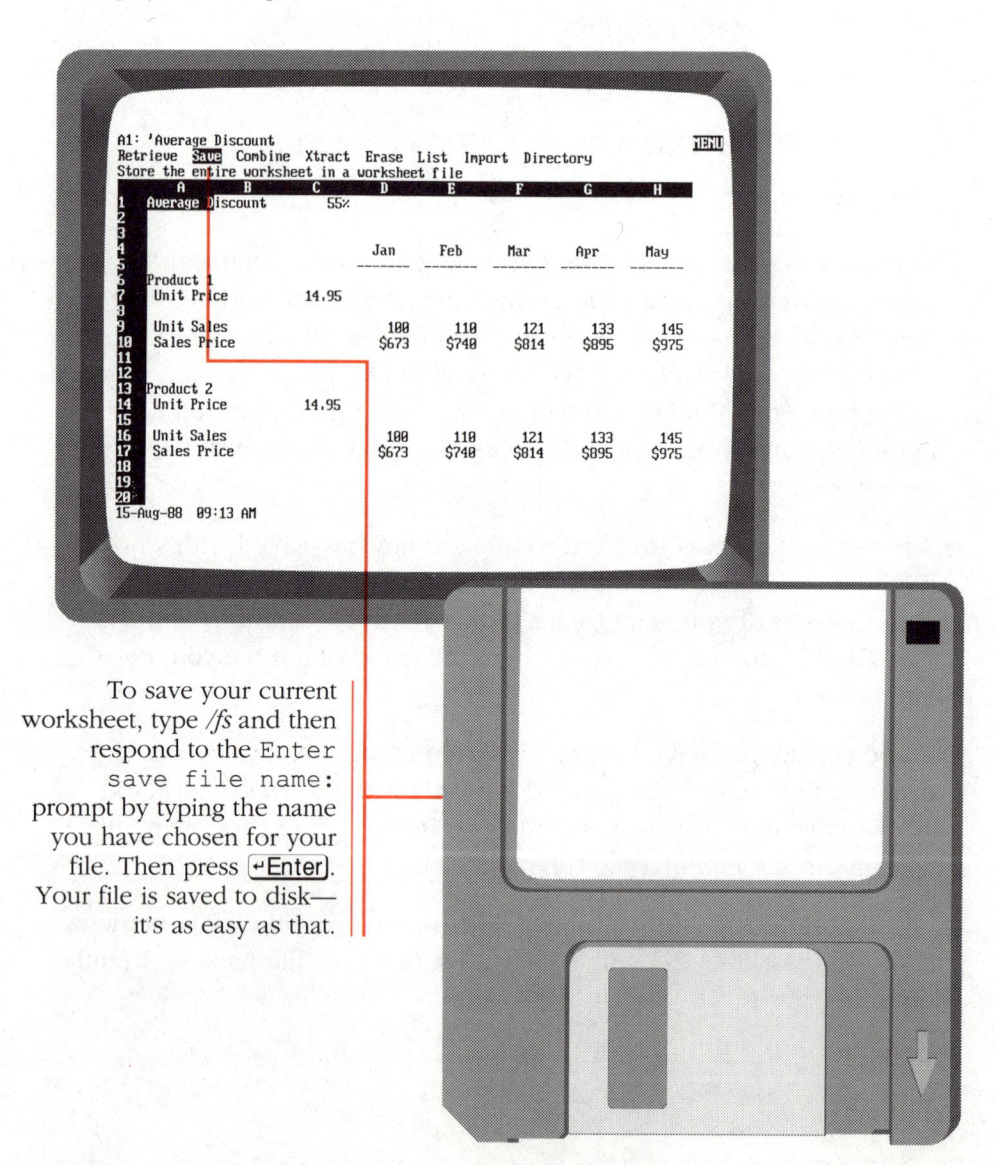

To save your current worksheet, type /fs and then respond to the Enter save file name: prompt by typing the name you have chosen for your file. Then press [←Enter]. Your file is saved to disk— it's as easy as that.

When you access DOS by selecting **/S**ystem, 1-2-3 allows you to get to the DOS level, perform basic DOS operations, and then return to the spreadsheet, right where you left it. Using **/Q**uit, on the other hand, requires a bit more foresight. Get used to issuing the **/F**ile **S**ave command before pressing Q for Quit. Otherwise, all information you've entered since the last time you saved the file will be lost.

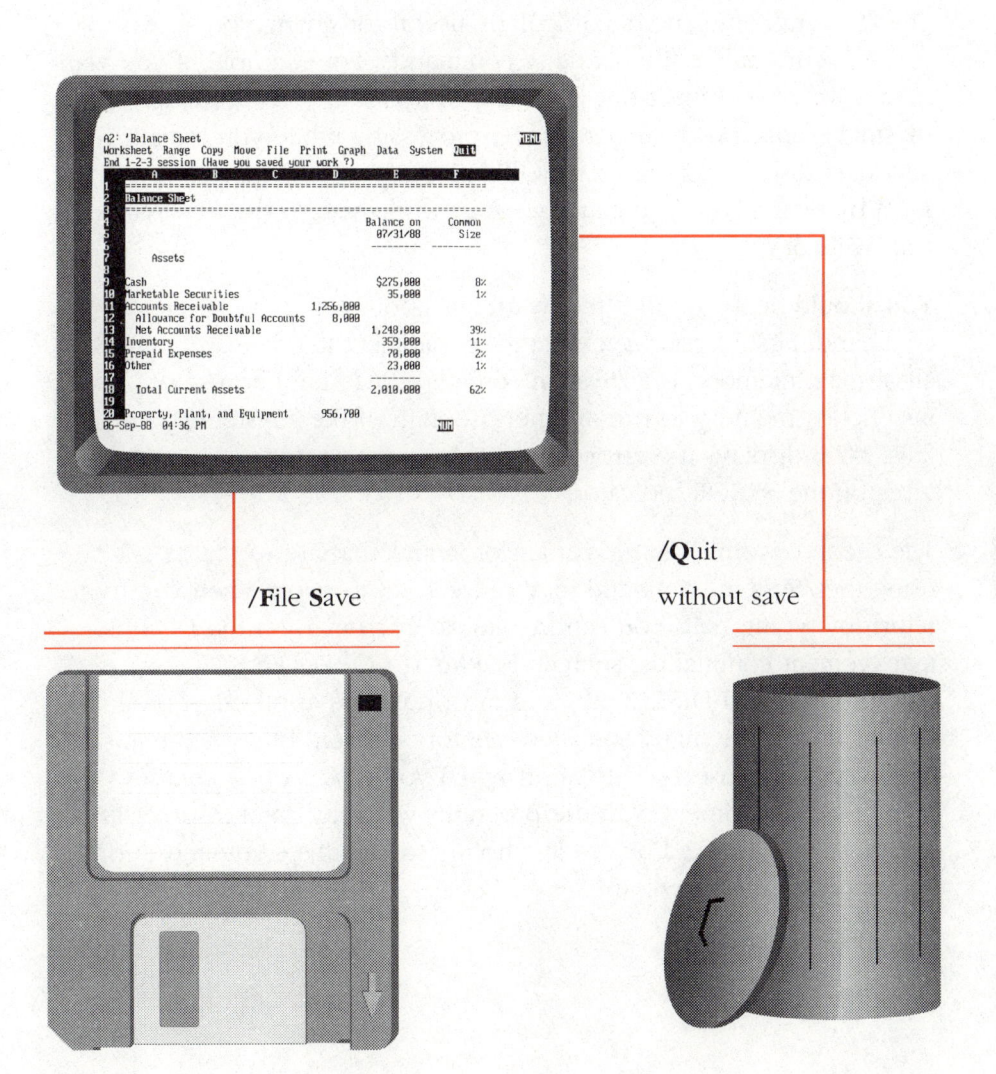

/File **S**ave

/Quit without save

215

Accessing DOS from 1-2-3

The **/S**ystem command suspends the operation of 1-2-3 and returns you to the system prompt (C> for hard disk systems, A> for floppy and microfloppy disk systems). Once at the system prompt, you can execute other programs and DOS commands. To return to 1-2-3, you type *exit* at the system prompt.

The **/S**ystem command is particularly useful for giving you access to your system's native file-handling commands. For example, if you want to save your worksheet but your data disk is full, you can use the **/S**ystem command to suspend 1-2-3 processing while you initialize a new data disk, using the DOS FORMAT command. After you return to 1-2-3 by typing *exit*, you can save your worksheet to the new data disk with **/F**ile **S**ave.

You should be aware of a few warnings about using the **/S**ystem command. First, if you have a large spreadsheet that takes up almost all of main memory, the **/S**ystem command may fail because of insufficient memory to run another program. If the **/S**ystem command fails, 1-2-3 displays the error message `Cannot Invoke DOS` and turns on the ERROR indicator.

The second warning is that certain programs that are run from 1-2-3 using the **/S**ystem command may cause 1-2-3 to abort when you try to return by typing *exit*. You can invoke safely from 1-2-3 the DOS file-management commands, such as FORMAT, COPY, DELETE, DIRECTORY, and DISKCOPY, and most business application programs. Calling one of the many so-called memory-resident utility programs, however, will cause 1-2-3 to abort when you type *exit*. Take a few minutes to experiment with the programs you may want to use with the **/S**ystem command before attempting to use this command during an important 1-2-3 session.

Things To Remember When Using /System

When you use the **/S**ystem command, you need to keep a couple of things in mind:

- If your spreadsheet takes up almost all available memory, you may not have enough memory to use the **/S**ystem command to run another program.

- Certain memory-resident programs run from 1-2-3 may cause 1-2-3 to abort.

- You can use DOS commands FORMAT, COPY, DELETE, DIRECTORY, and DISKCOPY safely from within 1-2-3.

Conclusion

This section marks the conclusion of this chapter. This chapter has covered a wealth of topics, including

>   Selecting commands
>   Using ranges
>   Using **/W**orksheet commands
>   Saving Files
>   Accessing DOS

If you need more information on any of these topics, refer to *Using 1-2-3,* Special Edition for full discussion of each of these subjects.

In the next chapter, you will learn how to create and print 1-2-3 reports.

5 *Printing Reports*

1-2-3 is a powerful tool for developing information presented in column-and-row format. You can enter and edit your spreadsheet and database files on-screen as well as store the input on disk. But to make good use of your data, you often need it in printed form: as a target production schedule, a summary report to your supervisor, or a detailed reorder list to central stores, for example.

By using 1-2-3's **/P**rint command, you can access many sublevels of print options to meet your printing needs. You can elect to write directly from 1-2-3 to the printer by using the **/P**rint **P**rinter command sequence. Or use the alternate **/P**rint **F**ile *filename* sequence to create a print (.PRN) file; later, you can produce a printout of the file from within 1-2-3 or from DOS, or you can incorporate the file into a word-processing file.

To target this chapter effectively so that we teach you the basics of printing and not just a complex series of options, we have assumed several things: (1) that you have not modified 1-2-3's preset printing defaults; (2) that you need to produce reports on 8 1/2-by-11-inch paper; and (3) that you want to learn basic report-enhancement techniques such as hiding columns and rows, adding headers and footers, and repeating column and row headings. If you want to explore and perhaps modify 1-2-3's default settings, consult *Using 1-2-3*, Special Edition.

Key Terms Covered in This Chapter

print defaults	The specifications included with 1-2-3 that control what 1-2-3 "assumes" about each print job.
range	A rectangle of cells specified as a group.
borders	Labels that border data and repeat on subsequent pages.
headers	Information displayed at the top of a page. May include date, name, and page number information.
footers	Information displayed at the bottom of a page. May include date, name, and page number information.

What Is Covered in This Chapter?

This chapter shows you how to

- Choose between **/P**rint **P**rinter and **/P**rint **F**ile
- Print single or multiple pages
- Exclude segments within a designated print range
- Control paper movement
- Change the default settings
- Print spreadsheet content cell-by-cell
- Prepare output for acceptance by other programs

/Print Printer and /Print File

You must start any **/P**rint command sequence from 1-2-3's main menu. After initiating a **/P**rint command from the main menu, you must select one of the two options displayed: **P**rinter or **F**ile. To indicate that you want to use a printer on-line, choose **P**rinter. Choose **F**ile to create a file on disk; later you can print the file from within 1-2-3 or incorporate it into a word-processing file.

If you choose **F**ile, respond to the prompt for a print-file name by typing a name that is up to eight characters long. You don't need to add a file extension because 1-2-3 will automatically assign the .PRN (print file) extension. You can again incorporate the file into a 1-2-3 spreadsheet by using the **/F**ile **I**mport command, although the file will not be the same as your original worksheet file; imported .PRN files are all long labels. You also can view a .PRN file by using the DOS TYPE command, a word-processor's print command, or a special printing routine.

After you select either **P**rinter or **F**ile, the second line of the control panel will display the main **P**rint menu. This menu presents the following choices:

    Range **L**ine **P**age **O**ptions **C**lear **A**lign **G**o **Q**uit

The following list gives you an overview of the various options on the /Print menu:

Menu Selection	Description
Range	Indicates what section of the worksheet is to be printed or saved to the disk as a print file.
Line	Adjusts the paper line-by-line in the printer
Page	Adjusts the paper page-by-page in the printer
Options	Makes available options to change default settings and enhance the appearance of the printout
Clear	Erases settings previously entered
Align	Signals the beginning of each page in the printer
Go	Starts printing
Quit	Exits the **P**rint menu

1-2-3 consistently positions the most frequently used (or least dangerous) command options to the left of a menu. In any /**P**rint command sequence, you start with /**P**rint, branch to either **P**rinter or **F**ile *filename*, and proceed to a common main **P**rint menu. Regardless of which branch you select, you must specify a **R**ange to print, activate **G**o, and then select **Q**uit to return to the worksheet. All other selections are optional.

/Print Printer and /Print File

When you first select **P**rint from 1-2-3's main menu, you are presented with two options: **P**rinter and **F**ile. If you want to print a paper copy of the worksheet, select **P**rinter. If you want to print the worksheet to a file, select **F**ile.

| Introduction | /Print Printer and /Print File | Printing Reports | Hiding Rows, Columns, and Ranges | Controlling Paper Movement | Adding Headers and Footers | Printing Cell Contents and Clearing Print Options | Preparing Output for Other Programs |

After you select **P**rinter, 1-2-3 displays the **P**rint menu.

```
A1: [W25] \=                                              MENU
Range Line Page Options Clear Align Go Quit
Specify a range to print
         A              B        C         D         E         F
 1 ========================================================
 2 REGIONAL INCOME REPORT      Qtr 1     Qtr 2     Qtr 3     Qtr 4
 3 ========================================================
 4 Sales
 5   Northeast               $30,336   $33,370   $36,707   $40,377
 6   Southeast                20,572    22,629    24,892    27,381
 7   Central                 131,685   144,854   159,339   175,273
 8   Northwest                94,473   103,920   114,312   125,744
 9   Southwest               126,739   139,413   153,354   168,690
10                          --------  --------  --------  --------
11 Total Sales               403,805   444,186   488,604   537,464
12 ::
13 Cost of Goods Sold
14   Northeast                10,341    11,272    12,286    13,392
15   Southeast                 6,546     7,135     7,777     8,477
16   Central                  65,843    71,769    78,228    85,269
17   Northwest                63,967    69,724    75,999    82,839
18   Southwest                72,314    78,822    85,916    93,649
19                          --------  --------  --------  --------
20 Total Cost of Goods Sold  219,011   238,722   260,207   283,626
01-Sep-88  09:54 AM
```

Range	Indicates what section of the worksheet is to be printed.
Line	Adjusts the paper line-by-line in the printer.
Page	Adjusts the paper page-by-page in the printer.
Options	Makes available options to change default settings and enhance the appearance of the printout.
Clear	Erases settings previously entered.
Align	Signals the beginning of each page in the printer.
Go	Starts printing.
Quit	Exits the **P**rint menu.

Introduction

An Overview of 1-2-3

Getting Started

1-2-3 Basics

Creating a Worksheet

Printing Reports

Creating and Printing Graphs

Managing Data

Understanding Macros

Appendix

223

Printing Reports

Printing doesn't have to be an arduous process. With 1-2-3, you can print out a quick report by issuing a few simple commands.

Printing a Screenful of Data (PrtSc)

Before you print any portion of a 1-2-3 spreadsheet, decide whether the output must be of "report" quality (suitable for official distribution or filing) or whether all you need is a "screen dump" (hard copy of the screen's contents).

If a copy of what you see on-screen is sufficient, you can send that data to the printer by pressing Shift-PrtSc. The resultant screen dump captures everything on the screen, even such unwanted items as the contents of the highlighted cell A1 and the mode indicator. Such "quick-and-dirty" printouts may be adequate for interoffice memos and, because these printouts capture the date-time display, for documenting model construction.

Printing Draft-Quality Reports on One Page or Less

If you don't change any of the default print settings, and you have not entered other print settings during the current worksheet session, then printing a page or less involves only a few steps. These steps include

1. Choosing to print to the printer or file
2. Highlighting on the worksheet the area you want printed
3. Choosing the command to begin printing

Two other steps may be necessary if another person uses your copy of 1-2-3 and has possibly changed either the default settings or has entered new settings in the **P**rint menu during the current worksheet session. First, you can check the default settings by selecting **/W**orksheet **G**lobal **D**efault **S**tatus. A quick review of the top left section of the **S**tatus screen will indicate whether the printer and page layout settings are the ones you need. Second, you can clear any settings that may have been entered by another user by selecting **/P**rint **P**rinter **C**lear **A**ll.

If you are certain that all default settings are correct and no other settings have been entered into the **P**rint commands, you can easily print a report of a page or less by completing the following sequence of operations. First, check that your printer is on-line and that your paper is positioned where you want the data to print. Next choose **/P**rint **P**rinter. The main **P**rint menu will then appear:

Range   **L**ine   **P**age   **O**ptions   **C**lear   **A**lign   **G**o   **Q**uit

Indicate what part of the worksheet you want to print by selecting **R**ange and highlighting the area. You can use the PgUp, PgDn, and End keys to designate ranges when you print. If you want to designate a range that includes the entire active area of the spreadsheet, anchor the left corner of the print range, press the End key, and then press the Home key.

After you have highlighted the exact range you want to print, select **G**o. If you accidentally press Enter after you have already used the **G**o option, the file will print a second time, an act which can be particularly disconcerting. If this problem occurs, you can stop printing by pressing Ctrl-Break.

225

Printing Reports

Printing with PrtSc

You can get a quick printout of what you see on-screen by pressing ⇧Shift PrtSc.

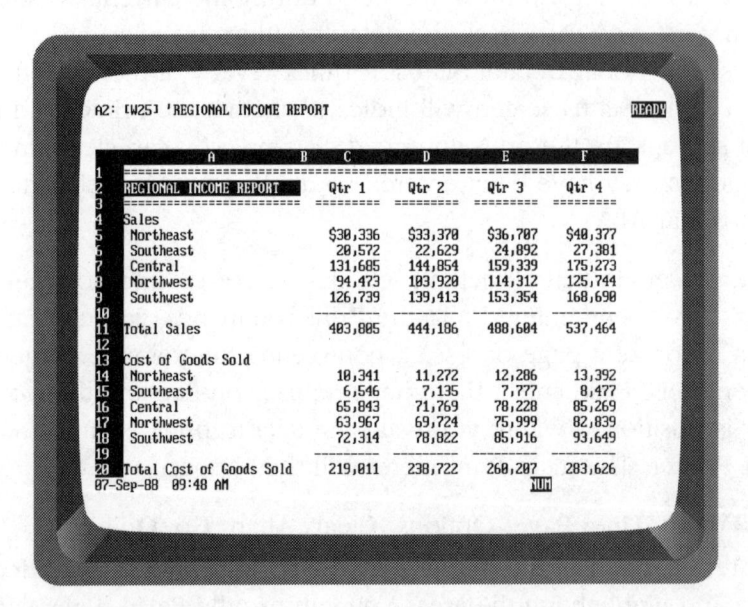

| Introduction | /Print Printer and /Print File | **Printing Reports** | Hiding Rows, Columns, and Ranges | Controlling Paper Movement | Adding Headers and Footers | Printing Cell Contents and Clearing Print Options | Preparing Output for Other Programs |

To print a draft-quality report with default settings, type / to access the 1-2-3 main menu and select **P**rint.

Next select **P**rinter.

Select **R**ange.

Finally, select **A**lign and **G**o.

Enter the range you want to print.

Introduction

An Overview of 1-2-3

Getting Started

1-2-3 Basics

Creating a Worksheet

Printing Reports

Creating and Printing Graphs

Managing Data

Understanding Macros

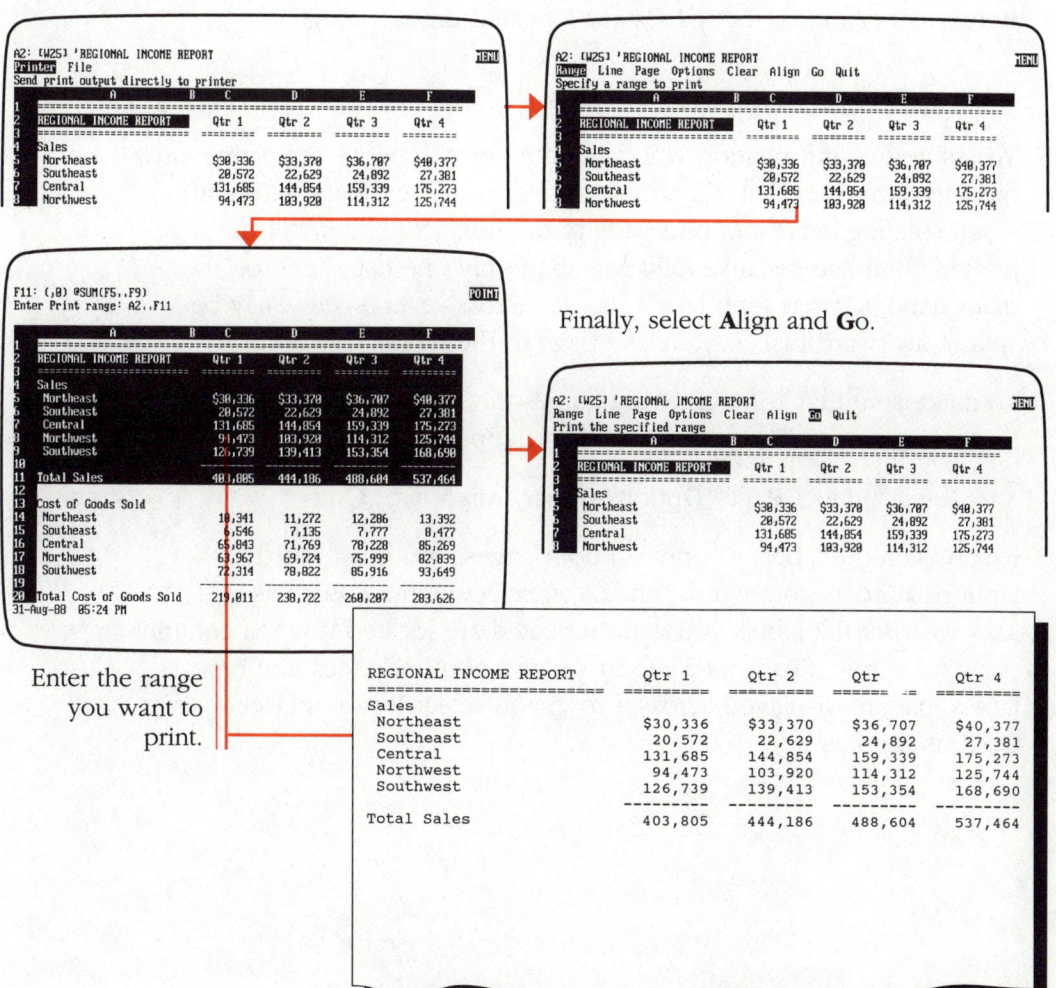

Appendix

227

Printing Reports

Even if the area of your worksheet has more rows and columns than can be printed on one page, you still can use the basic steps discussed above for printing reports on a page or less. Setting the print range, however, so that a new page begins exactly where you want it to begin can sometimes be a bit tricky. Also, if you want to print a section of a large worksheet, you may need to use the **/P**rint **P**rinter **O**ptions **B**order command so that labels are repeated on each page.

Adding Borders

To assure that information will be printed on the pages correctly, you'll need to remember that 1-2-3 treats numeric and text data differently when splitting data from one page to the next. Numbers will be printed complete because they can span only one cell. Text, on the other hand, such as long labels that lie across several cells, may be split in awkward places from one page to the next.

To make sure that 1-2-3 correctly copies the labels, choose the **/P**rint **P**rinter command. The main **P**rint menu appears:

Range   **L**ine   **P**age   **O**ptions   **C**lear   **A**lign   **G**o   **Q**uit

If you want the labels to print on both pages, you must use the **O**ptions **B**orders command. When you select **O**ptions **B**orders, 1-2-3 asks whether the labels you want repeated are located down a column or across a row. (To print a report on two or more pages and repeat labels that are displayed across a row, you select **R**ows after choosing **O**ptions **B**orders.)

Repeating labels on the second page of a report is often a frustrating problem for new 1-2-3 users. The procedure isn't difficult, however; you just have to know where to find the commands. To repeat labels down a column or across a row,

1. Type / to call up the 1-2-3 menu.
2. Choose **P**rint **P**rinter.
3. Select **O**ptions
4. Select **B**orders
5. Choose either **C**olumns or **R**ows
6. Indicate the position of the labels by moving the cell pointer to that location.

After you choose **C**olumns, the prompt `Enter Border Columns:` will appear. If your cell pointer is located in the column where the labels appear, press Enter; if not, move your cell pointer to the column and press Enter. To return to the main **P**rint menu, select **Q**uit. Once you have indicated which column or row of labels you want repeated on each page, you do not need to include those labels in your actual print range. 1-2-3 automatically places those labels in the first column or row on every page.

Completing the Print Specifications for Multi-Page Reports

When you set the print range for reports that will print on more than one page, you highlight all columns or rows except those columns or rows that you entered using the **O**ptions **B**orders command.

The last three steps involve moving the cursor to **A**lign on the main **P**rint menu, then selecting **G**o, and finally choosing **Q**uit after printing is completed. Choosing **A**lign assures that printing will begin at the top of all succeeding pages after the first. Make sure in particular that you reposition your printer paper and use the **A**lign command whenever you have aborted a print job.

Printing Reports

Repeating Labels

When you are working with a multi-page report, you need to make sure that the labels on the first page are repeated on the second page.

To repeat labels on subsequent pages of a report, type `/` to call up the 1-2-3 menu.

Choose **P**rint **P**rinter, and select **O**ptions.

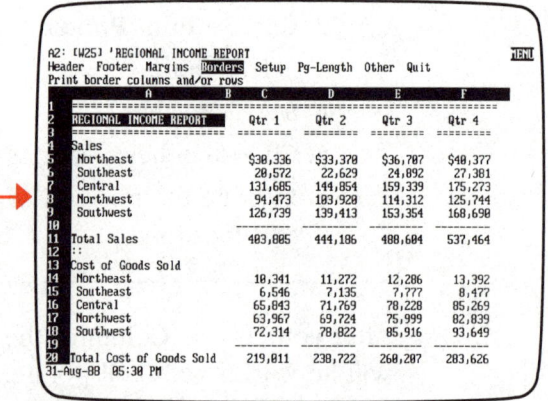

Next, select **B**orders.

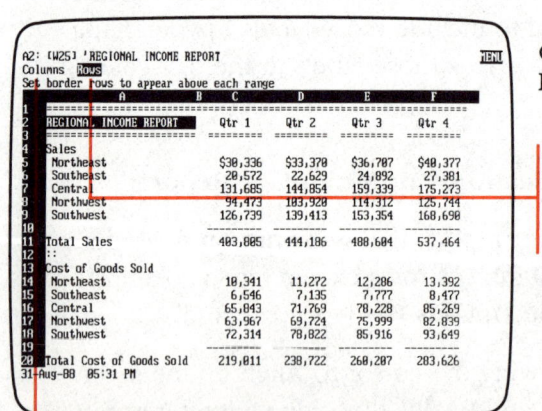

Choose either **C**olumns or **R**ows.

Use **/P**rint **P**rinter **O**ptions **B**orders **R**ows to tell 1-2-3 that the labels you want to repeat are across a row.

Use **/P**rint **P**rinter **O**ptions **B**orders **C**olumns to tell 1-2-3 that the labels you want to repeat are positioned down a column.

230

| Introduction | /Print Printer and /Print File | **Printing Reports** | Hiding Rows, Columns, and Ranges | Controlling Paper Movement | Adding Headers and Footers | Printing Cell Contents and Clearing Print Options | Preparing Output for Other Programs |

Next, indicate which rows (or columns) you want printed on each page by highlighting the rows or columns.

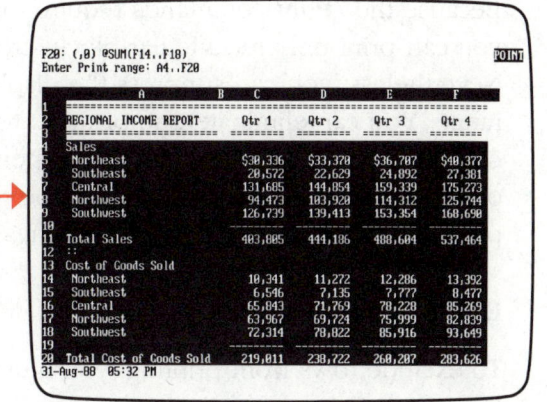

When you set the range to be printed, remember to exclude the rows (or columns) which you set with the **B**order command.

When you select **A**lign and then **G**o from the Printer menu, your printer will print a multiple-page report with row and/or column borders represented on each page.

```
REGIONAL INCOME REPORT      Qtr 1       Qtr 2       Qtr 3       Qtr 4
=======================  =========   =========   =========   =========
Sales
  Northeast                $30,336     $33,370     $36,707     $40,377
  Southeast                 20,572      22,629      24,892      27,381
  Central                  131,685     144,854     159,339     175,273
  Northwest                 94,473     103,920     114,312     125,744
  Southwest                126,739     139,413     153,354     168,690
                         ---------   ---------   ---------   ---------
Total Sales                403,805     444,186     488,604     537,464

Cost of Goods Sold
  Northeast                 10,341      11,272      12,286      13,392
  Southeast                  6,546       7,135       7,777       8,477
  Central                   65,843      71,769      78,228      85,269
  Northwest                 63,967      69,724      75,999      82,839
  Southwest                 72,314      78,822      85,916      93,649
                         ---------   ---------   ---------   ---------
Total Cost of Goods Sold   219,011     238,722     260,207     283,626
```

Introduction

An Overview of 1-2-3

Getting Started

1-2-3 Basics

Creating a Worksheet

Printing Reports

Creating and Printing Graphs

Managing Data

Understanding Macros

Appendix

231

Hiding Rows, Columns, and Ranges

Because the **/P**rint commands require that you specify a range to print, you can print only rectangular blocks from the spreadsheet. Nevertheless, you can suppress the display of cell contents within the range. You can eliminate one or more rows, hide one or more columns, or remove from view a segment that spans only part of a row or a column. The results of each of the following explanations will print on one page, using default settings.

Excluding Rows

To exclude rows from printing, you must mark the rows for omission. Do this omission by typing a double vertical bar (| |) in the blank leftmost cell of the print range of each row you want to omit. Only one of these vertical bars appears on-screen and neither appears on the printout. A row marked in this way will not print, but the suppressed data remains in the spreadsheet and is used in any applicable calculations.

To restore the spreadsheet after you have finished printing, delete the vertical bars from the leftmost cells of the marked rows.

Excluding Columns

As you learned in Chapter 4, you can use 1-2-3's **/W**orksheet **C**olumn **H**ide command to mark columns that you don't want to display on-screen. If these marked columns are included in a print range, they will not appear on the printout if the **/P**rint **P**rinter **O**ptions **O**ther setting is **A**s-Displayed.

To restore the columns, select **/W**orksheet **C**olumn **D**isplay. When the hidden columns (marked with an asterisk) reappear on-screen, you can specify which column or columns to display.

When you are printing reports, you can hide rows, columns, or ranges. The following list shows you the commands used for each of these operations:

rows	Mark the row to be hidden by entering two vertical bars (| |) in the leftmost cell.
columns	/**W**orksheet **C**olumn **H**ide /**P**rint **P**rinter **O**ptions **O**ther **A**s-Displayed
ranges	/**R**ange **F**ormat **H**idden

Excluding Ranges

If you want to hide only a partial row, a partial column, or an area that partially spans one or more rows and columns, use the /**R**ange **F**ormat **H**idden command to mark the ranges.

Perhaps your spreadsheet includes documentation that you want to save on disk but omit from the printout. Simply issue the /**R**ange **F**ormat **H**idden command, and specify the range you want to hide. Then specify the print range, and print the report.

After you finish printing, select /**R**ange **F**ormat **R**eset, and then specify the range to restore the information.

If you find yourself repeating print operations (hiding the same columns, suppressing and then restoring the same documentation messages, etc.), remember that you can save time and minimize frustration by developing and using print macros. (Note: Chapter 8 explains the basics about macros; for more detailed information, see Chapter 14 of *Using 1-2-3,* Special Edition.)

Hiding Rows, Columns, and Ranges

Hiding Columns and Rows

As you become proficient with 1-2-3, there will be times when you want to suppress the display of data. Whether you want to hide a column of sensitive financial information or simply want to compress the worksheet so that the most important data fits on a one-page report, you can use 1-2-3 to hide columns and rows.

After you mark the rows to be hidden by entering the double vertical bars, 1-2-3 produces the report without showing the specified rows.

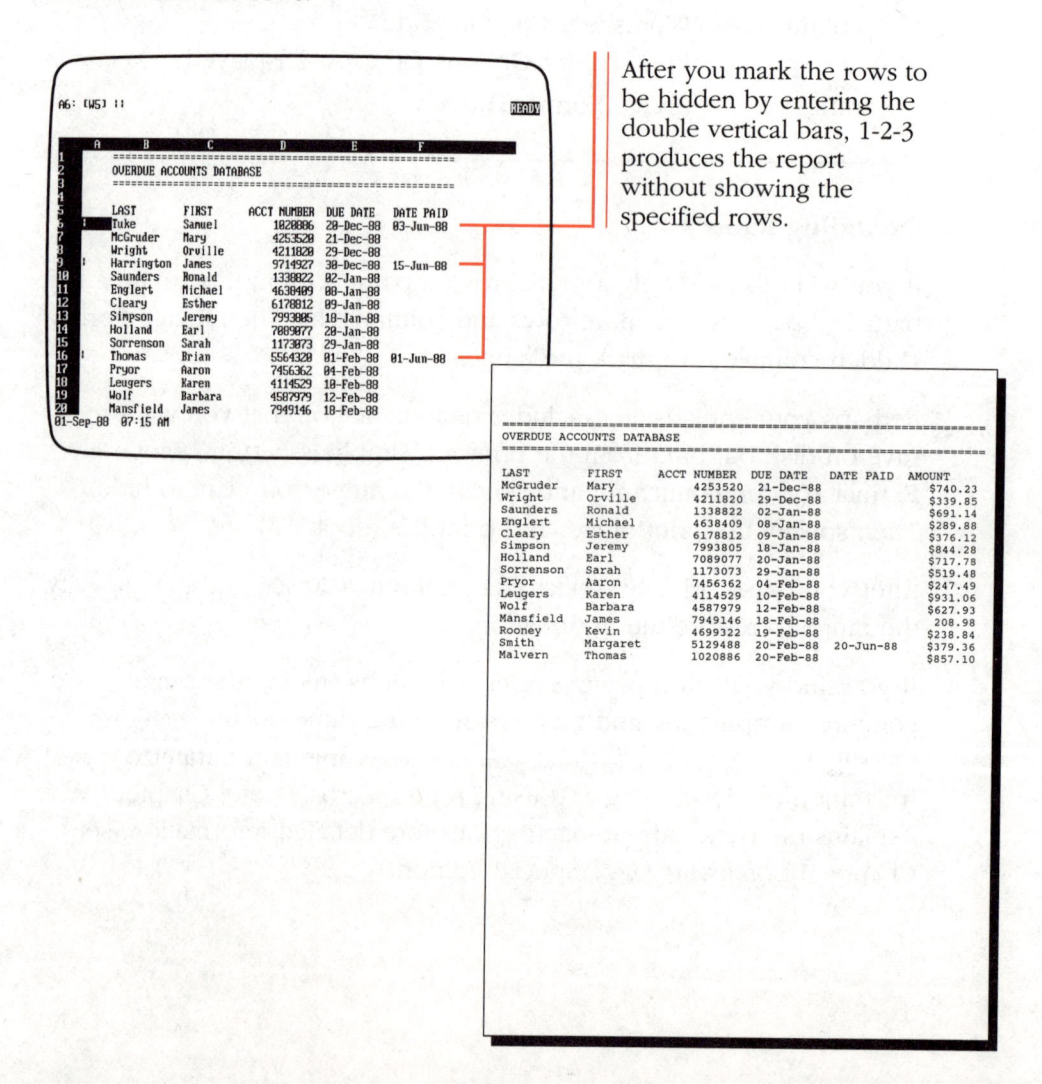

234

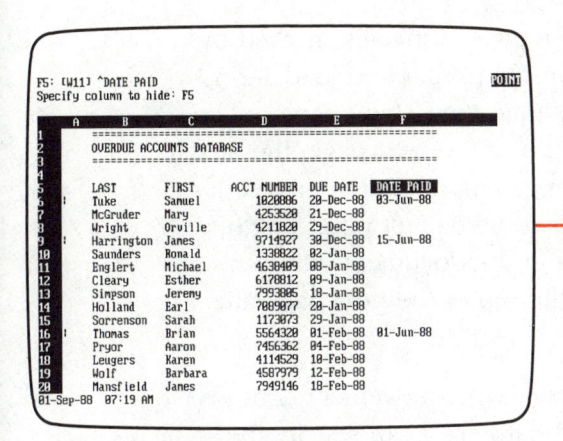

| Introduction | /Print Printer and /Print File | Printing Reports | **Hiding Rows, Columns, and Ranges** | Controlling Paper Movement | Adding Headers and Footers | Printing Cell Contents and Clearing Print Options | Preparing Output for Other Programs |

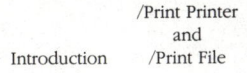

The columns hidden with the **/W**orksheet **C**olumn **H**ide command are not printed if you specify **/P**rint **P**rinter **O**ptions **O**ther **A**s-Displayed.

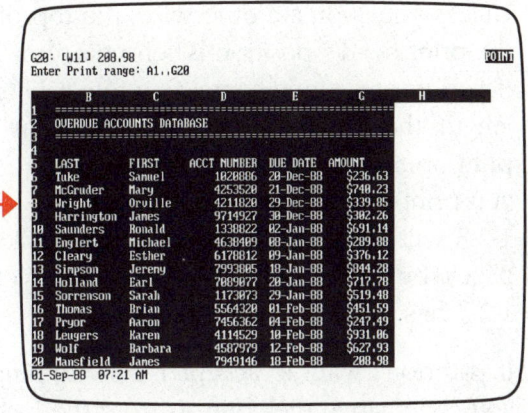

After the appropriate columns are hidden, choose **/P**rint **P**rinter **R**ange to assign the range to print.

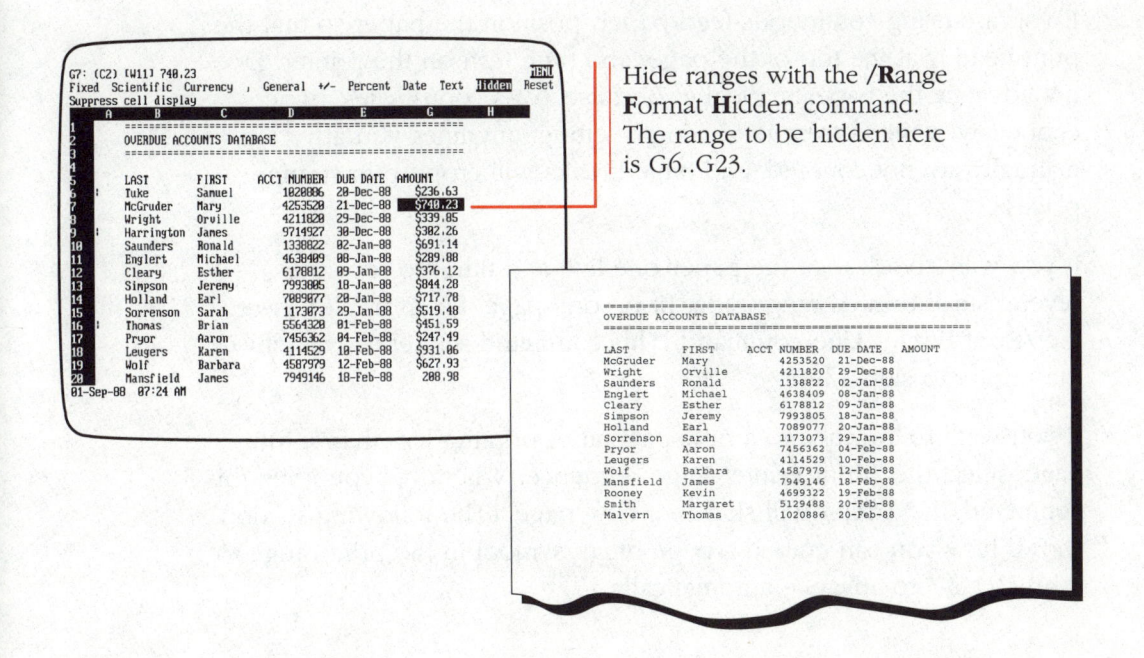

Hide ranges with the **/R**ange **F**ormat **H**idden command. The range to be hidden here is G6..G23.

Introduction

An Overview of 1-2-3

Getting Started

1-2-3 Basics

Creating a Worksheet

Printing Reports

Creating and Printing Graphs

Managing Data

Understanding Macros

Appendix

235

Controlling Paper Movement

Unless you stipulate otherwise, the top of a page is initially marked by the print head's position when you turn on the printer and load 1-2-3. If you print a range containing fewer lines than the default page length, the paper will not advance to the top of the next page; the next print operation will begin wherever the preceding operation ended. If you print a range containing more lines than the default page length, 1-2-3 will automatically insert page breaks in the document between pages, but the paper will not advance to the top of the next page after 1-2-3 has printed the last page.

If you don't want to accept 1-2-3's automatic paper-movement controls, you can change the controls from the keyboard. You can specify the "top" of a page in any paper position, advance the paper by line or by page, and insert page breaks exactly where you want them.

The Print Menu's Line, Page, and Align Options

If you are using continuous-feed paper, position the paper so that the print head is at the top of the page, and then turn on the printer. Do not advance the paper manually. Because 1-2-3 coordinates a line counter with the current page-length setting, any lines you advance manually are not counted, and page breaks will crop up in strange places.

If you want to advance the paper one line at a time (to separate several small printed ranges that fit on one page, for example), issue the **/P**rint **P**rinter **L**ine command. This command sequence will cause the printer to skip a line.

If you want to advance to a new page after printing less than a full page, select the **/P**rint **P**rinter **P**age sequence. Whenever you issue this command, the printer will skip to a new page. (The following section shows how you can embed a page-break symbol in the print range to instruct 1-2-3 to advance automatically.)

In many cases, a faster way to advance the paper is to take the printer off-line, adjust the paper manually, put the printer on-line, and then issue the **/P**rint **P**rinter **A**lign command.

Whenever you begin a print job at the top of a page, you should select **A**lign before selecting **G**o.

To print an existing footer option on the last page, use the **P**age command at the end of the printing session. If you select the **Q**uit command from the **/P**rint menu without issuing the **P**age command, this final footer will not print; although you can reissue the **/P**rint **P**rinter command, select **P**age, and the footer will still print.

Setting Page Breaks within the Spreadsheet

To enter a page break by using 1-2-3's commands, first move the cell pointer to the leftmost column of the range to be printed and then to the row that you want to begin on the new page. Then select the **/W**orksheet **P**age command, which automatically inserts a new blank row containing a page-break symbol (|::). You could instead insert a blank row into your worksheet where you want a page break, and then type a page-break symbol (|::) into a blank cell in the leftmost column of the print range in that row. The contents of cells in any row marked by the page-break symbol will not print.

Be careful when you alter a spreadsheet. You may alter formula results by inserting rows, or you may accidentally delete the wrong row after you finish printing. You may be able to avoid these problems by typing the page-break symbol into the leftmost column in the print range of a row that is already blank in your worksheet. First check to be sure the row is blank; use the End key and the arrow keys to scan across the row.

Controlling Paper Movement

When you first turn on the printer and load 1-2-3, the program notes the position of the print head and "remembers" that as the top of the page. If the print job takes only a fraction of a page, 1-2-3 does not advance the paper to the next page automatically; you will have to do that yourself. With 1-2-3, you can align and insert page breaks without relying on the program-supplied settings.

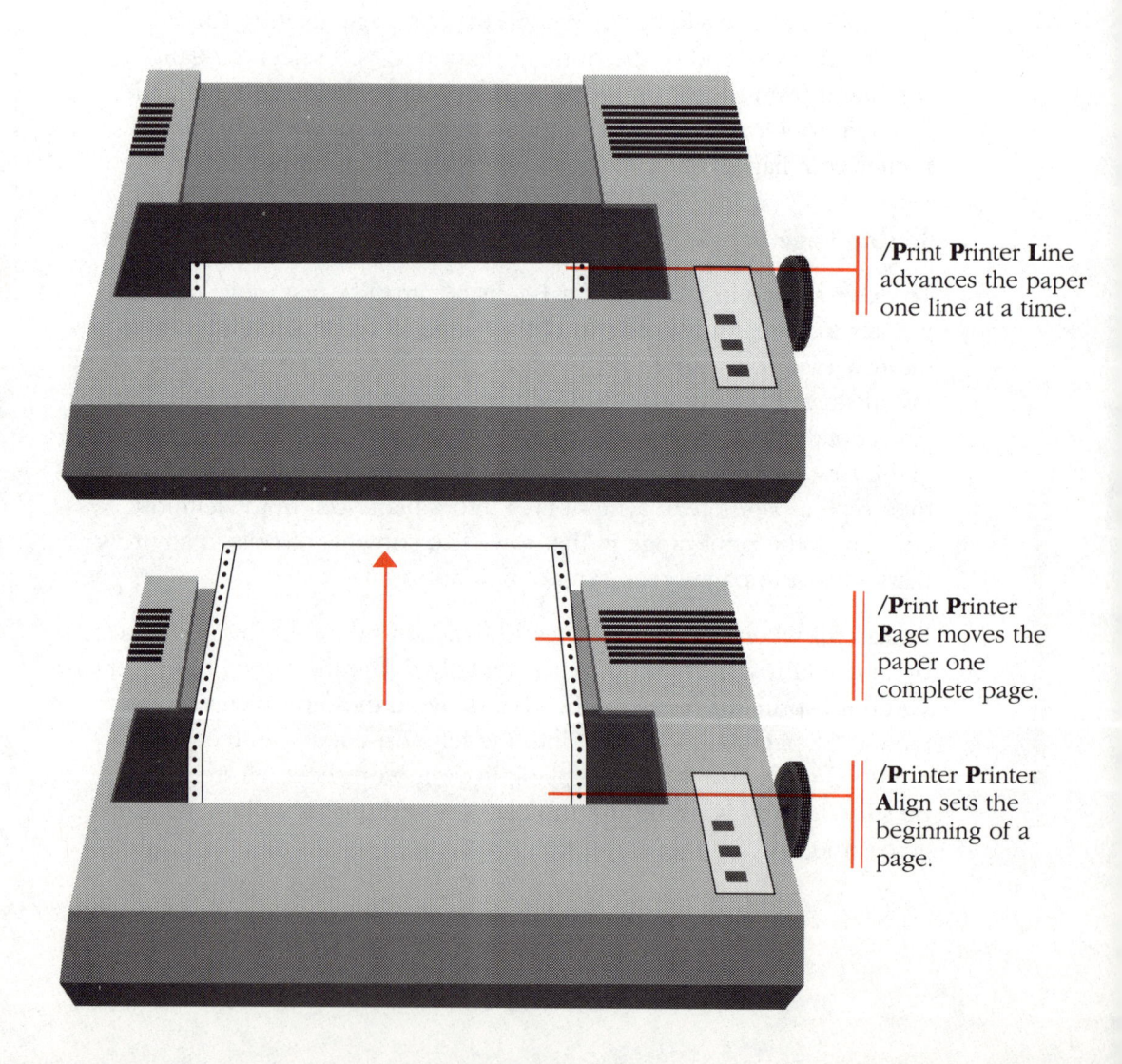

/Print Printer Line advances the paper one line at a time.

/Print Printer Page moves the paper one complete page.

/Printer Printer Align sets the beginning of a page.

| Introduction | /Print Printer and /Print File | Printing Reports | Hiding Rows, Columns, and Ranges | **Controlling Paper Movement** | Adding Headers and Footers | Printing Cell Contents and Clearing Print Options | Preparing Output for Other Programs |

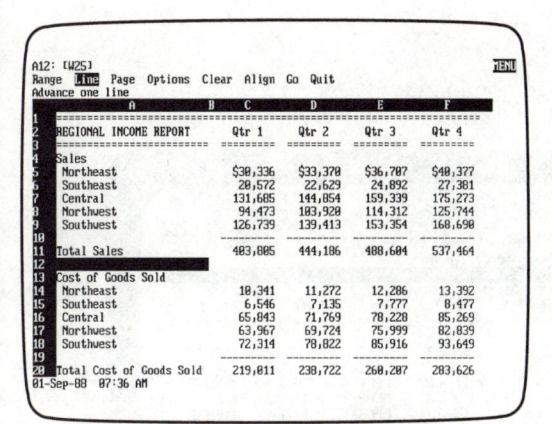

To advance the paper one line at a time, select **/P**rint **P**rinter **L**ine.

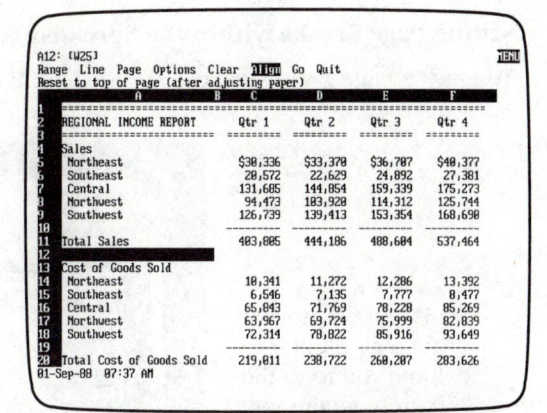

To align the paper, take the printer off-line, adjust the paper manually, put the printer on-line, and select **/P**rint **P**rinter **A**lign.

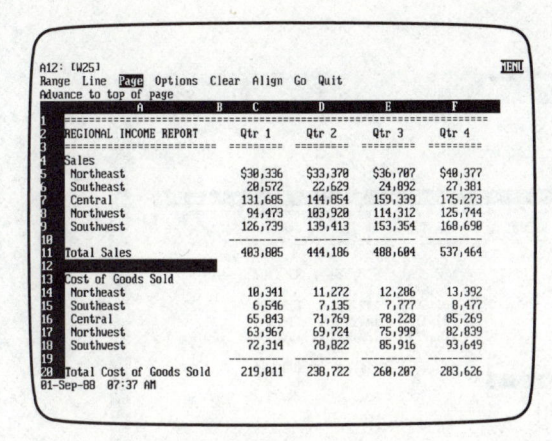

To move to a new page after printing less than a full page, select **/P**rint **P**rinter **P**age.

Introduction

An Overview of 1-2-3

Getting Started

1-2-3 Basics

Creating a Worksheet

Printing Reports

Creating and Printing Graphs

Managing Data

Understanding Macros

Appendix

239

Controlling Paper Movement

Setting Page Breaks within the Spreadsheet

To enter a page break, use the **/W**orksheet **P**age command.

Begin by moving the cell pointer to column A and to the row where you want the page to break. Select **/W**orksheet **P**age.

After selecting the command, 1-2-3 will enter a page-break symbol (|::) in the cell where the cell pointer is located.

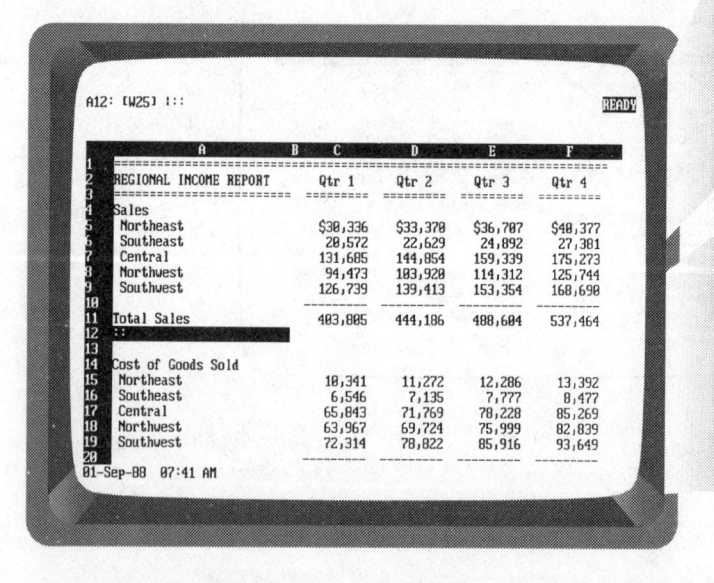

240

| Introduction | /Print Printer and /Print File | Printing Reports | Hiding Rows, Columns, and Ranges | **Controlling Paper Movement** | Adding Headers and Footers | Printing Cell Contents and Clearing Print Options | Preparing Output for Other Programs |

```
REGIONAL INCOME REPORT        Qtr 1      Qtr 2      Qtr 3      Qtr 4
============================ ========== ========== ========== ==========
Sales
  Northeast                  $30,336    $33,370    $36,707    $40,377
  Southeast                   20,572     22,629     24,892     27,381
  Central                    131,685    144,854    159,339    175,273
  Northwest                   94,473    103,920    114,312    125,744
  Southwest                  126,739    139,413    153,354    168,690
                            ---------  ---------  ---------  ---------
Total Sales                  403,805    444,186    488,604    537,464
```

When you print the range containing the page break symbol, 1-2-3 will automatically advance the paper at that point.

```
REGIONAL INCOME REPORT        Qtr 1      Qtr 2      Qtr 3      Qtr 4
============================ ========== ========== ========== ==========
Cost of Goods Sold
  Northeast                   10,341     11,272     12,286     13,392
  Southeast                    6,546      7,135      7,777      8,477
  Central                     65,843     71,769     78,228     85,269
  Northwest                   63,967     69,724     75,999     82,839
  Southwest                   72,314     78,822     85,916     93,649
                            ---------  ---------  ---------  ---------
Total Cost of Goods Sold     219,011    238,722    260,207    283,626
```

1-2-3 will begin to print the data following the page-break symbol on a new page.

Introduction

An Overview of 1-2-3

Getting Started

1-2-3 Basics

Creating a Worksheet

Printing Reports

Creating and Printing Graphs

Managing Data

Understanding Macros

Appendix

241

Adding Headers and Footers

As you know, 1-2-3 reserves three lines in a document for a header and an additional three lines for a footer. You can either retain the six lines (regardless of whether you use them) or eliminate all six lines by selecting **O**ther **U**nformatted (illustrated later in this chapter) from the **/P**rint **P**rinter **O**ptions menu.

Technically, either the **H**eader or **F**ooter option lets you specify up to 240 characters of text within one line in each of three positions: left, right, and center. But from a practical standpoint, the overall header or footer line cannot exceed the number of characters printed per inch multiplied by the width of the paper in inches minus the right and left margins.

The header text, which is printed on the first line after any blank top margin lines, is followed by two blank header lines (for spacing). The footer text line is printed above the specified bottom-margin blank lines and below two blank footer lines (for spacing).

Although you can enter manually all features of the text, 1-2-3 provides special characters for controlling page numbers, the current date, and the positioning of text within a header or footer. The pound sign (#) is used to print page numbers; the ampersand (@) prints the date; and the vertical bar (|) separates text and takes care of text alignment.

The following list gives you an overview of the characters used to place the page number and date in headers and to set the alignment of the header.

Character	Function
#	Automatically prints page numbers, starting with 1
@	Automatically includes (in the form 29-Jun-87) the date that you entered when you loaded DOS
|	Automatically separates text. (Absence of a | mark left-justifies all text. The first | mark centers text that follows. The second | mark right-justifies remaining text.)

To add a header, select **/P**rint **P**rinter, specify the **R**ange, and then select **O**ptions **H**eader. At the `Enter Header Line:` prompt, type

@|*YOUR FIRM NAME*|#

Then select **Q**uit from the **/P**rint **P**rinter **O**ptions menu; signal the top of the page to the printer, if necessary, by selecting **A**lign; and then select **G**o. The header will then appear on the report.

Whenever the print range exceeds a single-page output, the header will be reproduced on each succeeding page and the page number will increase by one. If you have used the special page-number character (#) and want to print your report a second time before you leave the **P**rint menu, you can reset the page counter and set the top of the form by simply selecting **A**lign before you select **G**o.

If you have specified a header line, but the centered or right-justified text doesn't print, make sure that the right-margin setting is appropriate for the current pitch and paper width. To change the header, simply repeat the sequence to establish the text, press Esc to remove the display of the existing header from the control panel, and press Enter. (You can delete a header or footer without removing other specified options.)

243

Adding Headers and Footers

Adding Headers and Footers

With 1-2-3's reports, you can also add headers and footers. The header text, which is printed on the first line after any blank top margin lines, is followed by two blank header lines (for spacing). The footer text line is printed above the specified bottom-margin blank lines and below two blank footer lines (for spacing).

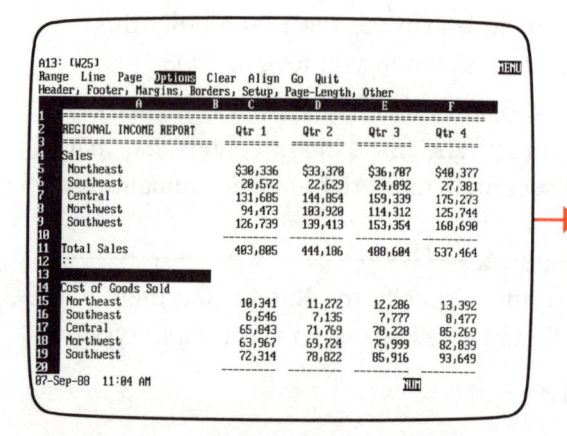

To add a header or footer, select **O**ptions after selecting **/P**rinter **P**rinter.

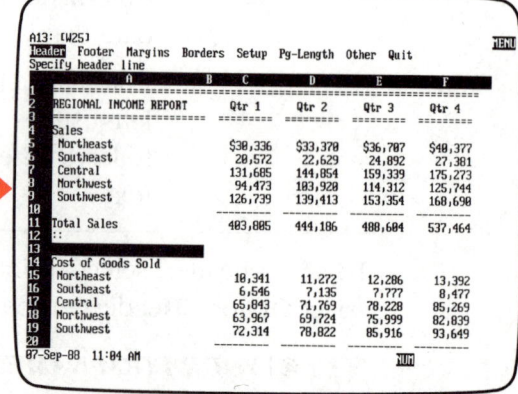

Select **H**eader or **F**ooter from the **O**ptions menu.

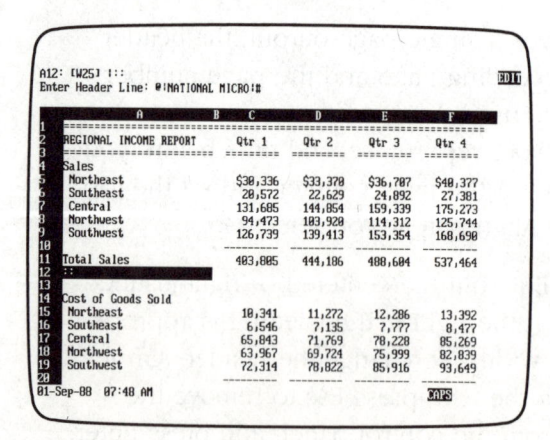

Finally, enter the text and/or codes for date and page number.

244

| Introduction | /Print Printer and /Print File | Printing Reports | Hiding Rows, Columns, and Ranges | Controlling Paper Movement | **Adding Headers and Footers** | Printing Cell Contents and Clearing Print Options | Preparing Output for Other Programs |

@ ¦ NATIONAL MICRO ¦

The **@** sign tells 1-2-3 to include the date in your header. (Make sure your computer is set to the correct date.)

The **¦** character tells 1-2-3 how to align the different items in this header line.

The **#** symbol tells 1-2-3 to print a page number.

```
07-Sep-88                   NATIONAL MICRO                          1

REGIONAL INCOME REPORT      Qtr 1       Qtr 2       Qtr 3       Qtr 4
==========================  =========   =========   =========   =========
Sales
  Northeast                 $30,336     $33,370     $36,707     $40,377
  Southeast                  20,572      22,629      24,892      27,381
  Central                   131,685     144,854     159,339     175,273
  Northwest                  94,473     103,920     114,312     125,744
  Southwest                 126,739     139,413     153,354     168,690
                            ---------   ---------   ---------   ---------
Total Sales                 403,805     444,186     488,604     537,464
```

Introduction

An Overview of 1-2-3

Getting Started

1-2-3 Basics

Creating a Worksheet

Printing Reports

Creating and Printing Graphs

Managing Data

Understanding Macros

Appendix

245

Adding Headers and Footers

Changing Page Layout: Margins and Page Length

Before you change the page layout defaults, you should be aware of the current settings. 1-2-3 initially assumes 8 1/2-by-11-inch paper and a printer output of 6 lines per inch; the default length of a page is 66 lines. 1-2-3 saves 2 lines at the top and bottom of each page for the top and bottom margins. Also, 1-2-3 automatically saves 3 lines at the top and bottom for headers and footers. The three lines reserved for a header and footer cannot be controlled by the user.

To change page layout temporarily, use the **/P**rint **P**rinter **O**ptions menu. To change the margins, select the **M**argins option and then select **L**eft, **R**ight, **T**op, or **B**ottom from the submenu.

When you select **L**eft, you are asked to enter a new left margin setting. You can enter a value from 0 to 240 in response to this prompt.

To change the right margin, select **R**ight and enter a value from 0 to 240 at the `Enter Right Margin` prompt. For the top and bottom margins, respectively, you select **T**op or **B**ottom and enter the margin specification from 0 to 32. You can check the default settings for margins and page length by selecting **/W**orksheet **G**lobal **D**efault **S**tatus.

```
A12: [W25] ':':                                                    STAT

     Printer:                         International:
        Interface..... Parallel 1        Punctuation..... A
        Auto-linefeed. No                    Point Dot
                                         Argument Comma
     Margins                             Thousands Comma
        Left 8      Top 2
        Right 72    Bottom 2          Currency......... $ (Prefix)
                                      Date format D4.. A (MM/DD/YY)
     Page length... 66                Time format D8.. A (HH:MM:SS)
     Wait.......... No
     Setup string..
     Name.......... HP LaserJet or LaserJet+

     Directory at startup: A:

     Help access method: Instant

     Clock on screen: Standard


     01-Sep-88  07:53 AM
```

Be sure that you set left and right margins that are consistent with the width of your paper and the printer's established pitch (characters per inch). The right margin must be greater than the left margin. And make sure that settings for the top and bottom margins are consistent with the paper's length and the established number of lines per inch.

The following list shows you the keystrokes and messages involved in changing margin settings.

▼

Option	Keystroke	Message
Left	**L**	`Enter Left Margin (0..240):xx`
Right	**R**	`Enter Right Margin (0..240):xx`
Top	**T**	`Enter Top Margin (0..32):xx`
Bottom	**B**	`Enter Bottom Margin (0..32):xx`

The xx at the end of each line denotes the current setting, which you can change. The right margin must be greater than the left margin.

▲

The specified page length must not be less than the top margin *plus* the header lines *plus* one line of data *plus* the footer lines *plus* the bottom margin, unless you use the **/P**rint **P**rinter **O**ptions **O**ther **U**nformatted command to suppress all formatting. (Information about this command is included in the following section, "Printing a Listing of Cell Contents.") To maximize the output on every printed page of a large spreadsheet, you can combine the **U**nformatted option with setup strings that condense print and increase the number of lines per inch. (The **U**nformatted option ignores margins, headers, and footers.)

Adding Headers and Footers

Changing Page Layout

You can also control the way your report appears on paper by changing the page layout options and resetting the margins.

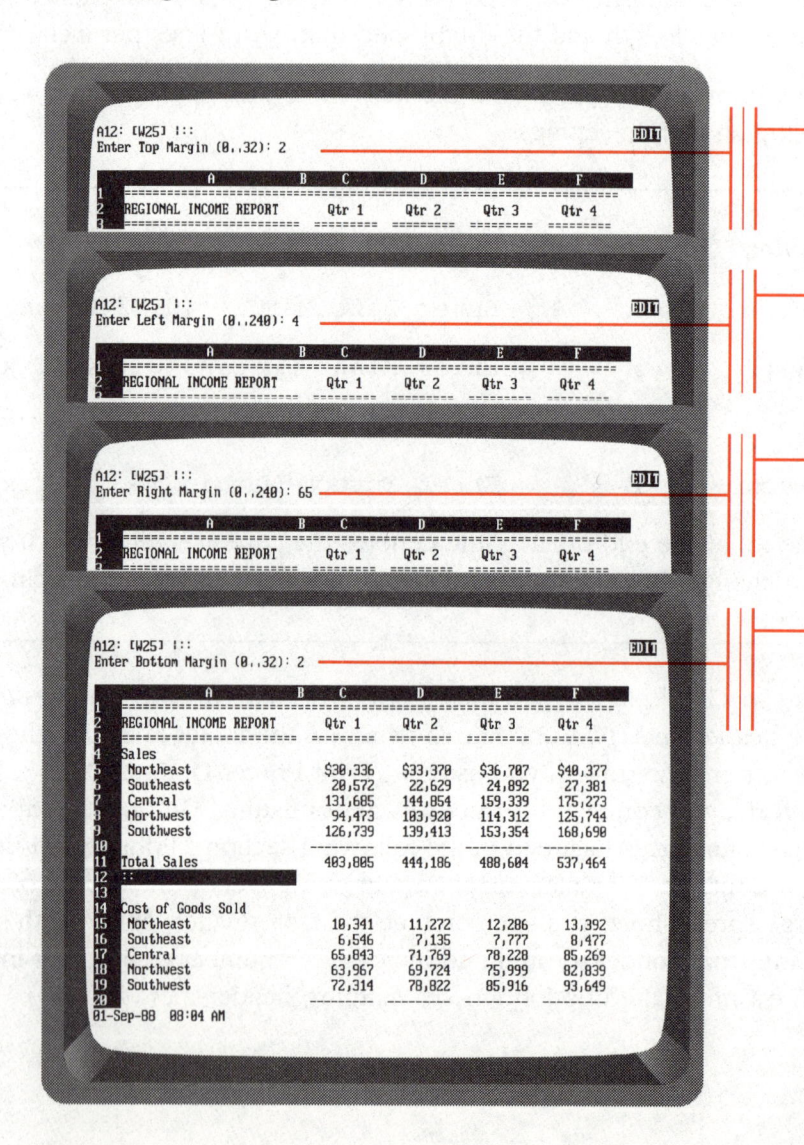

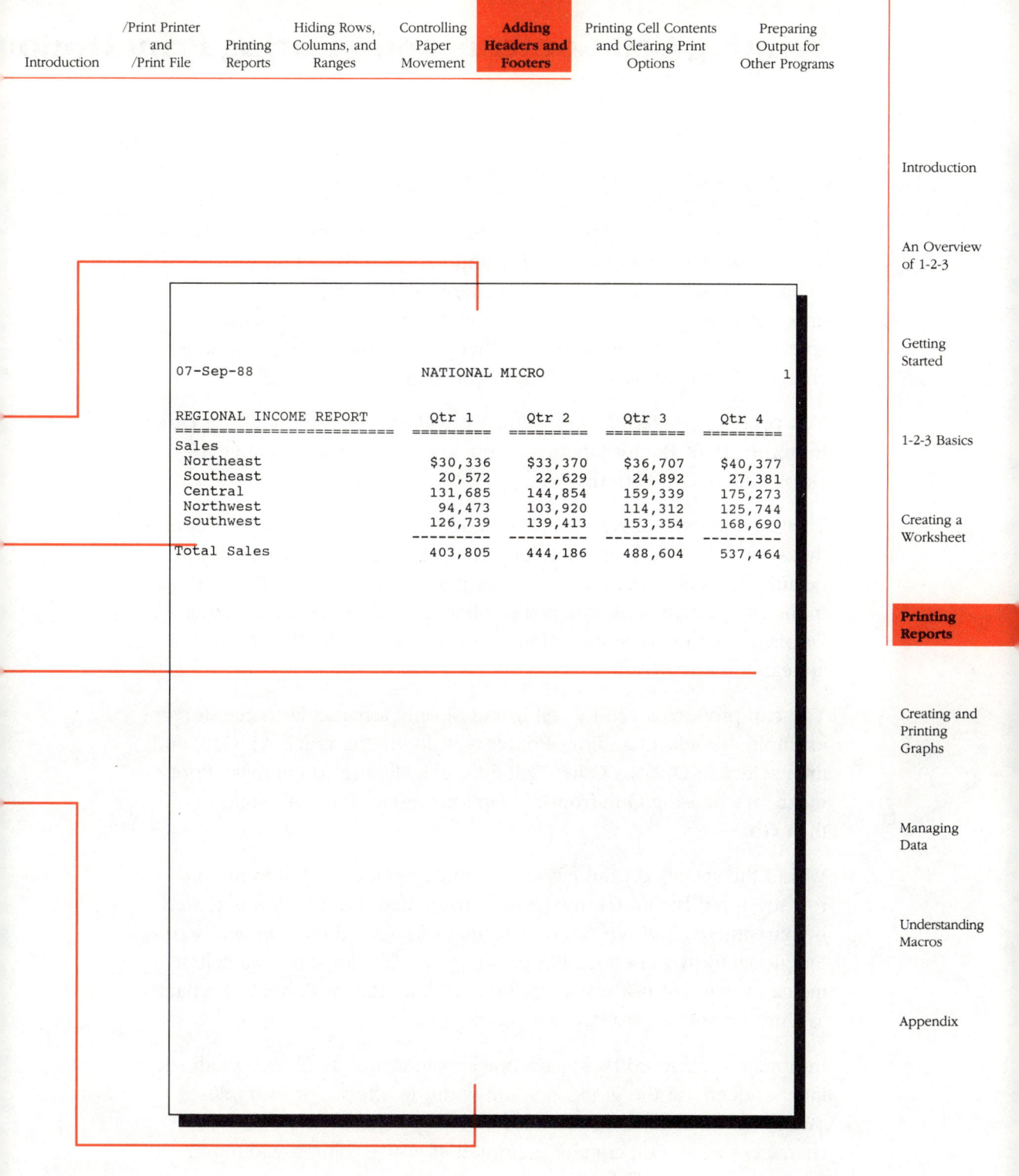

```
07-Sep-88                    NATIONAL MICRO                         1


REGIONAL INCOME REPORT       Qtr 1       Qtr 2       Qtr 3       Qtr 4
==========================   =========   =========   =========   =========
Sales
  Northeast                  $30,336     $33,370     $36,707     $40,377
  Southeast                   20,572      22,629      24,892      27,381
  Central                    131,685     144,854     159,339     175,273
  Northwest                   94,473     103,920     114,312     125,744
  Southwest                  126,739     139,413     153,354     168,690
                             ---------   ---------   ---------   ---------
Total Sales                  403,805     444,186     488,604     537,464
```

Printing Cell Contents and Clearing Print Options

You can spend hours developing and debugging a model spreadsheet and much additional time entering and verifying data. You should safeguard your work not only by making backup copies of your important files but also by printing the cell contents of important spreadsheets. Be aware, however, that this print job can eat up large chunks of time if you have a large worksheet.

You produce printed documentation of cell contents by selecting **O**ther from the **/P**rint **P**rinter **O**ptions menu, and then selecting either **A**s-Displayed or **C**ell-Formulas.

The two options are related. Choosing **C**ell-Formulas produces a listing that shows the width of the cell (if the cell width is different from the default), the cell format, cell-protection status, and the contents of cells in the print range, with one cell per line. By subsequently selecting **A**s-Displayed, you restore the default instructions to print the range as it appears on-screen.

You can produce a cell-by-cell listing of only a particular range, for example, by selecting **/P**rint **P**rinter, specifying the range A1..G18, and then selecting **O**ptions **O**ther **C**ell-Formulas. Return to the main **P**rint menu by choosing **Q**uit from the **O**ptions menu. Press **A**lign and then **G**o.

Within the specified print range, the contents of each cell in the first row are listed before the next row is presented. Information enclosed by parentheses indicates a range format established independently of the global format in effect. For example, if (C0) appears in a cell, it indicates that that cell was formatted (with a **/R**ange **F**ormat command) as **C**urrency, with zero decimal places.

Information enclosed by square brackets indicates a column width set independently of the global column width in effect. For example, [W11] indicates that the column was set specifically to be 11 characters wide. Cell content is printed after the column-width and format information.

Clearing the Print Options

Selecting **/P**rint **P**rinter **C**lear lets you eliminate all or a portion of the **P**rint options that you chose earlier. The **C**lear options are

All   **R**ange   **B**orders   **F**ormat

You can clear every **P**rint option, including the print range, by selecting **A**ll, or you can be more specific by using the other choices:

Menu Selection	Keystroke	Description
Range	**R**	Removes the previous print-range specification
Borders	**B**	Cancels **C**olumns and **R**ows specified as borders
Format	**F**	Eliminates **M**argins, **P**g-Length, and **S**etup string settings, returning settings to the default settings displayed in the **/W**orksheet **G**lobal **D**efault screen.

Remember that you can automate many routine print operations by setting up the print macros. **/P**rint **P**rinter **C**lear **A**ll is usually the first instruction in this type of macro.

Printing Cell Contents and Clearing Print Option

Listing Cell Contents

To help document your model and to debug the formulas in a part of your worksheet, 1-2-3 gives you the option of printing a list of the worksheet contents through the **/P**rint **P**rinter (or **F**ile) **O**ptions **O**ther **C**ell-Formulas command.

To print a list of cell contents, begin by selecting **/P**rint **P**rinter (or **F**ile) **O**ptions **O**ther.

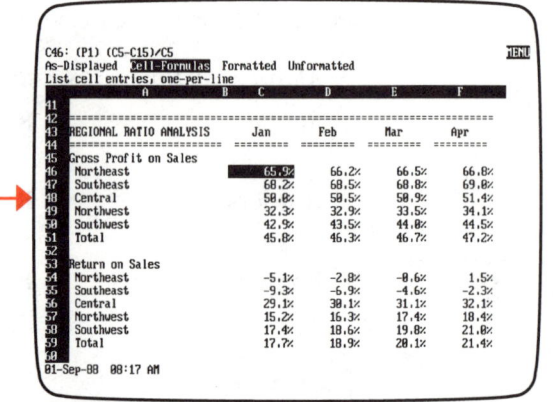

Choose **C**ell-Formulas to print a listing of formulas in cells. **A**s-Displayed, the default, prints the range as it appears on the screen.

Enter the print range for the cells that you want printed in **C**ell-Formulas format.

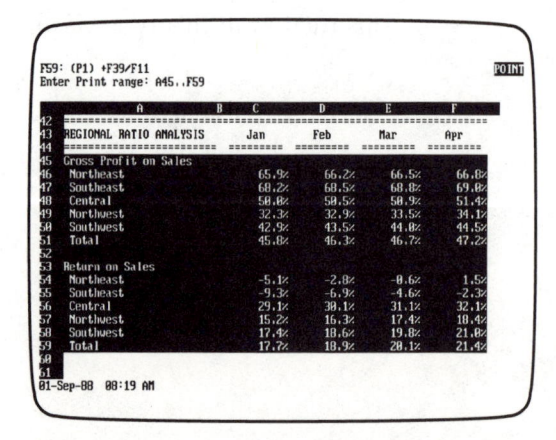

252

| Introduction | /Print Printer and /Print File | Printing Reports | Hiding Rows, Columns, and Ranges | Controlling Paper Movement | Adding Headers and Footers | **Printing Cell Contents and Clearing Print Options** | Preparing Output for Other Programs |

1-2-3 prints the cell contents horizontally, moving across each row of the print range.

```
A45: [W25] 'Gross Profit on Sales
A46: [W25] ' Northeast
C46: (P1) (C5-C15)/C5
D46: (P1) [W11] (D5-D15)/D5
E46: (P1) [W11] (E5-E15)/E5
F46: (P1) (F5-F15)/F5
A47: [W25] ' Southeast
C47: (P1) (C6-C16)/C6
D47: (P1) [W11] (D6-D16)/D6
E47: (P1) [W11] (E6-E16)/E6
F47: (P1) (F6-F16)/F6
A48: [W25] ' Central
C48: (P1) (C7-C17)/C7
D48: (P1) [W11] (D7-D17)/D7
E48: (P1) [W11] (E7-E17)/E7
F48: (P1) (F7-F17)/F7
A49: [W25] ' Northwest
C49: (P1) (C8-C18)/C8
D49: (P1) [W11] (D8-D18)/D8
E49: (P1) [W11] (E8-E18)/E8
F49: (P1) (F8-F18)/F8
A50: [W25] ' Southwest
C50: (P1) (C9-C19)/C9
```

Each entry begins with the location of the cell.

If the column width of the cell is different from the default column width, 1-2-3 indicates the width.

D49:(P1)[W11](D8-D18)/D8

If the format of the cell is different from the default format, 1-2-3 prints a notation for the cell's format.

The printed entry ends with the actual contents of the cell, in this case a formula.

Introduction

An Overview of 1-2-3

Getting Started

1-2-3 Basics

Creating a Worksheet

Printing Reports

Creating and Printing Graphs

Managing Data

Understanding Macros

Appendix

253

Preparing Output for Other Programs

Many word-processing and other software packages accept ASCII text files. You can maximize your chances of successfully exporting 1-2-3 files to other programs if you select several **P**rint command sequences that eliminate unwanted specifications for page layout and page breaks.

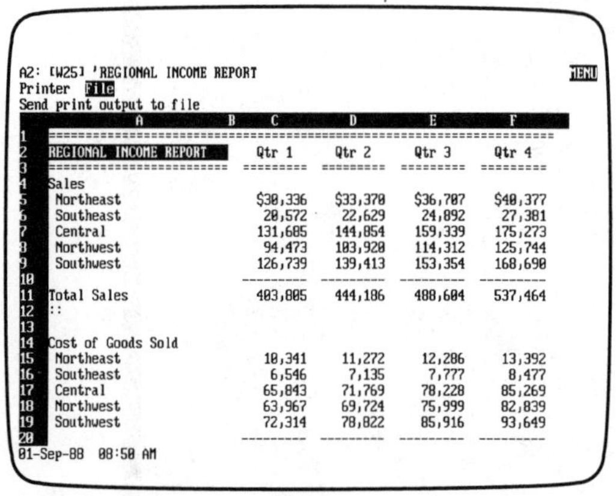

Begin by selecting **/P**rint **F**ile.

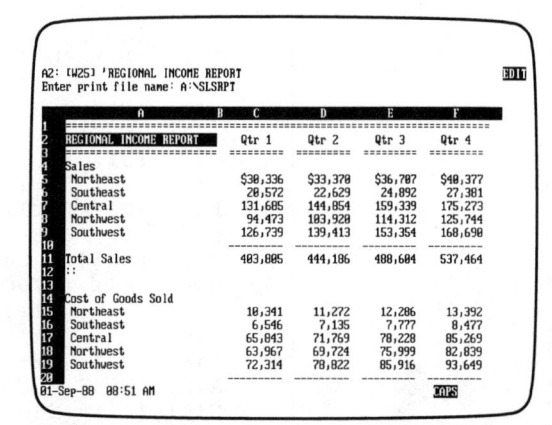

Direct output to a .PRN file instead of to a printer by specifying a file name.

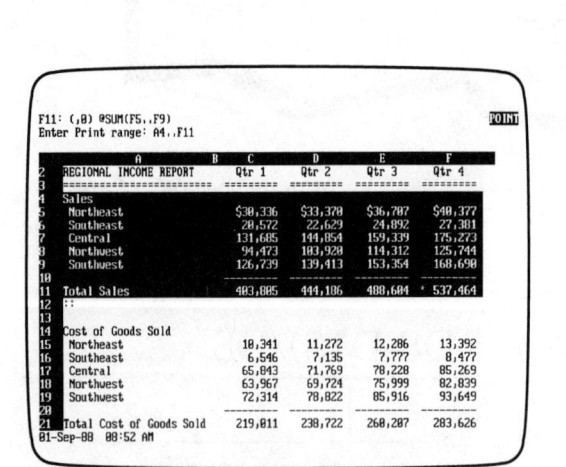

Specify the **R**ange to print.

| Introduction | /Print Printer and /Print File | Printing Reports | Hiding Rows, Columns, and Ranges | Controlling Paper Movement | Adding Headers and Footers | Printing Cell Contents and Clearing Print Options | **Preparing Output for Other Programs** |

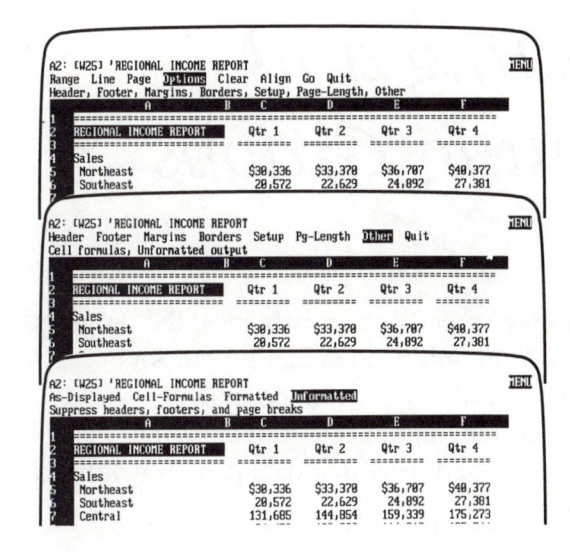

Choose **O**ptions **O**ther **U**nformatted. Selecting **U**nformatted removes all headers, footers, and page breaks from a print operation.

Then **Q**uit the **O**ptions menu, create the .PRN file on disk by selecting **G**o, and **Q**uit the **/P**rint **F**ile menu. Follow the instructions in your word-processing or other software package to import the specially prepared 1-2-3 disk files.

Introduction

An Overview of 1-2-3

Getting Started

1-2-3 Basics

Creating a Worksheet

Printing Reports

Creating and Printing Graphs

Managing Data

Understanding Macros

Appendix

255

6 Creating and Printing Graphs

Even if Lotus 1-2-3 provided only spreadsheet capabilities, the program would be extremely powerful. More information can be quickly assembled and tabulated electronically than could possibly be developed manually. But despite the importance of keeping detailed worksheets that show real or projected data, that data can be worthless if you can't readily understand it.

To help decision-makers who are pressed for time or unable to draw conclusions from countless rows of numeric data and who may benefit from seeing key figures displayed graphically, Lotus offers graphics capabilities. The program offers five types of basic business graphs as well as limited options for enhancing the graphs' appearance. Although no match for the capabilities of many stand-alone graphics packages, 1-2-3's strength lies in its integration with the spreadsheet.

Key Terms Used in This Chapter

graph type   A 1-2-3 graph can be one of five types: line, bar, XY, stacked bar, and pie.

y-axis   The vertical left edge of a graph.

x-axis   The horizontal bottom edge of a graph.

legend   Description of the shading, color, or symbols assigned to data ranges in line or bar graphs, appearing across the bottom of those graphs.

tick marks   Small marks on the y-axis of a graph that indicate the increments between the minimum and maximum graph values.

What Is Covered in This Chapter?

This chapter shows you how to do the following:

- Meet minimum requirements for constructing graphs
- Select a graph type
- Create a basic graph
- Enhance the appearance of a graph
- Preserve the graph on disk

An Overview of Creating a Graph

Before creating your first graph, you must determine whether your hardware supports viewing and printing graphs, whether your 1-2-3 software is correctly installed and loaded, and whether the spreadsheet on-screen contains data you want to graph. And you should understand which type of graph is best suited for presenting specific numeric data in picture form.

We will use 1-2-3's graphics feature to create and view a graph, store its specifications for later use, and print it. Creating and storing a graph requires only that you have the Lotus system software installed on your equipment and that you correctly select options from the Graph menu.

Hardware Requirements

To view a graph on-screen, you need a graphics monitor or a monitor with a graphics-display adapter. (Without such a monitor, you can construct and save a 1-2-3 graph, but you must print the graph to view it.) If you have two graphics monitors installed, one monitor will display the spreadsheet while the other displays the graph.

To print a graph, you need a graphics printer supported by 1-2-3 and a separate set of PrintGraph instructions. (These instructions are explained later in this chapter.)

Creating a Graph

To create a 1-2-3 graph, you begin by selecting the **/G**raph command from the main menu while the worksheet containing the data you want to graph is displayed. Selecting **/G**raph from the main 1-2-3 menu produces the following menu:

Type **X A B C D E F** **R**eset **V**iew **S**ave **O**ptions **N**ame **Q**uit

You will use some of these commands every time you create a graph; you'll use other commands (particularly some subcommands provided by **O**ptions) less frequently, only when you need to enhance or customize your graph or when you want to save your graph in a form so that it can be printed. If you do not need to enhance, customize, or print the graph, creating a graph that displays nothing more than data points in bar (or stacked-bar), line (or XY), and pie forms is easy. Only four steps are required to produce a simple graph:

1. Selecting the type of graph (if different from the default type Line) by using the **T**ype command.
2. Indicating the data ranges from your worksheet that you want to graph by using the **A-F** options from the **/G**raph menu (To create a pie graph, you use the **A** option to indicate what data range you want to graph and use the **B** option to set the hatching for each part of the pie graph. To create an XY graph, you use the **A-F** options to plot the dependent variables.)

An Overview of Creating a Graph

   3. Indicating the data range for labeling the tick marks along the x-axis in a line, bar, or stacked-bar graph; for labeling each part of a pie graph; and for plotting the dependent variable in an XY graph by using the **X** option from the **/G**raph menu.
   4. Displaying the graph by selecting the **V**iew command from the **/G**raph menu or pressing F10 (Graph).

To improve the appearance of your graphs and produce final-quality output suitable for business presentations, you can select one or more choices from the **/G**raph **O**ptions menu. In addition to the four steps needed for creating and viewing a basic graph, other steps needed to enhance, customize, and save a graph for printing include the following:

   1. Entering the titles you want displayed (and printed) at the top of your graph, below the x-axis, and to the left of the y-axis by using the **/G**raph **O**ptions **T**iles command.
   2. Entering the legends identifying the different data ranges in a line, bar, stacked-bar, or XY graph by using the **/G**raph **O**ptions **L**egend command.
   3. Adding a horizontal and vertical grid to your graph by using the **/G**raph **O**ptions **G**rid command.
   4. Drawing lines or symbols in a line or XY graph by using the **G**raph **O**ptions **F**ormat command.

5. Controlling the scaling and the format of values along the x-axis or y-axis by using the **/G**raph **O**ption **S**cale command.

6. Resetting the graph display from monochrome to color or vice versa by using the **/G**raph **O**ptions **C**olor or **/G**raph **O**ptions **B**&W commands.

7. Adding labels that will appear within the graph, identifying different data points.

8. Naming each graph you create for a worksheet by using the **/G**raph **N**ame command so that you can redisplay each graph anytime you retrieve the worksheet file.

9. Saving your graph in a special file format by using the **/G**raph **S**ave command so that you can print the graph with 1-2-3's PrintGraph program.

The following sections of this chapter describe and illustrate how you can create basic graphs by using only a few commands and how you can create final-quality graphs by using many of the commands from the **/G**raph **O**ptions menu.

An Overview of Creating a Graph

Creating a Graph

To create a 1-2-3 graph, you begin by selecting the /Graph command from the main menu.

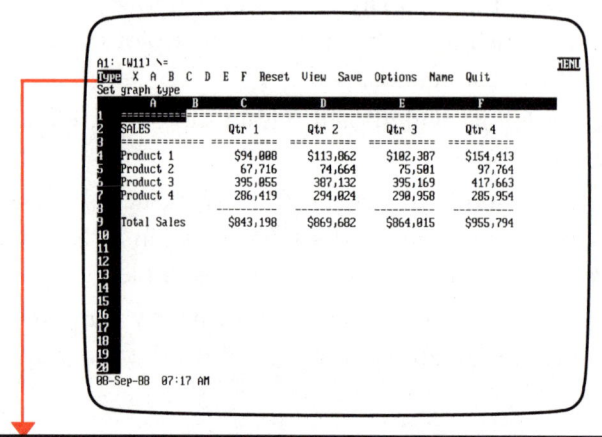

Options on the /Graph Main Menu

Type Provides options for creating five types of graphs.

X-F Let you enter the ranges of data you want to display in a graph.

Reset Clears the current graph settings.

View Displays a graph on your computer monitor.

Save Saves a graph in the file format needed for printing the graph with the 1-2-3 PrintGraph program.

Options Provides choices for labeling, enhancing, or customizing a graph.

Name Lets you assign a name to one or more graphs and store the graph settings so that you can redisplay the graph(s) whenever you retrieve the worksheet file.

Quit Quits the /Graph menu and returns the worksheet to READY mode.

Creating a Simple Graph

If you want to create a graph quickly for your own analysis, you only need to complete four steps.

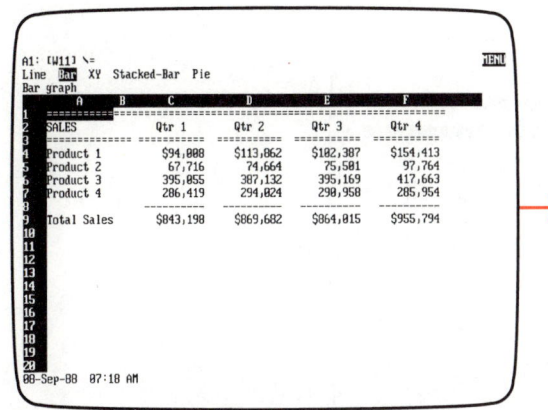

First, select **/G**raph **T**ype to select the type of graph you want to create. (Because the line graph is the default type, you do not need to select the **T**ype command if you want to create the line graph.)

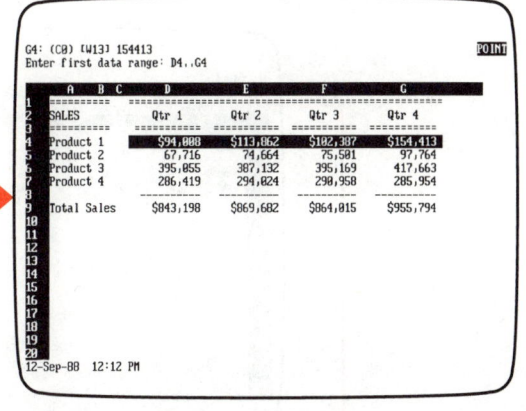

Second, indicate the data range(s) in your worksheet that you want to graph. For example, to graph the quarterly sales for Product 1, select **A**. When the `Enter first data range:` prompt appears, highlight the range for Product 1 sales.

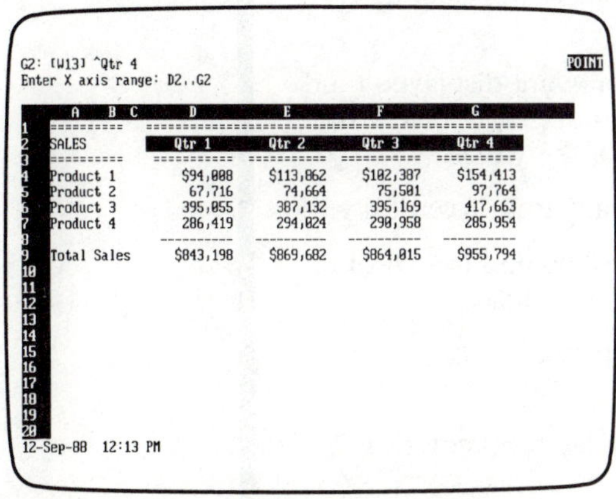

Third, choose **X** to label the x-axis in a line, bar, or stacked-bar graph.

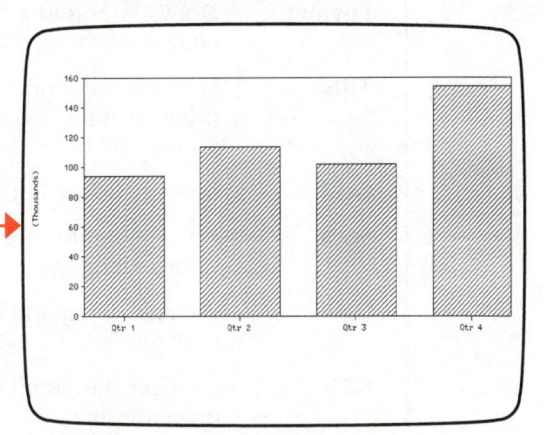

Finally, display the graph by selecting **V**iew or by pressing [F10] (Graph). Press [Esc] to return to the worksheet..

263

An Overview of Creating a Graph

Enhancing a Graph

To improve the appearance of your graphs and produce final-quality output suitable for business presentations, you need to use the choices provided by **/G**raph **O**ptions.

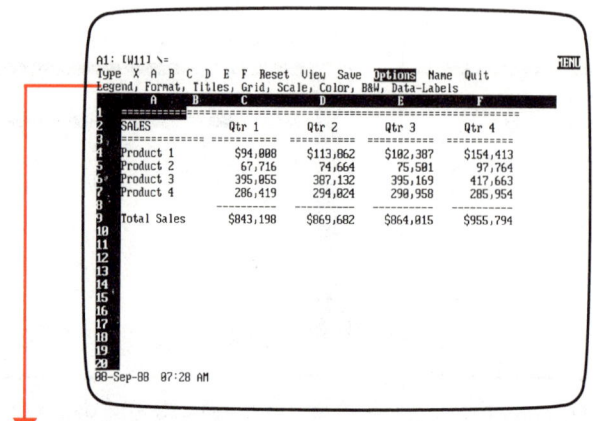

```
A1: [W11] \=                                                    MENU
Type  X  A  B  C  D  E  F  Reset  View  Save  Options  Name  Quit
Legend, Format, Titles, Grid, Scale, Color, B&W, Data-Labels
        A              B           C           D           E           F
  1  ===============================================================
  2  SALES            Qtr 1       Qtr 2       Qtr 3       Qtr 4
  3  ===============================================================
  4  Product 1       $94,008    $113,062    $102,387    $154,413
  5  Product 2        67,716     74,664      75,501      97,764
  6  Product 3       395,055    387,132     395,169     417,663
  7  Product 4       286,419    294,024     290,958     285,954
  8                  --------   --------    --------    --------
  9  Total Sales    $843,198   $869,682    $864,015    $955,794
 10
 11
 12
 13
 14
 15
 16
 17
 18
 19
 20
08-Sep-88  07:28 AM
```

Options on the **/G**raph **O**ptions Menu

Legends	Lets you specify descriptions to link shadings or colors on a graph to specific y-axis data ranges.
Format	Draws lines and symbols to present and connect data points.
Titles	Lets you enter titles you want displayed (and printed) at the top of your graph, below the x-axis, and to the left of the y-axis.
Grid	Lets you add a horizontal and/or vertical grid.
Scale	Lets you control the scaling and format of values along the x-axis or y-axis.
Color	Changes the graph display to color if available.
B&W	Changes the graph display from color to monochrome.
Data-Labels	Lets you add labels that will appear within the graph identifying different data points.

To enhance and customize a graph after you have selected the graph type and have identified the data ranges to be graphed, use the commands provided by **/G**raph **O**ptions. Some of the frequently used **/G**raph **O**ptions commands include the following:

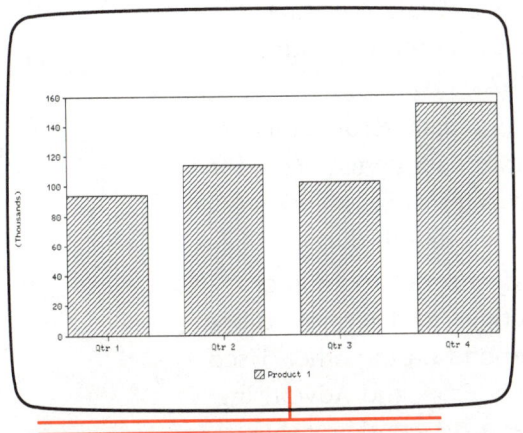

Select **/G**raph **O**ptions **L**egend if you want to identify the data ranges on your graph.

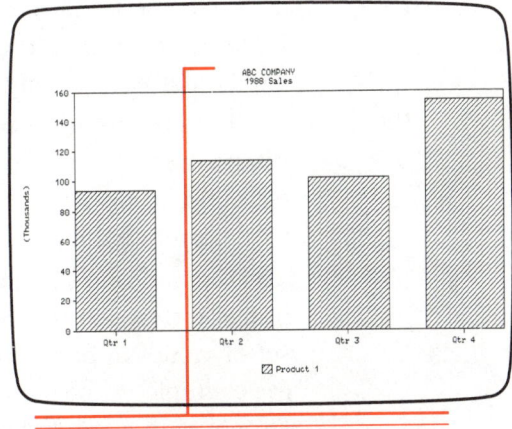

Choose **/G**raph **O**ptions **T**itles to add titles at the top of your graph, below the x-axis, or to the left of the y-axis.

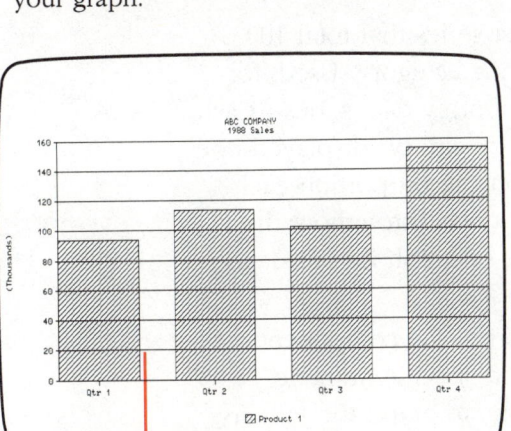

Choose **G**rid to add a vertical and/or horizontal grid.

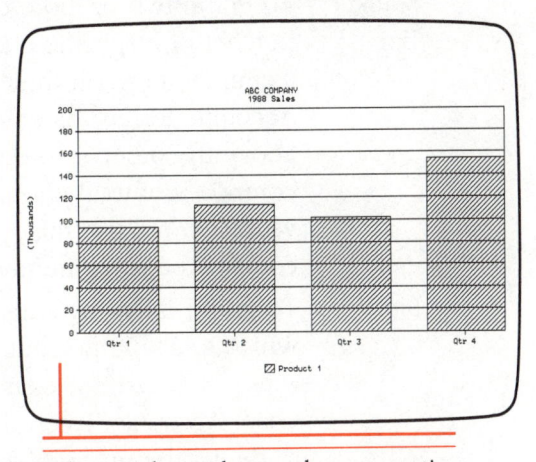

Select **S**cale to change the automatic scaling or default format of values along the x-axis and y-axis.

See "Enhancing the Appearance of a Basic Graph" later in this chapter for explanations and illustrations of other **/G**raph **O**ptions commands.

265

Selecting a Graph Type

You can create five different graph types with 1-2-3. The following list highlights the differences of each of these types:

Type	*Purpose*
Line	To show the trend of numeric data across time. Used, for example, to display monthly working-capital amounts during 1987.
Bar	To show the trend of numeric data across time, often comparing two or more data items. Used, for example, to display total current assets compared to total current liabilities for each month during 1987.
XY	To compare one numeric data series to another numeric data series across time, to determine if one set of values appears to depend on the other. Used, for example, to plot monthly Sales and Advertising Expenses to assess whether a direct relationship exists between the amount of sales and the dollars spent for advertising.
Stacked Bar	To graph two or more data series that total 100 percent of a specific numeric category. Used, for example, to graph three monthly data series—Cash, Accounts Receivable, and Inventory (displayed one above the other)—to depict the proportion each comprises of total current assets throughout the year. (Do not use this type of graph if your data contains negative numbers.)
Pie	To graph only one data series, the components of which total 100 percent of a specific numeric category. Used, for example, to graph the January Cash, Accounts Receivable, and Inventory amounts to depict the proportion each comprises of the January current assets. (Do not use this type of graph if your data contains negative numbers.)

Selecting one of the five available graph types is easy. When you select **T**ype from the Graph menu, 1-2-3 displays the following options:

Line **B**ar **X**Y **S**tacked-Bar **P**ie

By selecting one of these options, you set that graph type, and automatically restore the **G**raph menu to the control panel.

To understand which type will best display specific numeric data, you must know something about plotting points on a graph. Let's review the two basic terms *x-axis* and *y-axis*.

All graphs (except pie graphs) have two axes: the y-axis (the vertical left edge) and the x-axis (the horizontal bottom edge). 1-2-3 automatically provides tick marks for both axes. The program also scales the adjacent numbers on the y-axis, based on the minimum and maximum figures included in the plotted data range(s).

Every point plotted on a graph has a unique location (x,y): *x* represents the time period or the amount measured along the horizontal axis; *y* measures the corresponding amount along the vertical axis. The intersection of the y-axis and the x-axis is called the *origin*. To minimize misinterpretation of graph results and to make graphs easier to compare, use a zero origin in your graphs. Later in this chapter, you will learn how to manually change the upper or lower limits of the scale initially set by 1-2-3.

Of the five 1-2-3 graph types, all but the pie graph display both x- and y-axes. Line, bar, and stacked-bar graphs display figures (centered on the tick marks) along the y-axis only. The XY graph displays figures on both axes.

Selecting a Graph Type

1-2-3's Graphic Capabilities

1-2-3's graphic capabilities increase the program's power by giving you a way to visually represent your data. Do you want to see whether there is a trend in the latest sales increase of a particular product? A 1-2-3 graph can show you the answer quickly when deciphering that type of information from columns of numbers would be difficult. 1-2-3 offers five basic graph types: line, bar, XY, stacked bar, and pie graphs.

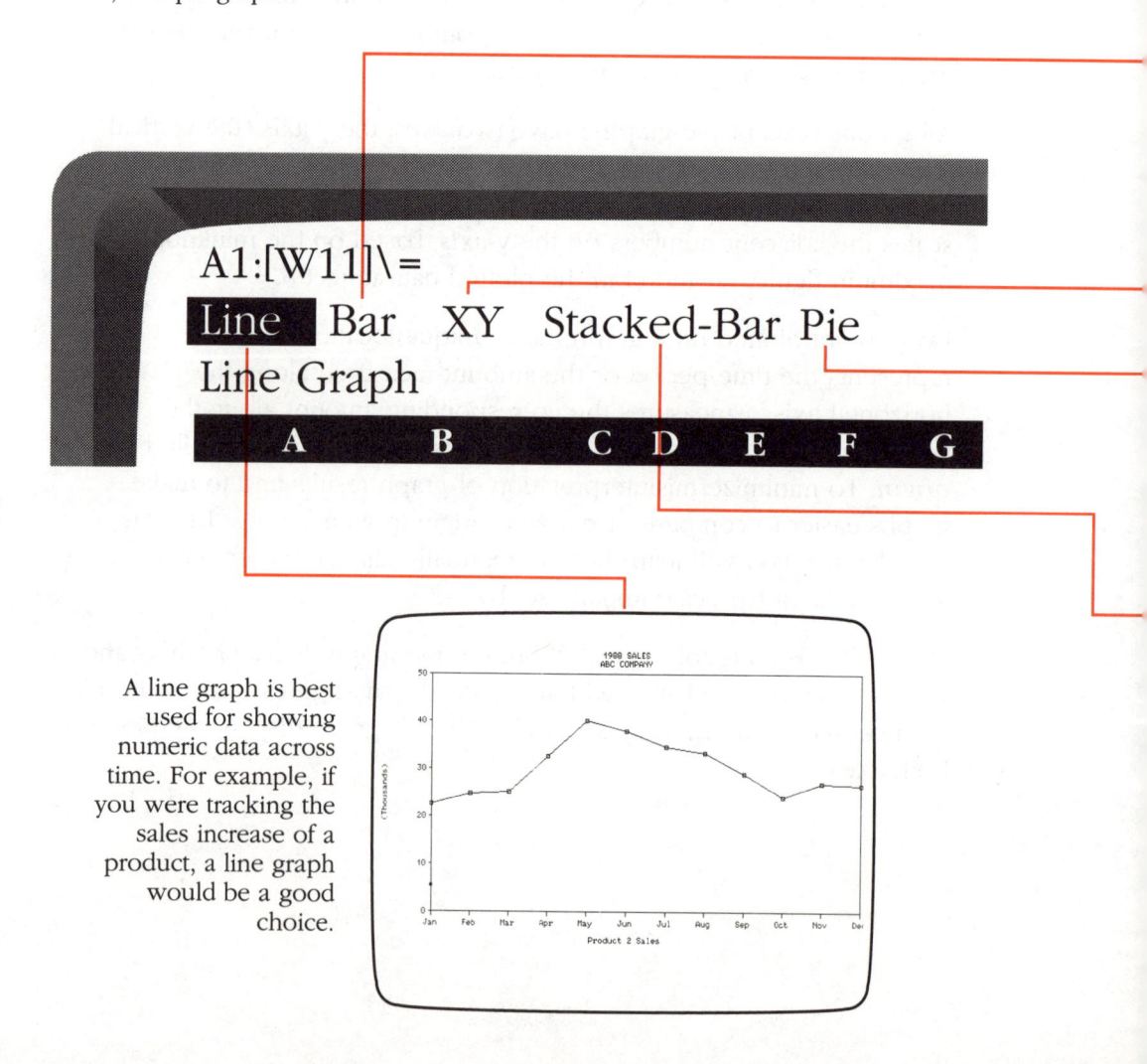

A line graph is best used for showing numeric data across time. For example, if you were tracking the sales increase of a product, a line graph would be a good choice.

268

A bar graph compares two or more data items across time. Use a bar graph, for example, to track the progress of two or more products.

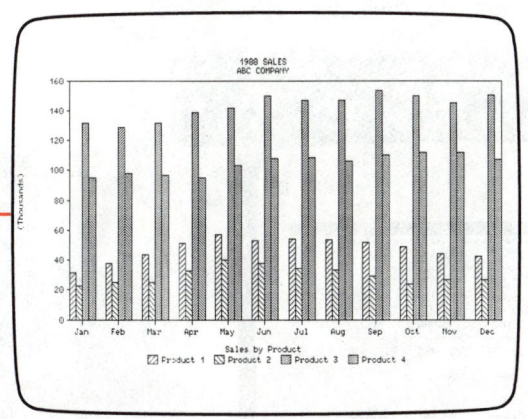

An XY graph compares one numeric data series to another, to determine whether one set of values depends on the other.

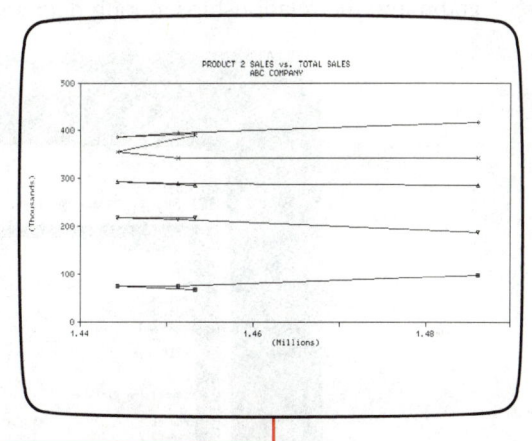

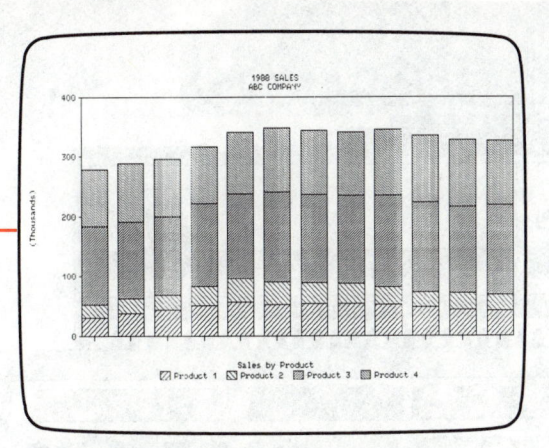

A stacked bar graph shows two or more data series that total 100 percent of a specific category.

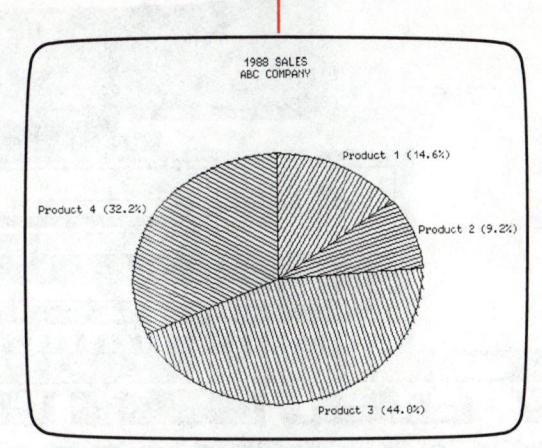

A pie graph is used to graph only one data series in which the components total 100 percent.

Selecting a Graph Type

Choosing the Type of Graph

Because more than one type of graph can accomplish the desired presentation, you need to consider what data ranges you want to graph and the relationships among data you want to show.

| Introduction | An Overview of Creating a Graph | **Selecting a Graph Type** | Specifying a Data Range | Enhancing the Appearance of a Basic Graph | Preserving the Graph on Disk | Accessing and Exiting PrintGraph | Printing Graphs |

Because 1-2-3 sets a scale based on minimum and maximum values, the program automatically displays the Thousands indicator along the y-axis.

The y-axis measures the amount along the vertical axis.

1-2-3 automatically scales the adjacent numbers on the y-axis, based on the minimum and maximum values.

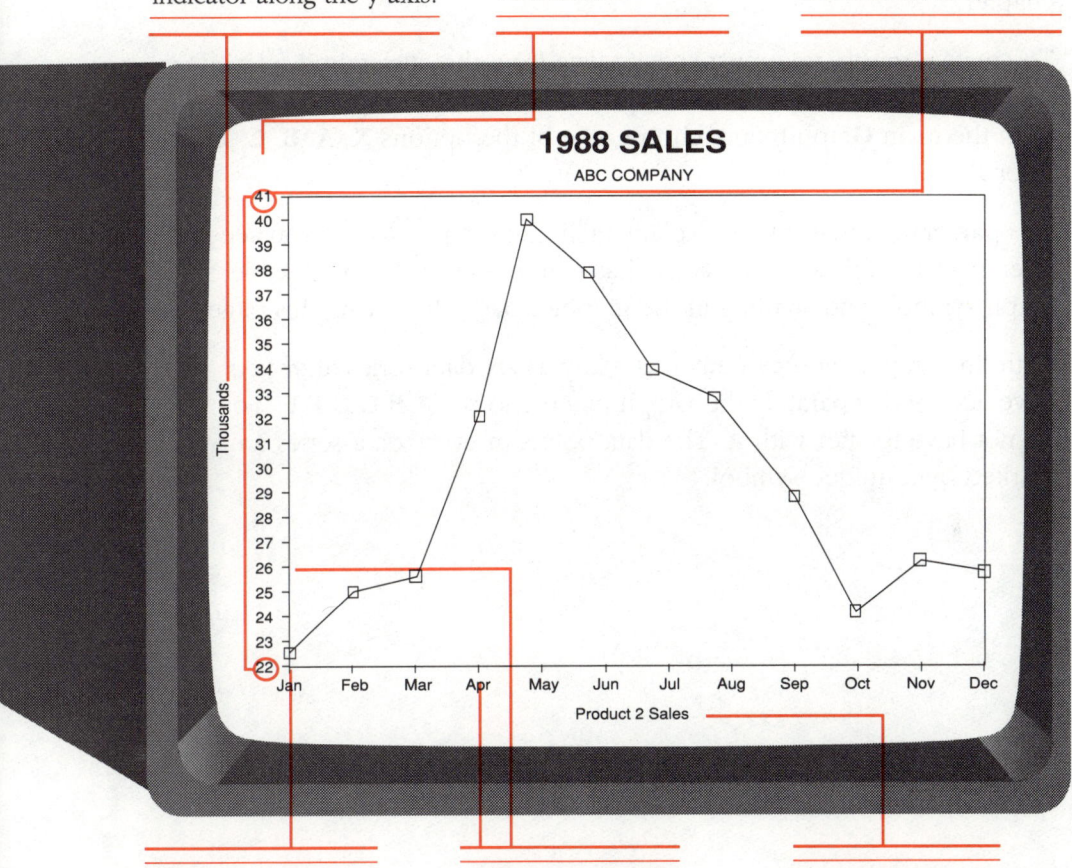

1988 SALES
ABC COMPANY

The origin of the x and y-axis. Notice that if the origin on the graph is not zero, the upward trend will seem larger than it really is.

1-2-3 automatically provides tick marks.

The x-axis represents the time period of the amount measured along the horizontal axis.

Introduction

An Overview of 1-2-3

Getting Started

1-2-3 Basics

Creating a Worksheet

Printing Reports

Creating and Printing Graphs

Managing Data

Understanding Macros

Appendix

271

Specifying a Data Range

Specifying a Worksheet Data Range

1-2-3 does not permit you to type in data to be plotted on a graph. Do not confuse the process of plotting data points with that of typing descriptions, such as titles, a process that is illustrated later in this chapter.

To create a graph, you must specify data from the currently displayed spreadsheet as a data series in range form. To enter a data series from the main **G**raph menu, choose one of the options **X, A, B, C, D, E**, or **F**.

The paragraphs that follow explain each graph type. Where you see references to various symbols used as data points, refer to the table of graph symbols and shading in the graphics pages following this page.

With line graphs, you can enter as many as six data series after you have accessed separately the **G**raph menu choices **A B C D E F**. You do not have to start with **A**. The data points in every data series are marked by a unique symbol.

With bar graphs, you can enter as many as six data series after you have accessed separately the **G**raph menu choices **A B C D E F**. You do not have to start with **A**. Multiple data ranges appear on the graph from left to right in alphabetical order. Every data series displayed in black and white has unique shading. Every data series displayed in color is assigned one of three colors.

With XY graphs, to enter the data series being plotted as the independent variable, select **X** from the main **G**raph menu. Plot at least one dependent variable (you would usually select **A**). The unique symbols that mark the data points depend on which data series (**A-F**) is used with **X**.

With stacked-bar graphs, follow the bar graph instructions. In a stacked-bar graph, multiple data ranges appear from bottom to top in alphabetical order.

With pie graphs, enter only one data series by selecting **A** from the main **G**raph menu. (To shade and "explode" pieces of the pie, also select **B**.)

273

Specifying a Data Range

Specifying a Data Range

To create a graph, you must specify the cells in your worksheet containing the data you want to graph.

To enter a data series, choose one of the **X**, **A**, **B**, **C**, **D**, **E**, or **F** options.

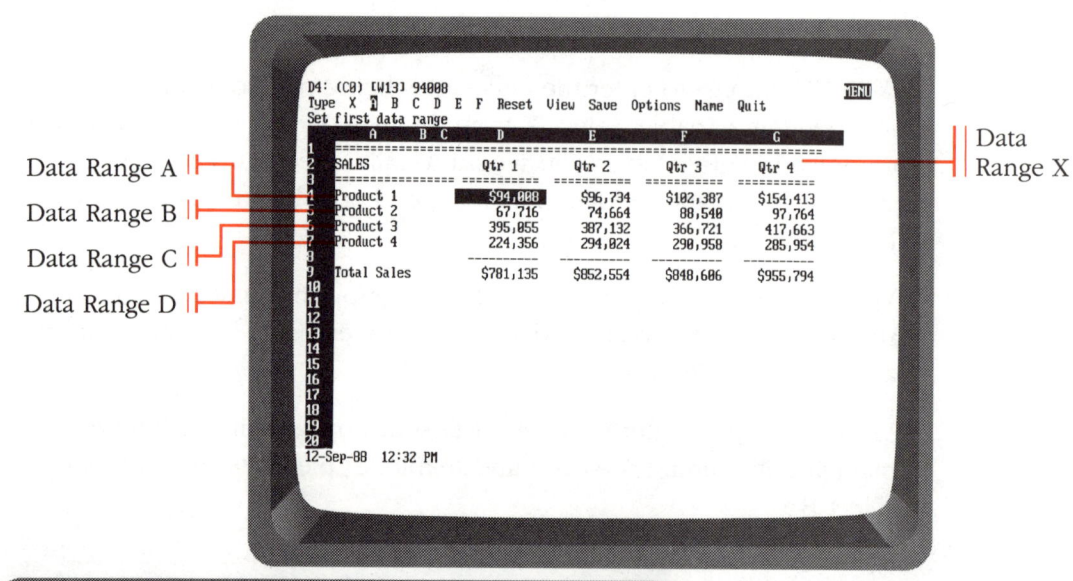

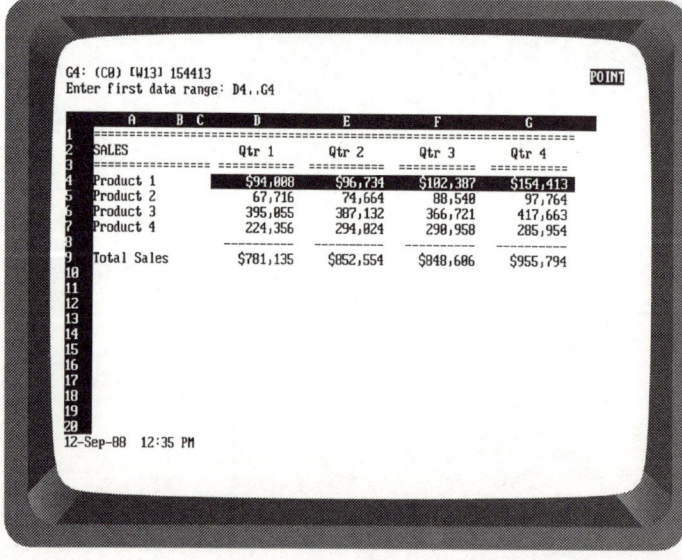

```
D4: (C0) [W13] 94000                                          MENU
Type X A B C D E F Reset View Save Options Name Quit
Set first data range
     A     B C     D           E           F           G
 1  ================================================================
 2  SALES             Qtr 1       Qtr 2       Qtr 3       Qtr 4
 3  ================================================================
 4  Product 1        $94,000     $96,734    $102,387    $154,413
 5  Product 2         67,716      74,664      88,540      97,764
 6  Product 3        395,055     387,132     366,721     417,663
 7  Product 4        224,356     294,024     290,958     285,954
 8                   -------     -------     -------     -------
 9  Total Sales     $781,135    $852,554    $848,606    $955,794
10
...
20
12-Sep-88  12:32 PM
```

Data Range A — Product 1 row
Data Range B — Product 2 row
Data Range C — Product 3 row
Data Range D — Product 4 row
Data Range X — Qtr 1–Qtr 4 header row

```
G4: (C0) [W13] 154413                                        POINT
Enter first data range: D4..G4
     A     B C     D           E           F           G
 1  ================================================================
 2  SALES             Qtr 1       Qtr 2       Qtr 3       Qtr 4
 3  ================================================================
 4  Product 1        $94,000     $96,734    $102,387    $154,413
 5  Product 2         67,716      74,664      88,540      97,764
 6  Product 3        395,055     387,132     366,721     417,663
 7  Product 4        224,356     294,024     290,958     285,954
 8                   -------     -------     -------     -------
 9  Total Sales     $781,135    $852,554    $848,606    $955,794
10
...
20
12-Sep-88  12:35 PM
```

When you select one of the **X-F** options, 1-2-3 will prompt you for the cell or range of cells containing the data you want to graph. You cannot enter data directly at the prompt.

| Introduction | An Overview of Creating a Graph | Selecting a Graph Type | **Specifying a Data Range** | Enhancing the Appearance of a Basic Graph | Preserving the Graph on Disk | Accessing and Exiting PrintGraph | Printing Graphs |

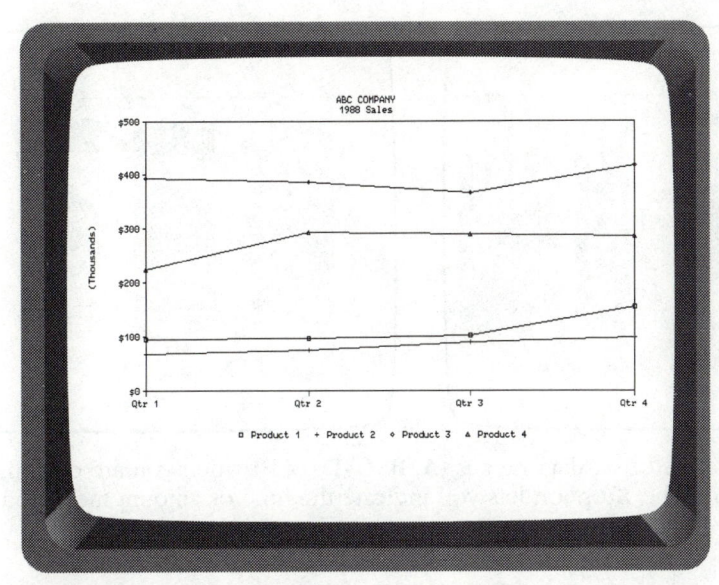

When you create a line graph, you can enter from one to six data ranges.

When creating a line graph, use the **X** option to plot the time or amount measured along the x-axis.

Data Range Symbols for Line Graphs

Data Range	Line Graph Symbols
A	□
B	◇
C	+
D	△
E	×
F	▽

Introduction

An Overview of 1-2-3

Getting Started

1-2-3 Basics

Creating a Worksheet

Printing Reports

Creating and Printing Graphs

Managing Data

Understanding Macros

Appendix

275

Specifying a Data Range

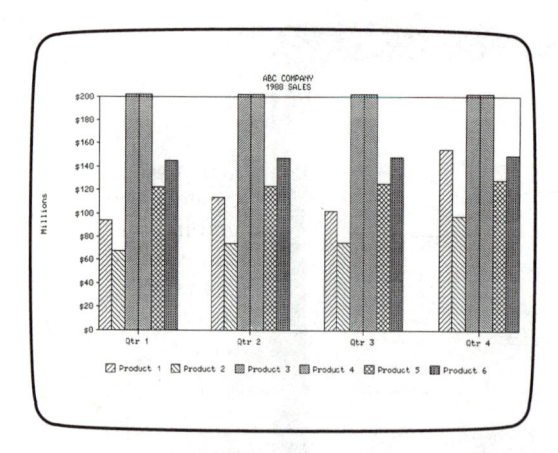

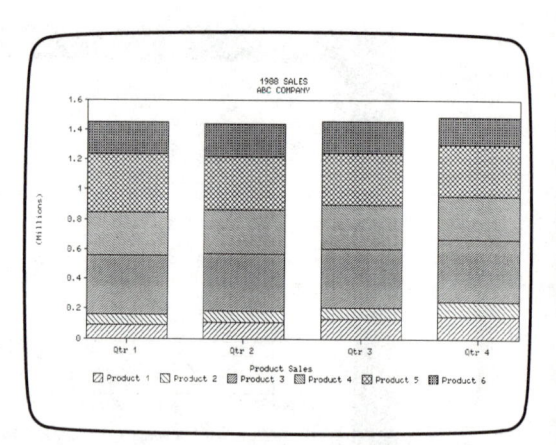

You can enter from one to six data ranges (**A**, **B**, **C**, **D**, **E**, **F**) when you are creating a bar or stacked-bar graph. The **X** option lets you indicate the time or amount measured along the x-axis.

Data Range Symbols for Bar Graphs

Data Range	Bar Graph Symbols	On-Screen Color
A	▨	Red
B	▨	Blue
C	▨	White
D	▨	Red
E	▨	Blue
F	▨	White

| Introduction | An Overview of Creating a Graph | Selecting a Graph Type | **Specifying a Data Range** | Enhancing the Appearance of a Basic Graph | Preserving the Graph on Disk | Accessing and Exiting PrintGraph | Printing Graphs |

To create an XY graph, you select **X** to graph the independent variable and select at least one **A-F** option to graph the dependent variable(s).

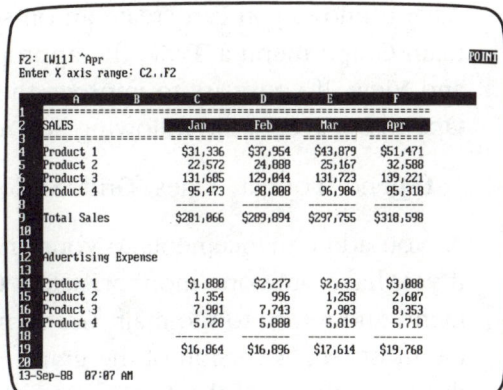

To create a pie graph, choose **X** to identify each piece of the pie. Then, enter only one data range by selecting **A**. Other than the **X** and **A** options, the only other option in the **X-F** selections you need for creating a pie graph is **B**. By selecting **B**, you can shade pieces and explode pieces of the graph.

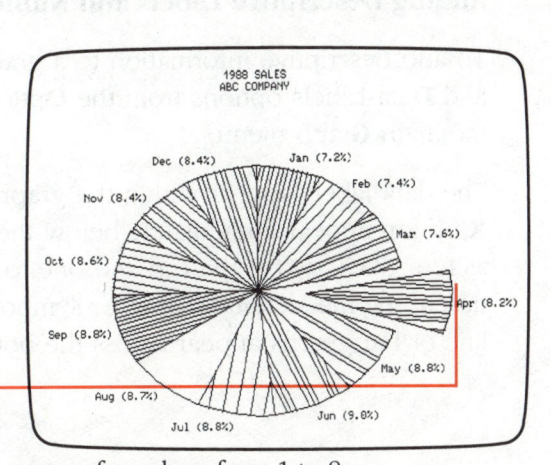

To shade the pieces of the pie graph, enter a range of numbers from 1 to 8 corresponding to data range **A** of the graph. To explode a piece of the pie, multiply one of the numbers between 1 and 8 by 100. Select **B** from the menu, and highlight the range of numbers.

Introduction

An Overview of 1-2-3

Getting Started

1-2-3 Basics

Creating a Worksheet

Printing Reports

Creating and Printing Graphs

Managing Data

Understanding Macros

Appendix

277

Enhancing the Appearance of a Basic Graph

As you know, you can create an on-screen graph by selecting from the main Graph menu a **T**ype, the appropriate data series (**X A B C D E F**), and **V**iew. If you want to improve the appearance of your graph, select **O**ptions to access the following submenu:

Legend **F**ormat **T**itles **G**rid **S**cale **C**olor **B**&W **D**ata-Labels **Q**uit

As you add enhancements to your graphs, check the results frequently. If you have only one monitor, select **Q**uit to leave the **G**raph **O**ptions menu and return to the main **G**raph menu. Then select **V**iew to check the most recent version of the graph. Press any key to exit the graph display and restore the **G**raph menu to the screen.

To view the current graph from the worksheet's READY mode, press the F10 (Graph) key, which instantly redraws the graph with any updated information. Whenever you are not in MENU mode, you can use the F10 (Graph) key to "toggle" between the worksheet and the graph.

Adding Descriptive Labels and Numbers

To add descriptive information to a graph, you use the **L**egend, **T**itles, and **D**ata-Labels options from the **O**ptions menu and the **X** option from the main **G**raph menu.

The data labels appear within the graph. Descriptions entered with the **X** option appear immediately below the x-axis. You can enter as many as four titles: two at the top and one to describe each axis. Legends describing the shading, color, or symbols assigned to data ranges in line or bar graphs appear across the bottom of those graphs.

Using the Titles Option

If you select **/G**raph **O**ptions **T**itles, the following options will be displayed in the control panel:

First   **S**econd   **X**-Axis   **Y**-Axis

You can enter one or two centered titles at the top of your graph. If you enter two titles, both will be the same size on-screen. But on the printed graph, the title you enter by selecting **F**irst will be twice the size of any other title specified. You can enter titles by typing a new description, by specifying a range name, or by referencing the cell location of a label or a number already in the worksheet. Although all titles appear on-screen in the same print style, when you print the graph you can select one font (such as italic) for the top title and another font for other titles and labels.

To edit a title, use the command sequence that you used for creating the title. The existing text, cell reference, or range name will appear in the control panel, ready for editing. If you want to eliminate a title, press Esc and then press Enter. The **X**-Axis and **Y**-Axis titles have no significance when you construct a pie graph.

Entering Labels within a Graph

After you have graphed a data series, you can enter values or labels to explain each point plotted on the graph. You do so by first selecting **O**ptions **D**ata-Labels from the main **G**raph menu and then specifying the data series (**A B C D E F**) to which the data labels apply. Instead of typing the labels (as you typed the titles), you must specify each data-label range by pointing to an existing range in the worksheet, providing cell coordinates, or specifying a previously determined range name.

Placing labels within a graph often produces less than desirable results. Particularly on line graphs, the first and last labels tend to overlap the

Enhancing the Appearance of a Basic Graph

graph's edges. To solve this problem, you can expand any data ranges defined for a line graph by including blank cells at each end of the ranges defined.

If you graph more than one data series, attach the data labels to the data series with the largest figures. Then select **A**bove to position the data labels above the data points plotted. To enter text or numbers as the plotted points, use the **C**enter option with line graphs that display **N**either lines nor symbols.

To edit either the range or position of the data label, use the same command sequence you used to create the data label. Edit the current range, or specify a different position.

To eliminate a data label, use one of two methods. If you remember both the data series (**A B C D E F**) and the position (**C**enter, **L**eft, and so on) that you specified when you entered the data label, you can follow the original setup sequence, overriding the existing data-label range by substituting any single blank cell in the worksheet. (You cannot eliminate the existing range by pressing Esc, as you did to eliminate an unwanted title.)

Entering Labels below the X-Axis

Instead of placing descriptive information within a graph, you may prefer to enter label information along the x-axis in bar, stacked-bar, and line graphs. For pie graphs, use the **X** option to label each slice. The main **G**raph menu's **X** option has two distinct functions. Use it to position labels below the x-axis in line, bar, and stacked-bar graphs, or to enter a data series in an XY graph. (XY graphs are discussed later in this chapter.) You can use the **X** option also to identify slices of a pie chart.

If the x-axis labels or numbers are longer than 9 or 10 characters, parts of the extreme right or left descriptions may not be displayed. To edit the x-axis labels, select **X** from the main **G**raph menu and then override the current range by typing or pointing to a different range.

The **/G**raph **R**eset **X** command will clear x-axis labels from your graph.

Using the Legend Option

Whenever a graph contains more than one set of data, you need to be able to distinguish between those sets. If you are using a color monitor and select **C**olor from the main **G**raph menu, 1-2-3 differentiates data series with color. If the main **G**raph menu's default option **B**&W (black and white) is in effect, data series in line graphs will be marked with special symbols; data series in bar-type graphs will be marked with unique patterns of crosshatches.

If you intend to print the graph on a black-and-white printer, even if you have a color monitor, choose **B**&W before saving the graph. A graph saved under the **C**olor option will print on a black-and-white printer as all black.

You might pick a data series (**A B C D E F**) because you want certain symbols or shadings or, more often, to avoid using certain combinations of symbols or shadings. For example, if you entered only two data items in a line graph and used data ranges **D** and **F**, you would have difficulty distinguishing between the two three-sided assigned symbols—one pointing up and the other pointing down. On the other hand, pairing the **A** range (widely spaced crosshatches) with the **D** range (narrowly spaced crosshatches extending in the opposite direction) on a bar graph produces a distinctly different display. To provide explanatory text for data that is represented by symbols or shadings, use legends below the x-axis.

If you want to edit a legend, use the same command sequence you used to create that legend. The existing text, cell reference, or range name will appear in the control panel, ready for you to edit. To eliminate a legend, press Esc and then press Enter. You cannot use the **L**egend option for pie graphs, which can have only one data series.

281

Enhancing the Appearance of a Basic Graph

Using the Titles Option

The **/G**raph **O**ptions **T**itles command lets you add titles at the top, below the x-axis, and to the left of the y-axis.

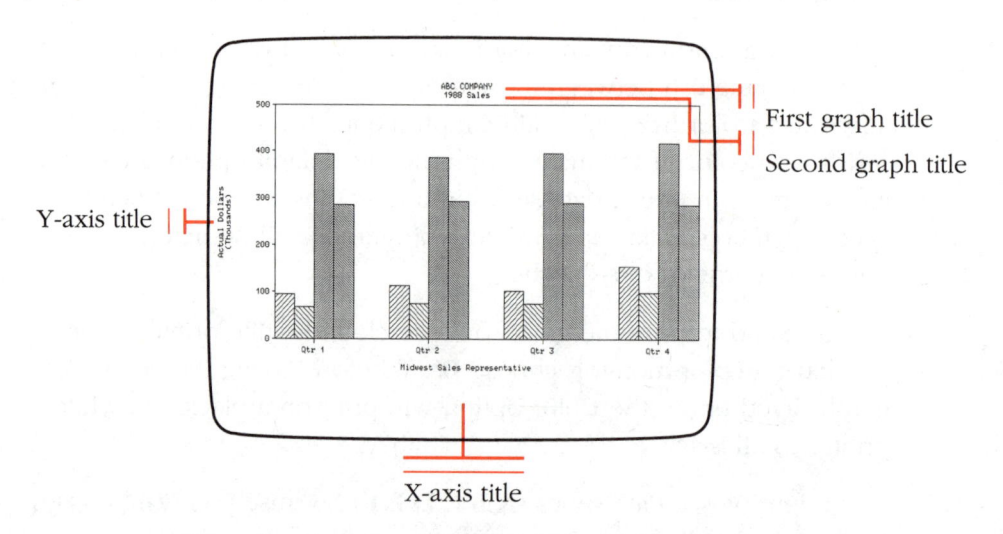

[Illustration of a graph screen with callouts labeling: First graph title, Second graph title, Y-axis title, X-axis title]

To add titles to your graph (after you have chosen the graph type and entered data ranges), complete the following steps:

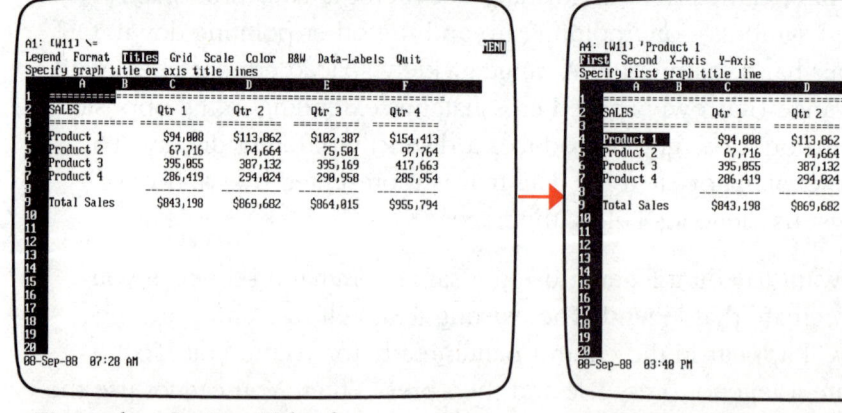

[Two screen images showing the /Graph menu with Titles selected, and the Titles submenu]

First, select **O**ptions **T**itles from the **/G**raph menu.

When the **T**itles menu appears, choose one of the four options.

| Introduction | An Overview of Creating a Graph | Selecting a Graph Type | Specifying a Data Range | **Enhancing the Appearance of a Basic Graph** | Preserving the Graph on Disk | Accessing and Exiting PrintGraph | Printing Graphs |

To display and print a title on the top line of your graph, select **F**irst, and enter the title at the prompt.

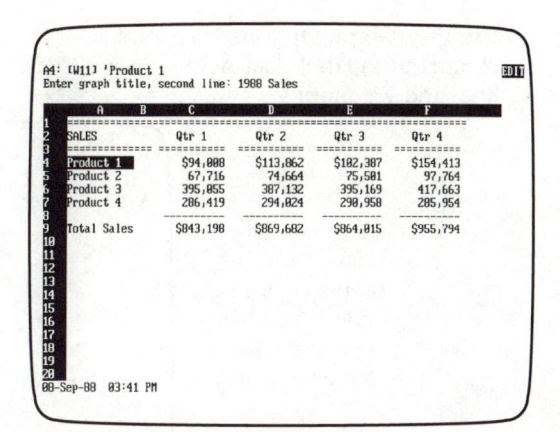

To display and print a title on the second line of your graph, select **S**econd, and enter the title at the prompt.

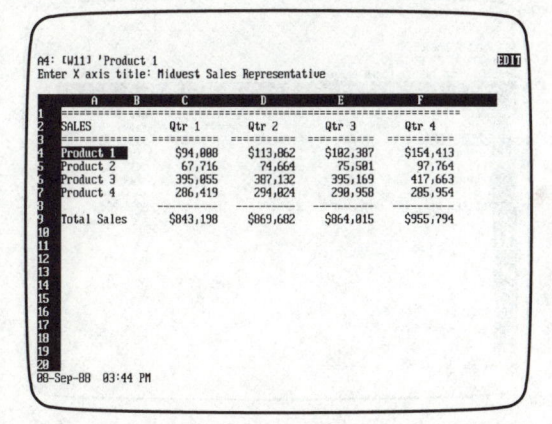

To display and print a title below the x-axis, select **X**-Axis, and enter the title at the prompt.

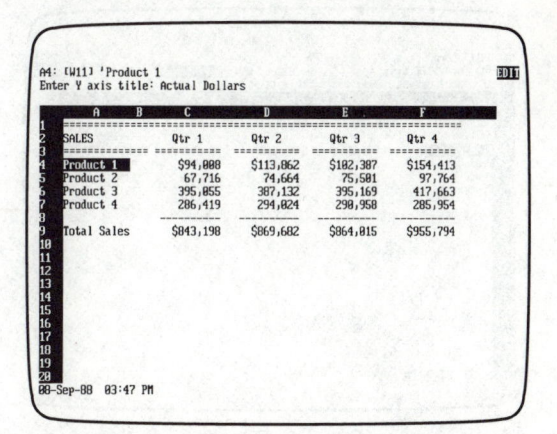

To display and print a title to the left of the y-axis, select **Y**-Axis, and enter the title at the prompt.

283

Enhancing the Appearance of a Basic Graph

Entering Labels within a Graph

Use the **/G**raph **O**ptions **D**ata-Labels command to label data points on your bar, line, and XY graphs.

You can label, for example, points on a line graph with the specific values for each point.

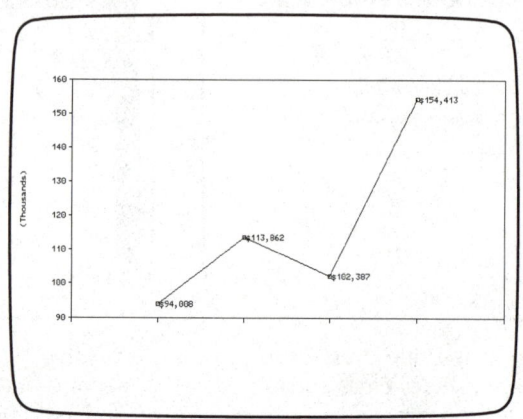

Using the **/G**raph **O**ptions **D**ata-Labels Command

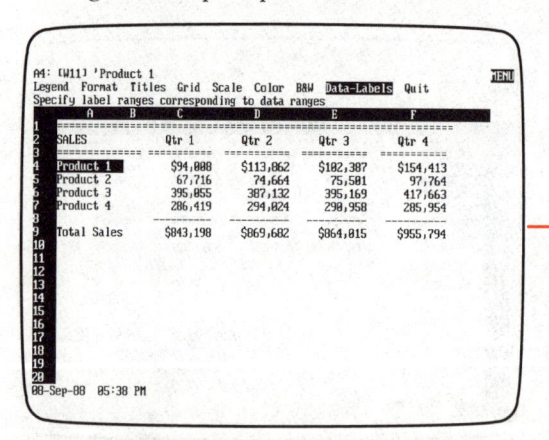

First, choose **O**ptions **D**ata-Labels from the **/G**raph menu.

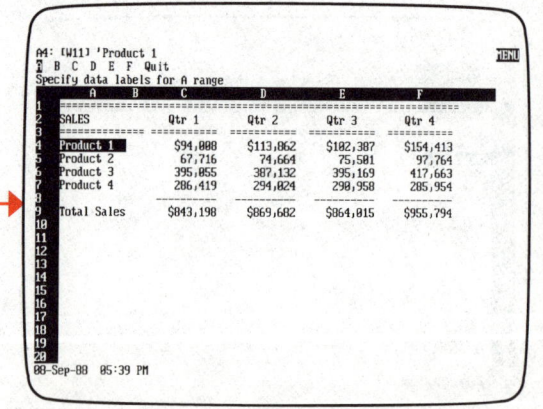

Second, select the data range that you want to label. In the line graph pictured above, for example, only one data range (**A**) is graphed. To assign labels to this range, choose **A**.

284

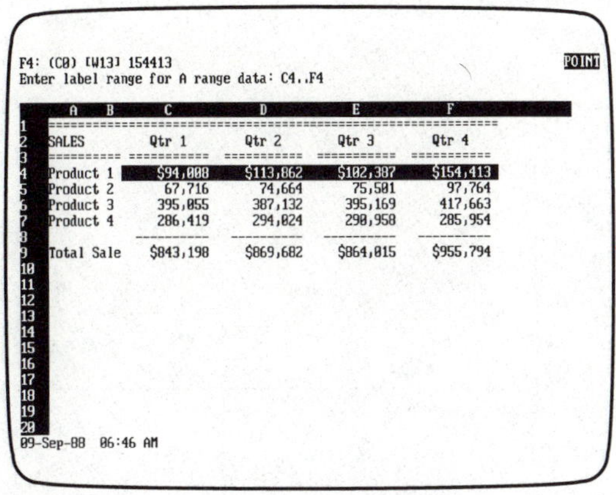

| Introduction | An Overview of Creating a Graph | Selecting a Graph Type | Specifying a Data Range | **Enhancing the Appearance of a Basic Graph** | Preserving the Graph on Disk | Accessing and Exiting PrintGraph | Printing Graphs |

Enter the range containing the text or values you want to use as labels for your graph. To label data points in the sales graph pictured on the previous page, highlight the range containing the sales figures.

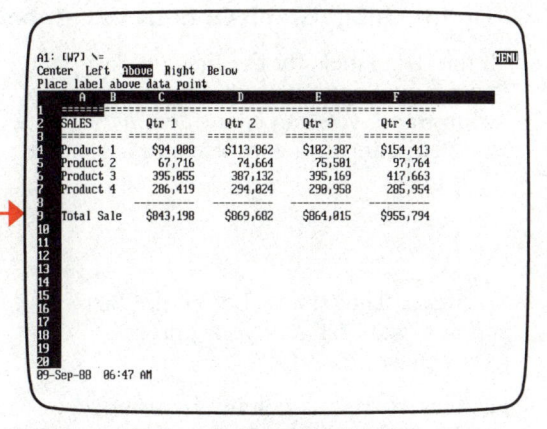

After you have entered the range containing labels, you must indicate the location of the data labels. You may need to test two or more positions for data labels to determine which position is best for your graph.

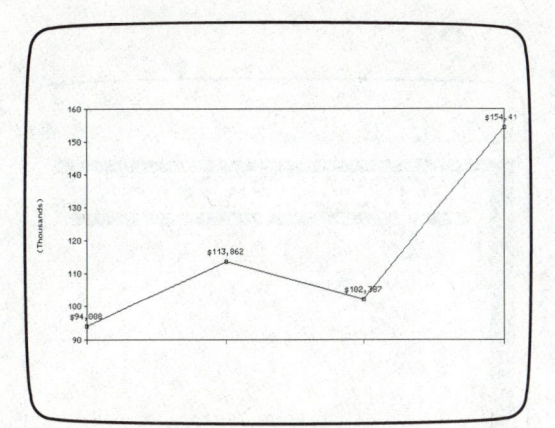

This graph shows the result of choosing the **A**bove option for the location of data labels.

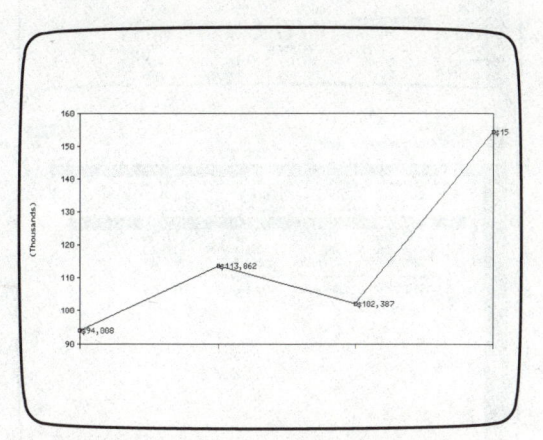

This graph shows the result of choosing the **R**ight option for the location of data labels. You can solve the problem of having data labels overlap the right and left borders of your graph by using the technique described on the next page.

Introduction

An Overview of 1-2-3

Getting Started

1-2-3 Basics

Creating a Worksheet

Printing Reports

Creating and Printing Graphs

Managing Data

Understanding Macros

Appendix

285

Enhancing the Appearance of a Basic Graph

Tip for Using /Graph Options Data-Labels

If the data labels for the first and last data points overlap the left and right borders of your graph, you can create "empty" cells at the beginning and end of your data range.

To create blank spaces before the first and last data points of your graph, follow these steps.

First, insert a blank column by using the **/W**orksheet **I**nsert **C**olumn command at the beginning and end of your data range.

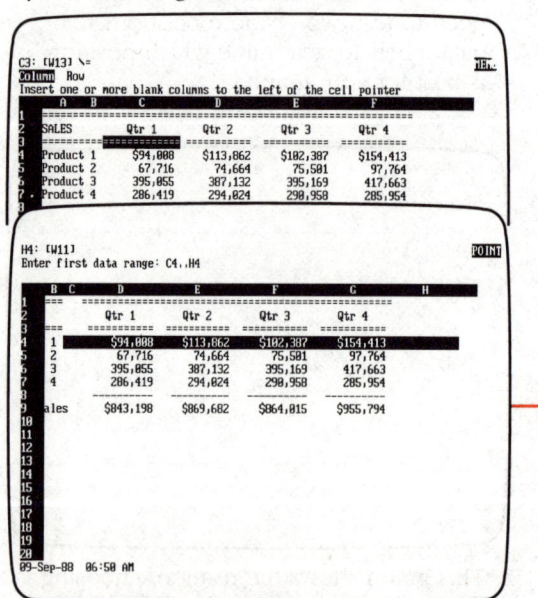

Second, re-enter all data ranges for your graph using the **/G**raph **X-F** options, making sure that the ranges include the blank columns.

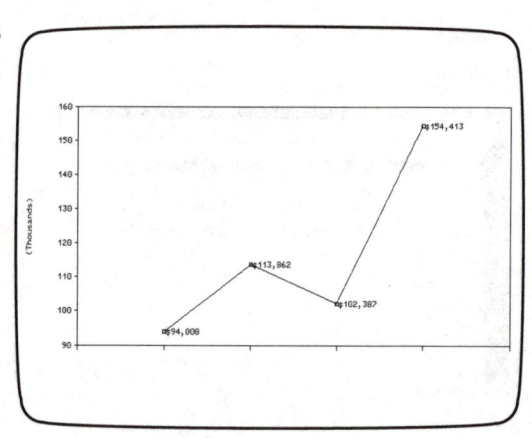

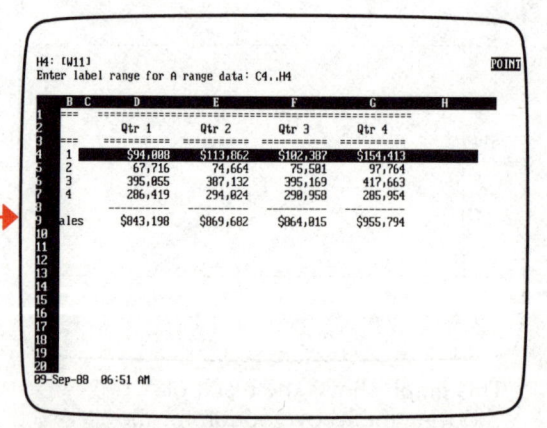

Finally, re-enter the ranges for data labels by using the **/G**raph **O**ptions **D**ata-Labels command. Again, make sure your ranges include the blank columns.

| Introduction | An Overview of Creating a Graph | Selecting a Graph Type | Specifying a Data Range | **Enhancing the Appearance of a Basic Graph** | Preserving the Graph on Disk | Accessing and Exiting PrintGraph | Printing Graphs |

Entering Labels Below the X-Axis and on Pie Graphs

The **X** option listed in the **/G**raph main menu lets you label the x-axis points for bar, stacked-bar, and line graphs.

You should also use the **X** option to label the slices of a pie graph.

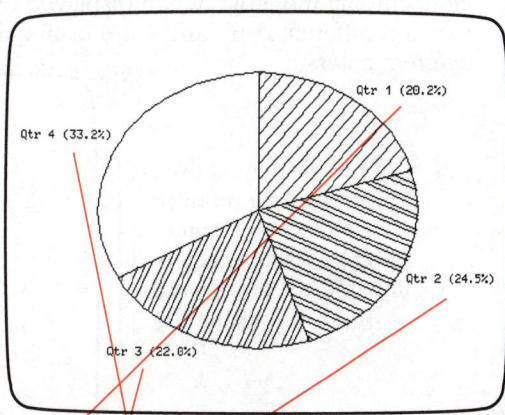

To display labels below the x-axis, select **/G**raph **X**, and enter the range containing the values or text you want to use as x-axis labels.

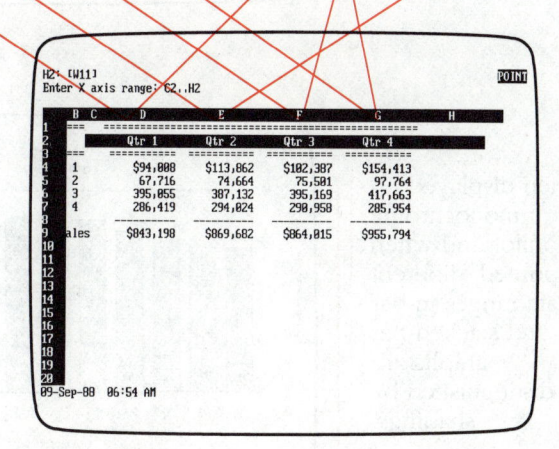

Note: For pie graphs, do not enter empty cells for the data range and for the labels identifying each part of the graph.

Introduction

An Overview of 1-2-3

Getting Started

1-2-3 Basics

Creating a Worksheet

Printing Reports

Creating and Printing Graphs

Managing Data

Understanding Macros

Appendix

287

Enhancing the Appearance of a Basic Graph

Using the Legend Option

When displaying graphs on your computer monitor, 1-2-3 identifies different data ranges depending on whether you are using (and have installed 1-2-3 for) a color or monochrome monitor. When displayed on a color monitor, different data ranges are distinguished by different colors.

When displayed on a monochrome monitor and when printed, different data ranges in line and XY graphs are distinguished by symbols.

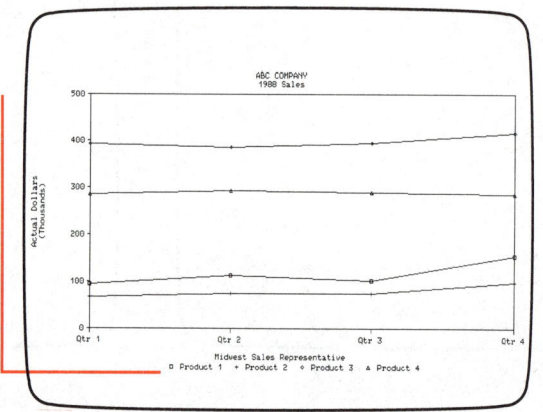

When displayed on a monochrome monitor and when printed, different data ranges in bar and stacked-bar graphs are distinguished by shadings.

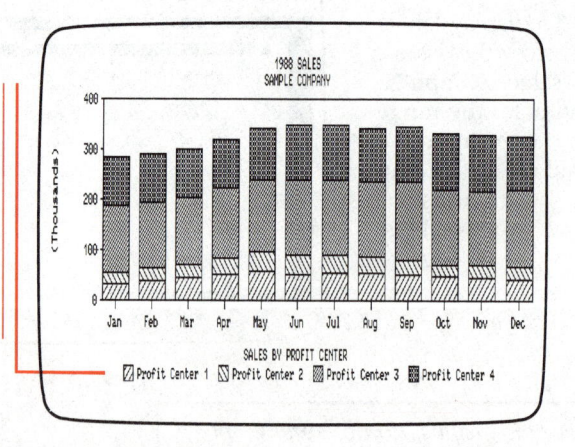

The **/G**raph **O**ptions **L**egend command lets you display a legend below the x-axis indicating the symbols or shading for your data ranges.

288

To display symbol or shading legends for your graph, follow these steps:

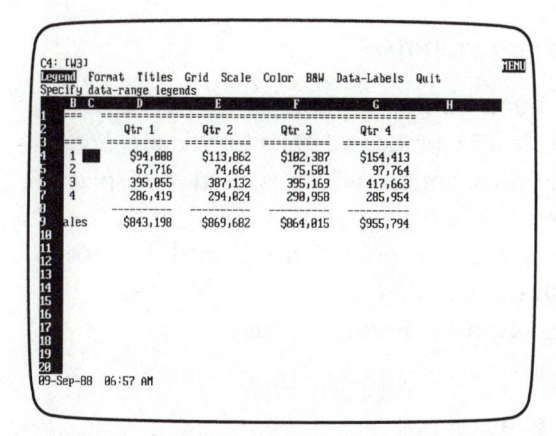

First, select **/G**raph **O**ptions **L**egend.

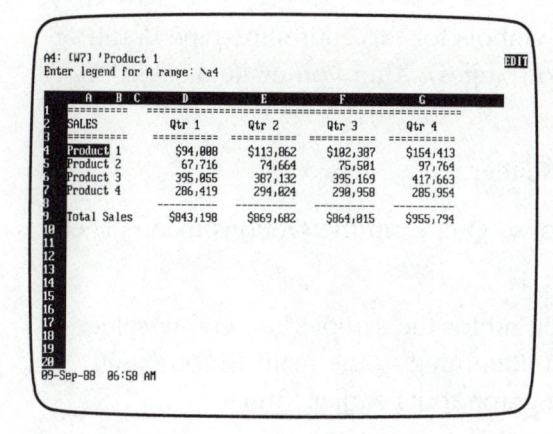

Second, enter the cell address containing the label for identifying each data range. When the `Enter legend for (A-F) range:` prompt appears, type `\` and then type the cell address containing the label.

Repeat the first and second steps for each data range.

After you have entered all legends and then view the graph, the legends will appear below the x-axis.

289

Enhancing the Appearance of a Basic Graph

All the previously described enhancements involve adding label or number descriptions to the basic minimal graph. You can also change any of the additional default graph display items.

Specifying Connecting Lines or Symbols

A few choices on the Options menu do not apply to all graphs. For example, you've learned that **T**itles, **L**egend, and **D**ata-Labels are not applicable to pie graphs. The **F**ormat option, which is used to display connecting lines and symbols on a line-type graph, is appropriate for only two types of graphs: Line and XY (a form of line graph). Do not confuse this **F**ormat option with the **O**ptions **S**cale **X**- (or **Y**-) Axis **F**ormat option. Selecting /**G**raph **O**ptions **F**ormat produces this submenu:

    Graph **A** **B** **C** **D** **E** **F** **Q**uit

You can control the lines and symbols for the entire line-type graph or for only a specific data range (or ranges). After you make a selection, this final submenu appears:

    Lines **S**ymbols **B**oth **N**either

After you make a selection, choose **Q**uit from the **O**ptions menu. Then select **V**iew to check the graph.

To restore the default format setting for the sample line graph, select /**G**raph **O**ptions **F**ormat **A** **B**oth. Returning to the main **G**raph menu and selecting **V**iew restores the graph to its earlier form.

Note: You cannot use the **F**ormat option from the **G**raph **O**ptions menu for bar, stacked-bar, or pie graphs.

Setting a Background Grid

Ordinarily, you'll use the default (clear) background for your graphs. But you'll have times when you'll want to impose a grid on a graph so that the data-point amounts are easier to read. Selecting /**G**raph **O**ptions **G**rid produces this menu:

    Horizontal   **V**ertical   **B**oth   **C**lear

The first option creates a series of horizontal lines across the graph, spaced according to the tick marks on the y-axis. The second option creates a series of vertical lines across the graph, spaced according to the tick marks on the x-axis. The third option causes both horizontal and vertical lines to appear, and the fourth clears all grid lines from the graph.

To add horizontal lines to the sample graph, select /**G**raph **O**ptions **G**rid **H**orizontal. Then select **Q**uit from the **O**ptions menu and press **V**iew.

Experiment with different grids, repeating the command sequence and specifying other options. Whenever you want to eliminate a grid display, select /**G**raph **O**ptions **G**rid **C**lear.

Note: You cannot use the **G**rid option from the **G**raph **O**ptions menu for a pie graph.

Enhancing the Appearance of a Basic Graph

Specifying Connecting Lines or Symbols

The **/G**raph **O**ptions **F**ormat command lets you modify line and XY graphs so that they display and print in one of four formats:

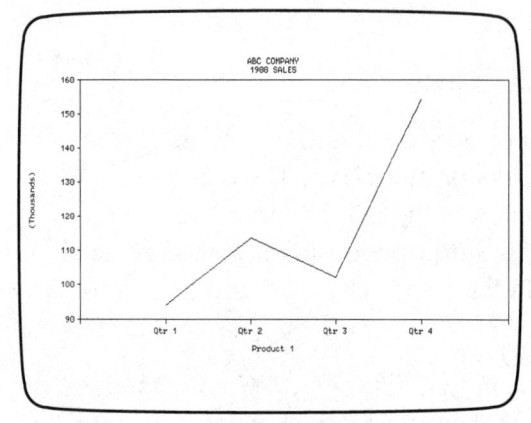

With lines connecting data points

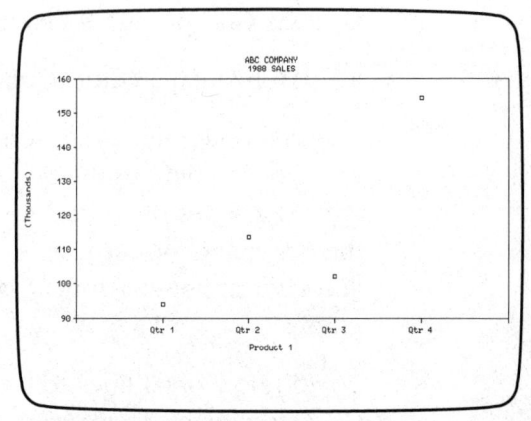

With symbols alone marking data points

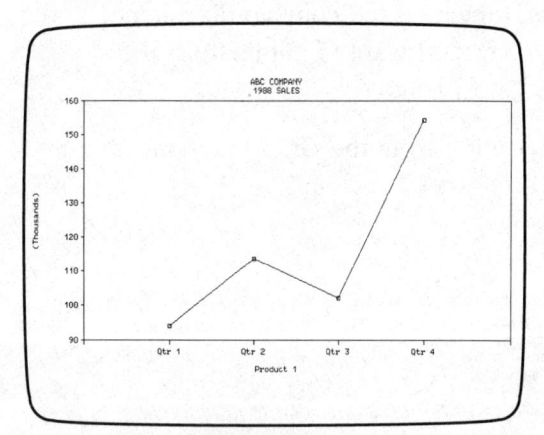

With both lines and symbols

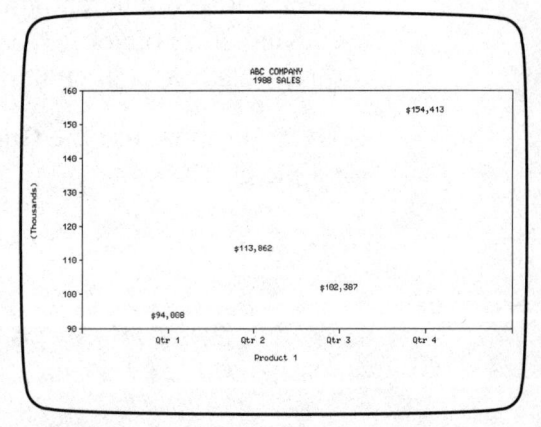

With neither lines nor symbols. (This option is useful when you want to mark data points with data labels alone.)

292

Specifying Lines and Symbols with the /Graph Options Format Command

To specify connecting lines or symbols for line and XY graphs,

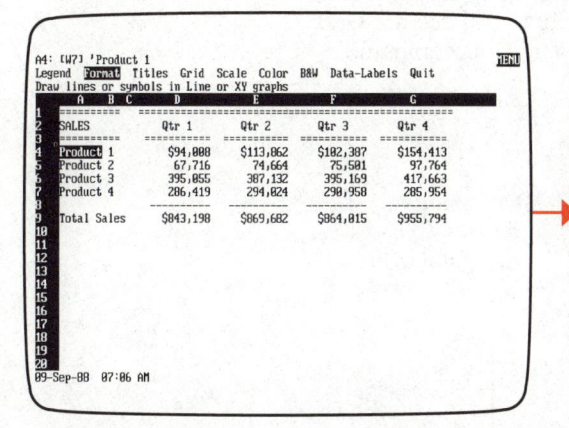

First, select **O**ptions and then **F**ormat from the **/G**raph menu.

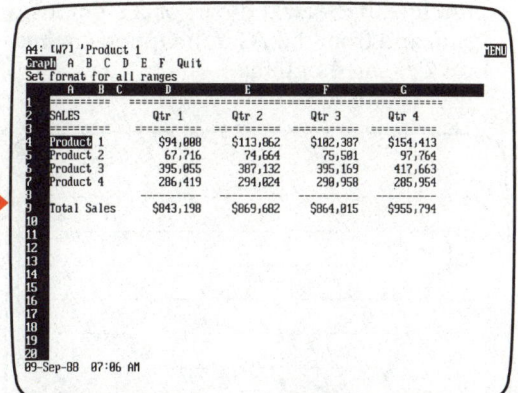

Second, after you select **F**ormat, 1-2-3 will display seven choices for drawing lines and/or symbols. You can assign lines and/or symbols to the whole graph or assign lines and/or symbols to individual data ranges (**A-F**).

Third, choose **L**ines if you want data points connected by lines alone, choose **S**ymbols for symbols alone, choose **B**oth for both lines and symbols, and choose **N**either if you do not want lines or symbols, but only data labels.

Enhancing the Appearance of a Basic Graph

Setting a Background Grid

When 1-2-3 displays a line, bar, stacked-bar, or XY graph, data ranges are displayed without background grids. To display and print line, bar, stacked-bar, or XY graphs wtih a grid, use the **G**rid command from the **/G**raph **O**ptions menu. The **G**rid command provides three options:

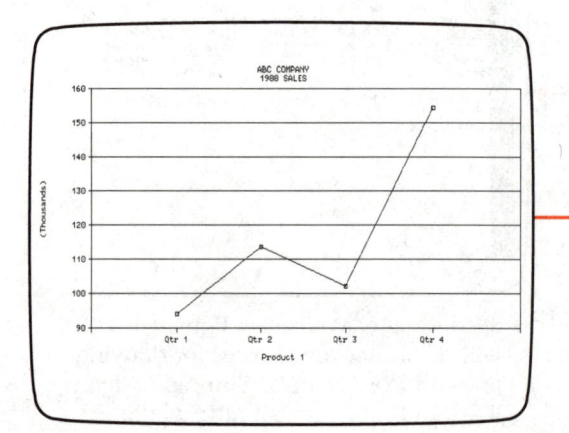

Displaying a graph with a horizontal grid

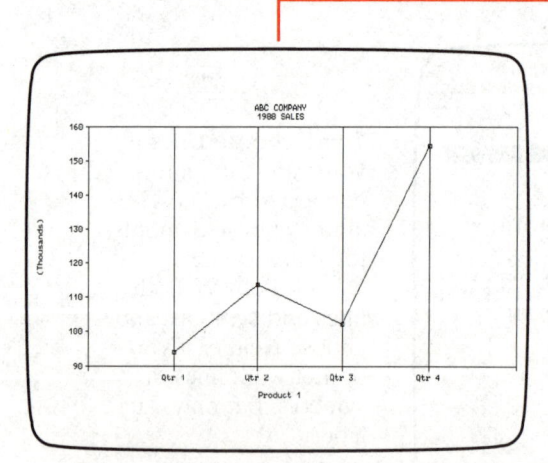

Displaying a graph with a vertical grid

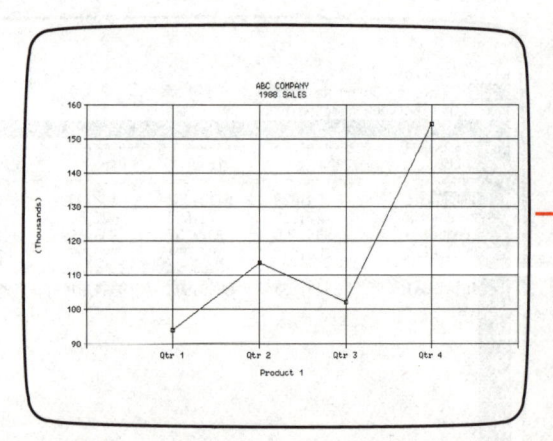

Displaying a graph with both horizontal and vertical lines

Using the /Graph Options Grid Command

To add a grid to your line, bar, stacked-bar, or XY graphs, follow these two steps:

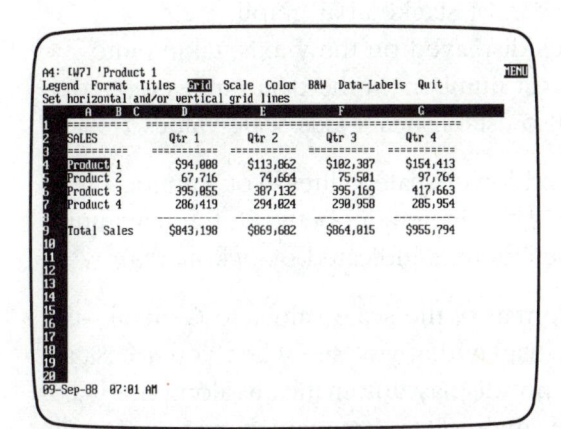

First, select **G**rid from the **/G**raph **O**ptions menu.

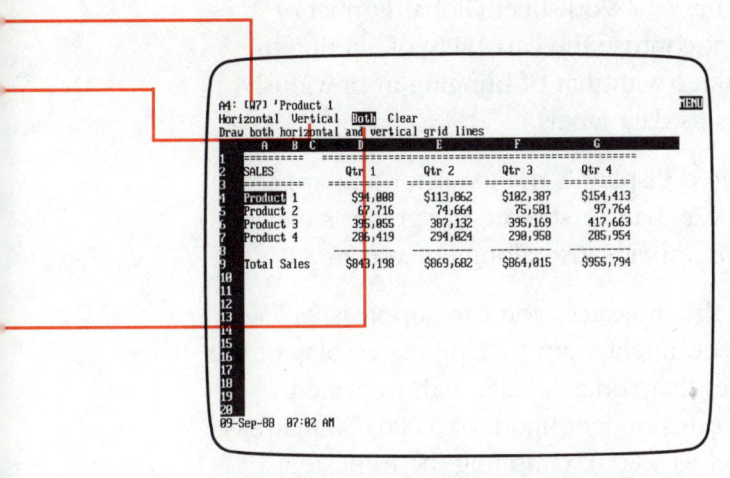

Second, choose the type of grid you want displayed: **H**orizontal, **V**ertical, or **B**oth.

The **C**lear option will erase the grid setting for a particular graph. You can then either display the graph without a grid or enter a new grid setting.

Enhancing the Appearance of a Basic Graph

Changing Axis Scale Settings

You can use the **S**cale option to alter three distinct default settings associated with the values displayed along a graph's x- and y-axes.

When you create a line, XY, bar, or stacked-bar graph, 1-2-3 automatically sets scale values displayed on the y-axis, taking into account the smallest and largest numbers in the data ranges plotted. (For XY graphs only, 1-2-3 also establishes x-axis scale values.)

You can change the upper and lower scale values. You cannot, however, determine the size of the increment between the maximum and minimum values (this increment is indicated by tick marks).

1-2-3 automatically sets the format of the scale values to **G**eneral—the same default global numeric display that you see when you access a blank worksheet. 1-2-3 does not display automatically along the y-axis dollar signs, commas, and decimal points. You can change the format to any of the styles available under **/W**orksheet **G**lobal **F**ormat or **/R**ange **F**ormat menus. Do not confuse the capability of altering the default format of the scale values with that of bringing in previously formatted worksheet numbers as data labels.

The third automatic scale-related display is the indicator that appears along the y-axis when a line, XY, bar, or stacked-bar graph is created. (On an XY graph, an indicator appears also along the x-axis.)

Although you cannot change the indicator, you can suppress its display. To understand why you might want to suppress display of the indicator, imagine a worksheet that contains data with truncated trailing zeros (for example, a sales budget figure of 5,000,000 that has been entered in the worksheet as 5,000). Graphing the truncated figures will produce the y-axis indicator (`Thousands`), but you need (`Millions`). You can suppress display of the indicator and type an appropriate indicator as part of the y-axis title. Select **/G**raph **O**ptions **S**cale to produce this menu:

    Y Scale   **X** Scale   **S**kip

To initiate changes in the upper or lower scale values, changes in the format of the scale values, or suppression of the scale indicator, select either of the first two options. (The **S**cale **S**kip command sequence is discussed in the following section.) Selecting either **Y** Scale or **X** Scale produces the following submenu:

Automatic **M**anual **L**ower **U**pper **F**ormat **I**ndicator **Q**uit

The **A**utomatic and **M**anual options work as a set. To specify maximum (**U**pper) or minimum (**L**ower) axis values, select **M**anual; select **A**utomatic to restore control to 1-2-3. When you select **M**anual, the entire submenu remains on the screen. Simply select **U**pper or **L**ower and respond to the prompt for a new figure.

If you elect to establish manual limits, remember two basic rules: (1) you must specify both upper and lower settings, and (2) the upper limit must be larger than the lower limit.

You can use negative figures for scale values in line, XY, and bar graphs, but not in stacked-bar or pie graphs.

Choose **/G**raph **O**ptions **S**cale **X** Scale only when the graph type is XY. Choose **Y** Scale for line, XY, bar, and stacked-bar graph types. The **F**ormat, **I**ndicator, and **M**anual scale capabilities are not applicable to pie graphs.

Spacing the Display of X-Axis Labels

You've seen how to use the first two options on the **/G**raph **O**ptions menu. The **S**kip option determines the spacing of displayed labels. The default setting of 1 causes every label to display. If you set the skip factor to 3, every third label will be displayed.

If the labels are so long that they crowd together or overlap, use this option to improve the display. Technically, you can set a skip factor of 1 to 8,192, but you will seldom need to set the factor higher than 4.

Enhancing the Appearance of a Basic Graph

Changing Axis Scale and Label Settings

The **S**cale command from the **/G**raph **O**ptions menu lets you make four types of changes to your line, XY, bar, or stacked-bar graphs. **/G**raph **O**ptions **S**cale lets you

Change the y-axis scale on line, bar, and stacked-bar graphs.

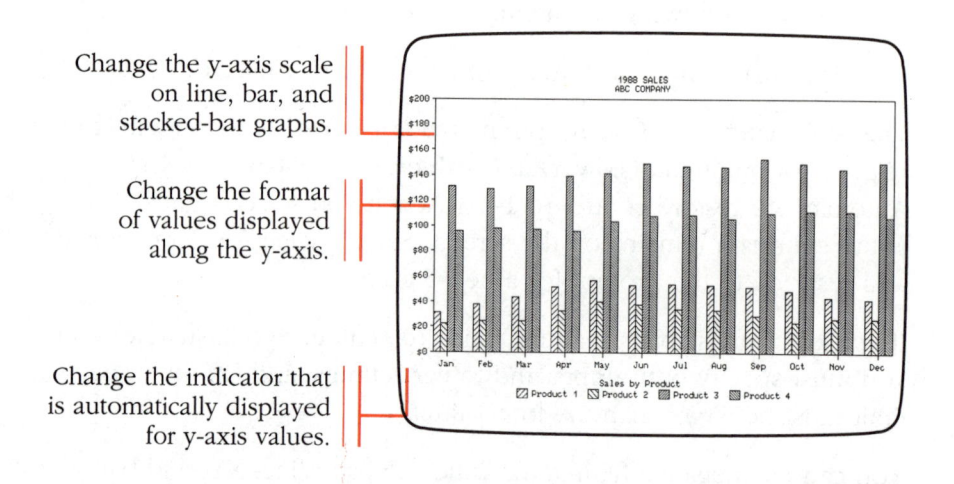

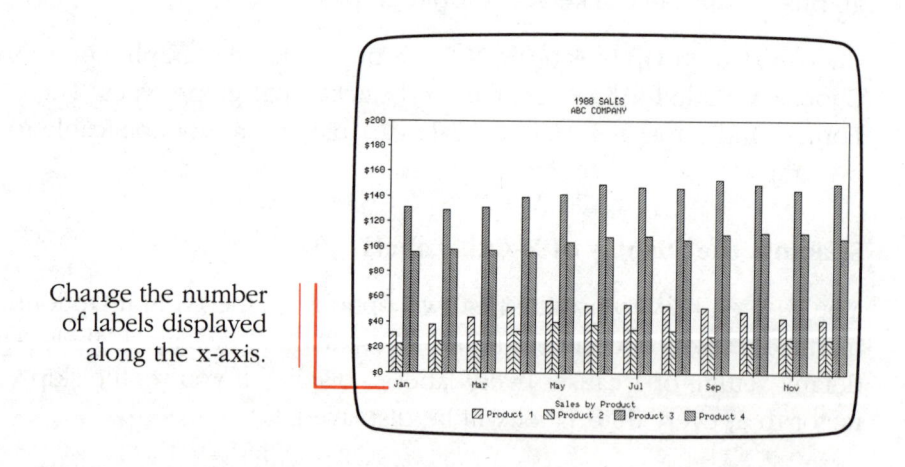

Change the format of values displayed along the y-axis.

Change the indicator that is automatically displayed for y-axis values.

Change the number of labels displayed along the x-axis.

Changing the Scale and Format

To change the scale and format of values displayed along the y-axis, follow these steps:

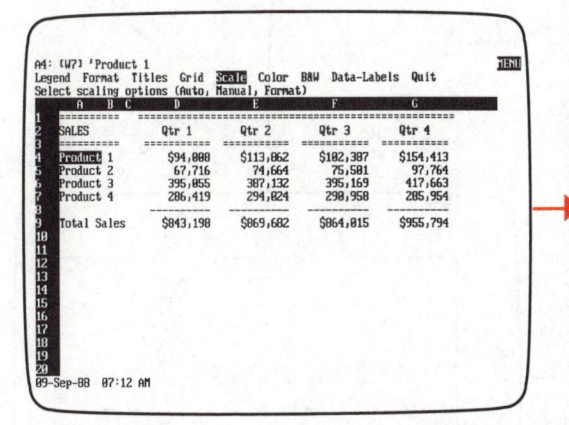

First, select **S**cale from the **/G**raph **O**ptions menu.

Second, select the **Y** Scale option if you want to change the y-axis scale on a bar, stacked-bar, or line graph. Choose the **X** Scale option to change the x-axis scale on XY graphs.

Third, choose **M**anual to change from 1-2-3's automatic scaling to your own scaling.

Fourth, choose **L**ower to assign the lower value of the scale.

Fifth, choose **U**pper to assign the upper value of the scale.

Optional: Select **F**ormat if you want to change the display format of values along the y-axis (or x-axis for XY graphs).

When you choose **F**ormat, 1-2-3 displays the same options that are displayed when you use **/R**ange Format.

299

Enhancing the Appearance of a Basic Graph

Suppressing the Y-Axis or X-Axis Indicators

1-2-3 automatically displays a value indicator for y-axis values on line, bar, and stacked-bar graphs.

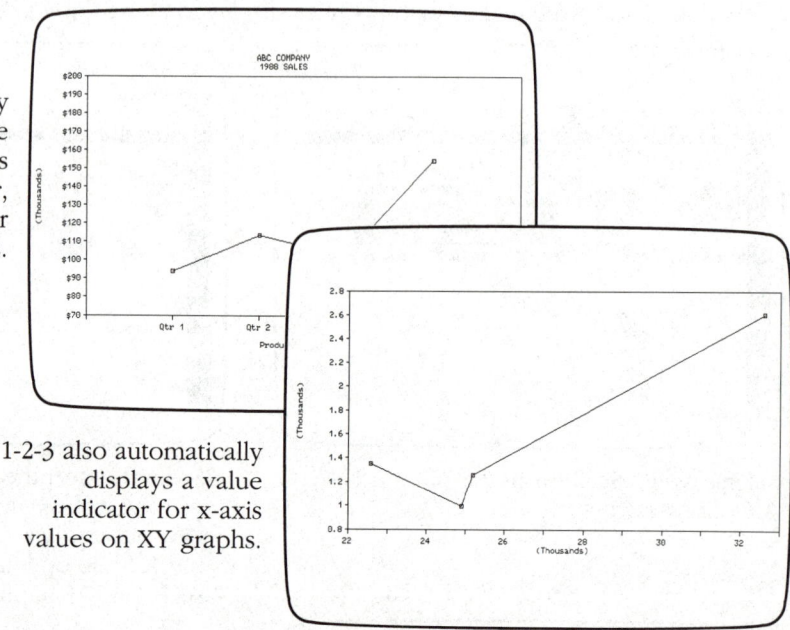

1-2-3 also automatically displays a value indicator for x-axis values on XY graphs.

To suppress either type of indicator, follow these steps:

Choose **S**cale, then select **Y** Scale or **X** Scale, and finally choose **I**ndicator.

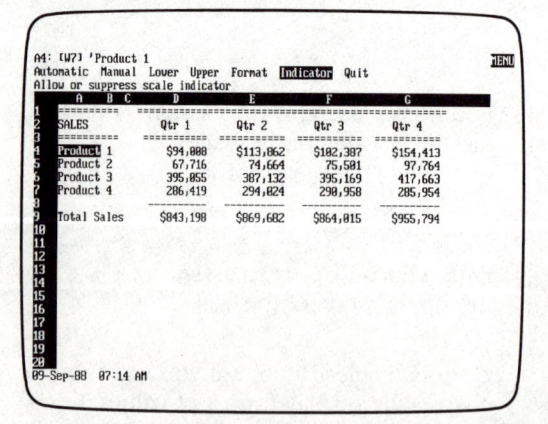

Select **N**o to suppress the indicator.

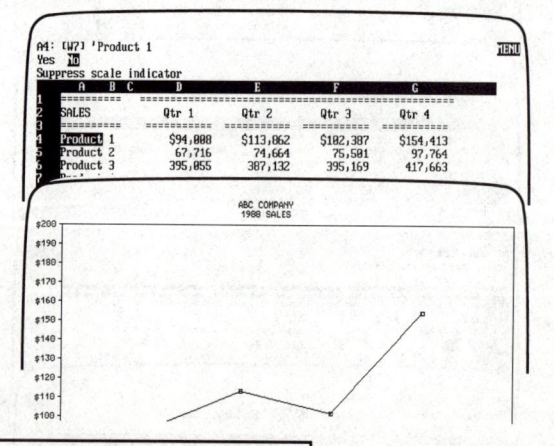

> Note: After suppressing the y-axis or x-axis indicator, you can supply your own indicator by using the /**G**raph **O**ptions **T**itles command.

300

Spacing the Display of X-Axis Labels

Use the **/G**raph **O**ptions **S**cale **S**kip command to control the number of labels displayed along the x-axis. This command, for example, lets you change the display of x-axis labels from displaying every month to displaying every other month.

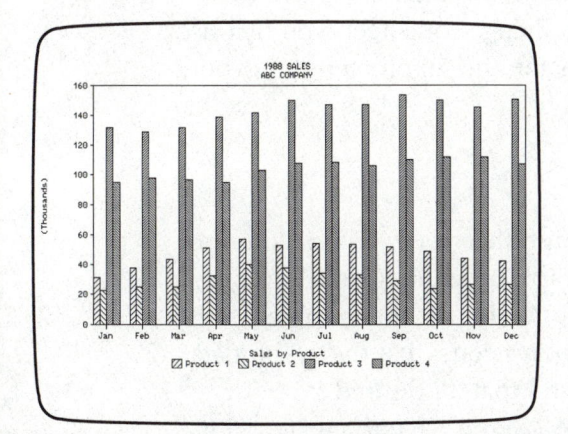

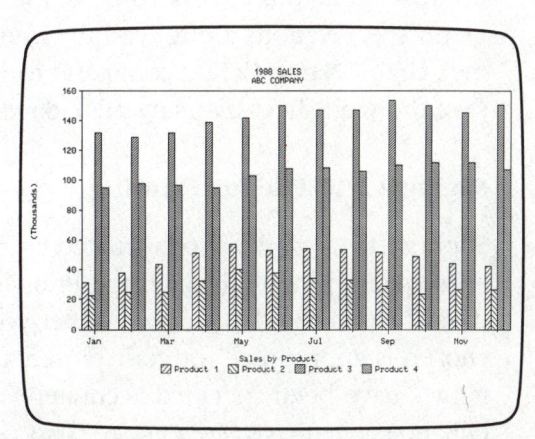

When you select **/G**raph **O**ptions **S**cale **S**kip, 1-2-3 will prompt you to enter a skip factor from 1 to 8192.

Preserving the Graph on Disk

Although using 1-2-3 to construct a graph from existing data in a spreadsheet is easy, having to rebuild the graph whenever you want to print or display it on-screen would be tedious.

To create a disk file (with the file extension .PIC) that can be used only to print the graph, you use the /Graph Save command. To save the graph specifications along with the underlying worksheet, you first use the /Graph Name Create command to name the graph, and then you save the worksheet by using /File Save.

Saving a .PIC File for Printing

Suppose that you have constructed a graph that you want to store for subsequent printing through the PrintGraph program. (PrintGraph is discussed later in this chapter.) After you verify that the graph type chosen is appropriate for your presentation needs, that the graph data ranges have been specified accurately, and that all desired enhancements have been added, choose /Graph Save to create a .PIC file on disk. 1-2-3 prompts you for a file name and displays (in menu form across the top of the screen) a list of the .PIC files in the current directory.

You can either use the arrow keys to highlight an existing name or type a name that is as many as eight characters long. (1-2-3 will automatically add the extension.) If a .PIC file by the same name already exists in the current directory, you'll see a Cancel/Replace menu similar to that which appears when you try to save a worksheet file under an existing name. To overwrite the contents of the existing .PIC file, select Replace. To abort storage of the current graph as a .PIC file, select Cancel.

Remember two points. First, /Graph Save stores only an image of the current graph, locking in all data and enhancements, for the sole purpose of printing it with the PrintGraph program. When it is time to print, you cannot access this print file to make changes such as adding a label or editing an underlying worksheet figure. Second, you cannot recall the graph to screen unless you have named the graph and saved the worksheet (unless the graph is the last active graph on the current worksheet).

Creating Graph Specifications for Reuse

If you want to be able to view on-screen a graph that you created in an earlier graphing session, you must have given the graph a name when you originally constructed the graph (and you must have saved the worksheet, unless the same worksheet is still active). To name a graph, you issue the **/G**raph **N**ame command to access the following menu:

    Use   **C**reate   **D**elete   **R**eset

Only one graph at a time can be the current graph. If you want to save a graph that you have just completed (for subsequent recall to the screen) as well as build a new graph, you must first issue a **/G**raph **N**ame **C**reate command. The only way to store a graph for later screen display is to issue this command, which instructs 1-2-3 to remember the specifications used to define the current graph. If you don't name a graph and subsequently either reset the graph or change the specifications, you cannot restore the original graph without having to rebuild it.

When 1-2-3 prompts you for a graph name, provide a name that is up to 15 characters long. To recall any named graphs from within the active spreadsheet, select **/G**raph **N**ame **U**se.

To delete a single named graph, issue the **/G**raph **N**ame **D**elete command. Again, 1-2-3 will list all the graph names stored in the current worksheet. You can select the graph you want to delete by either typing the appropriate name or pointing to the name on the list.

303

Preserving the Graph on Disk

Using /Graph Save

/Graph **S**ave stores only an image of the current graph, locking in all data and enhancements, for the sole purpose of printing it with the PrintGraph program.

To use **/G**raph **S**ave, follow these steps:

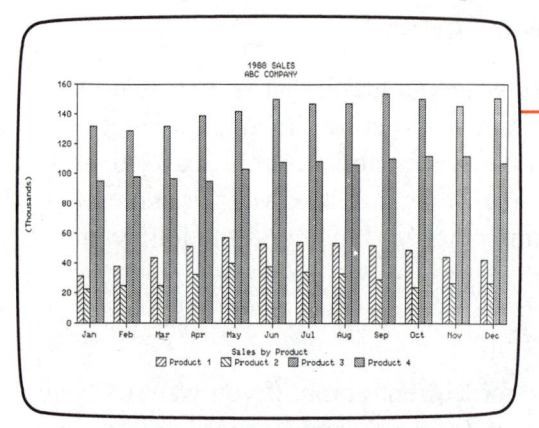

First, view your graph by using **/G**raph **V**iew or by pressing [F10] to make sure the graph is drawn as you want it.

Second, select **/G**raph **S**ave, and then enter a name when the `Enter save file name:` prompt appears. 1-2-3 will add the PIC extension for you.

After you have saved the graph settings for printing, you can print the graph with 1-2-3's PrintGraph program.

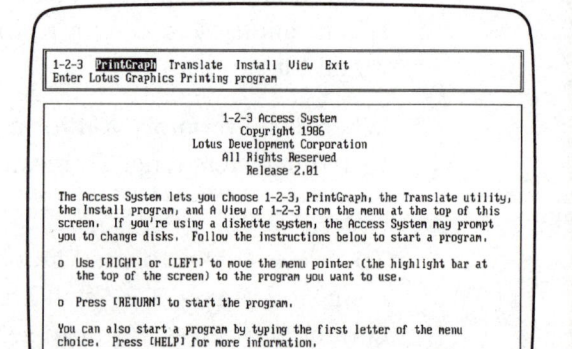

304

Using /Graph Name

Use **/G**raph **N**ame when you want to save the graph along with the underlying worksheet. **/G**raph **N**ame lets you store the settings for each graph you create so that you can access and change the graph in the future.

To save the graph with the underlying worksheet, first name the graph with **/G**raph **N**ame **C**reate.

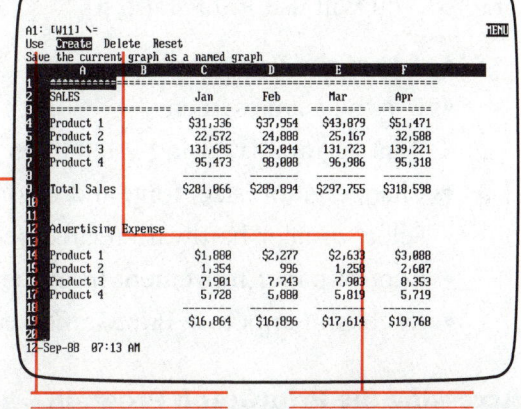

Select **U**se when you want to view a graph whose settings are saved through **/G**raph **N**ame **C**reate.

Select **D**elete to erase individual name; select **R**eset to erase all graph names.

When the Enter graph name: prompt appears, enter a name up to 15 characters in length.

*Note: If you want graph names to be stored with their worksheet, remember to save the worksheet file by using /**F**ile **S**ave after creating the names.*

Accessing and Exiting PrintGraph

The first half of this chapter showed you how to use 1-2-3 to create and display graphs. Because the main 1-2-3 program cannot print graphics, you must use the PrintGraph program to print the graphs you saved as graph (.PIC) files. You can use the PrintGraph program for quick and easy printouts of graphs. You can also choose from a variety of optional print settings for enhancing the appearance of printed graphs. You will use PrintGraph to

- Access the PrintGraph program
- Use the status screen
- Print a graph by using PrintGraph default settings
- Change graph size, font, and color settings
- Select or alter hardware-related settings
- Control paper movement from the keyboard
- Establish temporary PrintGraph settings

Accessing the PrintGraph Program

To access PrintGraph directly from DOS, type *pgraph* at the DOS prompt. (The PrintGraph program should reside in the current directory for a hard disk system; for a floppy disk system, the disk containing the PrintGraph program should be in the active drive.) If you use a printer driver set other than the default 1-2-3 set, you must also type name of that driver set (*pgraph hp*, for example) to reach the main PrintGraph menu.

However, you are more likely to use PrintGraph immediately after you have created a graph. If you originally accessed 1-2-3 by typing *lotus*, select **/Q**uit **Y**es to return to the Access menu. Then select **P**rintGraph instead of exiting to the DOS prompt. If you are using 1-2-3 on a floppy disk system, the program will prompt you to remove the 1-2-3 System disk and insert the PrintGraph disk, unless you use a member of the IBM PS/2 family. For the PS/2, the PrintGraph program resides on the System disk.

Alternatively, if you have sufficient RAM, you can use PrintGraph after you have issued the **/S**ystem command. Then, instead of having to reload 1-2-3 after you leave PrintGraph, you can return directly to 1-2-3 by typing *exit* at the system prompt. But be careful. Before you use this technique, save your worksheet. And, because you must have at least 256K of remaining RAM to run PrintGraph and 1-2-3 simultaneously without overwriting your worksheet, use the **/W**orksheet **S**tatus report to check remaining internal memory (RAM) before you attempt to use **/S**ystem.

Exiting the PrintGraph Program

To leave the PrintGraph program, choose **E**xit from the main **P**rintGraph menu. The next screen to appear depends on the method you used to access PrintGraph. If you entered PrintGraph from the 1-2-3 Access System, the Access menu reappears. Select **E**xit to restore the DOS prompt, or select another Access menu option. If you entered PrintGraph by typing *pgraph* from the DOS prompt, the DOS prompt is restored.

If you want to enter 1-2-3 after you have exited PrintGraph and restored the DOS prompt, remember how you originally accessed the DOS prompt (before you typed *pgraph*). If you were using 1-2-3 and selected **/S**ystem to reach the DOS prompt, type *exit* and press Enter to return to the 1-2-3 worksheet. If you were not using 1-2-3 before the PrintGraph session, type *123* or *lotus* and then select **123** from the Access menu.

Accessing and Exiting PrintGraph

Accessing PrintGraph

Most likely, you will use PrintGraph immediately after creating a graph. Remember to use either **/G**raph **S**ave or **/G**raph **N**ame **C**reate and **/F**ile **S**ave before exiting the program.

If you originally accessed 1-2-3 by typing *lotus*, select **/Q**uit **Y**es to return to the Access menu.

Then select **P**rintGraph.

To access PrintGraph directly from DOS, type *pgraph* at the DOS prompt. The PrintGraph program should be in your current directory, or, on a floppy system, in the current drive.

```
C:\123>pgraph
```

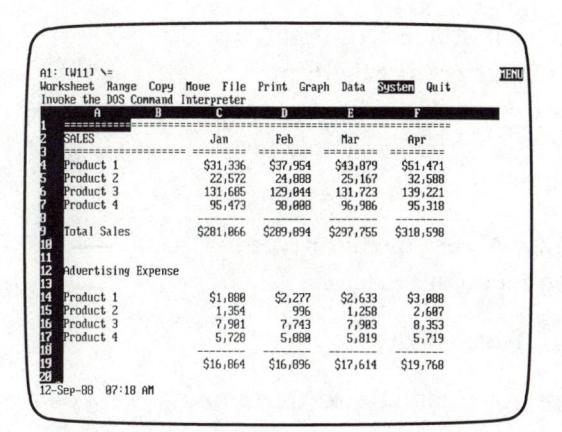

| Introduction | An Overview of Creating a Graph | Selecting a Graph Type | Specifying a Data Range | Enhancing the Appearance of a Basic Graph | Preserving the Graph on Disk | **Accessing and Exiting PrintGraph** | Printing Graphs |

If you have enough RAM, you can use **P**rint**G**raph with the **/S**ystem command. Then, instead of having to reload 1-2-3 after you leave PrintGraph, you can return to 1-2-3 by typing *exit*.

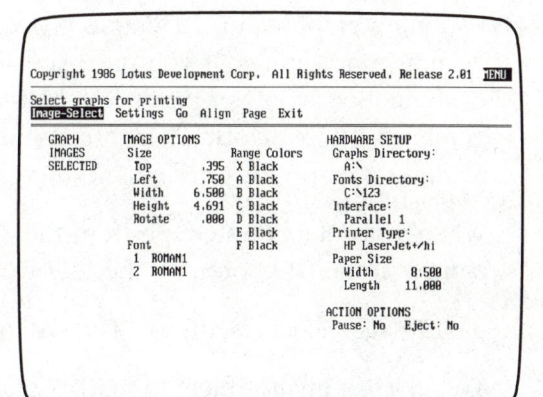

When the opening screen of the **P**rint**G**raph program is displayed, you can choose the options you want to set and print your graph.

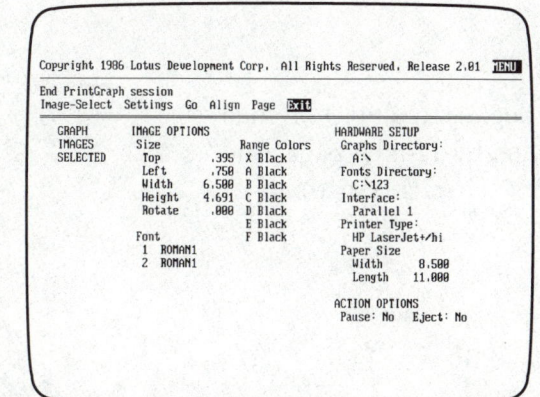

Exiting PrintGraph

When you are ready to leave the **P**rint**G**raph program, choose **E**xit from the main **P**rint**G**raph menu. If you accessed **P**rint**G**raph from the 1-2-3 Access System, you will be returned to the Access System screen. If you entered **P**rint**G**raph by typing *pgraph* at the DOS prompt, you will be returned to the DOS prompt.

Introduction

An Overview of 1-2-3

Getting Started

1-2-3 Basics

Creating a Worksheet

Printing Reports

Creating and Printing Graphs

Managing Data

Understanding Macros

Appendix

309

Printing Graphs

Printing a graph can be a simple procedure if you accept PrintGraph's default print settings. If you have specified the correct hardware configuration, you can produce a half-size, block-font, black-and-white graph on 8 1/2-inch-by-11-inch continuous-feed paper simply by marking a graph for printing and then printing it.

When you select PrintGraph from the 1-2-3 Access menu or type *pgraph* at the DOS prompt, the following menu appears:

Image-Select   **S**ettings   **G**o   **A**lign   **P**age   **E**xit

You choose **I**mage-Select to mark a graph for printing, and **G**o to print the graph.

Suppose, for example, that you want to print a line graph saved in a file called 88SALES. Make sure that the current printer and interface specifications accurately reflect your hardware, that you're using continuous-feed paper, and that the printer is on-line and positioned at the page's top. Then you can print the default graph by issuing the following command sequences:

Image-Select **88SALES**
Go

This graph will be centered upright (zero degrees rotation) on the paper and will fill about half of an 8 1/2-inch-by-11-inch page. The titles are printed in the default BLOCK1 font (character style).

If you want to enhance this default graph, you can do so by using any or all of PrintGraph's many special features. These special capabilities (which are not available in the main 1-2-3 program) include the production of high-resolution output on special printers and plotters; enlargement, reduction, and rotation of graph printouts; and the use of several additional colors and font types.

To illustrate what happens if you use PrintGraph's size and font options with the same hardware settings that you used for the graph, you could issue the following command sequences:

Image-Select **88SALES**
    Settings   **I**mage   **S**ize   **F**ull
                                    Quit
                           Font **1** **ITALIC1**
                           Font **2** **ROMAN1**
                           Quit
            Quit
    Align
    Go

The resulting graph is printed automatically on its side (90 degrees rotation) and almost fills an 8 1/2-inch-by-11-inch page. The top center title is printed in the italic font; the other titles, in the roman font. (These font options, as well as other nondefault settings, are described in detail later in this chapter.)

Printing Graphs

Printing a Graph

If you use PrintGraph's default settings, printing a graph is easy. The default values produce a half-size, black-and-white graph with titles printed in black font on 8 1/2-by-11-inch continuous-feed paper.

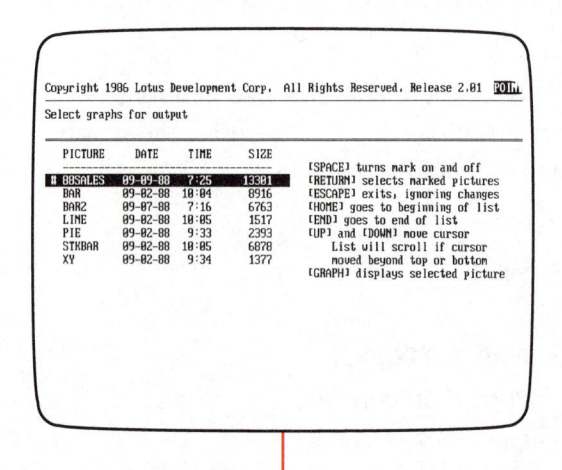

Choose **I**mage-Select to mark a graph for printing. When a list of PIC files appears, move the cursor to the you want to print, and press the space bar. Finally, press `↵Enter` to return to the **P**rintGraph menu.

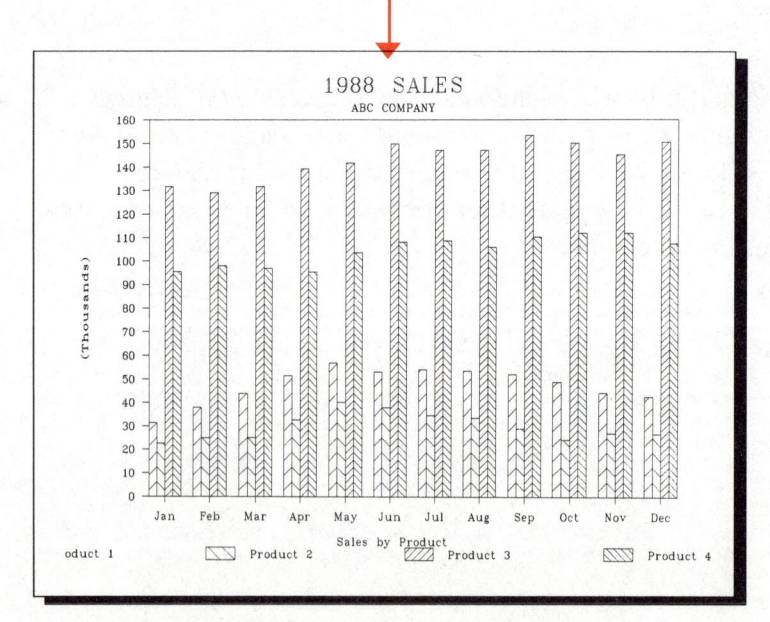

Select **G**o to print the graph.

Enhancing the Basic Graph

When you select **S**ettings **I**mage from the **P**rintGraph menu, 1-2-3 provides three options for changing the printout of your graph: changing the size, changing fonts used to print graph titles, and changing colors.

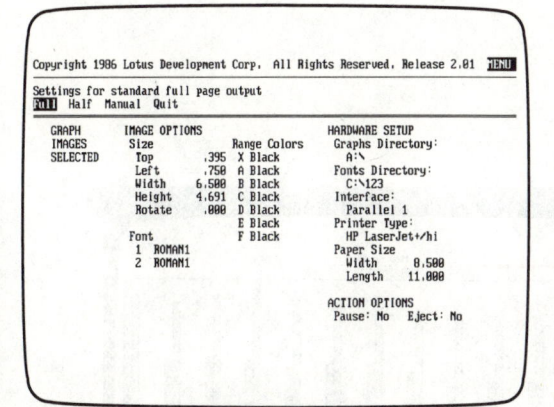

After having selected an image to print, select **S**ettings **I**mage **S**ize **F**ull, and 1-2-3 resets the dimensions and rotation of your graph.

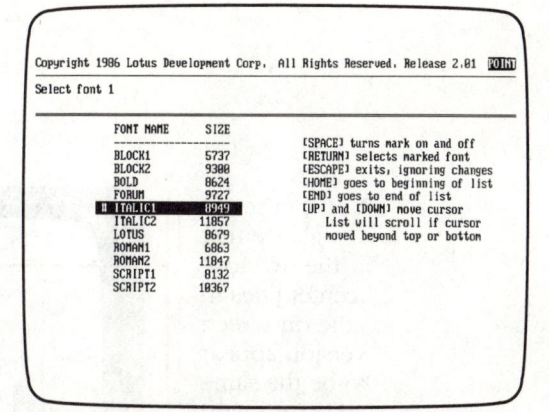

Select **S**ettings **I**mage **F**ont **1** (or **2**), and 1-2-3 displays a list of font options for first and second graph titles.

After you change size and font options, your printed graph will look like this.

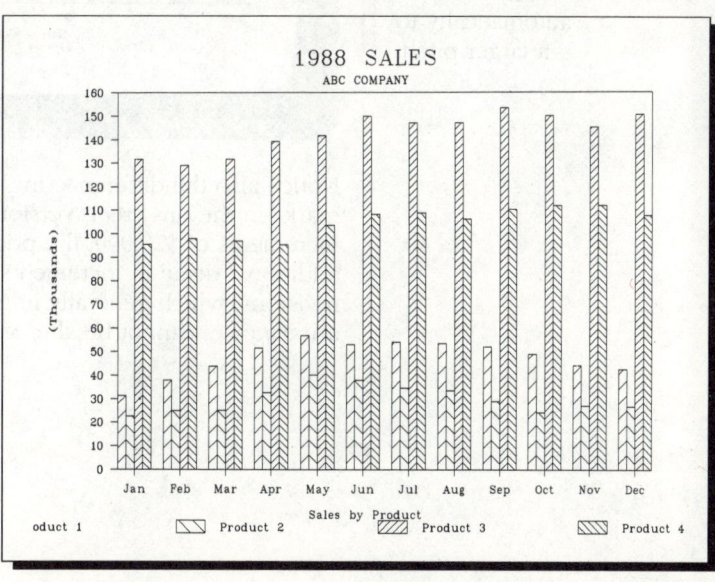

Printing Graphs

A printed graph looks different from its on-screen display. For example, if you compare the figure on this page (which captures the on-screen display of a stacked-bar graph) with the figure on the next page (which shows the same graph printed), two differences are immediately apparent.

You can see at a glance that the two top-center titles in the on-screen version appear to be the same size (or pitch) but that, in the printed graph, the first title has been changed automatically to a larger pitch.

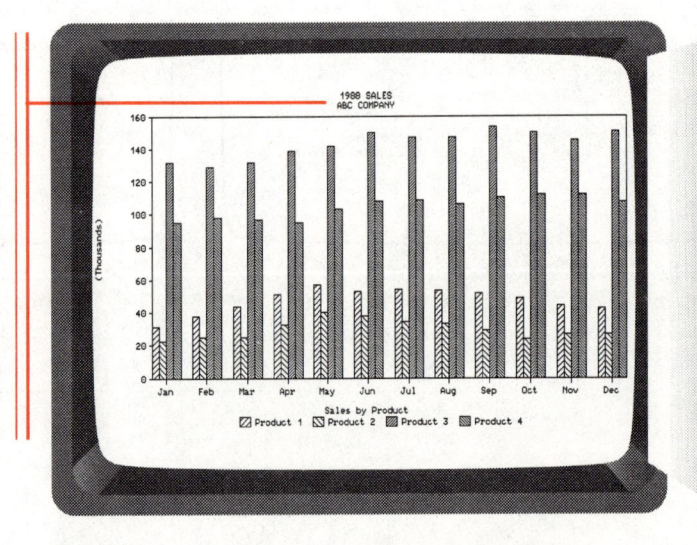

Notice also the difference in the y-axis—the tick marks in the on-screen version are scaled in increments of $20,000; the printed graph provides additional detail in increments of $10,000. These revisions, which generally improve graph appearance, cannot be altered.

Notice a third difference between the two graphs—the legends. Although the four legends in the figure on page 314 are centered neatly below the graph, the legends in the figure on page 315 are spread out so that the first and last legends are not printed. You can solve this problem by reducing the amount of text in each legend.

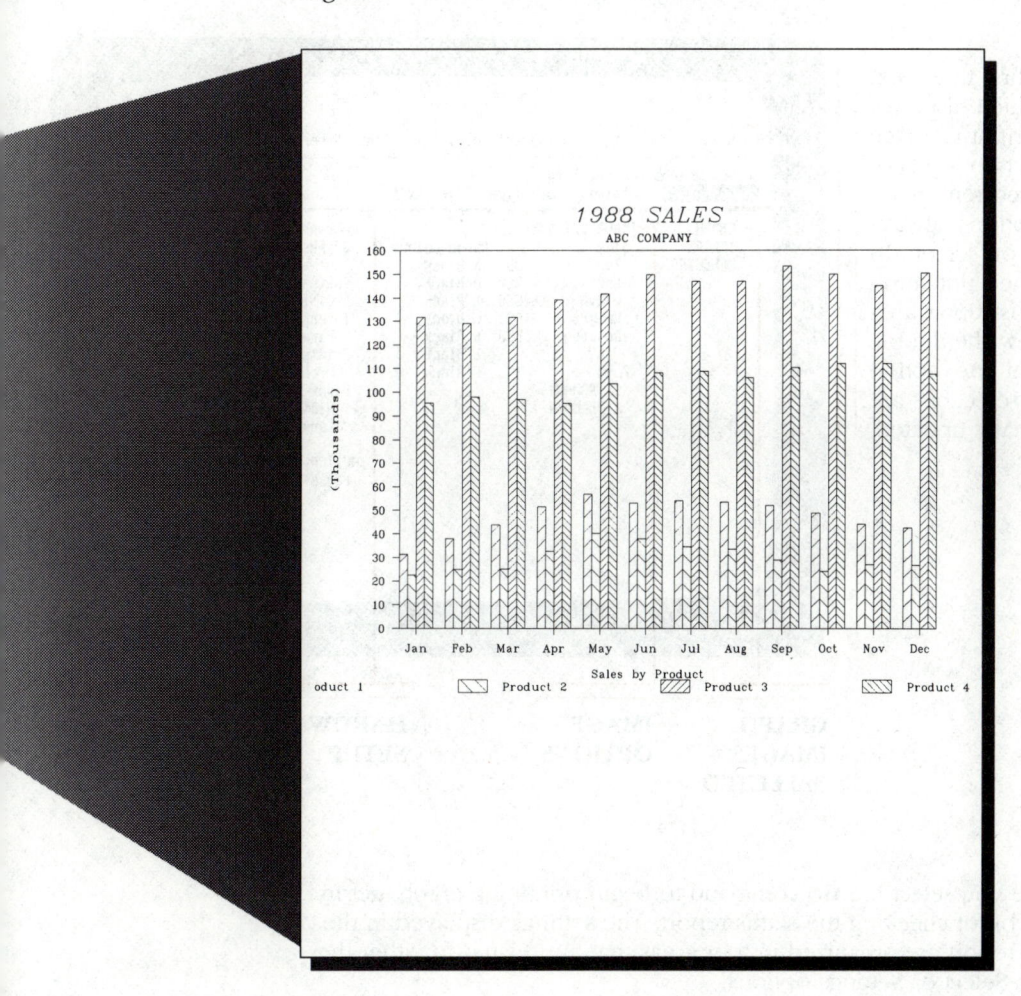

Printing Graphs

The PrintGraph Menu

PrintGraph is entirely menu-driven. The menu screens provide not only instructions for printing graph (.PIC) files but also information about current print conditions.

The first three text lines, which display a copyright message and two levels of current menu options, always remain on-screen. In the PrintGraph status-report area below the double solid line, option selections are continually updated.

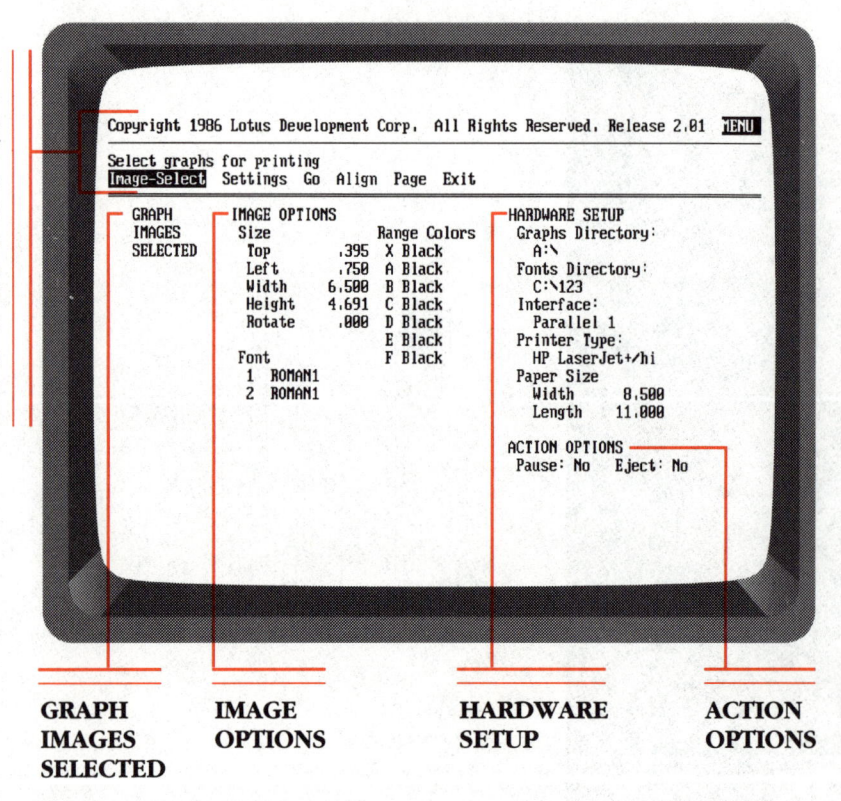

```
Copyright 1986 Lotus Development Corp. All Rights Reserved. Release 2.01  MENU
Select graphs for printing
Image-Select  Settings  Go  Align  Page  Exit

GRAPH      IMAGE OPTIONS                          HARDWARE SETUP
IMAGES     Size              Range Colors         Graphs Directory:
SELECTED   Top       .395    X Black                A:\
           Left      .750    A Black              Fonts Directory:
           Width    6.500    B Black                C:\123
           Height   4.691    C Black              Interface:
           Rotate    .000    D Black                Parallel 1
                             E Black              Printer Type:
           Font              F Black                HP LaserJet+/hi
           1 ROMAN1                                Paper Size
           2 ROMAN1                                  Width    8.500
                                                    Length  11.000

                                                  ACTION OPTIONS
                                                  Pause: No   Eject: No
```

GRAPH IMAGES SELECTED   **IMAGE OPTIONS**   **HARDWARE SETUP**   **ACTION OPTIONS**

Before you select the **G**o command to begin printing a graph, get in the habit of checking the status report. The settings displayed in the status report are organized in four areas that are related to either the **I**mage-Select or **S**ettings options.

316

A list of graphs that can be selected for printing appears under GRAPH IMAGES SELECTED, on the left side of the status report. To make changes in the other three status-report areas, you first select **S**ettings from the main **P**rintGraph menu. When you select **S**ettings, the following menu appears:

Image **H**ardware **A**ction **S**ave **R**eset **Q**uit

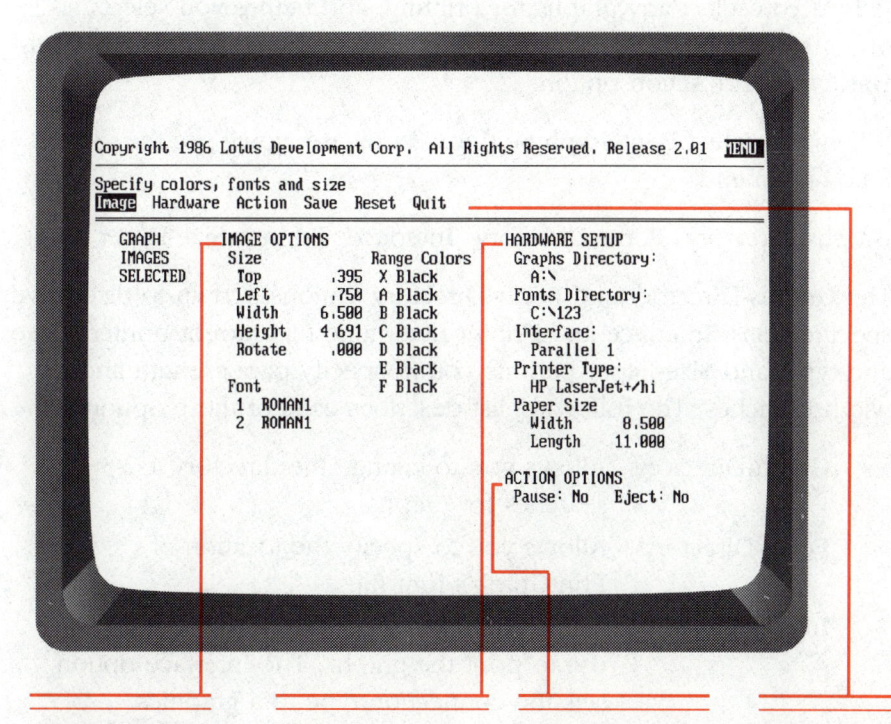

Image changes the size, font, and color of the graph; the updated revisions are displayed in the status report's **IMAGE OPTIONS** area.

Hardware alters the paper size, printer, or disk-drive specifications displayed in the **HARDWARE SETUP** area.

Action moves to a new page and pauses while you change specifications for the next graph.

Save, **Reset**, and **Quit** have the same functions they perform on other 1-2-3 menus.

317

Printing Graphs

The physical print environment includes the disk drives containing files applicable to the graph-printing operation, the printer type and name, paper size, and printer actions to control print delay and paper movement. Updates to these print environment settings are displayed in the status report's rightmost column.

Before you select any graphs for printing, and before you select options that will affect the printed image, you should understand each **H**ardware and **A**ction option.

When you select **P**rintGraph **S**ettings **H**ardware, you'll see the following menu:

Graphs-Directory **F**onts-Directory **I**nterface **P**rinter **S**ize-Paper **Q**uit

The **G**raphs-Directory and **F**onts-Directory options pertain to disk-drive specifications; **I**nterface and **P**rinter determine the current printer name and type; and **S**ize-Paper permits you to specify paper length and width in inches. The following list describes each of these options:

Graph-Directory	Allows you to change the directory 1-2-3 searches for graphs.
Fonts-Directory	Allows you to specify the location of PrintGraph's font files.
Interface	Helps you specify the printer or plotter you use to print the graphs. The Interface option sets the connection type to a graphics printer.
Printer	Establishes a connection to a specific type of printer.
Size-Paper	Allows you to set the size of paper you are using to produce the printed graph. (The default is 8 1/2-by-11 inches.)

Making the Printer Pause between Graphs

If you have selected more than one .PIC file for a single print operation, you can make the printer pause between printing the specified graphs. If you are using a manual sheet-feed printer, for example, you can pause to change the paper. Or you may want to stop printing temporarily so that you change the hardware settings, directing the output to a different printer. (You cannot change the font, color, and size options during the pause.)

If you want the printing operation to pause, select **S**ettings **A**ction **P**ause **Y**es before you select **G**o from the main **P**rintGraph menu. After each graph has been printed, the printer will pause and beep. To resume printing, press the space bar.

To restore the default setting so that all currently specified graphs will print nonstop, choose **S**ettings **A**ction **P**ause **N**o.

Ejecting the Paper To Start a New Page

The other **A**ction option applies to "batching" several graphs in one print operation. When you select **S**ettings **A**ction **E**ject **Y**es, continuous-feed paper advances to the top of a new page before the next graph is printed. Use the alternate default setting, **E**ject **N**o, to print two (or more) half-size (or smaller) graphs on a single page.

Do not confuse the **S**ettings **A**ction **E**ject **Y**es command sequence with the main **P**rintGraph menu's **P**age command. Both commands advance the paper to the top of a new page. **S**ettings **A**ction **E**ject **Y**es is appropriate when you use a single **G**o command to print more than one selected graph; the paper advances automatically after each graph has been printed. You select **P**rintGraph **P**age, on the other hand, whenever you want to advance the paper one page at a time before or after a printing session.

319

Printing Graphs

There's more to printing than just sticking a sheet of paper in a printer and pressing a key. Although the printing process is governed to some extent by your hardware and software, most of the initial decisions are up to you. You need to make decisions about the disk drives containing the print files, the printer type and name, size of paper, and the printer actions that control print delay and paper movement.

| Introduction | An Overview of Creating a Graph | Selecting a Graph Type | Specifying a Data Range | Enhancing the Appearance of a Basic Graph | Preserving the Graph on Disk | Accessing and Exiting PrintGraph | **Printing Graphs** |

Before you select any graphs for printing or change any options, you need to understand the options available on the **P**rintGraph **S**ettings **H**ardware menu.

Graphs-Directory is used to change directories.

Fonts-Directory allows you to specify location of PrintGraph's font files.

Interface lets you specify the printer or plotter.

Printer establishes a connection with a printer type.

Size-Paper sets the paper size.

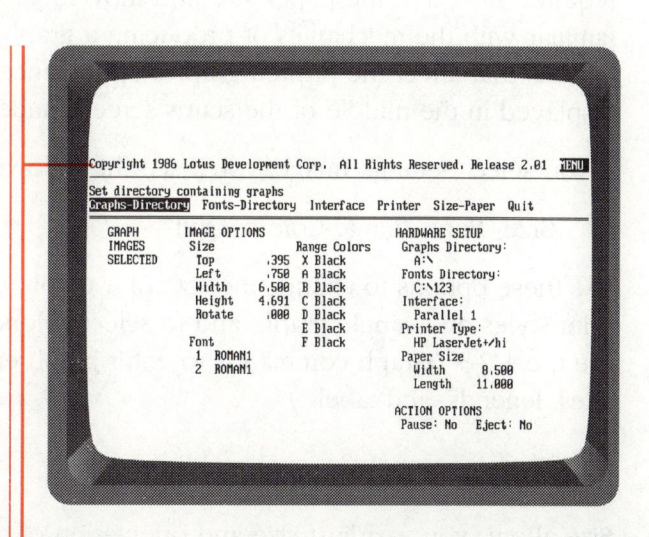

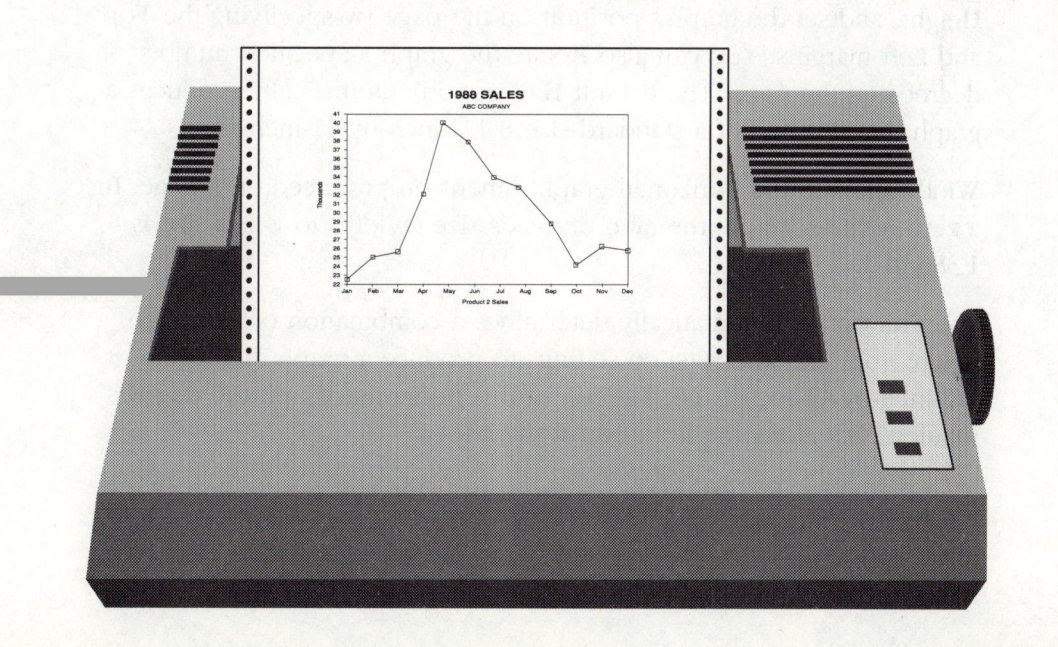

321

Printing Graphs

You've learned about the physical print environment needed to produce a graph: the printer type and name, the disk-drive location of required files, and the paper size and movement. Now that you're familiar with the mechanics of producing a graph, you'll learn about options that affect the printed graph's appearance. These options are displayed in the middle of the status screen, under IMAGE OPTIONS.

If you select **S**ettings **I**mage, you'll see the following submenu:

    Size **F**ont **R**ange-Colors **Q**uit

Use these options to change the size of a graph, to specify one or two print styles on a single graph, and to select colors. (As you know, you use the 1-2-3 /**G**raph commands to enter graph enhancements such as titles, legends, and labels.)

Adjusting Size and Orientation

Size allows you to adjust size and orientation of printed graphs. You determine the size of the graph by specifying the desired **W**idth and **H**eight, and set the graph's position on the page by specifying the **T**op and **L**eft margins. You can also **R**otate the graph a specified number of degrees on the page. The default **H**alf option automatically produces a graph that fills half of a standard-size 8 1/2-inch-by-11-inch page.

Width refers to the horizontal graph dimension produced on a page. In a zero-rotation graph, the ratio of x-axis size (Width) to y-axis size is 1.386 to 1.

The **F**ull option automatically determines a combination of the width, height, top, left, and rotation settings to produce a graph that fills an 8 1/2-inch-by-11-inch page. The top of this horizontal graph (90 degrees rotation) lies along the left edge of the paper.

If you want to change any or all of the size settings, select **M**anual from the **S**ettings **I**mage **S**ize submenu. Then select one or more of the following options:

Top **L**eft **W**idth **H**eight **R**otation **Q**uit

To change the location of a graph, change the margin settings. If you want to center a half-size graph at the top of 11-inch-by-14-inch paper, for example, specify a different left margin by selecting **S**ettings **I**mage **S**ize **M**anual **L**eft and typing *3.5* as the revised number of inches. When you press Enter, the updated left-margin specification will be displayed in the status report.

Determine the appropriate number of inches by working from the default values. You know that a half-size graph is centered automatically on an 8 1/2-inch page and that changing to paper 14 inches wide will add 5 1/2 inches to the width. Add half of the increase (2.75 inches) to the default left margin (.75 inches) to calculate the total number of inches (3.5) for the new dimension.

When you change the **W**idth and **H**eight settings, be sure to maintain the basic x- to y-axis ratio of approximately 1.38 to 1. For example, suppose that you want to produce an upright (zero rotation) graph that is only three inches high. You know that the x-axis dimension should exceed the y-axis dimension and that, at zero rotation, the x-axis is the width. Multiply the desired height of 3 inches by 1.38 to calculate the proportionate width (4.14 inches) of the graph.

Be sure that the combined dimensions (margin, width, and height) do not exceed the size of the paper. If a graph exceeds the paper's physical bounds, 1-2-3 will print as much of the graph as possible and then truncate the rest.

Although you can set rotation anywhere between zero and 360 degrees, you will use three settings (zero, 90, or 270) for most graphs. To print an upright graph, use zero; to position the graph's center titles along the left edge of the paper, use 90; to position the graph's center titles along the right edge of the paper, use 270.

Printing Graphs

Selecting Fonts

You can use different character types, or *fonts*, in a printed graph. For example, you can print a graph's top center title in one character type (Font 1) and then select a different font (Font 2) for the remaining titles, data-labels, x-labels, and legends. If you want to use only one print style, your Font 1 choice will be used for all descriptions.

BLOCK1 is the default font. The number after the font name indicates the darkness (density) of the printed characters. Notice that four of the fonts permit alternative print-density specifications. If you choose BLOCK2, for example, the printed characters will be darker than those produced by choosing BLOCK1.

Two of these fonts (italic and script) may be difficult to read, especially on half-size graphs produced on a nonletter-quality printer. Before you print a final-quality draft in darker density, print the graph at the lower density so that you can determine whether the font and size settings are correct.

Choosing Colors

If you have a color printing device, you can use the PrintGraph program to assign colors to all parts of a graph. Select **S**ettings **I**mage **R**ange-Colors to produce the following submenu:

   X A B C D E F Quit

For all graph types except Pie, use the **X** option to assign a single color to the edges of the graph, any background grid, and all displayed options other than legends and data-labels. Use **A**, **B**, **C**, **D**, **E** and **F** to assign a different color to every data range used. The color set for an individual data range is used also for any data-label or legend assigned to that data range.

You use a different method to determine the print colors for a pie graph. Because you create a pie graph by using only data in the **A** range, and because each wedge of the pie is assigned a **B**-range shading code, you must use the appropriate shading codes to determine which colors will print. First, associate each code with the following **I**mage **R**ange-Colors menu options:

Range-Colors Option	B-range Shading Code
X	Shading code ending in 1 (101 or 1)
A	Shading code ending in 2
B	Shading code ending in 3
C	Shading code ending in 4
D	Shading code ending in 5
E	Shading code ending in 6
F	Shading code ending in 7

When you select an option from the **S**ettings **I**mage **R**ange-Colors submenu, a menu of colors will be displayed. The number of colors displayed depends on the capabilities of the current printer (named in the hardware setup area of the PrintGraph status report). If your printer does not support color printing, only the **B**lack option will appear. To choose a color for each range, highlight that color and press Enter.

If you know that you will print a specific graph in color, select **/G**raph **O**ptions **C**olor before you store that graph as a .PIC file. If you store the graph in black and white and then print it in color, the crosshatch markings and the colors assigned to the ranges both will print.

Printing Graphs

Controlling the Appearance of the Printed Graph

Once you understand the mechanics of producing a graph, you may want to learn to use the options that affect the graph's appearance. These options are displayed in the center of PrintGraph's status screen, under IMAGE OPTIONS.

With **S**ize, you can adjust the size and orientation of printed graphs.

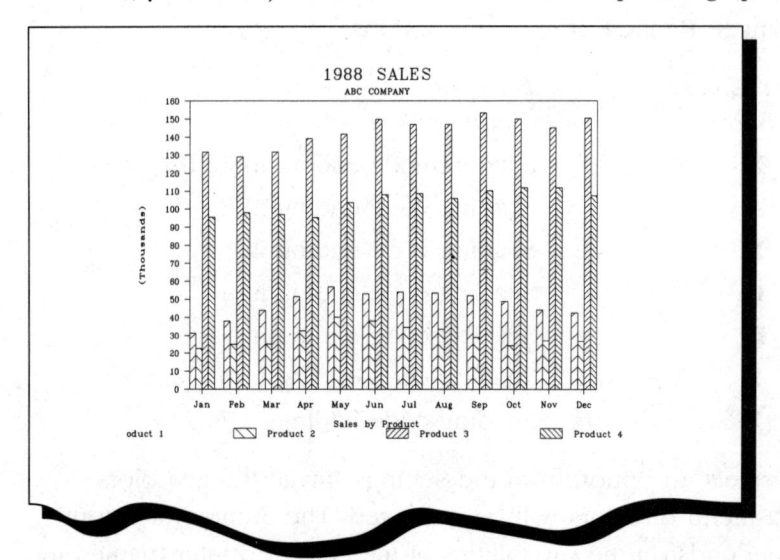

The default **H**alf options automatically produces a graph that fills half a standard-sized page.

The **F**ull option prints a full page graphic in landscape style.

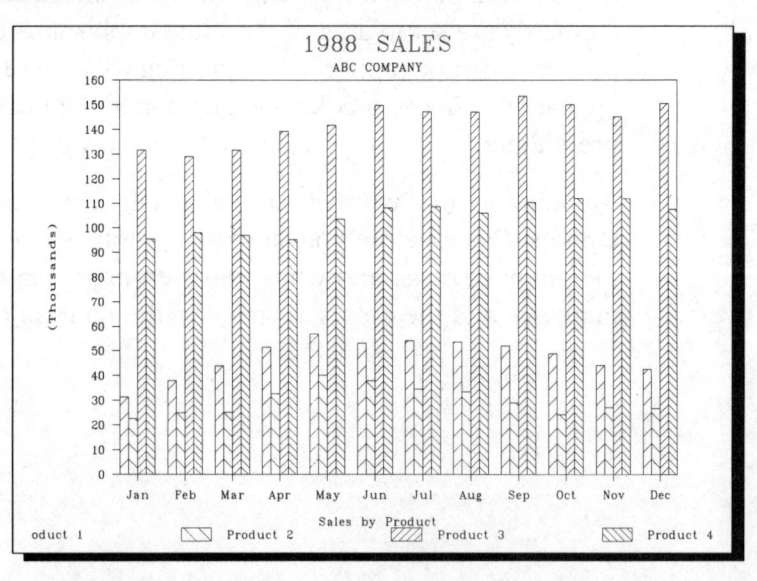

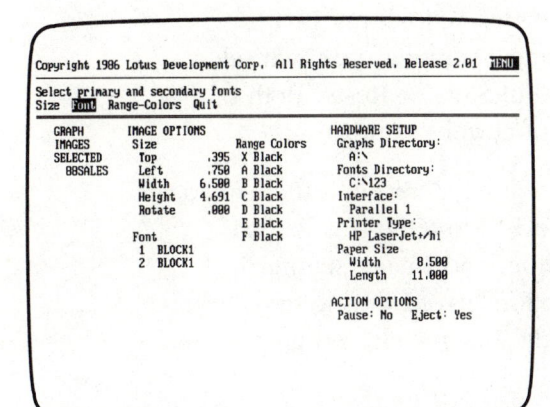

| Introduction | An Overview of Creating a Graph | Selecting a Graph Type | Specifying a Data Range | Enhancing the Appearance of a Basic Graph | Preserving the Graph on Disk | Accessing and Exiting PrintGraph | **Printing Graphs** |

You can use **F**ont to specify a font used on the graph. The default is BLOCK1.

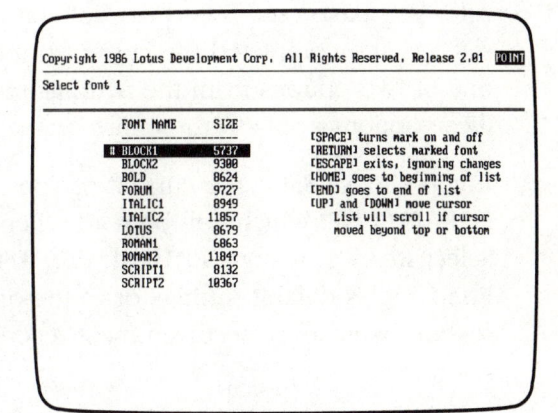

But you can choose from among several different font styles.

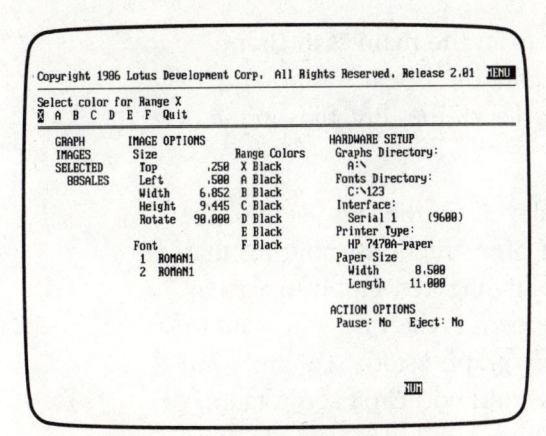

If you have a color printing device, you can use PrintGraph to print a graph in color. You will use **P**rintGraph **S**ettings **I**mage **R**ange-Colors to select the range.

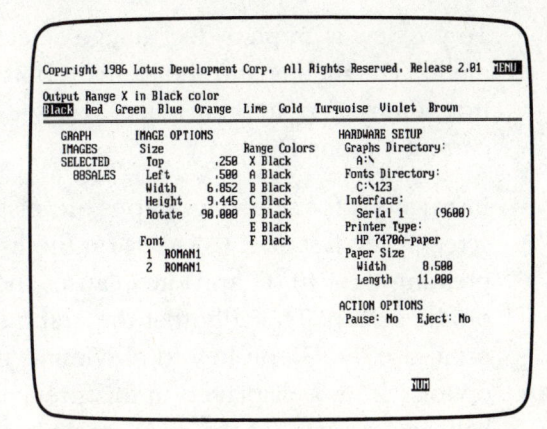

Finally, specify the colors.

Introduction

An Overview of 1-2-3

Getting Started

1-2-3 Basics

Creating a Worksheet

Printing Reports

Creating and Printing Graphs

Managing Data

Understanding Macros

Appendix

327

Printing Graphs

After you have established current Hardware, Action, and Image settings and completed the current printing operation, you will select one of two options from the **S**ettings menu: **S**ave or **R**eset. Both of these options apply to the entire group of current settings.

If you choose **S**ave, the current options will be stored in a file named PGRAPH.CNF, which will be read whenever PrintGraph is loaded. Select **R**eset to restore all **H**ardware, **A**ction, and **I**mage settings to PrintGraph's default settings or to the options saved during the current session, whichever occurred most recently. **I**mage-Selected graphs are not reset.

After you have accepted the default options or selected other **H**ardware, **A**ction, and **I**mage options, you access the main **P**rintGraph menu to complete the printing operation. From this menu, you select the graph(s) to be printed, adjust the paper alignment, and select **G**o.

Previewing a Graph

To preview a graph, select **I**mage-Select from the main **P**rintGraph menu. The menus and the status report area disappear temporarily from the screen; in their place, you see a list of the .PIC files in the current Graphs Directory.

Instructions for selecting graphs are displayed on the right side of the screen. The last item (GRAPH) on the list of instructions indicates that pressing the F10 (Graph) key causes the highlighted graph to appear on the screen. To verify that the graph shown is the one you want to print, use the Graph key to preview every graph listed. Size and font options are not displayed in this preview, and you can't see rotation or half-size results. But the preview does give a good idea of what the printed graph will look like—in some instances, a better idea than **/G**raph **V**iew. For example, legend titles that are too wide to print will appear complete when viewed on-screen with **/GV**, but not with the F10 preview.

Selecting a Graph

Selecting graphs that you want to print from the list of .PIC files is easy—to mark the files for printing, simply follow the directions on the right side of the screen. Use the cursor-movement keys to position the highlighted bar on the graph that you want to select. Then press the space bar to mark the file with a # symbol. The space bar acts as a toggle key; use the same action to remove any unwanted marks. If necessary, continue to mark additional graphs. After you press Enter to accept the currently marked graphs for printing, the updated status report will again be displayed.

Controlling Paper Movement from the Main Menu

The main **P**rintGraph menu's **A**lign option sets the program's built-in, top-of-page marker. When you choose **A**lign, PrintGraph assumes that the paper in the printer is aligned correctly at the top of the page. Using the page-length information you provided when you installed the graphics device, PrintGraph then inserts a form feed at the end of every page. Regularly selecting **A**lign before selecting **G**o is a good practice. The **P**age option advances the paper one page at a time. At the end of a printing session, this useful option advances continuous-feed paper to help you remove the printed output.

Go (and Wait!)

To print a graph, you must select **G**o from the main **P**rintGraph menu. After you select **G**o, you will see in the screen's menu area messages indicating that picture and font files are loading. Then 1-2-3 will print the graphs. If you want to interrupt the process of printing a graph or series of graphs, press the Ctrl-Break key combination. Then press Esc to access the **P**rintGraph menu options.

329

Printing Graphs

Saving PrintGraph Settings and Completing the Print Cycle

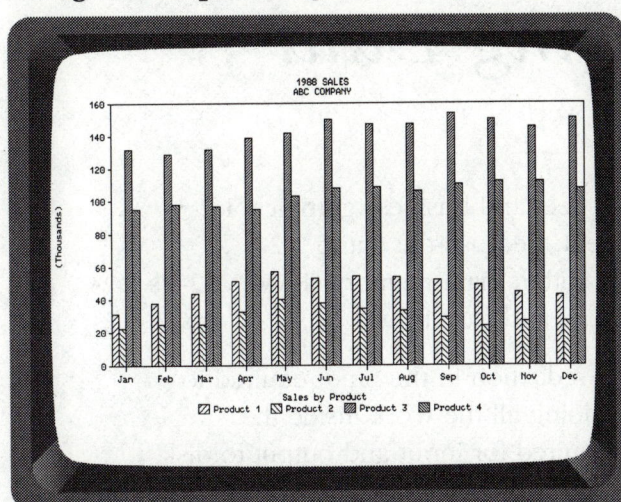

Now you've been through the process of creating a graph and specifying which options you want to use when printing. All that's left to do is save the PrintGraph settings and print the graph.

Saving PrintGraph Settings

When you choose to save the **P**rintGraph **S**ettings, you select **P**rintGraph **S**ettings **S**ave. The current options are then written to a file named PGRAPH.CNF.

Previewing a Graph

The last item (GRAPH) on the list of instructions on the PrintGraph screen indicates that pressing the [F10] (Graph) key causes the highlighted graph to appear on the screen.

Size and font options are not displayed in this preview, and you can't see rotation or half-size results. But the preview does give a good idea of what the printed graph will look like—in some instances, a better idea than /**G**raph **V**iew.

Selecting and Printing a Graph

When you want to select a graph for printing, you simply follow the instructions shown in the right side of the PrintGraph screen. Use the cursor-movement keys to highlight the file you want, press the space bar to mark the file with a # symbol. (The space bar acts as a toggle: the same action will remove the #.) When you press Enter, the status report is displayed. Then, after you select **A**lign (to make sure the paper is aligned) and **G**o, the graph is printed.

331

7 *Managing Data*

In addition to the electronic spreadsheet and business graphics, 1-2-3 has a third element: data management. Because the entire 1-2-3 database resides in the spreadsheet within main memory (RAM), 1-2-3's database feature is fast, easy to access, and easy to use.

The database's speed results from a reduction in the time required to transfer data to and from disks. By doing all the work inside the spreadsheet, 1-2-3 saves the time required for input and output to disk.

The 1-2-3 database is easily accessed because Lotus Development Corporation has made the entire database visible within the spreadsheet. You can view the contents of the whole database by using worksheet windows and cursor-movement keys to scroll through the database.

The ease of use is a result of integrating data management with the program's spreadsheet and graphics functions. The commands for adding, modifying, and deleting items in a database are the same ones you have already seen for manipulating cells or groups of cells within a worksheet. And creating graphs from ranges in a database is as easy as creating them in a spreadsheet.

Key Terms Used in This Chapter

database	A collection of data organized so that you can list, sort, or search its contents.
record	A collection of associated fields. In 1-2-3, a record is a row of cells within a database.
field	One information item, such as Address or Name. In 1-2-3, a field is a single cell.
keys	The fields to which you attach the highest precedence when the database is sorted.
input range	The range of the database on which data manipulation operations are performed.
output range	The range to which data is copied when extracted from the database.
criterion range	The range of the database in which you enter queries and criterion.

What Is Covered in This Chapter?

This chapter shows you how to

- Understand the advantages and limitations of 1-2-3's database
- Create, modify, and maintain data records
- Carry out **S**ort and **Q**uery operations
- Create data with other **/D**ata commands

333

What Is a Database?

A database is a collection of data organized so that you can list, sort, or search its contents. The list of data might contain any kind of information, from addresses to tax-deductible expenditures.

In 1-2-3, the word *database* means a range of cells that spans at least one column and more than one row. This definition, however, does not distinguish between a database and any other range of cells. Because a database is actually a list, its manner of organization sets it apart from ordinary cells. Just as a list must be organized to be useful, a database must be organized to permit access to the information it contains.

Remember nonetheless that in 1-2-3 a database is similar to any other group of cells. This knowledge will help you as you learn about the different **/D**ata commands that are covered in this chapter. In many instances, you can use these database commands in what you might consider "nondatabase" applications.

The smallest unit in a database is a *field*, or single data item. For example, if you were to develop an information base of present or potential corporate contributors for a not-for-profit organization, you might include the following fields of information:

    Company Name
    Company Address
    Contact Person
    Phone Number
    Last Contact Date
    Contact Representative
    Last Contribution Date

A database *record* is a collection of associated fields. For example, the accumulation of all contributor data about one company forms one record.

In 1-2-3, a *record* is a row of cells within a database, and a *field* is a single cell.

You must set up a database so that you can access the information it contains. Retrieval of information usually involves relying on key fields. A database *key field* is any field on which you base a list, sort, or search operation. For example, you could use Zipcode as a key field to sort the data in the contributor database and assign contact representatives to specific geographic areas. And you could prepare a follow-up contact list by searching the database for the key field Last Contact Date in which the date is less than one year ago.

Size Limitations of the 1-2-3 Database

The major disadvantage of Lotus's approach is the limitation it imposes on the database's size. With some popular database programs, you can get by with loading only portions of your database at once; with 1-2-3, the entire database must be in memory before you can perform any data-management operations.

If your computer has 640K of internal memory, you can store in a single database only about 1,000 400-byte (character) records or 8,000 50-byte records. Disk operating system commands and the 1-2-3 program instructions occupy the remaining memory. For large databases, you need to extend the internal memory capacity beyond 640K. If you use floppy disks for external storage of database files, you are limited to files that total approximately 360,000 characters (1.2 million characters on a high-density disk). On a hard disk, a database of 8,000 500-byte records occupies four million characters, or 4M.

What Is a Database?

What Is a Database?

A database is a collection of information that is organized so that you can list, sort, or search its contents. A Rolodex® is one form of database, as is an address book and a file cabinet full of employee records.

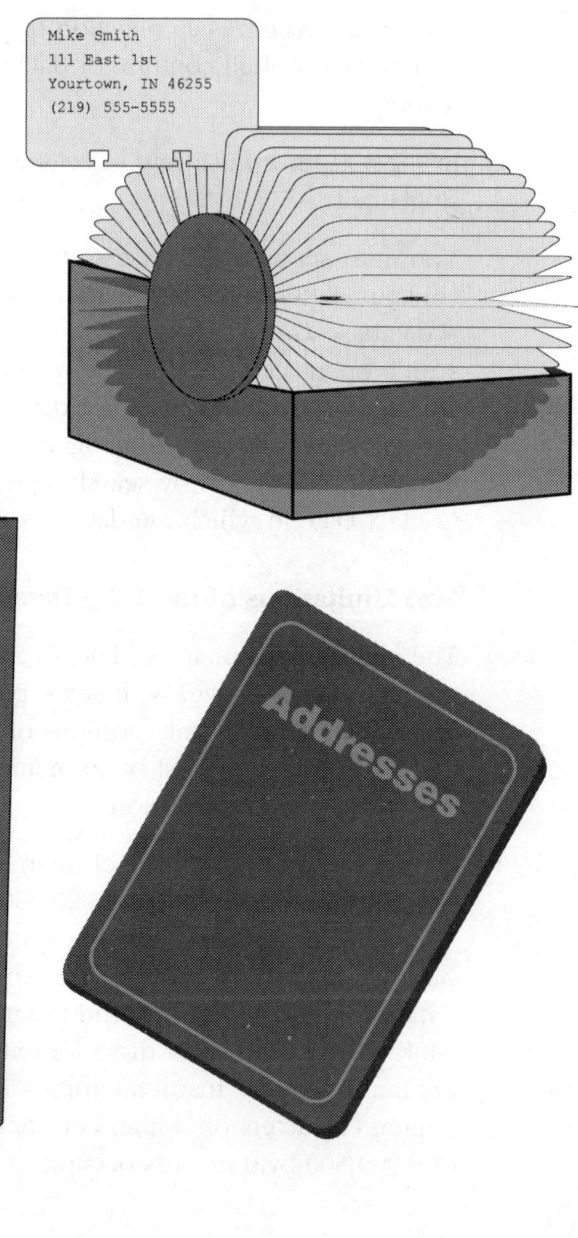

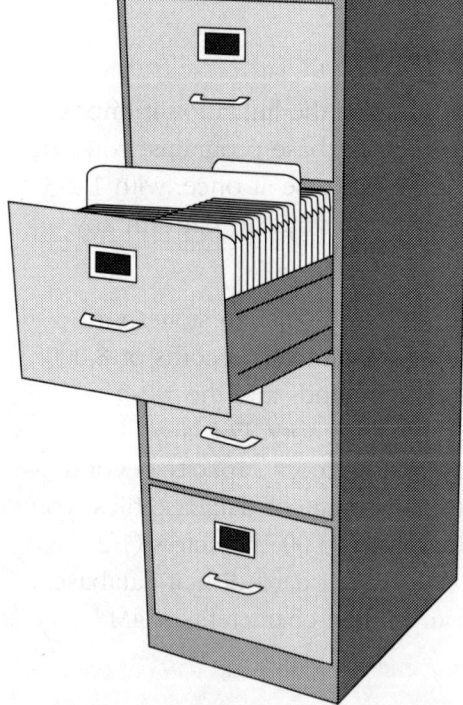

| Introduction | **What Is a Database?** | Creating a Database | Modifying a Database | Sorting Database Records | Searching for Records |

In 1-2-3, a database is a range of cells that covers at least one column and more than one row. So what makes a 1-2-3 database any different from any group of values on a worksheet? The organization of the data makes the difference. The information in a database must be sorted, searched, and organized in a manner that makes it easy to access.

A database key field is any field on which you base a list, search, or sort operation.

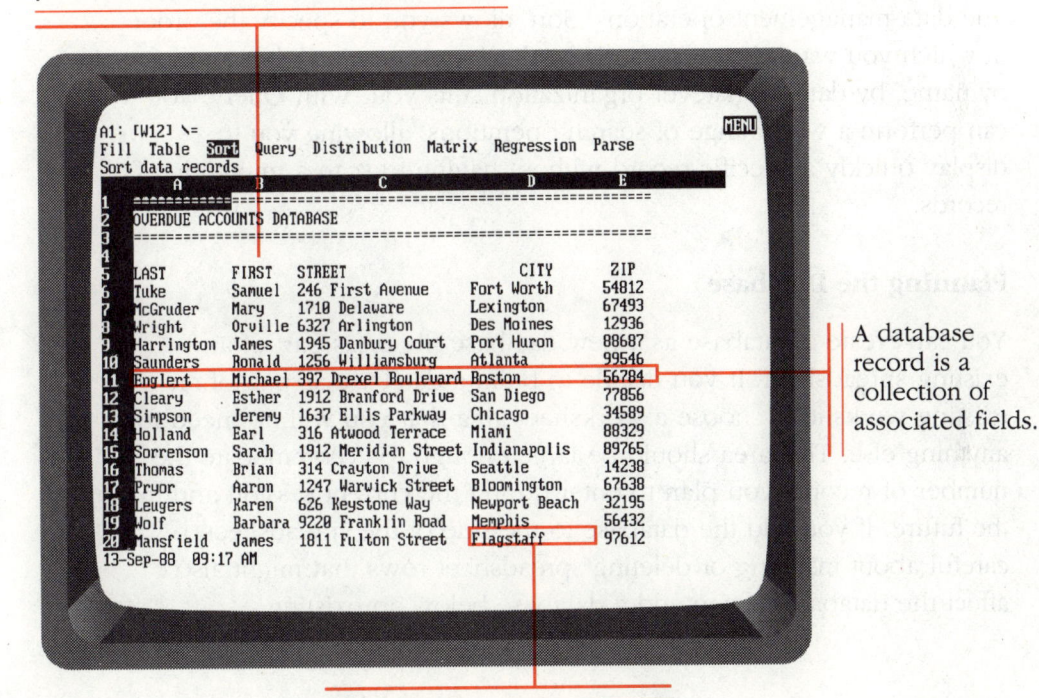

```
A1: [W12] \=                                              MENU
Fill Table Sort Query Distribution Matrix Regression Parse
Sort data records
         A         B         C              D            E
     ================================================
  1
  2   OVERDUE ACCOUNTS DATABASE
  3   ================================================
  4
  5   LAST      FIRST     STREET              CITY         ZIP
  6   Tuke      Samuel    246 First Avenue    Fort Worth   54812
  7   McGruder  Mary      1710 Delaware       Lexington    67493
  8   Wright    Orville   6327 Arlington      Des Moines   12936
  9   Harrington James    1945 Danbury Court  Port Huron   88687
 10   Saunders  Ronald    1256 Williamsburg   Atlanta      99546
 11   Englert   Michael   397 Drexel Boulevard Boston      56784
 12   Cleary    Esther    1912 Branford Drive San Diego    77856
 13   Simpson   Jeremy    1637 Ellis Parkway  Chicago      34589
 14   Holland   Earl      316 Atwood Terrace  Miami        88329
 15   Sorrenson Sarah     1912 Meridian Street Indianapolis 89765
 16   Thomas    Brian     314 Crayton Drive   Seattle      14238
 17   Pryor     Aaron     1247 Warwick Street Bloomington  67638
 18   Leugers   Karen     626 Keystone Way    Newport Beach 32195
 19   Wolf      Barbara   9220 Franklin Road  Memphis      56432
 20   Mansfield James     1811 Fulton Street  Flagstaff    97612
13-Sep-88  09:17 AM
```

A database record is a collection of associated fields.

The smallest unit in a database is a field, or single data item.

Introduction

An Overview of 1-2-3

Getting Started

1-2-3 Basics

Creating a Worksheet

Printing Reports

Creating and Printing Graphs

Managing Data

Understanding Macros

Appendix

337

Creating a Database

As you may know, you access the submenu of /**D**ata commands from the main 1-2-3 menu. All the options (**W**orksheet, **R**ange, **C**opy, **M**ove, **F**ile, **P**rint, and **G**raph) that precede **D**ata on the main menu work as well on databases as they do on spreadsheets. If you prefer to use a stand-alone program such as dBASE for your database, use 1-2-3's file-translation capabilities (introduced in Chapter 3) to take advantage of 1-2-3's data and graph commands.

In the **D**ata menu, the **S**ort and **Q**uery (search) options are considered true data-management operations. **S**ort allows you to specify the order in which you want the records of the database organized; by number, by name, by date—whatever organization suits you. With **Q**uery, you can perform a wide range of search operations, allowing you to display quickly a specific record without having to scan a multitude of records.

Planning the Database

You can create a database as a new database file or as part of an existing spreadsheet. If you decide to build a database as part of an existing worksheet, choose a worksheet area that you will not need for anything else. This area should be large enough to accommodate the number of records you plan to enter during the current session and in the future. If you add the database to the side of the spreadsheet, be careful about inserting or deleting spreadsheet rows that might also affect the database. If you add a database below an existing spreadsheet, be careful not to disturb predetermined column widths in the spreadsheet portion when you adjust column widths to the widths of database fields.

After you have decided which area of the worksheet to use, you create a database by specifying field names across a row and entering data in cells as you would for any other 1-2-3 application. The mechanics of entering database contents are simple; the most critical step in creating a useful database is choosing your fields accurately.

Determining Required Output

1-2-3's data-retrieval techniques rely on locating data by field names. Before you begin typing the kinds of data items you think you may need, write down the output you expect from the database. You'll also need to consider any source documents already in use that can provide input to the file.

When you are ready to set up the items in your database, you must specify for each information item a field name, the column width, and the type of entry. Before you set up the items, be sure to consider how you might look for data in that field. For example, consider how you will most likely look for a particular information item. Will you search by date? By last name? Knowing how you will use your database before you design it will save you a great amount of time that could be lost in redesigning the database after the fact.

Creating a Database

Understanding the Data Menu

You will use the **D**ata menu for many of 1-2-3's data management tasks. Remember, however, that a great number of worksheet commands can also be used for managing and manipulating data. When you select **D**ata from the 1-2-3 main menu, 1-2-3 displays the following options in the control panel's second menu line:

Fill **T**able **S**ort **Q**uery **D**istribution **M**atrix **R**egression **P**arse

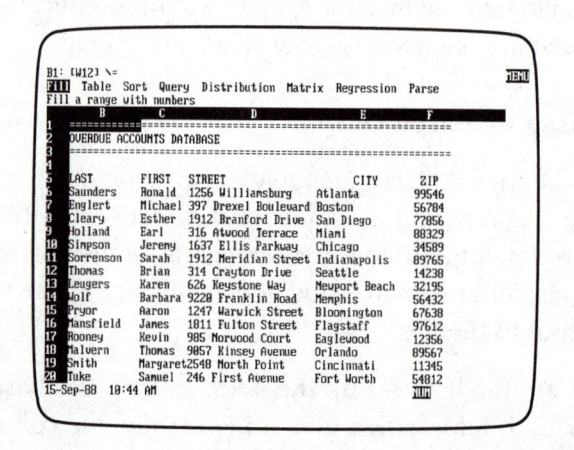

Fill	Is used to fill a specified range with values. You can choose the increment by which 1-2-3 increases or decreases successive numbers or dates.
Table	Often used for "what if" analysis, substitutes different values for a variable used in a formula.
Sort	Organizes the database in ascending or descending order.
Query	Is used for search operations and has different options for manipulating the found data items.
Distribution	Finds how often specific data occurs in a database.
Matrix	Lets you solve systems of simultaneous linear equations and manipulate the resulting solutions.
Regression	Performs multiple regression analysis on X and Y values.
Parse	Separates long labels resulting from **/F**ile **I**mport into discrete text and numeric cell entries.

If you decide to build a database as part of an existing worksheet, choose an area where changes to the database won't affect a spreadsheet or another database.

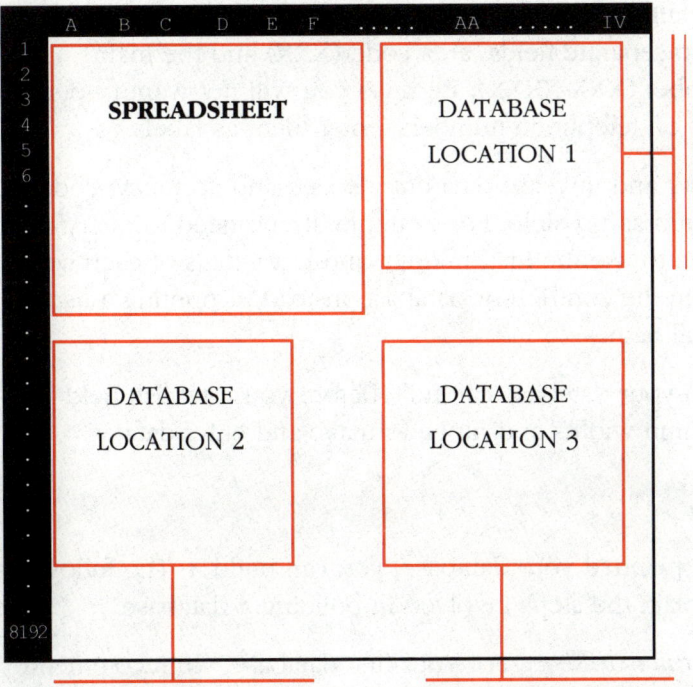

If you place a database to the right of a spreadsheet, inserting or deleting rows might affect the spreadsheet.

If you place a database directly below a spreadsheet, inserting and deleting columns might affect the spreadsheet.

An ideal location for a database is an area where inserting and deleting rows and columns or extracting data won't affect other applications above, below, to the right, or to the left of the database.

341

Creating a Database

After you decide on the fields, you then need to choose the level of detail needed for each item of information, select the appropriate column width, and determine whether you will enter data as a number or as a label. For example, if you want to be able to sort by area code all records containing telephone numbers, you should enter telephone numbers as two separate fields: area code (XXX) and the main telephone number (XXX-XXXX). Because you will not want to perform math functions on telephone numbers, enter them as labels.

To save memory and increase data-entry speed and accuracy, code as much information as possible. For example, if you need to query only workloads, plan to use the first, middle, and last initials of each contact representative in the contributor database instead of printing a list of the contacts' full names.

Be sure to plan your database carefully before you establish field names, set column widths and range formats, and enter data.

Entering Data

After you have planned your database, you can build it. The following paragraphs explain the steps involved in building a database.

Start with a blank worksheet. For your first database, we recommend that you start with a blank worksheet. If you'd rather use an existing worksheet, select an area that is out of the way of the spreadsheet, allows your database room to grow, and won't affect the spreadsheet when you insert or delete rows.

Enter the field names across a single row. The field names must be labels, even if they are numeric labels. Although you can use more than one row for the field names, 1-2-3 processes only the values that appear in the bottom row. For example, if you have the field name CONTRACT DATE assigned to column B with CONTRACT in row 3 and DATE in row 4, 1-2-3 will reference only DATE as a key field in sort or query operations. Also, keep in mind that all field names should be unique; any repetition of names confuses 1-2-3 when you search the database.

Set the cell display formats. Use 1-2-3's **F**ormat and **C**olumn **S**et-Width options to control the width of the cells and the way in which 1-2-3 displays the data. (For more information about these commands, see Chapter 4.) Note also that whenever a right-justified column of numeric data is adjacent to a left-justified column of label information, the data looks crowded. You can insert blank columns to change the spacing between fields, but if you plan to search values in the database, do not leave any blank rows.

Add records to the database. To enter the first record, move the cursor to the row directly below the field-name row and then enter the data across the row in the normal manner.

343

Creating a Database

Planning the Database

Plan what you want the database to do, what fields you will need, how wide the fields (columns) will have to be, and what type of output you want.

Remember that you must put the last and first names in separate columns if you want to sort the database according to the customers' last names.

Set up a separate area code field apart from your telephone number field if you want to search, sort, or extract records by zip code.

Customer Database

Item		Column Width	Type of Output
1.	Customer Last Name	12	Label
2.	Customer First Name	10	Label
3.	Street Address	15	Label
4.	City	12	Label
5.	State	2	Label
6.	Zip code	6	Number
7.	Area Code	6	Number
8.	Telephone	10	Label
9.	Account Number	10	Number
10.	Amount Due	6	Number
11.	Payment Due Date	12	Date
12.	Date Paid	12	Date

Because of the dash between the first three and last four digits of a telephone number, you must enter the number as a label.

344

Introduction | What Is a Database? | **Creating a Database** | Modifying a Database | Sorting Database Records | Searching for Records

Positioning the Database

If you don't want to start with a new worksheet, find a place on the worksheet where you will have enough room for the database, and where inserting or deleting lines on the spreadsheet won't affect the database information.

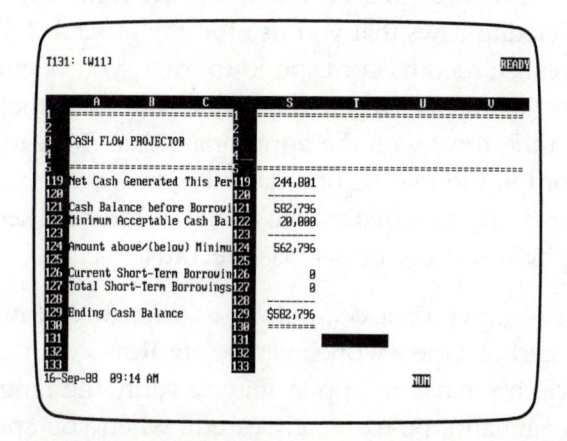

Once you've planned the database, you can get started by entering data. Enter the field names as labels across a single row, making sure that each field name is unique.

You can use two rows for field names, but 1-2-3 only processes the bottom row.

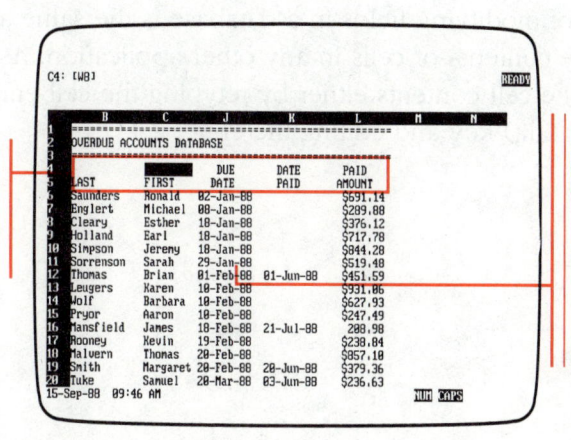

Change the column width to fit the information you will enter by using the **/W**orksheet **C**olumn **S**et-Width command.

Introduction

An Overview of 1-2-3

Getting Started

1-2-3 Basics

Creating a Worksheet

Printing Reports

Creating and Printing Graphs

Managing Data

Understanding Macros

Appendix

345

Modifying a Database

After you have collected the data for your database and decided which field types, widths, and formats to use, creating a database is easy. Thanks to 1-2-3, maintaining the accuracy of the database content is easy also.

To add and delete records in a database, use the same commands for inserting and deleting rows that you use for any other 1-2-3 application. Because records correspond to rows, you begin inserting a record with the **/W**orksheet **I**nsert **R**ow command. You then fill in the various fields in the rows with the appropriate data. Instead of inserting a record in the middle of a database, however, you probably will use 1-2-3's sorting capabilities, illustrated in the next section, to rearrange the physical order of database records.

To delete records, move your cell pointer to the row or rows that you want to delete and use the **/W**orksheet **D**elete **R**ow command. Because you will not have an opportunity to verify the range before you issue the command, be extremely careful when you specify the records to be deleted. If you want to remove only inactive records, consider first using the **E**xtract command to store the extracted inactive records in a separate file before you delete the records. (This chapter will teach you how.)

The process of modifying fields in a database is the same as that for modifying the contents of cells in any other application. As you know, you change the cell contents either by retyping the cell entry or by using the F2 (Edit) key and editing the entry.

Action	Use
add a record	**/W**orksheet **I**nsert **R**ow.
add a field	**/W**orksheet **I**nsert **C**olumn
delete a record	**/W**orksheet **D**elete **R**ow
delete a field	**/W**orksheet **D**elete **C**olumn
editing fields	F2 (Edit)

To add a new field to a database, position the cell pointer anywhere in the column that will be to the right of the newly inserted column. Issue the **/W**orksheet **I**nsert **C**olumn command, and then fill the field with values for each record.

Because maintaining data takes up valuable memory, you may not feel justified keeping certain seldom-used data fields in the database. To delete such a field, position the cell pointer anywhere in the column you want to remove and then use the **/W**orksheet **D**elete **C**olumn command.

All other commands, such as those for moving cells, formatting cells, displaying the contents of worksheets, etc., are the same for both database and other spreadsheet applications. For more about these commands, see Chapter 4.

Modifying a Database

Modifying a Database

As you update your 1-2-3 database, you may need to add or delete fields and records. Use the **/W**orksheet **I**nsert and **/W**orksheet **D**elete commands.

Inserting and Deleting Rows

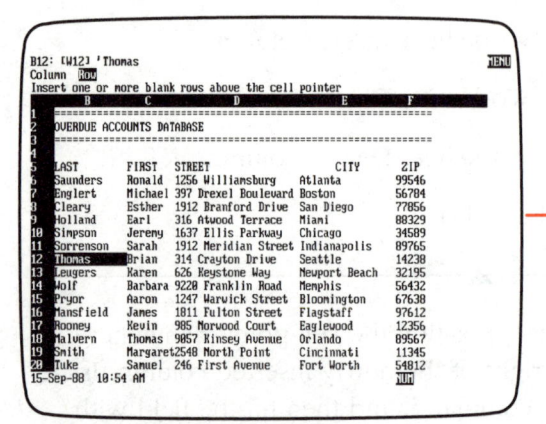

To insert a row (record) in the database, select **/W**orksheet **I**nsert **R**ow. When the `Enter row insert range:` prompt appears, move the cell pointer to or type the cell address of the location where you want the row inserted, and press `⏎Enter`.

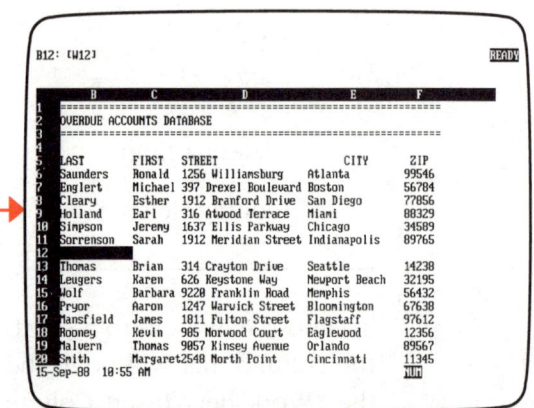

When you press `⏎Enter`, a blank row will appear ready for you to enter a new record.

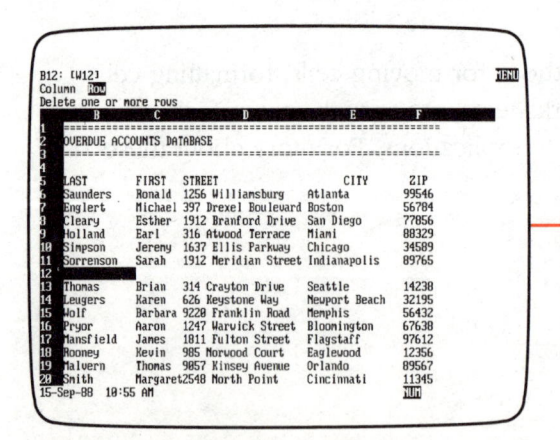

To delete a row, select **/W**orksheet **D**elete **R**ow.

When the `Enter range of rows to delete:` prompt appears, move the cell pointer to or type the cell address of the rows you want to delete and press `⏎Enter`.

348

	What Is a	Creating a	**Modifying a**	Sorting Database	Searching for
Introduction	Database?	Database	**Database**	Records	Records

Inserting and Deleting Columns

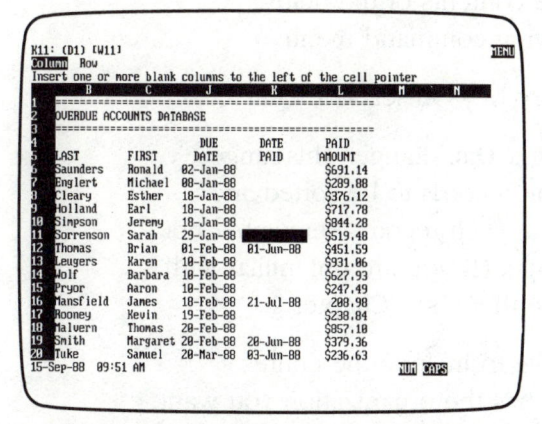

To insert a column (field) in the database, select **/W**orksheet **I**nsert **C**olumn. When the `Enter column insert range:` prompt appears, move the cell pointer to or type the cell address of the location you want the new column (field), and press ↵Enter.

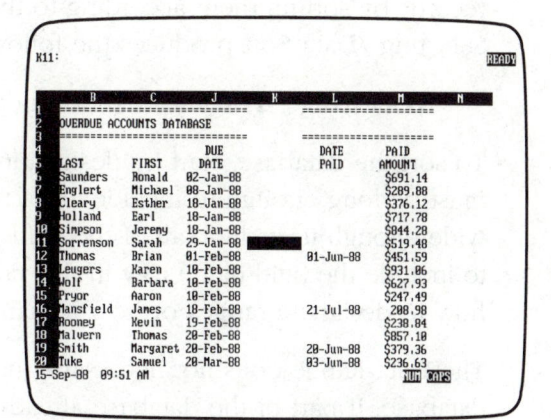

When you press ↵Enter, a blank column will appear ready for you to enter new data.

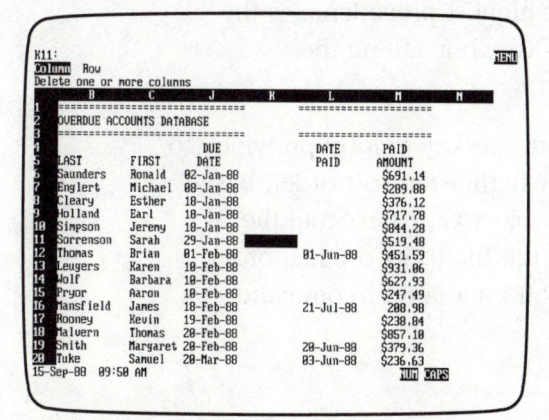

To delete a column, select **/W**orksheet **D**elete **C**olumn.

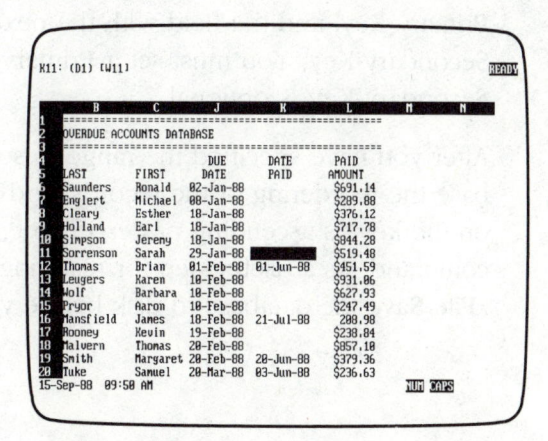

When the `Enter range of columns to delete:` prompt appears, move the cell pointer to the column you want to delete, and press ↵Enter.

Introduction

An Overview of 1-2-3

Getting Started

1-2-3 Basics

Creating a Worksheet

Printing Reports

Creating and Printing Graphs

Managing Data

Understanding Macros

Appendix

349

Sorting Database Records

1-2-3's data management capability lets you change the order of records by sorting them according to the contents of the fields. Selecting /Data Sort produces the following command menu:

Data-Range **P**rimary-Key **S**econdary-Key **R**eset **G**o **Q**uit

To sort the database, start by designating a **D**ata-Range. This range must be long enough to include all of the records to be sorted and wide enough to include all of the fields in each record. Remember not to include the field-name row in this range. (If you are unfamiliar with how to designate ranges or how to name them, see Chapter 4.)

The **D**ata-Range does not necessarily have to include the entire database. If part of the database already has the organization you want, or if you don't want to sort all the records, you can sort only a portion of the database. (Remember: When you sort, do not include the field names in your **D**ata-Range.)

After choosing the **D**ata-Range, you must specify the keys for the sort. *Keys* are the fields to which you attach the highest precedence when the database is sorted. The field with the highest precedence is the **P**rimary-Key, and the field with the next highest precedence is the **S**econdary-Key. You must set a **P**rimary-Key, but setting the **S**econdary-Key is optional.

After you have specified the range to sort, the key field(s) on which to base the reordering of the records, and whether the sort order, based on the key, is ascending or descending, select **G**o to execute the command. As a useful step for restoring the file to its original order, /**F**ile **S**ave the database to disk before you issue a **S**ort command.

The One-Key Sort

One of the simplest examples of a database sorted according to a primary key (often called a single-key database) is the White Pages of the telephone book. All the records in the White Pages are sorted in ascending alphabetical order using the last name as the primary key.

To use 1-2-3's **S**ort capability to reorder records alphabetically on the LAST name field, select **/D**ata **S**ort **D**ata-Range, and specify the range you want to sort. The **/D**ata **S**ort menu then returns to the screen. This menu is one of 1-2-3's "sticky" menus. (The **/P**rint **P**rinter menu is another.) Sticky menus remain displayed and active until you enter **Q**uit. This sticky menu is helpful because you don't have to enter **/D**ata **S**ort at the beginning of each command.

After choosing the **D**ata-Range, select **P**rimary-Key and then enter or point to the address of any entry (including blank or field-name cells) in the column containing the primary-key field. For example, if you want to sort the LASTNAME field in your database, and that field occupied column A, you could enter A1 as the address for the **P**rimary-Key. 1-2-3 then asks you to choose an ascending or descending sort order (**A** or **D**). If you choose ascending order, when you select **G**o, 1-2-3 sorts the database so that the last names are alphabetized from A to Z.

You can add a record to an alphabetized name-and-address database without having to insert a row manually to place the new record in the proper position. Simply add the new record to the bottom of the current database, expand the **D**ata-Range, and then sort the database again by last name.

351

Sorting Database Records

Sorting Data

Keeping data in a database would be meaningless if you were unable to alphabetize the data or sort it numerically. Sorting is an important function of any database. When you want to sort data, you will use the options available when you select /**D**ata **S**ort.

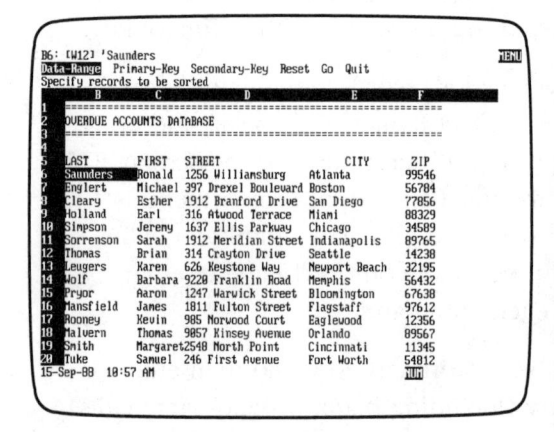

Data-Range	Specifies the range on which the sort operation will occur.
Primary-Key	First item on which the sort will be performed.
Secondary-Key	Second item on which the sort is performed.
Reset	Resets the sort options.
Go	Starts the search.
Quit	Leaves the /**D**ata **S**ort menu.

Steps for Sorting a Database

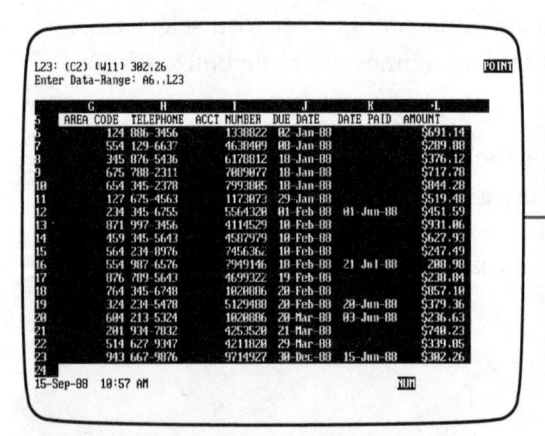

Follow these guidelines when entering a data-range:

1. The range should include only the records you want to sort. It should not include cells containing the field names or cells with data that are outside the database.
2. Make sure that your range includes all of the columns in your database.

First, select /**D**ata **S**ort **D**ata-Range. When the Enter Data Range: prompt appears, highlight, type the cell addresses, or enter the range name for the range you want to sort.

352

| Introduction | What Is a Database? | Creating a Database | Modifying a Database | **Sorting Database Records** | Searching for Records |

One-Key Sort

Specifying a one-key sort allows you to sort the records by one item. For example, in an employee database, an alphabetical sort by LASTNAME is a one-key sort. The field chosen as the sort key (LASTNAME) is known as the Primary-Key.

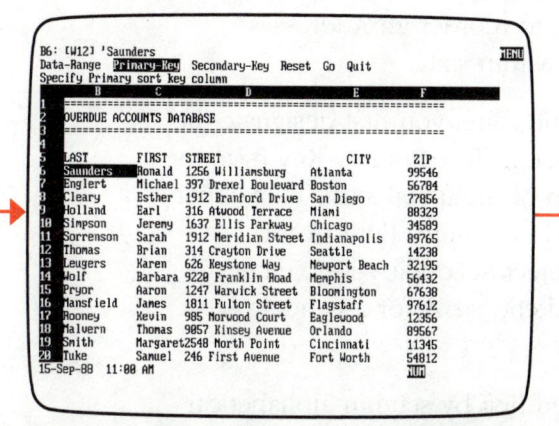

Second, after entering the data ranges containing the information you want sorted, select **P**rimary-Key from the **S**ort menu.

Third, move the cell pointer to any entry in the column containing the field upon which you want to sort. For example, move the cell pointer to an entry in the LAST (lastname) field if you want to sort the list by last name.

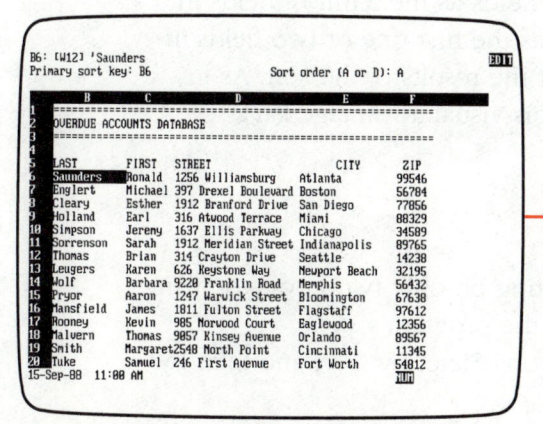

Fourth, type **A** or **D** to indicate whether you want your database sorted in ascending or descending order.

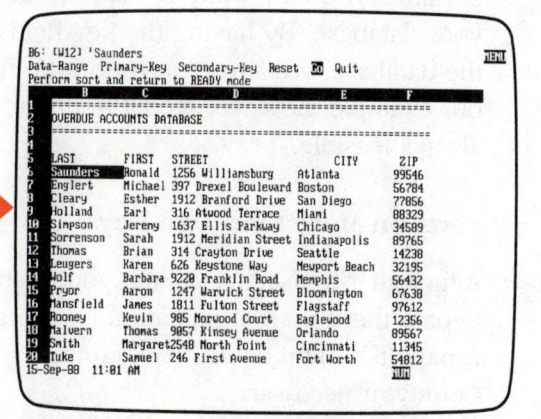

Finally, when the **S**ort menu returns, choose **G**o to have 1-2-3 sort the database.

Introduction

An Overview of 1-2-3

Getting Started

1-2-3 Basics

Creating a Worksheet

Printing Reports

Creating and Printing Graphs

Managing Data

Understanding Macros

Appendix

353

Sorting Database Records

The Two-Key Sort

A double-key database has both a primary and secondary key. In the Yellow Pages, records are sorted first according to business type (the primary key) and then by business name (the secondary key). Another example of a double-key sort (first by one key and then by another key within the first sort order) could be to reorder an Addresses database first by state and then by city within state.

To perform a double-key sort on city and state, you first designate the range you want to sort as the **D**ata-Range. Select **P**rimary-Key from the **S**ort menu and specify the field location of the initial sort. (Remember that you can specify any cell in the field's column.) Enter **A** for ascending order for the sort by state. Select **S**econdary-Key, enter the column location of the second sort, and choose **A** for ascending sort order by city.

After you select **G**o, records are grouped first by state in alphabetical order (California, Indiana, Kentucky, etc.) and then by city within state (Bloomington, Indiana, before Indianapolis, Indiana). When you determine whether to use a primary or secondary key, be sure to request a reasonable sort. Remember to make the primary key field the first field on which you want your data range sorted. Also, whenever possible, you may want to have the key fields as the leftmost fields in your database. By having the key fields as the first one or two fields in the database, you won't have to hunt for the results of the sort. As in our example, however, you'll find that this visual advantage isn't always feasible.

Sorts on More than Two Keys

Although 1-2-3 seems to limit you to sorting on only two keys, you can bypass this apparent limitation by using the program's *string* capabilities. You could, for example, sort by State, by City, and then by County, if necessary.

To generate accurate sorts by using 1-2-3 string capabilities, you must follow certain rules. You must create a new field and enter a string formula. All fields joined in the string operation must either be labels or be converted to labels. If the contents of the stringed fields are not all the same size, you must make appropriate adjustments to the string formula. You must copy the string formula to all records involved in the sort and convert the resultant formulas to values. After you complete the string setup, you will sort on the new field. For more about using string formulas for database operations, refer to Chapter 13 of *Using 1-2-3,* Special Edition.

Determining the Collating Sequence

The order in which the records appear after the sort depends on the ASCII numbers of the contents of the primary and secondary keys. For this reason, you should not include blank rows past the end of the database when you designate the **D**ata-Range. Because blanks have precedence over all the characters in a sort, these blank rows will appear at the top of your sorted database.

Use the Install program to determine the order of precedence that 1-2-3 uses for sorting text strings. You have three options: Numbers First (the default), Numbers Last, and ASCII.

Restoring the Presort Order

Once you sort the original contents of the database on any field, you cannot restore the records to their original order. If you add a "counter" column to the database before any sort, however, you will be able to reorder the records on any field and then restore the original order by resorting on the counter field. The counter field (often called Num) simply numbers each record so that you can restore the records back to their original order.

Sorting Database Records

The Two-Key Sort

The /Data Sort menu lets you sort your database on either one field or two fields. Sorting on one field is described on pages 351 - 353. To sort on two fields, follow these steps:

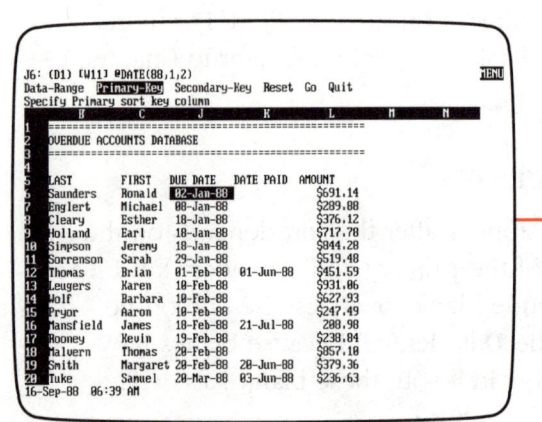

Primary-Key column

This database will be sorted first according to the DUE DATE column.

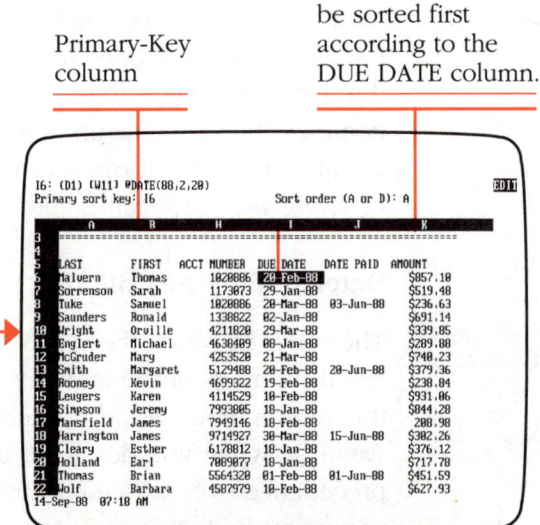

After you have entered the data range to be sorted, select **P**rimary-Key to indicate the main field upon which you want the data sorted.

Enter the cell address of a cell containing data in the column upon which the primary sort will occur. After entering the cell address, indicate the sort order: ascending (**A**) or descending (**D**).

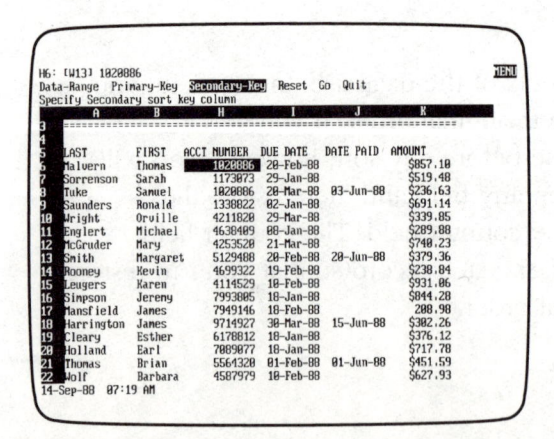

After establishing the primary key, select **S**econdary-Key to have the data sorted a second time within the primary sort order.

| Introduction | What Is a Database? | Creating a Database | Modifying a Database | **Sorting Database Records** | Searching for Records |

Secondary-Key

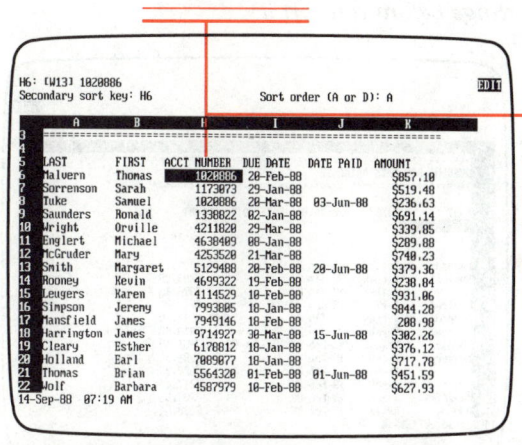

After being sorted according to DUE DATE, this database will be sorted according to ACCT NUMBER.

Enter the cell address of a cell containing data in the column upon which the secondary sort should occur, and indicate the sort order.

All records in the data range have been sorted first according to DUE DATE.

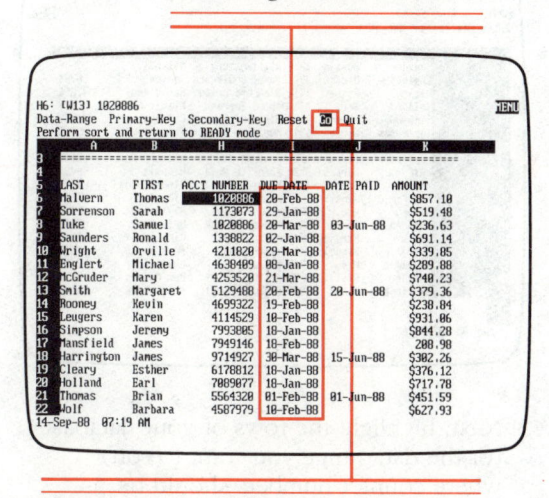

After setting the **P**rimary and **S**econdary keys, select **G**o to have the database sorted.

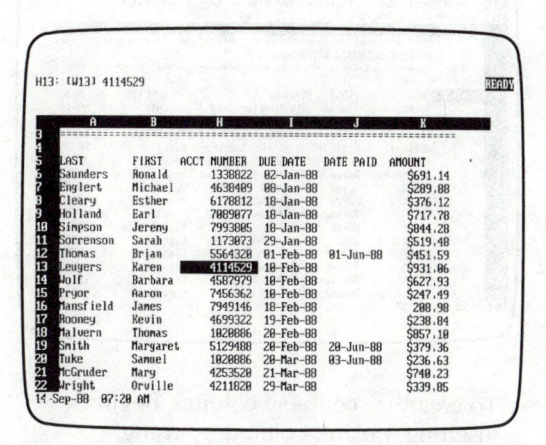

Accounts that are due on the same day are sorted according to ACCT NUMBER.

Introduction

An Overview of 1-2-3

Getting Started

1-2-3 Basics

Creating a Worksheet

Printing Reports

Creating and Printing Graphs

Managing Data

Understanding Macros

Appendix

357

Sorting Database Records

Tips for Sorting Database Records

Tip 1: Don't include blank rows in your data range before you sort it.

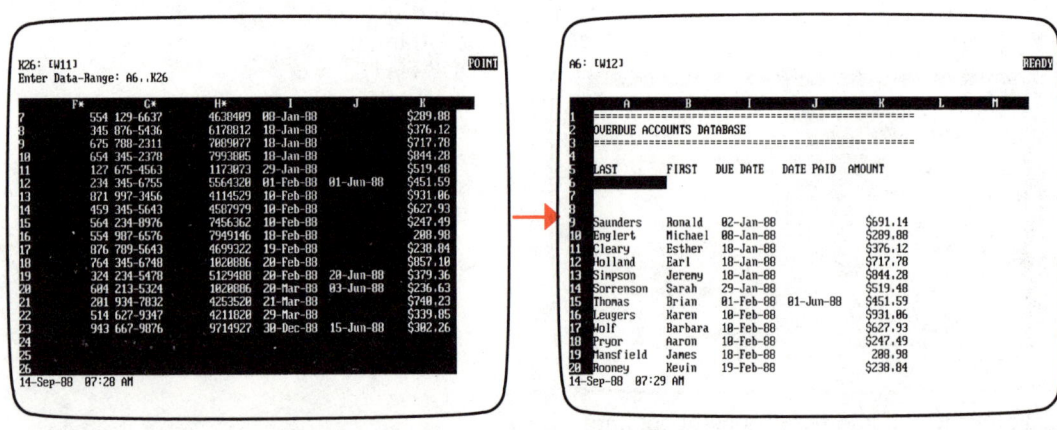

If you accidentally include one or more blank rows in your data range, the blank rows will appear at the top of your data range.

Tip 2: Use the /Data Fill Command to create a "counter" field so that you can easily re-sort the database to its original order if you need to.

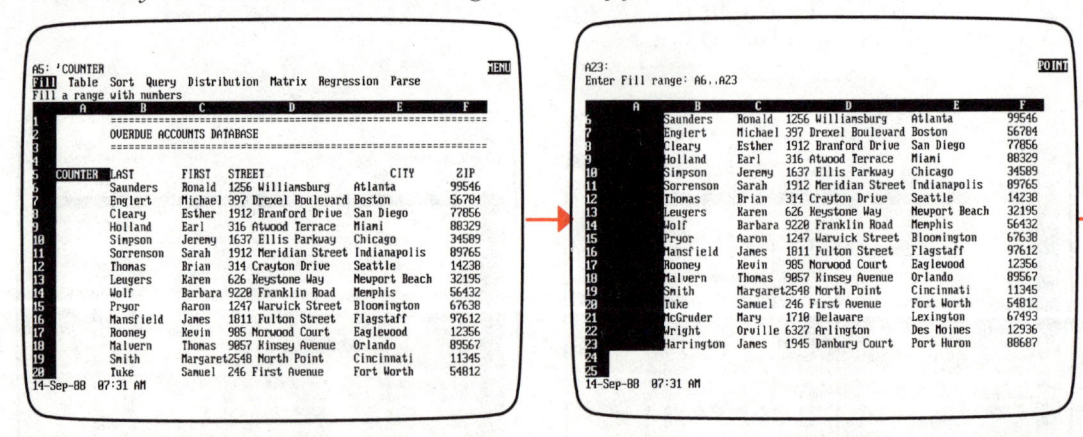

To create a "counter" column, begin by inserting a blank column by using /Worksheet Insert Column. Then, select /Data Fill.

Next, highlight the rows of your database (or the data range you want to sort) where counter numbers should be entered.

358

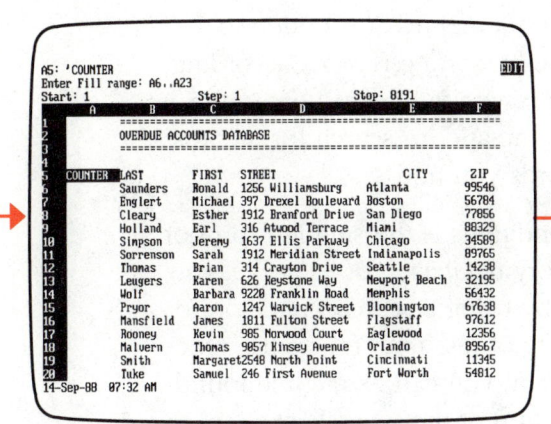

| Introduction | What Is a Database? | Creating a Database | Modifying a Database | **Sorting Database Records** | Searching for Records |

After indicating the /**D**ata **F**ill range, 1-2-3 will prompt you for Start and Stop numbers and for the increment of the numbers. Enter `1` for start and `1` for Step. (There's no need to change the Stop value).

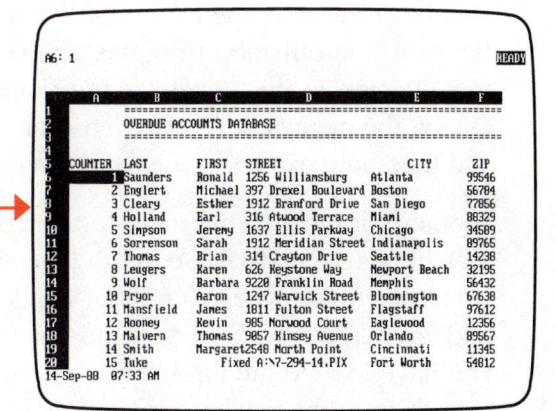

As soon as you enter Start and Step values, 1-2-3 will fill the range with consecutive numbers.

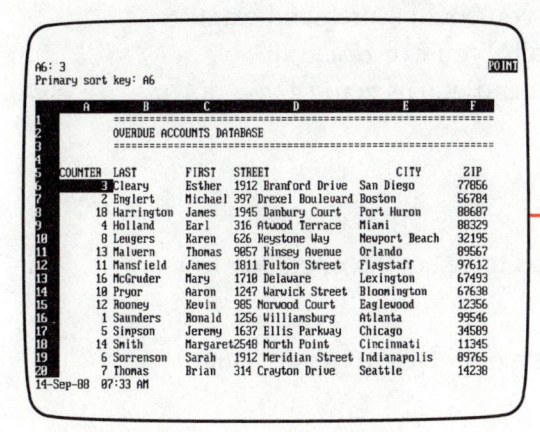

When you sort the database, be sure to include the COUNTER column in your data range. If you need to re-sort the database to its original order, sort the database with the COUNTER field as your primary key field.

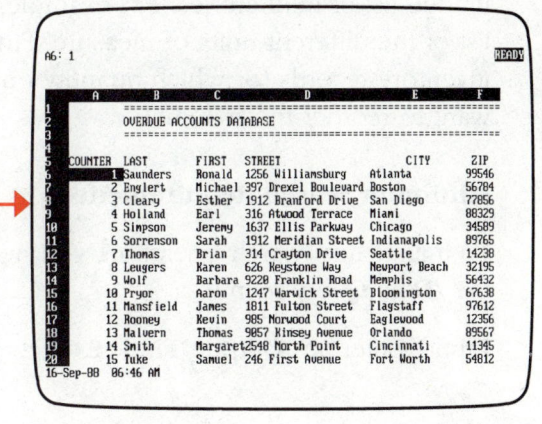

Using the COUNTER as your primary key field will return the database its original order.

Introduction

An Overview of 1-2-3

Getting Started

1-2-3 Basics

Creating a Worksheet

Printing Reports

Creating and Printing Graphs

Managing Data

Understanding Macros

Appendix

359

Searching for Records

You have learned how to use the main Data menu's Sort option to reorganize information from the database by sorting records according to key fields. In this section of the chapter, you will learn how to use Query, the menu's other data-retrieval command, to search for records and then edit, extract, or delete the records you find.

Looking for records that meet certain conditions is the simplest form of searching a 1-2-3 database. In an inventory database, for example, you could determine when to reorder items by using a search operation to find any records with an on-hand quantity of less than four units. Once you have located the information you want, you can extract the found records from the database to another section of the worksheet, separate from the database. For example, you can extract all records with a purchase order (P.O.) date, and print the newly extracted area as a record of pending purchases.

With 1-2-3's search operations, you also have the option of looking for only the first occurrence of a specified field value in order to develop a unique list of field entries. For example, you could search and extract a list of the different units of measure. Finally, you can *delete* all inventory records for which quantity on-hand equals zero (if you don't want to reorder these items).

Minimum Search Requirements

To initiate any search operation, you need to select the operation from the /Data Query menu:

Input Criterion Output Find Extract Unique Delete Reset Quit

You can use the first three options to specify ranges applicable to the search operations. **I**nput and **C**riterion, which give the locations of the search area and the search conditions, respectively, must be specified in all **Q**uery operations. An output range must be established only when you select a **Q**uery command that copies records or parts of records to an area outside the database.

The last two options signal the end of the current search operation. **R**eset removes all previous search-related ranges so that you can specify a different search location and conditions. **Q**uit restores the main **D**ata menu.

The four options in the middle of the **Q**uery menu perform the following search functions:

Find moves down through a database and positions the cursor on records that match given criteria. You can enter or change data in the records as you move the cursor through them. **E**xtract creates copies, in a specified area of the worksheet, of all or some of the fields in certain records that match given criteria. **U**nique is similar to **E**xtract, but recognizes that some of the field contents in the database may be duplicates of other cell entries in the same fields. **U**nique eliminates duplicates as entries are copied to output range. **D**elete deletes from a database all the records that match given criteria and shifts the remaining records to fill in the gaps that remain.

361

Searching for Records

The /Data Query Command

The **/D**ata **Q**uery **C**ommand lets you search for and extract data that meet a specific criterion.

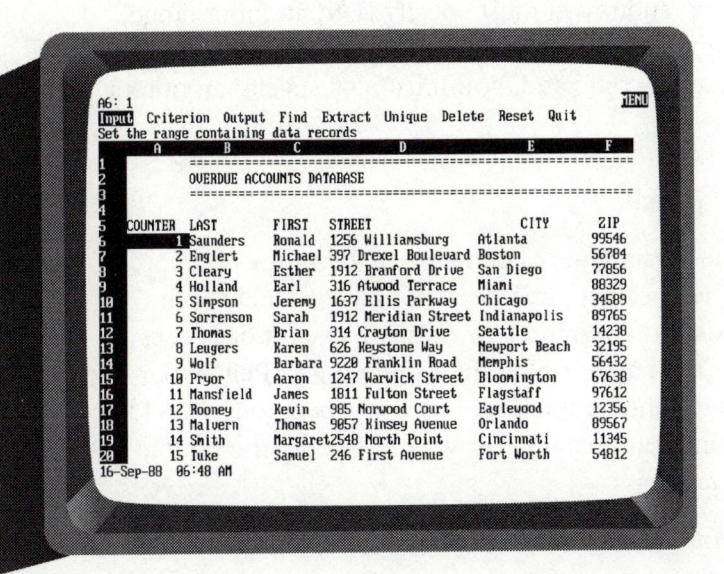

			Sorting	
	What Is a	Creating a	Modifying a	Database	**Searching for**
Introduction	Database?	Database	Database	Records	**Records**

After you choose **/D**ata **Q**uery, a menu of nine options is displayed for performing search and extract operations.

Introduction

An Overview of 1-2-3

Getting Started

1-2-3 Basics

Creating a Worksheet

Printing Reports

Creating and Printing Graphs

Managing Data

Understanding Macros

Appendix

/Data Query Menu

Input	Allows you to specify the input range.
Criterion	Lets you set the criterion on which the search is based.
Output	Is used to accept any ranges extracted from the database.
Find	Locates specified records.
Extract	Copies the specified records from the database and places them in the output range.
Unique	Finds only unique records based upon criterion.
Delete	Removes selected records.
Reset	Resets the search ranges.
Quit	Exits the **/D**ata **Q**uery menu.

363

Searching for Records

To perform a **Q**uery operation, you must specify both an input range and a criterion range and select one of the four search options. (Before issuing a **U**nique or **E**xtract command, you must also specify an output range.)

Determining the Input Range

The input range for the **/D**ata **Q**uery command is the range of records you want to search. The specified area does not have to include the entire database. Whether you search all or only a part of a database, you *must* include the field-name row in the input range. (Remember that you must *not* include the field names in a sort operation.) If field names occupy space on more than one row, specify only the bottom row to start the input range.

Select **/D**ata **Q**uery **I**nput, and specify the range by typing or pointing to a range name or by using an assigned range name. You do not have to specify the range again unless the search area changes.

Determining the Criterion Range

To search for data that meets a certain criterion, you must set up a special range, called a criterion range, that specifies the criterion upon which the search is conducted.

Suppose that in an addresses database, you want to identify all records that contain OH in the STATE field. When the database is on-screen and 1-2-3 is in READY mode, type *STATE* in cell H2, for example, and *OH* in cell H3. You can type *Criterion Range* in cell H1 if you want the documentation it provides; that cell will not be directly involved in the search command. You then select **/D**ata **Q**uery and specify A1..F19 as the input range. The **Q**uery submenu will be displayed in the control panel as soon as you enter the input range. Select **C**riterion, and then type, point to, or name the range H2..H3 as the location of your search condition. The **Q**uery menu will again return to the screen.

You can use numbers, labels, or formulas as criteria. A criterion range can be up to 32 columns wide and two or more rows long. The first row must contain the field names of the search criteria, such as STATE in the previous example. The rows below the unique field names contain the actual criteria, such as OH in row 3. The field names of the input range and the criterion range must match exactly.

By entering the input and criterion ranges, you have completed the minimum requirements for executing a **F**ind or **D**elete command. Be sure to enter the specific field names above the conditions in the worksheet (in READY mode) before you use the **/D**ata **Q**uery **C**riterion command sequence.

Issuing the Find Command

When you select **F**ind from the **Q**uery menu, a highlighted bar will rest on the first record (in the input range) that meets the conditions specified in the criterion range. In the example discussed in the last section, the highlighted bar would rest on the first record that includes OH in the STATE field.

By using the down-arrow cursor key, you can position the highlighted bar on the next record that conforms to the criterion. You can continue pressing the down-arrow key until the last record that meets the search conditions has been highlighted. Notice that the mode indicator changes from READY to FIND during the search.

The down-arrow and up-arrow keys let you position the cursor to the next and previous records that conform to the search criteria set in the criterion range. The Home and End keys can be used to position the cursor on the first and last records in the database, even if those records do not fit the search criteria. In FIND mode, you can use the right-arrow and left-arrow cursor keys to move the single-character flashing cursor to different fields in the current highlighted record. Then enter new values or use the Edit key to update the current values in the field.

To end the **F**ind operation and return to the **D**ata **Q**uery menu, press Enter or Esc. To return directly to READY mode, press Ctrl-Break.

365

Searching for Records

Searching for Specific Records

If you want to search for one or a number of specific records that meet a certain criterion, you need to use three commands from the /Data Query menu: Input, Criterion, and Find. If you wanted to search a database containing a list of customers to find a specific customer, you would follow these steps:

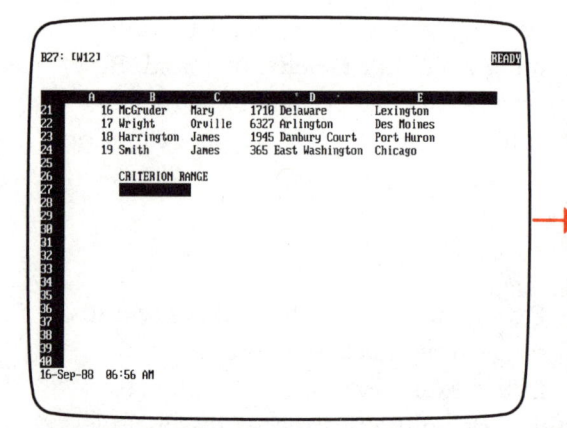

First, begin by locating an area where you can enter the criterion upon which you want to search the database, and type *Criterion Range* to mark the area.

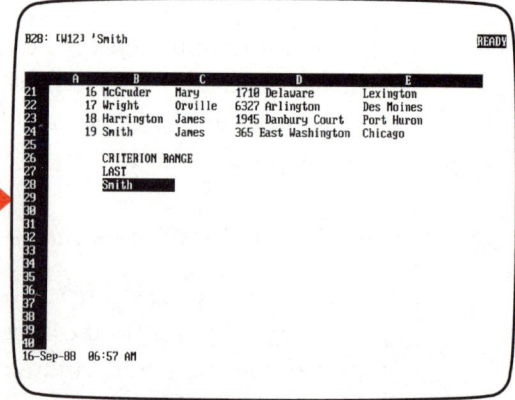

Second, enter the exact field name of the field upon which you want the search to take place. In this database, LAST is the field name. In the cell below the field name, enter the specific criterion.

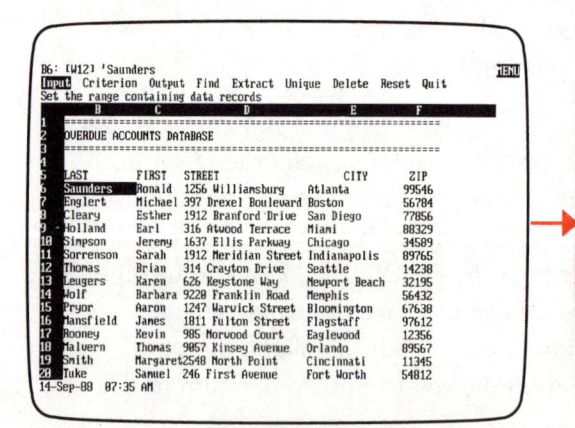

Third, indicate the range containing the records to be searched by using the /Data Query Input command.

Fourth, when the Enter Input range: prompt appears, enter the cell addresses of, highlight, or enter the range name for the range of cells to be searched.

Defining the Criterion Range

After you have located an area for your criterion range, use the **/D**ata **Q**uery **C**riterion command for specifying the criterion upon which 1-2-3 should search.

Choose **/D**ata **Q**uery **C**riterion.

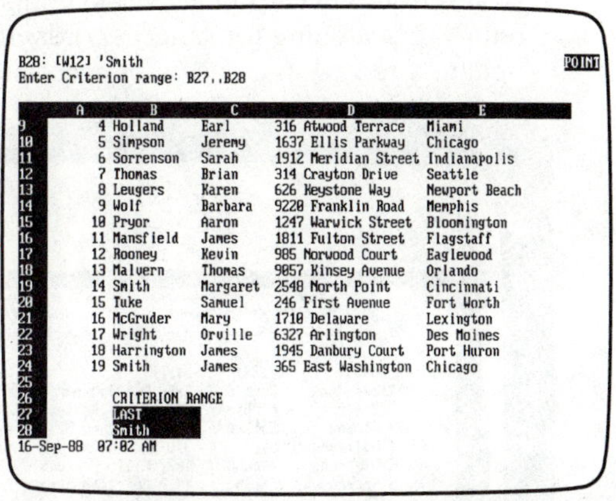

At the `Enter Criterion range:` prompt, enter the range of cells containing the field name and specific criterion. A criterion range can be up to 32 columns wide and two or more rows long.

Finding Records that Meet the Criterion

After you have defined the **I**nput and **C**riterion ranges, you're ready to search the database for records that meet the criterion you have set.

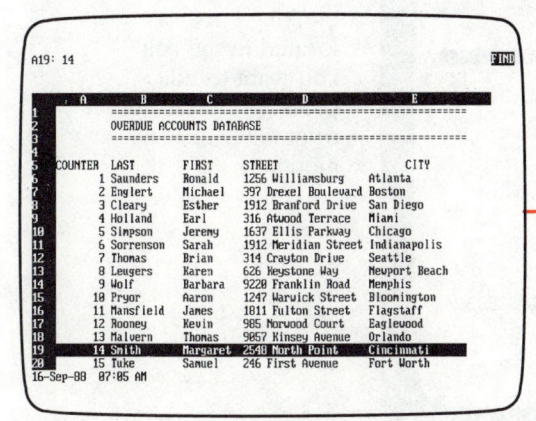

Select **F**ind from the **/D**ata **Q**uery menu, and 1-2-3 will highlight the first record meeting the criterion.

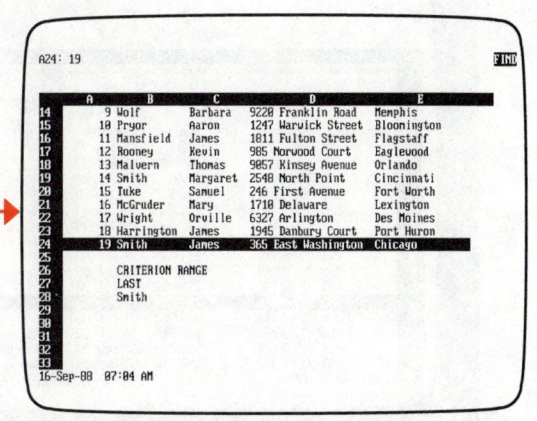

Move the down-arrow cursor to find other records that conform to the criterion. Press [Esc] if you want to end the search.

367

Searching for Records

Editing Records during a Search

If you need to change a record as you are conducting a search, you can switch from FIND to EDIT mode temporarily, edit the record, and then return to searching for other records. If you wanted, for example, to update a record in a customer account database, you follow these steps:

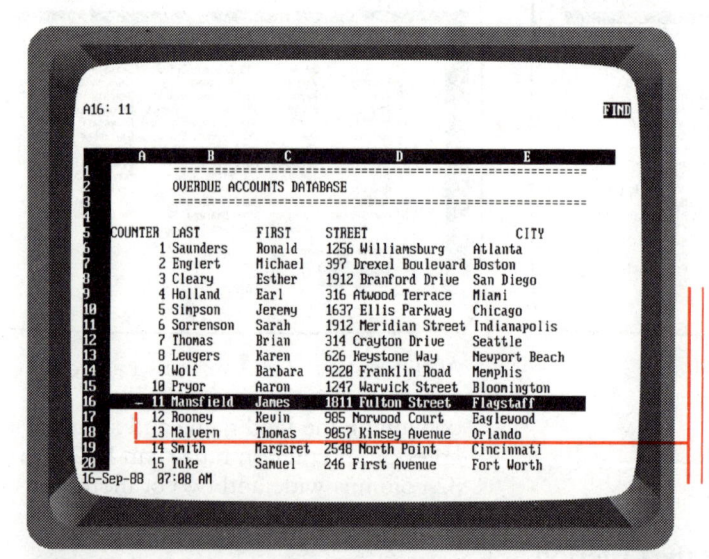

First, begin the search operation by choosing **/D**ata **Q**uery **F**ind.

In FIND mode, move the → or ← keys until the blinking cursor is located in the cell where you want to edit data.

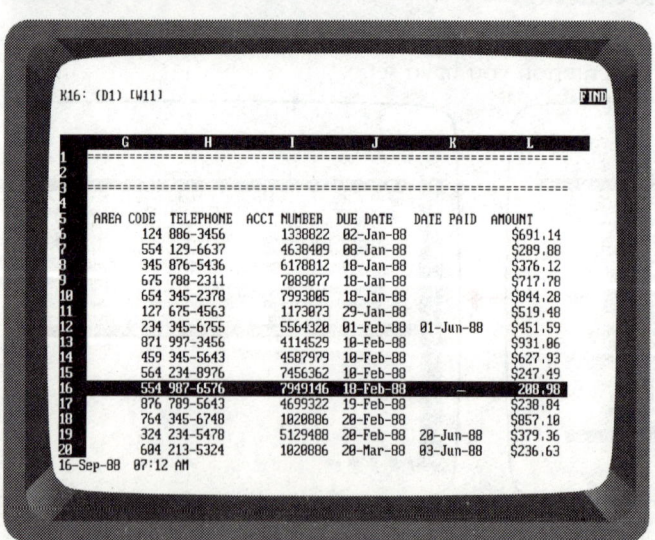

Second, when the blinking cursor is located in the cell you want to edit, press **F2** to change from FIND to EDIT mode.

368

					Sorting	
	What Is a	Creating a	Modifying a	Database	**Searching for**
Introduction	Database?	Database	Database	Records	**Records**

Third, enter new data or edit existing data.

After you edit the record, 1-2-3 will return to FIND mode.

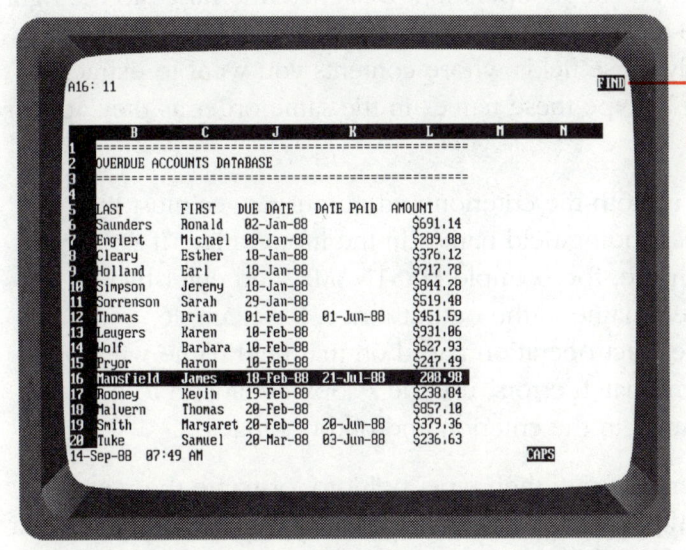

Finally, when you press ↵Enter the new or edited data will be displayed.

Introduction

An Overview of 1-2-3

Getting Started

1-2-3 Basics

Creating a Worksheet

Printing Reports

Creating and Printing Graphs

Managing Data

Understanding Macros

Appendix

369

Searching for Records

Listing All Specified Records

The **F**ind command has limited use, especially in a large database, because the command scrolls through the entire file so that you can view each record that meets the specified criterion. As an alternative to the **F**ind command, you can use the **E**xtract command to copy to a blank area of the worksheet only those records that meet specified conditions. (Before you issue the command, you must define the blank area of the worksheet as an output range.) You can view a list of all the extracted records, print the range of the newly extracted records, or even use the **/F**ile **X**tract command to copy only the extracted record range to a new file on disk.

Defining the Output Range

Choose a blank area in the worksheet as the output range to receive records copied in an extract operation. Designate the range to the right of, or below, the database. In the first row of the output range, type the names of only those fields whose contents you want to extract. You do not have to type these names in the same order as they appear in the database.

The field names in both the criterion and output ranges must match exactly the corresponding field names in the input range. If you enter a database field name, for example FIRSTNAME, and enter the corresponding field name in the output range, for example, FIRSTNAME, an extract operation based on that field name will not work. To avoid mismatch errors, use the /**C**opy command to copy the database field names in the criterion and output ranges.

Select **/D**ata **Q**uery **O**utput; then type, point to, or name the range location of the output area. You can create an open-ended extract area by entering only the field-name row as the range, or you can set the exact size of the extract area.

To limit the size of the extract area, enter the upper-left to lower-right cell coordinates of the entire output range. The first row in the specified range must contain the field names; the remaining rows must accommodate the maximum number of records you expect to receive from the extract operation. Use this method when you want to retain additional data that is located below the extract area. If you do not allow sufficient room in the fixed-length output area, the extract operation will abort and the message `too many records` will be displayed on-screen.

To create an open-ended extract area that does not limit the number of incoming records, specify as the output range only the row containing the output field names.

An extract operation first removes all existing data from the output range. If you use only the field-name row to specify the output area, all data below that row will be destroyed to make room for the unknown number of incoming extracted records.

Executing the Extract Command

To execute an **E**xtract command, you must type the search conditions in the worksheet, type the output field names in the worksheet, and set the input, criterion, and output ranges from the **D**ata **Q**uery menu.

To accelerate what seems to be a time-consuming setup process, establish standard input, criterion, and output areas and then store the range names for these locations. Keeping in mind the limit of 32 criterion fields, you might establish a single criterion range that encompasses all the key fields on which you might search. By establishing such a range, you will save the time needed to respecify a criterion range for each extract on different field names; but if the criterion range contains many unused field names, you will lose some execution speed.

You do not have to extract entire records or maintain the order of field names within the extracted records.

371

Searching for Records

Listing All Specified Records

In addition to searching for records that meet a specified criterion, you can copy all of those records to another part of the worksheet. To copy records to another part of the worksheet, begin by entering the input and criterion ranges as described in the previous sections, and then follow these steps:

First, copy the field names of your database to the section of the worksheet where you want specified records copied.

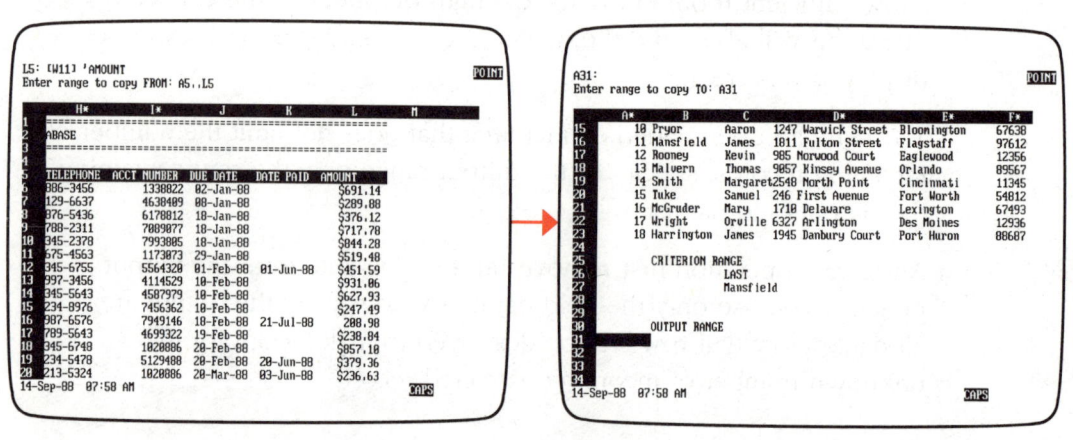

Second, select **/D**ata **Q**uery **O**utput and indicate the output range where the records should be copied. You can either indicate an unlimited range or range limited to a specific block of cells.

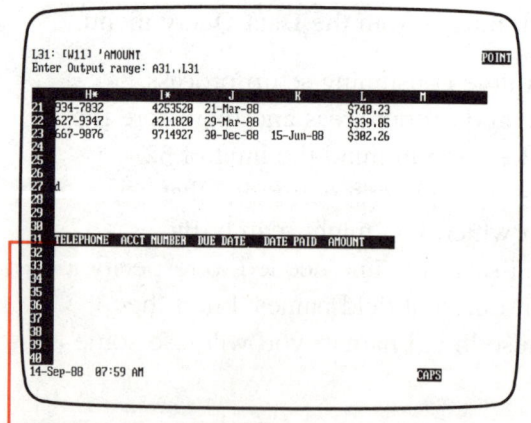

To enter an unlimited output range, highlight only the cells containing field names.

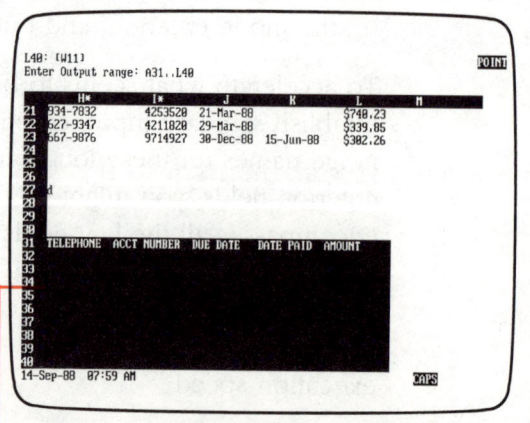

If you enter a limited range, the range must be as large or larger than the range of data you want copied to the range.

				Sorting	
	What Is a	Creating a	Modifying a	Database	**Searching for**
Introduction	Database?	Database	Database	Records	**Records**

Introduction

An Overview of 1-2-3

Getting Started

Third, choose **E**xtract from the **/D**ata **Q**uery menu.

1-2-3 Basics

Creating a Worksheet

Printing Reports

Creating and Printing Graphs

Managing Data

When you press ⏎**Enter**, all records that meet the specified criterion in the criterion range will be copied to the output area.

Understanding Macros

Appendix

The criterion for finding records in this output range is all accounts with overdue charges greater than $500.

373

Searching for Records

Copying Extracted Records to a New File

If you want to copy extracted records to their own special file, follow these steps:

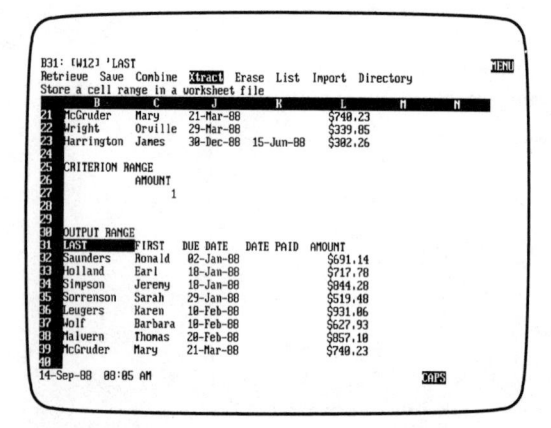

First, select the **X**tract command from the **/F**ile menu.

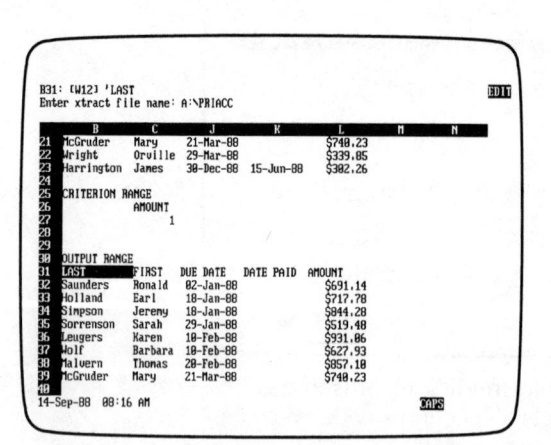

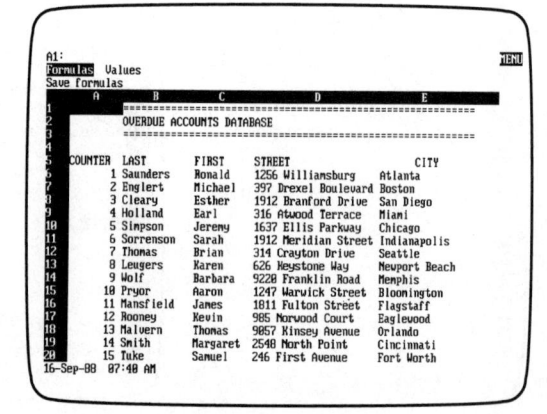

Second, select either **F**ormulas or **V**alues, depending on whether the data contains formulas you want retained in the new file.

Third, enter the name you want to give to the new file.

| Introduction | What Is a Database? | Creating a Database | Modifying a Database | Sorting Database Records | **Searching for Records** |

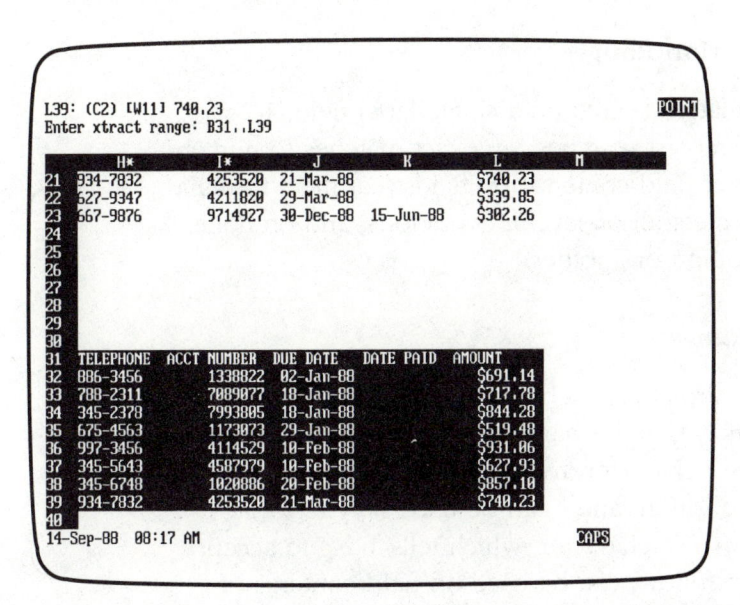

Introduction

An Overview of 1-2-3

Getting Started

1-2-3 Basics

Creating a Worksheet

Printing Reports

Creating and Printing Graphs

Managing Data

Understanding Macros

Appendix

Fourth, enter the cell addresses of, highlight, or enter the range name for the range of records you want to copy to a new file.

When you press ⏎Enter, a new file will be created containing the data from your extract range.

375

Searching for Records

More Complicated Criterion Ranges

In addition to an "exact match" search on a single label field, 1-2-3 permits a wide variety of record searches: on exact matches to numeric fields; on partial matches of field contents; on fields that meet formula conditions; on fields that meet all of several conditions; and on fields that meet either one condition or another.

Wild Cards in Criterion Ranges

You can use 1-2-3's wild cards for matching labels in database operations. The characters ?, *, and ~ have special meaning when used in the criterion range. The ? character instructs 1-2-3 to accept any character in that specific position, and ? can be used only to locate fields of the same length. The * character, which tells 1-2-3 to accept any and all characters that follow, can be used on field contents of unequal length. By placing a tilde (~) symbol at the beginning of a label, you tell 1-2-3 to accept all values *except* those that follow.

Use the ? and * wild card characters when you are unsure of the spelling used in field contents. Be sure that the results of any extract operation that uses a wild card are what you need. And be extremely careful when you use wild cards with a **D**elete command. If you are not careful, you may remove more records than you intend.

Formulas in Criterion Ranges

To set up formulas that query numeric fields in the database, you can use the following relational operators:

>	Greater than	<=	Less than or equal to
>=	Greater than or equal to	=	Equal to
<	Less Than	<>	Not equal to

Create a formula that references the first field entry in the numeric column you want to search. 1-2-3 will test the formula on each cell down the column until the program reaches the end of the specified input range.

You can place the formula anywhere below the criterion range's field-name row (unlike text criteria, which must appear directly below the associated field name).

If you want to use a formula to reference cells outside the database, use formulas that include absolute cell addressing.

With the program still in READY mode, press the F7 (Query) key to repeat the most recent query operation (**Extract**, in this example) and eliminate the need to select **/D**ata **Q**uery **E**xtract. Use the shortcut method only when you do not want to change the locations of the input, criterion, and output ranges.

AND Conditions

Now that you have seen how to base a **F**ind or **E**xtract operation on only one criterion, you will learn how to use multiple criteria for your queries. You can set up multiple criteria as AND conditions (in which *all* the criteria must be met) or as OR conditions (in which any *one* criterion must be met). For example, searching a music department's library for sheet music requiring drums AND trumpets is likely to produce fewer selections than searching for music appropriate for drums OR trumpets. Indicate two or more criteria, ALL of which must be met, by specifying the conditions on the criterion row immediately below the field names.

When you maintain a criterion range that includes many fields, you can quickly extract records based on an alternative condition.

You also can continue to add conditions that must be met. Enter the additional criteria only in the row immediately below the field-name row.

377

Searching for Records

OR Conditions

Criteria placed on the *same* row have the effect of a logical AND; they tell 1-2-3 to find or extract on this field condition AND this field condition AND this field condition, etc. Criteria placed on *different* rows have the effect of a logical OR; that is, find or extract on this field condition OR that field condition, and so on. You can set up a logical OR search on one or more fields.

Searching a single field for more than one condition is the simplest use of an OR condition. For example, you could extract from an inventory database only the records whose unit of issue is either KT (kit) or ST (set).

To do this search, under the ISSUE criterion field, you would type one condition immediately below the other. Be sure to expand the criterion range to include the additional row.

You can also specify a logical OR condition on two or more different field conditions. Building on the preceding example, perhaps you want to find the records with values of KT or ST OR with costs of more than $4.

To add additional OR criteria, drop to a new row, enter each new condition, and expand the criterion range. If you reduce the number of rows involved in an OR logical search, be sure to contract the criterion range.

Although no technical reason prevents you from mixing AND and OR logical searches, the results of such a mixed query operation may not be of much use. AND conditions do not have to be in the row immediately below the field name row. However, they do have to be contained in an individual row. OR conditions are done in separate rows. Follow the format of placing each AND condition in the row immediately below the criterion field name row, and each OR condition in a separate row below.

String Searches

If you want to search on the partial contents of a field, you can use functions in a formula. For example, suppose that you can remember only the street name "Keystone" for a record you want to extract from the Addresses database. If you can safely assume that all street addresses start with a number and have a space before the street name (XXX Streetname) and that your Addresses field occupies column C, you could use a formula similar to the following one as the search criterion:

```
@MID(C2,@FIND(" ",C2,0)+1,8)="keystone"
```

The double quotation marks (" ") in the formula instruct 1-2-3 to start the search after a blank space is encountered (between the street number and street name). The 1,8 portion of the formula instructs the program to search on the first through the eighth character positions matching "Keystone," thereby eliminating any need to know whether "Street," "Ave.," "Avenue," etc., is part of the field. You also could use compound criteria and search on both CITY and part of the STREET ADDRESS field.

Searching for Records

Wild Cards and Formulas in Criterion Ranges

Depending on the complexity of your database operations, you may need to be a bit more inventive when you are specifying criterion ranges in 1-2-3. For that reason, 1-2-3 allows you to use wild cards and formulas in criterion ranges. The following table shows how to use wild cards in search operations.

Using Wild cards in Search Operations

Enter	To find
N?	NC, NJ, NY, etc.
BO?L?	BOWLE but not BOWL
BO?L*	BOWLE, BOWL, BOLLESON, BOEING, etc.
SAN*	SANTA BARBARA, SAN FRANCISCO
SAN *	SAN FRANCISCO only
~N*	Strings in specified fields that *do not* begin with the letter *N*

Introduction | What Is a Database? | Creating a Database | Modifying a Database | Sorting Database Records | **Searching for Records**

AND Conditions

An AND condition tells 1-2-3 "search for the records that meet this AND that criterion." You would use this, for example, when you want to locate all employees in the database who are male AND who live in Boston.

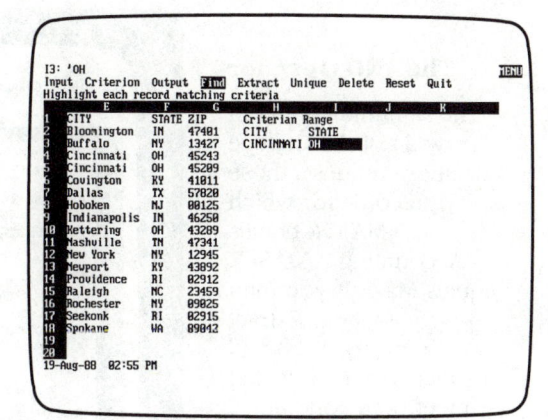

OR Conditions

An OR condition tells 1-2-3 "find the records in which this OR that is true." OR could be used when you want to find all employees who live in Boston OR Chicago.

String Searches

Even more complicated is the prospect of using strings in criterion ranges. By using the functions in a formula, you can search for a particular part of an entry. For more information, see *Using 1-2-3,* Special Edition.

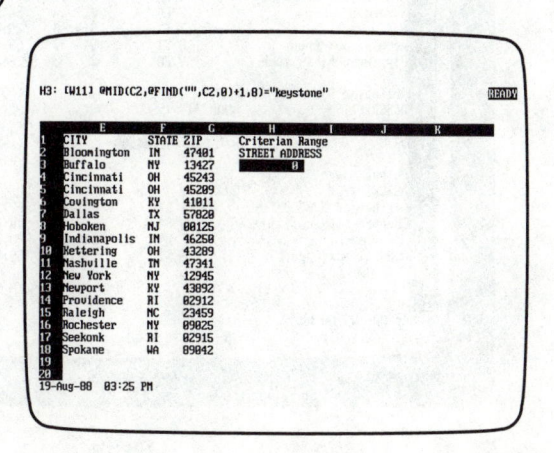

Introduction

An Overview of 1-2-3

Getting Started

1-2-3 Basics

Creating a Worksheet

Printing Reports

Creating and Printing Graphs

Managing Data

Understanding Macros

Appendix

381

Searching for Records

The AND Operator

The multiple criteria in row 24 of the College database requests those records for which MAJOR equals Accounting *AND* SEX equals Male. If you then issue an **E**xtract command, 1-2-3 will extract two records that meet both conditions.

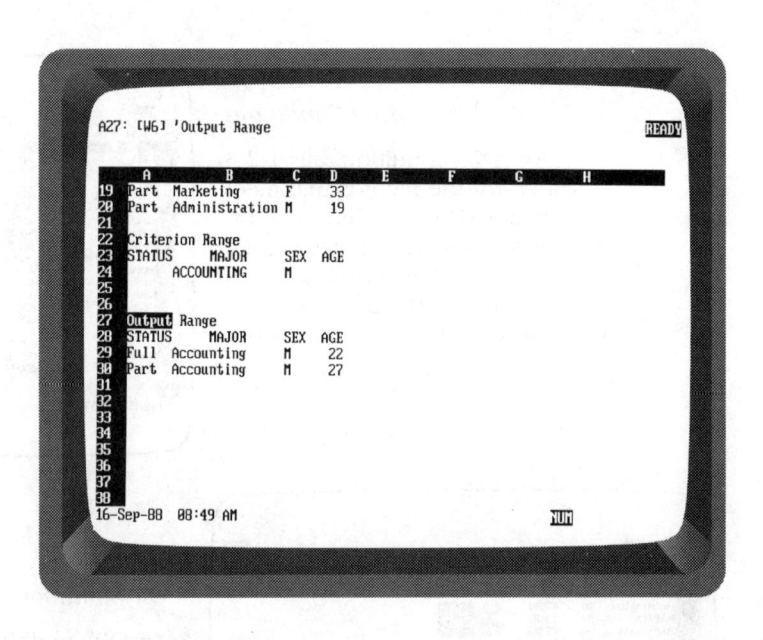

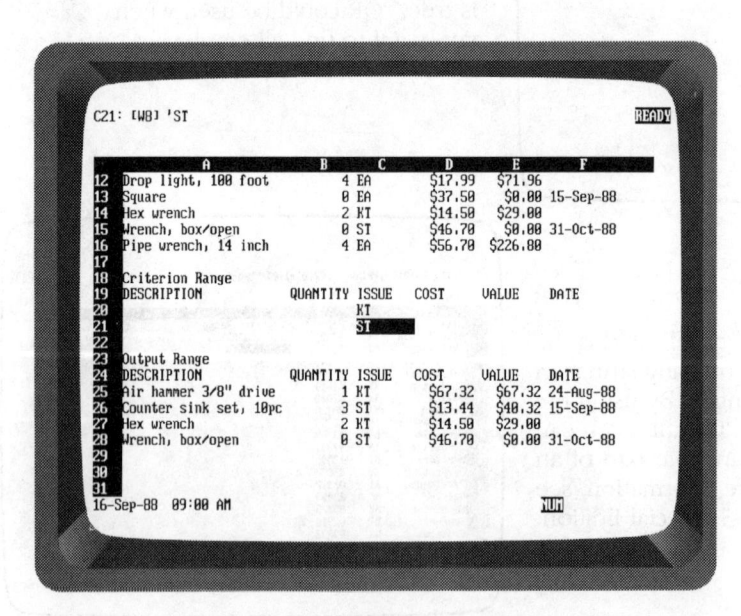

The **OR** Operator

The OR operator can be used to find the items in an inventory database that have either KT or ST in the ISSUE criterion field.

382

Using AND/OR Searches

This mixed query operation searches a database for records in which BUY equals Y (Yes) and INCOME is either less than $10,000 or greater than $30,000.

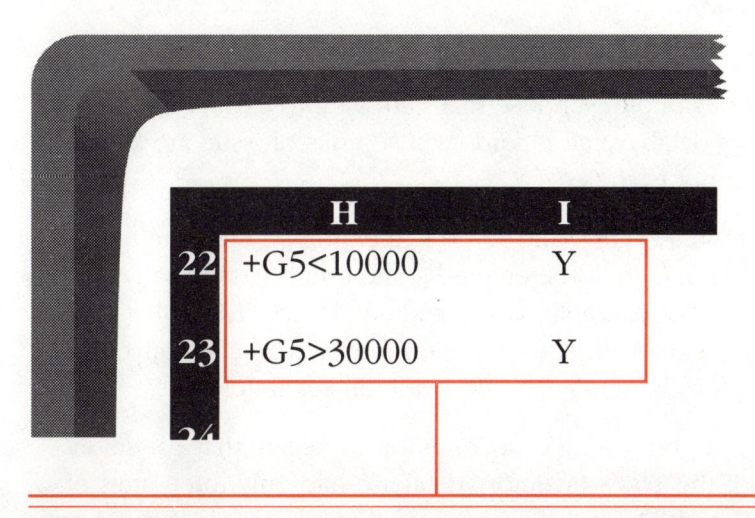

	H	I
22	+G5<10000	Y
23	+G5>30000	Y

These conditions tell 1-2-3 to search for records in which INCOME is less than $10,000 and the BUY response is "Yes" (row 22) OR for records in which INCOME is greater than $30,000 and the BUY response is "Yes" (row 23). Repeating the Y in cell I23 is critical (even though you have entered Y in cell I22) because if 1-2-3 finds a blank cell within a criterion range, the program selects all records for the field name above that blank cell.

Searching for Records

Special Operators

To combine search conditions within a single field, use the special operators #AND# and #OR#. Use the special operator #NOT# to negate a search condition.

Use #AND# or #OR# to search on two or more conditions within the same field. For example, suppose that you want to extract from the Tools Inventory database all records whose units of issue are kit (KT) or set (ST), but not each (EA).

You use the #AND#, #OR#, and #NOT# operators to enter (in one field) conditions that could be entered some other way (usually in at least two fields). For example, you could enter +C5="KT"#OR#C5="ST" in a single cell in any cell in the criterion range as an alternative criterion entry for entering each OR condition separately.

Use #NOT# at the beginning of a condition to negate that condition. For example, if the Tools Inventory database had only three units of issue—KT, ST, and EA (each)—you could find all records that did not have the EA value in the ISSUE field by specifying the criterion #NOT#EA in the criterion range.

Other Types of Searches

In addition to the **Q**uery and **F**ind commands, you can use the **D**ata menu's **U**nique and **D**elete commands for searches. By issuing the **U**nique command, you can produce (in the output range) a copy of only the first occurrence of a record that meets a specified criterion. And you can update the contents of your 1-2-3 database by deleting all records that meet a specified criterion. After entering the conditions, you need to specify only the input and criterion ranges before you issue the **D**elete command.

Searching for Unique Records

Ordinarily, the **U**nique command is used to copy into the output area only a small portion of each record that meets the criterion. For example, if you want a list of measurements used in the Tools Inventory database, set up an output range that includes only the unit of ISSUE. To search all records, leave blank the row below the field-name row in the criterion range. Then, define the input and output ranges, select **U**nique.

Deleting Specified Records

As you know, you can use the **/W**orksheet **D**elete **R**ow command sequence to remove records from a spreadsheet. If you want a fast alternative to this "one-by-one" approach, use the **D**elete command to remove unwanted records from your database files. Before you select **D**elete from the **Q**uery menu, simply specify the range of records to be searched (input range) and the conditions for the deletion (criterion).

Be extremely careful when you issue the **D**elete command. To give you the opportunity to verify that you indeed want to select the **D**elete command, 1-2-3 asks you to select **C**ancel or **D**elete. Choose **C**ancel to abort the delete command. Select **D**elete to verify that you want to execute the delete operation. To keep from deleting wanted data, we suggest you make another copy of the database, using **/F**ile Save, or use **/E**xtract so that you can view the sections you want to delete before performing the **/D**elete operation.

Searching for Records

Using Special Operators

Here, the formula condition has been entered in cell A20. The extracted records are displayed in rows 25 through 27.

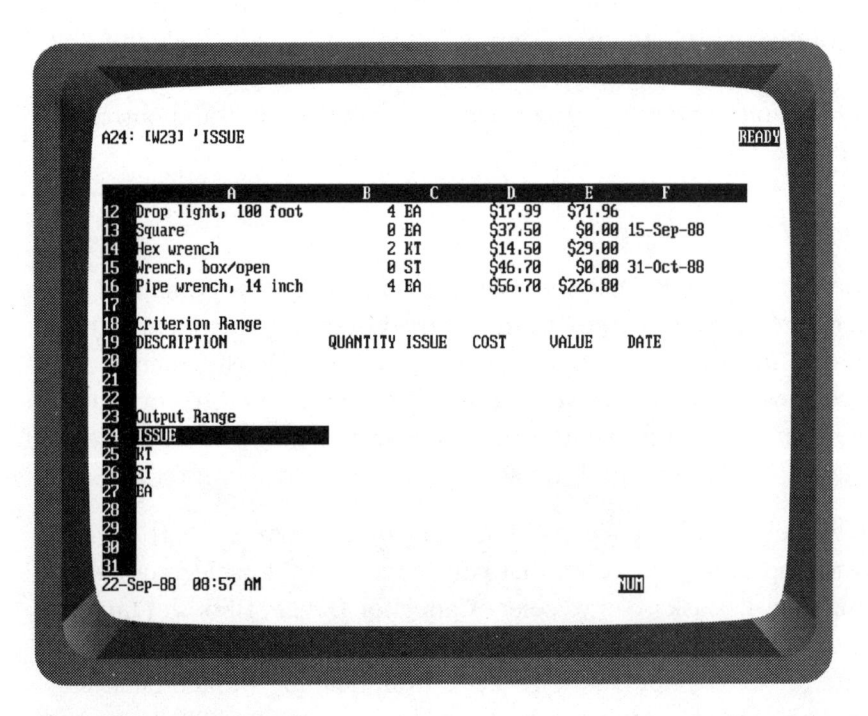

```
A24: [W23] 'ISSUE                                              READY

         A                    B       C       D       E       F
12  Drop light, 100 foot      4 EA   $17.99  $71.96
13  Square                    0 EA   $37.50   $0.00 15-Sep-88
14  Hex wrench                2 KT   $14.50  $29.00
15  Wrench, box/open          0 ST   $46.70   $0.00 31-Oct-88
16  Pipe wrench, 14 inch      4 EA   $56.70 $226.80
17
18  Criterion Range
19  DESCRIPTION         QUANTITY ISSUE  COST    VALUE   DATE
20
21
22
23  Output Range
24  ISSUE
25  KT
26  ST
27  EA
28
29
30
31
22-Sep-88  08:57 AM                                     NUM
```

The Unique Command

Ordinarily, the **U**nique command is used to copy into the output area only a small portion of each record that meets the criterion. For example, if you want a list of measurements used in the Tools Inventory database, set up an output range that includes only the unit of ISSUE. To search all records, leave blank the row below the field-name row in the criterion range A19..F20. Then, with the input range defined as A4..F16 and the output range set at A24, select **U**nique to produce (in rows 25 through 27) a list of the three units of measure.

The Delete Command

After you specify a criteria for deleting a set of records, 1-2-3 acts on the **D**elete commands without displaying the records that will be deleted. Although you are asked to verify that you indeed want to delete records, you won't have the opportunity to view the records that match the criteria you specified. For this reason, use **/F**ile **S**ave to make a copy of the database—just in case. Or, you can use the **E**xtract command to move the records you plan to delete, view them, and then proceed with the delete operation when you are sure that those records should be removed from the database.

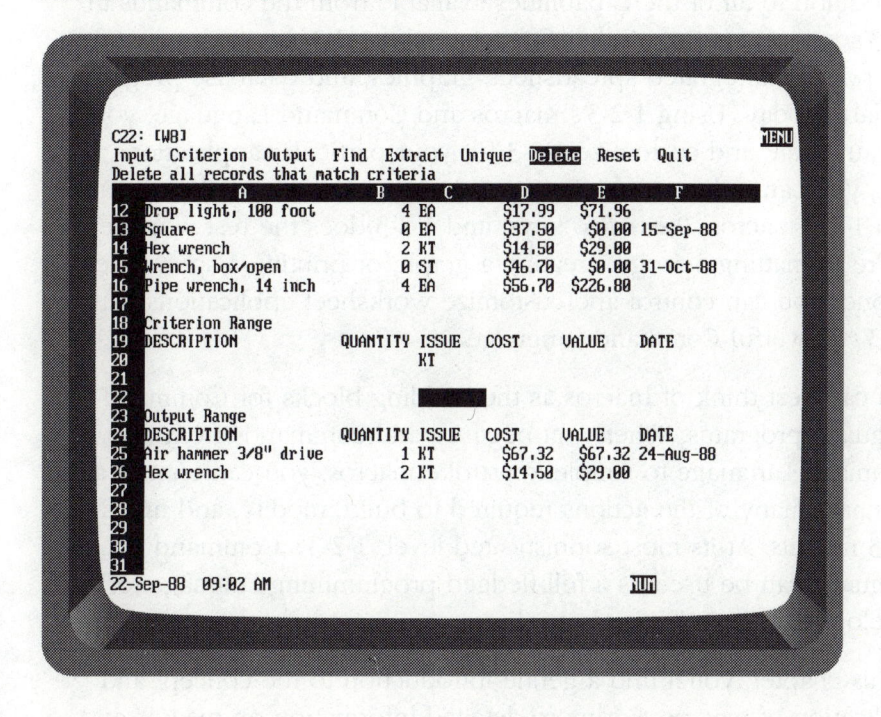

8 *Understanding Macros*

In addition to all of the capabilities available from the commands in 1-2-3's main menu, two other features make 1-2-3 the most powerful and popular integrated spreadsheet, graphics, and database program available today. Using 1-2-3's macros and Command Language, you can automate and customize 1-2-3 for your particular applications. First, you can reduce multiple keystrokes to a two-keystroke operation with 1-2-3 macros: Press two keys, and 1-2-3 does the rest, whether you're formatting a range, creating a graph, or printing a spreadsheet. Second, you can control and customize worksheet applications with 1-2-3's powerful Command Language.

You can best think of macros as the building blocks for Command Language programs. When you begin to add commands from the Command Language to simple keystroke macros, you can control and automate many of the actions required to build, modify, and update 1-2-3 models. At its most sophisticated level, 1-2-3's Command Language can be used as a full-fledged programming language for developing custom business applications.

In this chapter, you'll find a gentle introduction to the concept and application of macros. For more detailed information on macros and the Lotus Command Language, consult *Using 1-2-3,* Special Edition.

| Introduction | What Is a Macro? | The Elements of Macros | Planning and Positioning Your Macro | Documenting and Naming Your Macros | Executing Macros and Using Automatic Macros |

Key Terms Used in This Chapter

macro	A series of keystrokes or commands that can be carried out with the press of one key combination.
Command Language	1-2-3's powerful language consisting of over 40 "hidden" commands inaccessible from the 1-2-3 menu system.
tilde (~)	The symbol used in a macro to indicate the Enter keystroke.
self-documenting program	A program or macro that contains information explaining the steps in the program.
bug	An error in a program or macro.
debugging	The process of identifying and fixing the errors in a program or macro.

What Is Covered in This Chapter?

In this chapter, you'll find information on each of the following topics:

- Planning macros
- Positioning macros on the worksheet
- Naming macros
- Creating macros
- Executing macros
- Editing macros

What Is a Macro?

Before releasing 1-2-3 to the general public in 1983, Lotus decided to describe macros as *typing alternatives*. This name was later de-emphasized in favor of the term *macros*.

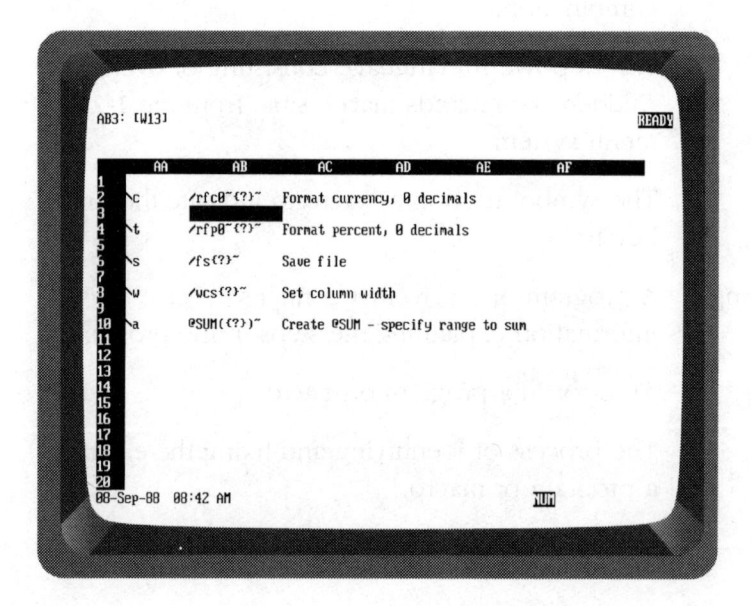

```
AB3: [W13]                                                    READY

        AA        AB          AC          AD        AE        AF
 1
 2    \c        /rfc0~{?}~   Format currency, 0 decimals
 3
 4    \t        /rfp0~{?}~   Format percent, 0 decimals
 5
 6    \s        /fs{?}~      Save file
 7
 8    \w        /wcs{?}~     Set column width
 9
10    \a        @SUM({?})~   Create @SUM - specify range to sum
11
12
13
14
15
16
17
18
19
20
08-Sep-88  08:42 AM                                           NUM
```

In its most basic form, a macro is simply a collection of keystrokes. These keystrokes can be commands or simple text and numeric entries. Macros provide an alternative to typing data and commands from the keyboard—hence the name "typing alternative."

390

| Introduction | **What Is a Macro?** | The Elements of Macros | Planning and Positioning Your Macro | Documenting and Naming Your Macros | Executing Macros and Using Automatic Macros |

By creating a simple macro, for example, you can automate the sequence of seven keystrokes necessary for formatting a cell in Currency format.

You can execute the seven keystrokes by pressing two keys.

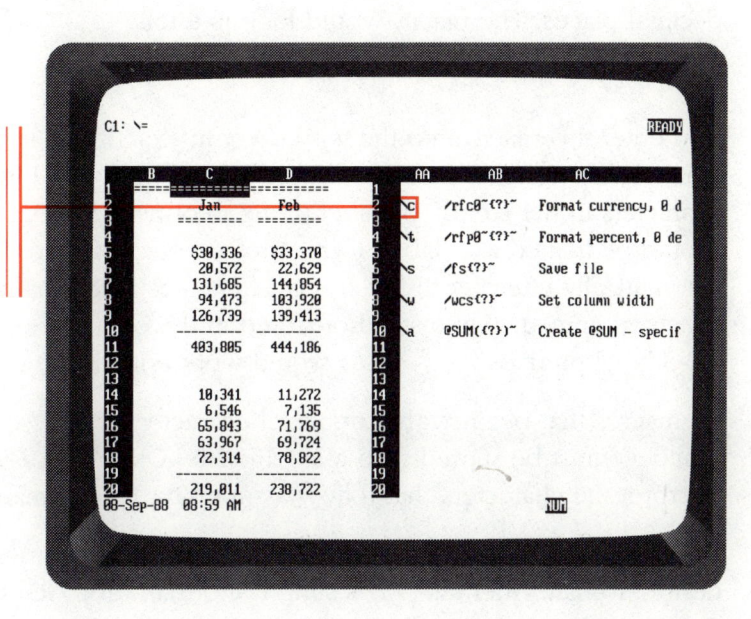

The Elements of Macros

A macro is nothing more than a specially named text cell. All macros are created by entering the keystrokes (or representatives of those keystrokes) to be stored into a worksheet cell. For example, suppose that you want to create the very simple typing alternative macro that will format the current cell to appear in the currency format with no decimal places. The macro would look like this:

    '/rfc0~~

You enter this macro into the worksheet in exactly the same way that you would any other label: by typing a label prefix, followed by the characters in the label. The label prefix informs 1-2-3 that what follows should be treated as a label. If this prefix were not used, 1-2-3 would automatically interpret the next character, /, as a command to be executed immediately instead of stored in the cell. Any of the three 1-2-3 label prefixes (', ", or ^) would work equally well.

All macros that begin with a nonlabel character (/, \, +, -, or any number) must be started with a label prefix. Otherwise 1-2-3 will interpret the characters that follow as numbers or commands.

The next four characters represent the command used to create the desired format. After all, */rfc* is simply shorthand for **/R**ange **F**ormat **C**urrency. The **0** ("zero") informs 1-2-3 that we want no digits to be displayed to the right of the decimal. If you were entering this command from the keyboard, you would type the *0* in response to a prompt. In the macro, the **0** is simply assumed by 1-2-3.

At the end of the macro are two characters called *tildes* (~~). When used in a macro, the tilde (~) represents the Enter key. In this case, the two tildes signal that the Enter key should be pressed twice.

1-2-3 also uses symbols other than the ~ to stand for keystrokes. For example, look at the following macro:

```
'/rfc0~.{END}{RIGHT}~
```

This macro is similar to the one we just looked at, except that the command here causes the cursor to move. This command can be used to format an entire row instead of just one cell.

Once again, notice the ' at the beginning of the macro and the ~ symbol at the end. Notice also the phrase {END}{RIGHT} in the macro. The {END} in this phrase stands for the End key on the keyboard. The {RIGHT} represents the right-arrow key. This phrase has the same effect in the macro as these two keys would have if they were typed in sequence from the keyboard. The cursor would move to the next boundary between blank and nonblank cells in the row.

Symbols like these are used to represent all of the special keys on the IBM PC keyboard. In every case, the name of the function key (that is, RIGHT for the right arrow, or CALC for function key F9) is enclosed in braces. For example, {UP} represents the up-arrow key, the symbol {END} stands for the End key, and {GRAPH} represents the F10 graph key. If you enclose in braces a phrase that is not a key name or a command keyword, 1-2-3 will return the error message Unrecognized key Range name {...}(A1) where {...} represents the invalid key name and (A1) says the error occurred in cell A1.

Function-Key Grammar

To specify more than one use of a special key, you can include repetition factors inside the braces of a special-key phrase. For example, you can use the following statements:

{PGUP 3}	Press the PgUp key three times in a row.
{RIGHT JUMP}	Press the right-arrow key the number of times indicated by the value in the cell called JUMP.

393

The Elements of Macros

1-2-3 macros follow a specific format, whether they are basic typing alternative macros or macros that perform complex tasks. Every macro that starts with a nontext character (/, \, +, -, or a number) must begin with a label prefix (', ", or ^). Otherwise, 1-2-3 interprets the characters that follow as numbers or commands.

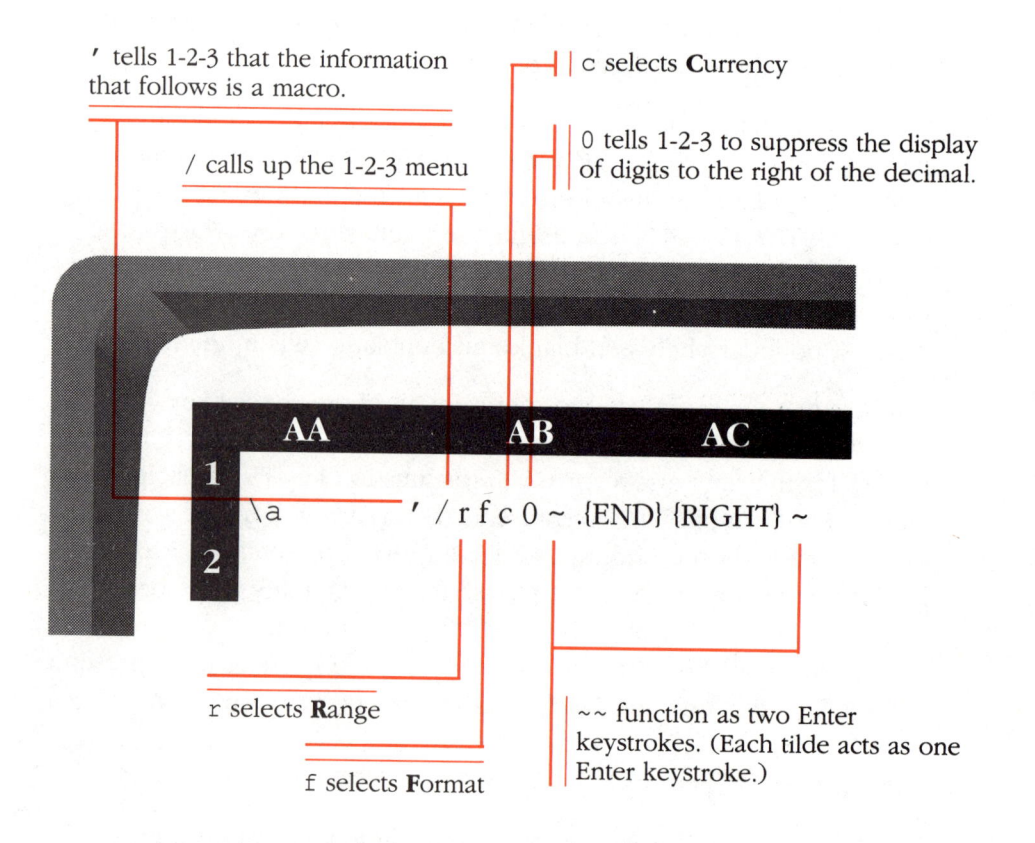

' tells 1-2-3 that the information that follows is a macro.

/ calls up the 1-2-3 menu

c selects **C**urrency

0 tells 1-2-3 to suppress the display of digits to the right of the decimal.

	AA	AB	AC
1	\a	' / r f c 0 ~ .{END} {RIGHT} ~	
2			

r selects **R**ange

f selects **F**ormat

~~ function as two Enter keystrokes. (Each tilde acts as one Enter keystroke.)

Special Key Representations in Macros

Function Keys   Action

{EDIT}	Edits contents of current cell (same as F2)
{NAME}	Displays list of range names in the current worksheet (same as F3)
{ABS}	Converts relative reference to absolute (same as F4)
{GOTO}	Jumps cursor to cell coordinates (same as F5)
{WINDOW}	Moves the cursor to the other side of a split screen (same as F6)
{QUERY}	Repeats most recent query operation (same as F7)
{TABLE}	Repeats most recent table operation (same as F8)
{CALC}	Recalculates worksheet (same as F9)
{GRAPH}	Redraws current graph (same as F10)

Cursor-Movement Keys

{UP}	Moves cursor up one row
{DOWN}	Moves cursor down one row
{LEFT}	Moves cursor left one column
{RIGHT}	Moves cursor right one column
{BIGLEFT}	Moves cursor left one screen
{BIGRIGHT}	Moves cursor right one screen
{PGUP}	Moves cursor up 20 rows
{PGDN}	Moves cursor down 20 rows
{HOME}	Moves cursor to cell A1
{END}	Used with {UP}, {DOWN}, {LEFT}, or {RIGHT} to move cursor to next boundary between blank and nonblank cells in the indicated direction. Used with {HOME} to move cursor to lower right corner of the defined worksheet.

Editing Keys

{DELETE} or {DEL}	Used with {EDIT} to delete a single character from a cell definition
{INSERT}	Toggles the editor between insert and overtype modes
{ESCAPE} or {ESC}	Esc key
{BACKSPACE} or {BS}	Backspace key

Special Keys

~	Enter key
{~}	Causes tilde to appear as ~
{{} and {}}	Causes braces to appear as { and }

395

Planning and Positioning Your Macro

As discussed previously, a macro can be thought of as a substitute for keyboard commands. Because a macro is a substitute for keystrokes, the best way to plan a macro is to step through the series of instructions you intend to include in the macro from the keyboard, one keystroke at a time. Do this stepping exercise before you start creating the macro. Take notes about each step as you go, and then translate the keystrokes that you've written down into a macro that conforms to the syntax rules.

The keystroke approach usually works well for simple macros. Stepping through an operation at the keyboard is an easy way to build simple macros.

For more complex macros, the best approach is to break a large macro into smaller macros that execute in series. Each small macro performs one simple operation; the series of simple operations together perform the desired application.

This approach starts with an application's results. What is the application supposed to do or to produce? What form must the results take? If you start with the desired results and work backward, you lower the risk of producing the wrong results with your application.

Next, consider input. What data is needed? What data is available and in what form? How much work is involved in going from the data to the results?

Finally, look at the process. How do you analyze available data and, using 1-2-3, produce the desired results? How can necessary calculations be divided into a series of tasks, for which each can have a simple macro?

This "divide-and-conquer" method of breaking a complex task into simpler pieces is the key to successful development of complex worksheets, whether they include macros. Although this method entails initial work, as you analyze and plan your macros, less work is required by the time your application functions properly.

Where To Put the Macro

In most cases, you will want to place your macros outside the area that will be occupied by your main model. This method of location will help to keep you from accidentally overwriting or erasing part of a macro as you create your model.

Depending on how much space you want to leave on your worksheet for applications, you can reserve either the topmost rows of the worksheet or a few columns to the right of the area where you build most applications.

We frequently put macros in column AA in our models. We selected this column for several reasons. First, because our models rarely require more than 26 columns, we don't have to worry about overwriting the macros area with the model. Second, column AA is close enough to the origin that you can easily reach the macros area with the Tab key.

1-2-3 has no rule that says you must place your macros in the same place in every model. In models that you'll use more than once, you'll want to place the macros wherever you find most convenient. In small models, you may want to put your macros in column I, which lies just off the home screen when all of the columns have a width of 9.

We typically apply the range name MACROS to the area of our sheet that contains the macros. This addition allows us to get at the macros quickly with the GOTO command and the range name MACROS.

Planning and Positioning Your Macro

The best way to plan a macro is to think about the steps involved in a process as you do it. A good candidate for a macro would be a process that involved a sequence of command selections that you wind up repeating again and again. Stepping through an operation at the keyboard is an easy way to build macros.

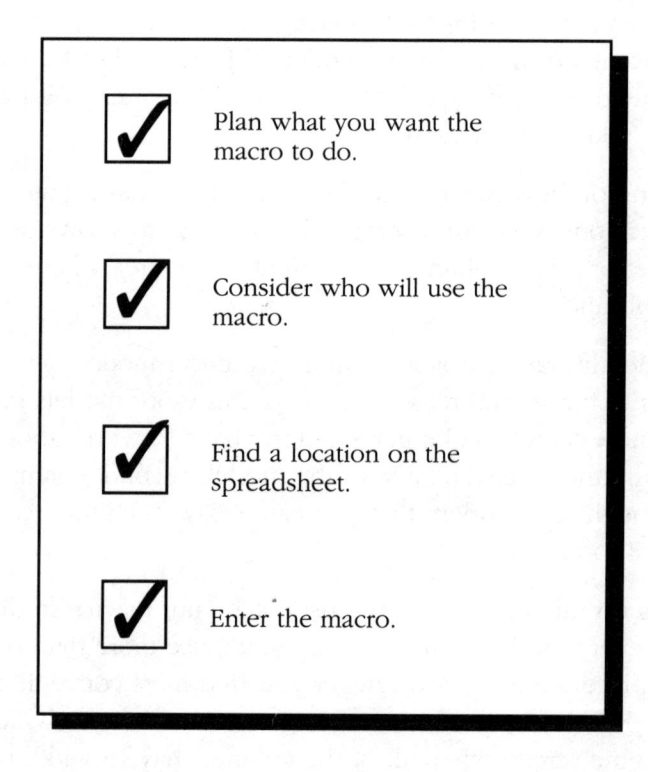

- ✓ Plan what you want the macro to do.

- ✓ Consider who will use the macro.

- ✓ Find a location on the spreadsheet.

- ✓ Enter the macro.

Planning and Positioning Your Macro

Position your macro so that it is out of the way of the worksheet. This will keep you from accidentally overwriting or erasing part of a macro as you create your model.

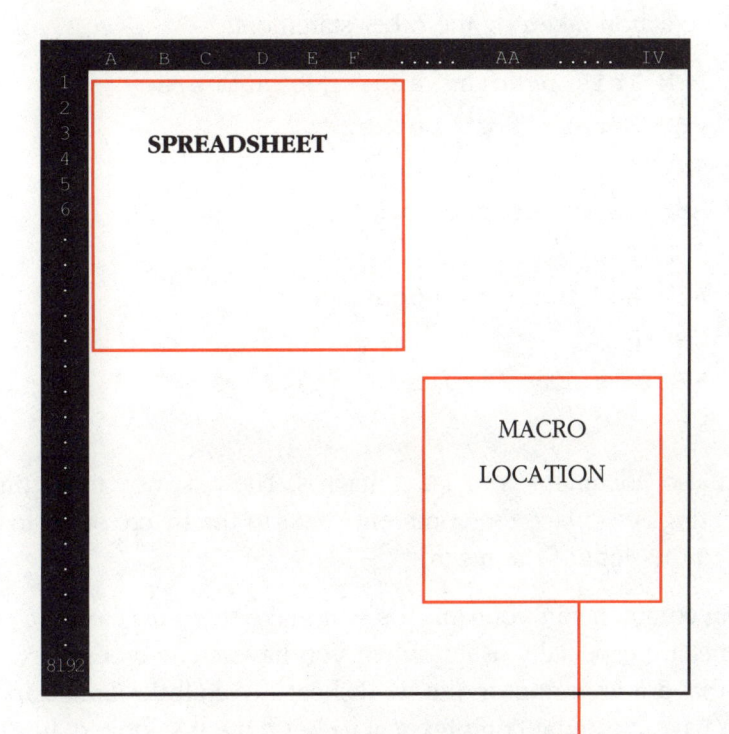

SPREADSHEET

MACRO LOCATION

The macro in this example is positioned far to the right of the actual worksheet. This lessens the possibility that the macro's range could accidentally be included in worksheet operations.

Documenting and Naming Your Macros

Professional programmers usually write programs that are *self-documented*, or *internally documented*. This term means that the program contains comments that help to explain each step in the program. In BASIC, these comments are in REM (for REMark) statements. For example, in the following program, the REM statements explain the action taken by the other statements.

```
10 REM This program adds two numbers
20 REM Enter first number
30 INPUT A
40 REM Enter second number
50 INPUT B
60 REM Add numbers together
70 C=A+B
80 REM Display Result
90 Print C
```

You can also document your 1-2-3 macros. The best way to do this documenting is to place the comments next to the macro steps in the column to the right of the macro.

Including comments in your macros will make them far easier to use. Comments are especially useful when you have created complex macros that are important to the worksheet's overall design. Suppose that you have created a complex macro but have not looked at it for a month. Then you decide that you want to modify the macro. Without built-in comments, you might have a difficult time remembering what each step of the macro does.

Naming Macros

A macro that has been entered in the worksheet as a label (or a series of labels) must be given a name. Ranges containing macros are assigned names just like every other range. The only difference is that the name you assign to a macro which you will invoke directly from the keyboard must meet certain special conditions: it must be only one character, it must be an alphabetic character (or 0), and it must be preceded by a backslash (\).

You can assign any legal range name to a macro that will be either used only as a subroutine or called with a BRANCH statement from another macro. A few examples of valid macro names include

Invoked from Keyboard	*Invoked Only from Macros*
\a	\ABC
\b	ABC
\0	\?
	\1

When you name a macro, choose any one-letter name that in some way describes the macro. For example, if you create a macro that adds a dollar sign in the appropriate place, you could name the macro \d. To do this, select **/R**ange **N**ame **C**reate, type \d, and press Enter. You then need to specify the range to be used for the macro.

Documenting and Naming Your Macros

Documenting Macros

When professional programmers write programs, they often include in the programs information that explains the various steps involved. This documentation of the program helps other users—and the programmers themselves—understand what function is performed by a particular line in the program.

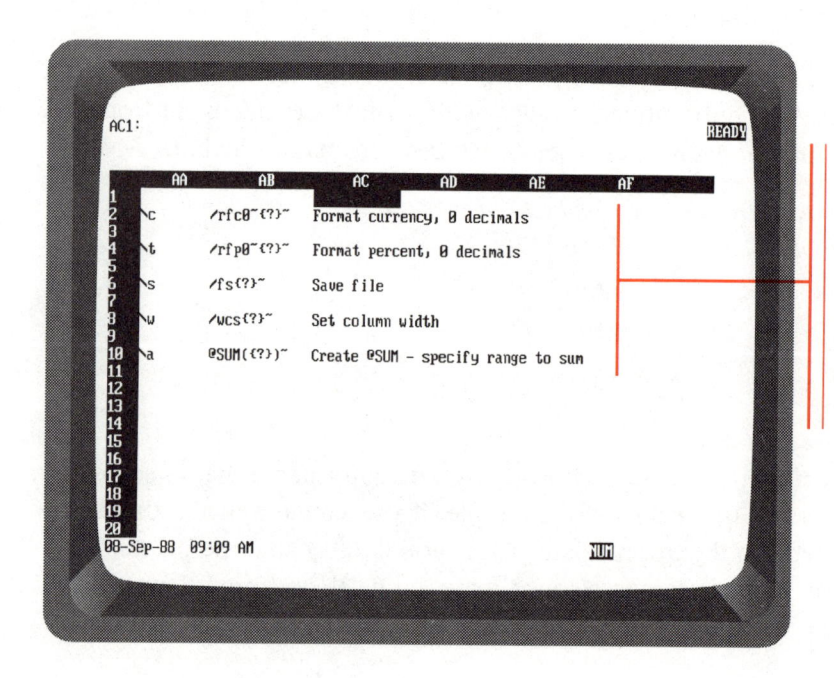

```
AC1:                                                          READY
        AA      AB         AC       AD      AE      AF
1
2    \c      /rfc0~{?}~  Format currency, 0 decimals
3
4    \t      /rfp0~{?}~  Format percent, 0 decimals
5
6    \s      /fs{?}~     Save file
7
8    \w      /wcs{?}~    Set column width
9
10   \a      @SUM({?})~  Create @SUM - specify range to sum
11
12
13
14
15
16
17
18
19
20
08-Sep-88  09:09 AM                                    NUM
```

Similarly, you can document your 1-2-3 macros. The best way to do this is to place the comments in the column to the right of the macro.

Each macro that is invoked directly from the keyboard must have a name, and the name must follow certain conventions: it must be only one character, it must be an alphabetic character (or 0), and it must be preceded by a backslash (\).

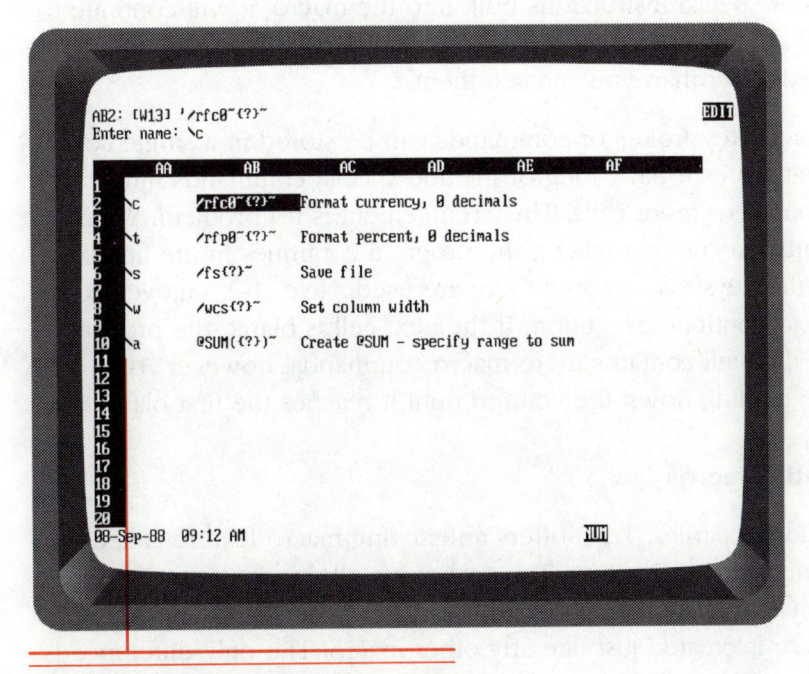

```
AB2: [W13] '/rfc0~{?}~                                    EDIT
Enter name: \c
         AA         AB         AC         AD         AE         AF
 1
 2      \c        /rfc0~{?}~   Format currency, 0 decimals
 3
 4      \t        /rfp0~{?}~   Format percent, 0 decimals
 5
 6      \s        /fs{?}~      Save file
 7
 8      \w        /wcs{?}~     Set column width
 9
10      \a        @SUM({?})~   Create @SUM - specify range to sum
11
12
13
14
15
16
17
18
19
20
08-Sep-88  09:12 AM                                        NUM
```

Remember to select a one-letter name that in some way describes the macro.

Executing Macros and Using Automatic Macros

All macros except those named \0 (which is executed automatically when the file is retrieved) are executed, or invoked, by pressing and holding the Alt key and the macro letter name. Then you release the letter key and finally release the Alt key. For example, if the macro we wanted to use were named \a, we would invoke it by pressing Alt-a. The \ symbol in the name is a representation of the Alt key.

As soon as the command is issued, the macro starts to run. If you have no bugs or special instructions built into the macro, it will continue to run until it is finished. You will be amazed at its speed. The commands are issued faster than you can see them.

Many macro keystrokes or commands can be stored in a single cell. Some that are especially long or include special commands must be split into two or more cells. This arrangement is no problem. When 1-2-3 starts executing a macro, the program continues in the first cell until all the keystrokes stored there are used. Next, 1-2-3 moves down one cell to continue execution. If the next cell is blank, the program stops. If that cell contains more macro commands, however, 1-2-3 will continue reading down the column until it reaches the first blank cell.

Automatic Macros

As mentioned earlier, 1-2-3 offers an exciting macro feature called *automatic macro execution*. This technique allows the user to create a special macro that will execute automatically when the sheet is loaded. This macro is created just like any other macro. The only difference is in its name. The macro that you want to execute automatically must have the name \0 ("backslash zero").

An even more powerful feature of 1-2-3 is its ability to load a model automatically into the 1-2-3 worksheet. When 1-2-3 loads, it automatically searches the default disk drive and subdirectory for a special worksheet file named AUTO123.WK1. If this file is on the disk, 1-2-3 will automatically load it into the worksheet. If the file contains a macro named \0, the macro will automatically execute.

You can use these features of 1-2-3 to create completely self-contained programs in the 1-2-3 worksheet. Pressing the Alt key is not required to start the macro in this case. When combined with menus and the other useful macro commands, the automatic execution feature makes macros a remarkably user-friendly tool.

Note one thing about the automatic macro: it cannot be executed by the Alt-0 key combination. If you need to be able to execute the macro from the keyboard, however, there is no reason why the macro you've named \0 could not also have another name, such as \a. One macro then becomes, in effect, two: one that executes automatically, and one that can be executed from the keyboard.

You can have only one automatic macro in each worksheet. This macro can be as large as you want, however, and can include as many steps as you wish. It can also include subroutine calls that access other macros in the sheet.

405

Executing Macros and Using Automatic Macros

Executing Macros

When you want to run a macro, you simply press the Alt key and then press the letter name of the macro. For example, if the macro were named \A, you would press [Alt][A].

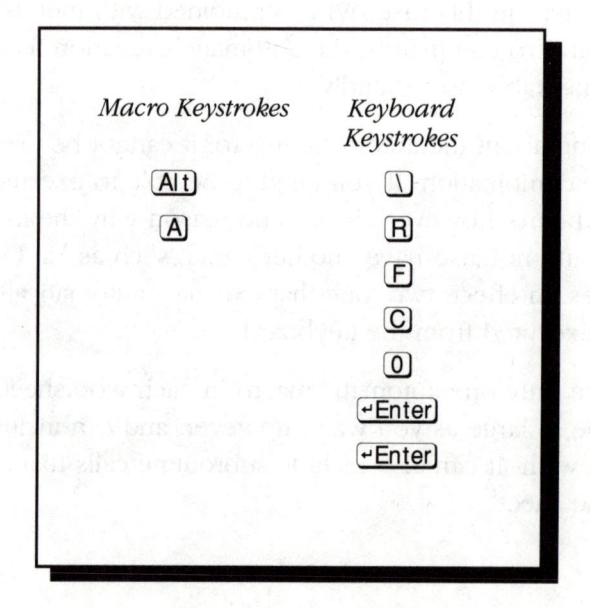

Macro Keystrokes	Keyboard Keystrokes
[Alt]	[\]
[A]	[R]
	[F]
	[C]
	[0]
	[↵Enter]
	[↵Enter]

Automatic Macros

An automatic macro executes automatically as soon as the worksheet is loaded. Perhaps you want a macro to take you to cell Z24 of the worksheet each time you start.

Automatic macros are named 0, and they execute when the file is opened. You cannot start these macros by typing Alt 0. You also can have only one automatic macro in a file at one time.

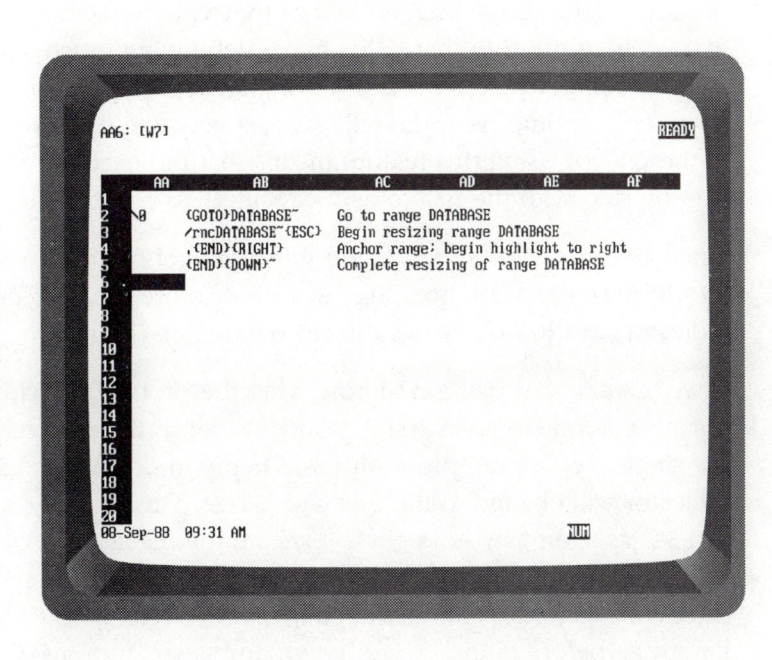

Executing Macros and Using Automatic Macros

Debugging and Editing Macros

Almost no program works perfectly the first time. In nearly every case, errors will cause programs to malfunction. Programmers call these problems *bugs*, and programmers call the process of eliminating bugs *debugging the program.*

Like programs written in other programming languages, 1-2-3 macros usually need to be debugged before they can be used. 1-2-3 has an extremely useful tool that helps make debugging much simpler: the Step function. When 1-2-3 is in STEP mode, all macros are executed one step at a time. 1-2-3 literally pauses between each keystroke stored in the macro. Using this feature means that the user can follow along step by step with the macro as it executes.

Once an error is discovered, you must first get out of the macro and into READY mode by pressing Esc one or more times. When the mode indicator says READY, you can start debugging the macro.

If we assume that we don't know what the problem is with the macro, our next step is to enter STEP mode and rerun the macro. To invoke the single-step mode, press Alt-F2. When you do this, the mode indicator will change to the message STEP. This message will change to SST as soon as you begin to execute the macro. In execution after the command, the macro will move forward only one step at a time. After each step, the macro will pause and wait for you to type any keystroke before going on. Although any key can be used, we prefer using the space bar to step through a macro. As you step through the macro, you will see each command appear in the control panel.

Common Errors in Macros

Like all computer programs, macros are literal creatures. They have no ability to discern an error in the code. For example, you will recognize immediately that {GOTI} is a misspelling of {GOTO}. But a macro cannot make this distinction. The macro will try to interpret the misspelled word and, being unable to, will deliver an error message. Here are two reminders to help you avoid some of the most common macro errors:

- Remember to use tildes (~) to represent all required Enter keystrokes in macros.
- Cell references in macros are always absolute.

Thanks to single-step mode, when the error occurs, it is easy to pinpoint the location in the macro. Once the error is identified, you can exit STEP mode by pressing Alt-F2 again. Then abort the macro by pressing Esc one or more times.

Editing the Macro

You are now ready to repair the error. Fixing an error in a macro is as simple as editing the cell that contains the erroneous code. You don't need to rewrite the cell. You need only to change the element in error.

Although editing complex macros can be tougher than editing a simple one, the concept is exactly the same. Just use 1-2-3's cell editor (F2) to correct the cell that contains the error.

Executing Macros and Using Automatic Macros

Using STEP Mode To Debug Macros

Most programs need to be debugged before they can be used. 1-2-3's Step function goes through a macro, one step at a time, pausing between each step so that you can locate the problem.

Each command appears in the control panel.

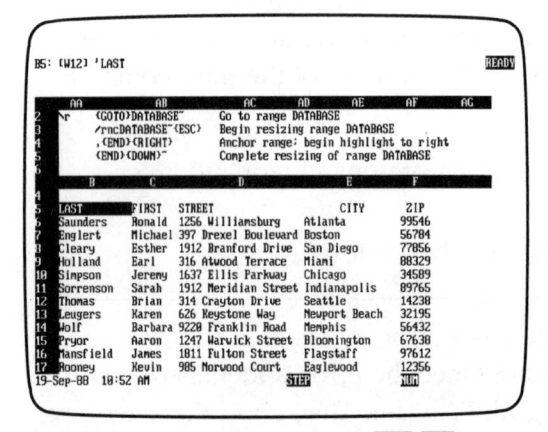

To initiate STEP mode, press [Alt][F2]. The mode indicator at the bottom of the screen changes to the message STEP.

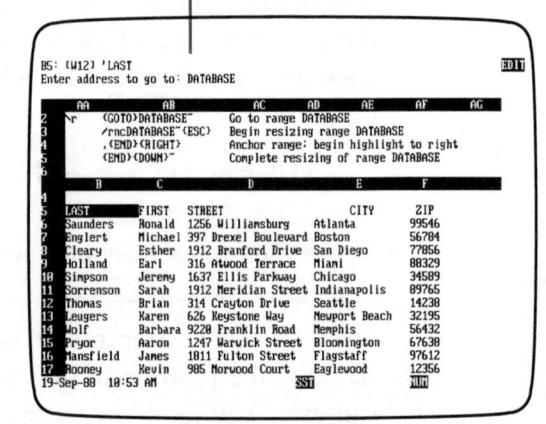

When you begin to execute the macro, the message will change to SST. You then step through the macro, pressing the space bar after you evaluate each step.

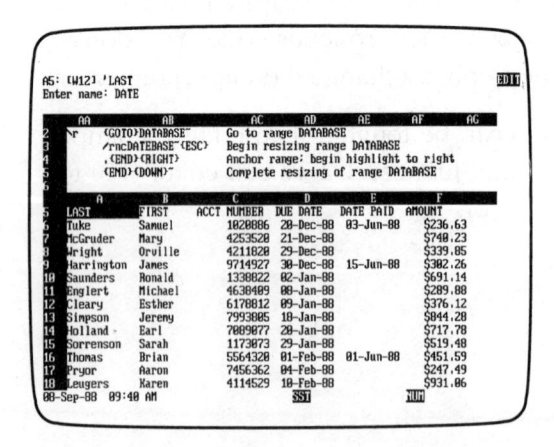

Once an error is discovered, you must first get out of the macro and into READY mode by pressing [Esc] one or more times. When the mode indicator says READY, you can start debugging the macro.

410

| Introduction | What Is a Macro? | The Elements of Macros | Planning and Positioning Your Macro | Documenting and Naming Your Macros | **Executing Macros and Using Automatic Macros** |

"Tips for Debugging" on "Common Errors in Macros"

✓ Is there a misspelling in your macro?

✓ Have you correctly used tildes to represent Enter keystrokes?

✓ Are any of the cell references relative?

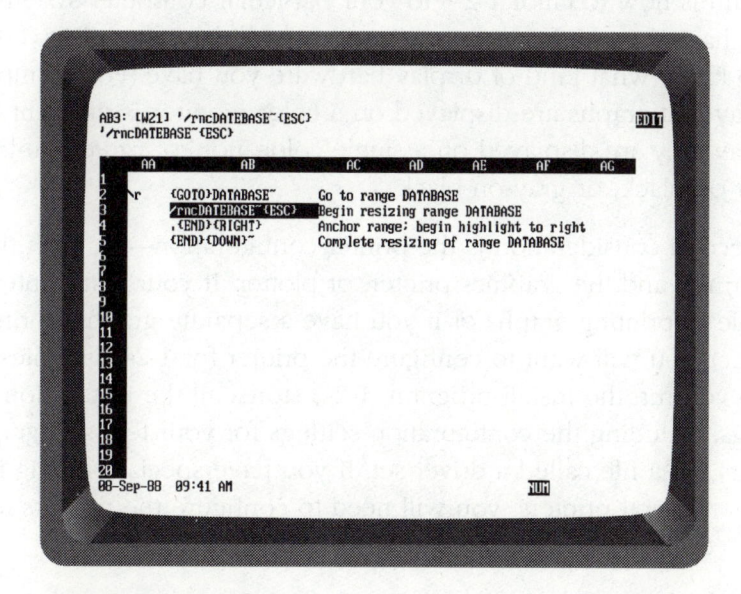

```
AB3: [W21] '/rncDATABASE~{ESC}                                    EDIT
'/rncDATABASE~{ESC}

        AA          AB              AC      AD      AE      AF      AG
   1
   2 r          {GOTO}DATABASE~         Go to range DATABASE
   3           /rncDATABASE~{ESC}       Begin resizing range DATABASE
   4           .{END}{RIGHT}            Anchor range; begin highlight to right
   5           {END}{DOWN}~             Complete resizing of range DATABASE
   6
   7
   8
   9
  10
  11
  12
  13
  14
  15
  16
  17
  18
  19
  20
08-Sep-88   09:41 AM                                              NUM
```

Editing Macros

After you identify where the error is, you need to fix it. Fixing an error in a macro is as easy as editing the cell. Use [F2] (Edit) to correct the cell that contains the error.

411

Appendix

Installing 1-2-3

Before you run the Install program to install 1-2-3 for your computer system, you need to copy the 1-2-3 disks to your hard disk, if you have one, or prepare the 1-2-3 disks for use on a two floppy or two microfloppy (PS/2) system. Preparing the disks consists of making backup copies and copying the DOS COMMAND.COM file to the disks you will be using.

The first matter to consider when you prepare to run the Install program is how to tailor 1-2-3 to your particular computer system. You'll have three different considerations with this issue. First, 1-2-3 has to know what kind of display hardware you have. For example, the way that graphs are displayed on a color monitor is different from the way they are displayed on a single-color monitor (green-on-black, amber-on-black, or gray-on-black).

The second consideration is the printer configuration—for both the text printer and the graphics printer, or plotter. If your text printer is capable of printing graphs or if you have a separate graphics printer (plotter), you will want to configure the printer for 1-2-3 graphics. When you run the Install program, 1-2-3 stores all the installation settings, including the configuration settings for your text and graphics printers, on a file called a driver set. If you have special printing needs and use several printers, you will need to configure the printers for 1-2-3. You may need to create additional driver sets.

When you know how you want to tailor 1-2-3 for your system, you run the Install program to complete installation.

When you install 1-2-3 on a hard disk system, you have the option of placing the copy-protection information on your hard disk, which makes it easier, but riskier, to start up 1-2-3. This appendix explains the use of the COPYHARD program to install and uninstall the copy-protection information.

Finally, after you have run the Install program and installed 1-2-3 for your system, you will need to prepare data disks for use with 1-2-3.

The 1-2-3 Disks

Lotus delivers 1-2-3 with two different sets of disks: (1) six 5 1\4-inch floppy disks for use on the IBM PC and PC-compatible computers; and (2) four 3 1/2-inch microfloppy disks encased in hard plastic for use on the IBM PS/2 family of computers. The programs contained on the two sets of disks are exactly the same, but the programs are divided among the disks somewhat differently.

The 1-2-3 System disk in both sets of disks contains a hidden copy-protection scheme. Individual files on the System disk can be copied, but you cannot use a "copy" of the System disk to start up the program. When 1-2-3 starts up, the program checks the System disk for the copy-protection scheme. If 1-2-3 can't find the scheme, the program won't run. Lotus provides a Backup *System disk* in case the System disk is lost or damaged.

Note that in this appendix, for the PS/2 the term *System disk* means *System disk with PrintGraph*.

Installing 1-2-3

The 1-2-3 Disks for the IBM PC and PC-Compatible Computers

The 1-2-3 package for the IBM PC and PC-compatibles contains six floppy disks. They are

- System disk
- Backup System disk
- PrintGraph disk
- Utility disk
- Install Library disk
- A View of 1-2-3 disk

The most important of these disks, the System disk, contains all the 1-2-3 operations except one: the commands for printing graphs. Printing graphs requires the use of the separate PrintGraph disk (see Chapter 6).

The Utility disk contains programs for installation and data transfer. With the Install program, you can tailor 1-2-3 to your computer system. The Utility disk also contains a Translate program that you use to transfer data between 1-2-3 and dBASE II, dBASE III, dBASE III Plus, Symphony, Jazz, earlier releases of 1-2-3, DIF, and VisiCalc.

The Install Library disk contains the library of drivers that you use with the Install program to set up 1-2-3 for your system. Drivers, briefly, are programs that 1-2-3 uses to control your hardware. For example, different drivers are used to control a color monitor and a black-and-white monitor.

The remaining disk, which contains A View of 1-2-3, presents a brief, on-line demonstration of some of 1-2-3's features. If you are a new user, you should spend a few minutes with this demonstration to become familiar with the program.

Before you can run the Install program to set up 1-2-3 for your system, you must take several steps to prepare your disks. The steps required depend on whether you are going to use 1-2-3 on a computer with a hard disk drive or on a computer with two floppy disk drives. You can now skip to the section "Installing 1-2-3 on a Hard Disk System" or the section "Installing the 1-2-3 Disks for a Two Floppy or a Two Microfloppy Disk System," whichever is appropriate.

The 1-2-3 Disks for the IBM PS/2

The 1-2-3 package for the IBM Personal System/2 family of computers contains four microfloppy disks. They are

>   System disk with PrintGraph
>   Backup System disk with PrintGraph
>   Install disk
>   View of 1-2-3 with Translate

These four disks contain the same programs as the six floppy disks for use on PCs and PC-compatibles. The programs on the PrintGraph, Utility disks and the Install Library disks have been distributed among the System, Install, and View of 1-2-3 disks.

The System disk contains all the 1-2-3 operations, including the commands for printing graphs. You can run 1-2-3 entirely from the System disk. For most PS/2 machines, this setup is not important because you will probably install 1-2-3 on the hard disk. However, for the Model 25 and Model 30, which may not have a hard disk, this grouping of programs on the System disk helps you avoid annoying disk-swapping.

Installing 1-2-3

The Install disk contains the Install program, which you use to tailor 1-2-3 to your computer system. The Install disk also contains the library of drivers that you use with the Install program to set up 1-2-3 for your system. Drivers, briefly, are programs that 1-2-3 uses to control your hardware. For example, different drivers are used to control a color monitor and a black-and-white monitor. This grouping of the Install program and the library of drivers allows you to complete installation from one disk.

The View of 1-2-3 with Translate disk presents a brief, on-line demonstration of some of 1-2-3's features. If you are a new user, you should spend a few minutes with this demonstration to become familiar with the program. This disk also contains the Translate program, which you use to transfer data between 1-2-3 and dBASE II, dBASE III, dBASE III Plus, Symphony, Jazz, earlier releases of 1-2-3, and VisiCalc.

Before you can run the Install program to set up 1-2-3 for your system, you must take several steps to prepare your disks. Because most PS/2 computers have hard disks, the appropriate installation instructions are included in the following section, "Installing 1-2-3 on a Hard Disk System." The steps required to install 1-2-3 for a Model 25 and 30, which may have two microfloppy disk drives, are found in the section "Installing the 1-2-3 Disks for a Two Floppy or a Two Microfloppy Disk System."

Copying the 1-2-3 Disks to a Hard Disk

The following steps are required to copy the 1-2-3 disks onto your hard disk so that all the 1-2-3 programs can be started from the hard disk. The instructions in this section are appropriate for the IBM PC, PC-compatibles, and the PS/2.

The following instructions assume that your hard disk is formatted, DOS is installed, and drive C is your default drive.

1. Start your computer; the C> prompt will appear.
2. Create a subdirectory to hold the 1-2-3 files. To create a subdirectory of the current directory (the root directory), use the DOS Make Directory command. For example, type *MD\123* to create a subdirectory named 123.
3. Make this subdirectory the current directory. In this case, you type *CD\123*.
4. Starting with the System disk, copy the contents of each 1-2-3 master disk onto the hard disk, following this procedure:
    a. Place, in turn, each master disk in drive A.
    b. Type cop*y a:*.*/v* and press Enter. The /v will verify the copy. (DOS recognizes that you want the files copied to the current directory—C:\123.)
    c. When copying is completed, remove the master disk from drive A.

For the IBM PC and PC-compatibles: Do steps 4a through 4c for the PrintGraph disk, the Utility disk, the Install Library disk, and the disk containing A View of 1-2-3.

For the IBM PS/2: Do steps 4a through 4c for the Install disk and the View of 1-2-3 with Translate disk.

Put all the master disks *except* the System disk in a safe place.

417

Installing 1-2-3

Preparing To Install 1-2-3 on a Two Floppy or a Two Microfloppy Disk System

Preparing to install 1-2-3 for a two floppy or a two microfloppy system is a fairly easy procedure and a necessary part of configuring the program to your system. Without this step, the 1-2-3 program will run, but you will not be able to use your printer with 1-2-3 or display graphs on the screen.

If you have a system with two floppy or two microfloppy disk drives, the general procedure for preparing and then using the disks that come with 1-2-3 consists of making backup copies of the 1-2-3 disks and then adding the COMMAND.COM file to the disks you will use to run the 1-2-3 programs. More specifically,

For the IBM PC and PC-compatibles:

1. Make backup copies of the PrintGraph disk, the Utility disk, the Install Library disk, and the disk containing A View of 1-2-3.
2. Add the COMMAND.COM file to the System disk, the Backup System disk, and the copies of the PrintGraph disk, the Utility disk, and the disk containing A View of 1-2-3.

For the IBM PS/2:

1. Make backup copies of the Install disk and the View of 1-2-3 with Translate disk.
2. Add the COMMAND.COM file to the System disk with PrintGraph, the Backup System disk with PrintGraph, and the copies of the Install disk and the View of 1-2-3 with Translate disk.

Making Backup Copies of the 1-2-3 Disks

Lotus provides you with a backup copy of the System disk, but you should make backup copies of the other disks if you work with a two floppy or two microfloppy disk system. You cannot copy the System disk or the Backup System disk, either one of which must be used to start the program. You frequently will need to use the other 1-2-3 disks as well, however, so it is a good idea to work with backup copies of the master disks and store the masters in a safe place. Should you damage one of the backup disks in any way, you can use the master disk to make a replacement copy.

Before making backup copies, you should become familiar with your computer's disk operating system. For specific explanations of formatting disks and copying files, refer to Que's books *Using PC DOS,* 2nd Edition or *MS-DOS User's Guide,* 3rd Edition, or check your system's manual. Keep in mind that you can use Release 2 of 1-2-3 with DOS V2.0 or later, but not with DOS V1.0 or V1.1.

Use the following steps to create backup copies of the 1-2-3 disks.

For the IBM PC and PC-compatibles:

1. Format four blank disks, using the DOS FORMAT.COM program.
2. Label the four blank disks as follows:
   Backup Copy: PrintGraph disk
   Backup Copy: Utility disk
   Backup Copy: Install Library disk
   Backup Copy: A View of 1-2-3 disk

Installing 1-2-3

3. Copy each 1-2-3 master disk, with the exception of the System disk and the Backup System disk, onto the appropriate formatted blank disk as follows:
    a. With DOS operating, place, in turn, each master 1-2-3 disk in drive A and the formatted blank disk in drive B.
    b. At the A> prompt, type *copy a:*.* b:/v* and press Enter. The /v will verify the copy. (Lotus suggests using the COPY command instead of the DISKCOPY command.)
    c. After all files have been copied from the master disk onto the formatted disk, remove the master disk from drive A and the backup copy from drive B.

Follow steps 3a through 3c for the PrintGraph Disk, the Utility disk, the Install Library disk, and the disk containing A View of 1-2-3.

For the IBM PS/2:

1. Format two blank disks, using the DOS FORMAT.COM program.
2. Label the two blank disks as follows:

    Backup Copy: Install disk

    Backup Copy: View of 1-2-3 with Translate disk
3. Copy the Install and the View of 1-2-3 with Translate master disks onto the appropriate formatted blank disk as follows:
    a. With DOS operating, place the master Install disk in drive A and the appropriate formatted blank disk in drive B.

b. At the A> prompt, type *copy a:*.* b:/v* and press Enter. The /v will verify the copy. (Lotus suggests using the COPY command instead of the DISKCOPY command.)

c. After all files have been copied from the master disk onto the formatted disk, remove the master disk from drive A and the backup copy from drive B.

Repeat steps 3a through 3c for the View of 1-2-3 with Translate disk.

Adding COMMAND.COM to the 1-2-3 Disks

For a two floppy or a two microfloppy disk system, Lotus suggests that you copy the COMMAND.COM file from your DOS disk to the System disk and the Backup System disk, and to your copies of the other 1-2-3 disks, except the Install Library disk (the Install disk for PS/2). If you try to exit 1-2-3 when drive A contains a disk that does not hold the COMMAND.COM file, the message `Insert disk with COMMAND.COM in drive A and strike any key when ready` appears on the screen. By having COMMAND.COM on your 1-2-3 disks, you avoid this problem.

In Release 2.01 of 1-2-3, COMMAND.COM is not required on the Utility disk. You may get an error message indicating insufficient disk space if you attempt to make the copy. If you decide that you want to copy COMMAND.COM onto the Utility disk, first delete an unneeded file, such as the VCWRK.XLT Translate files, from the backup copy of the Utility disk. Then copy COMMAND.COM to the backup.

Installing 1-2-3

To copy COMMAND.COM onto each of your 1-2-3 disks, proceed as follows. With the DOS A> prompt on the screen and your DOS disk in drive A:

1. Place the 1-2-3 System disk in drive B. Make sure there is no write-protect tab on the disk.
2. Type the command *copy a:command.com b:/v* and press the Enter key.
3. Remove the disk from drive B.

   For the IBM PC and PC-compatibles: Repeat steps 1 through 3 for the Backup System disk and your backup copies of the PrintGraph disk, the Utility disk (unless you have Release 2.01), and the disk containing A View of 1-2-3.

   For the IBM PS/2: Repeat steps 1 through 3 for the Backup System disk with PrintGraph and your backup copy of the View of 1-2-3 with Translate disk.

Put all the master disks except the System disk in a safe place.

Installing Driver Programs

Installing driver programs is the next step in tailoring the 1-2-3 disks to your particular system. The drivers are small programs that reside in the driver library on the Install Library disk.

The driver files store information about your computer system, such as information about the display(s), printer(s), and plotter. You can create one or many driver files, depending on your needs. For example, if you want to run 1-2-3 on an IBM Personal Computer that is capable of displaying graphics in color, and also run 1-2-3 on a COMPAQ that displays graphics and text in one color, creating two separate driver files will enable you to run 1-2-3 on both computers whenever you like.

When you make your driver selection, carefully review the options. Whether your system can display graphs and text at the same time and in color depends on a number of factors: the type of monitor(s) you will use; the type of video adapter card(s) (whether the monitor will produce only text or also graphics and color); and the number of colors that are displayed.

Some equipment selections enable you to view text and graphics only at different times on the screen (One-Monitor mode). An IBM color monitor with a color/graphics card, for example, will display both graphs and text in color, but not at the same time. On the other hand, some dual-monitor combinations enable you to view color graphs on one screen and text on the other at the same time (Two-Monitor mode).

Before you run the Install program, prepare a list of your equipment. When you run Install, you will first need to indicate to 1-2-3 what display hardware you have. For example, a color/graphics card uses graphics control characters to display graphs, but a monochrome adapter displays regular green-on-black text.

Second, you will need to indicate to the program what kind of text printer(s) you have. You can specify more than one printer at installation, and then select the proper one from within 1-2-3.

Third, 1-2-3 will ask you to indicate the graphics printer(s) or plotter(s) you will be using. Again, if you specify several graphics printers during installation, you can later select the appropriate one from within 1-2-3. Note that the same printer can be installed as both the text printer and the graphics printer.

Installing 1-2-3

If you do not have a hard disk, keep in mind that multiple drivers take up space on your 1-2-3 disk. If disk space is a problem, keep the list of printers to a minimum, or store your additional driver files on a separate disk. When you want to use another driver, place the system disk containing your usual driver set (123.SET) into drive A and the disk containing your other drivers into drive B. At the A> prompt type

> *123 B:name.SET*

where *name* is the name of the particular driver set you want to use. 1-2-3 will then load onto your computer using the specified driver.

Another installation option you can choose is the sort order, an option that is not affected by the kind of equipment you are using. (Note: To set the sort order, you must select the Advanced Options at the main Installation menu.)

Two data sort options are available:

1. English-like language with numbers first
2. English-like language with numbers last

The data sort selection regulates whether 1-2-3 sorts database entries beginning with numbers before (selection 1) or after (selection 2) it sorts entries beginning with letters. For example, suppose that you have a database containing inventory codes, some beginning with numbers and some beginning with letters. If you accept the default selection (*numbers first*) for your driver set, 1-2-3 will sort the codes that begin with numbers before those that begin with letters.

The following steps give detailed instructions for installing drivers. Notice that the Install program asks you to provide information for required equipment and any optional equipment you plan to use. The monitor you specify is considered required equipment. If you do not plan to use any optional equipment, you can skip the Install program steps that address optional equipment. For example, if you are not going to use a graphics printer or a plotter, you can skip the 1-2-3 Install program steps for adding these pieces of equipment to the driver set.

Select drivers to run 1-2-3 with your computer system as follows:

Hard Disk Systems

1. Make sure that your current directory is 123 by typing *cd \123* at the DOS C> prompt.
2. Type *install*.
3. When the main Install menu appears, select First Time Installation. Then create your driver set by following the step-by-step instructions that appear on your computer screen.
4. If you are creating only one driver set, use the default driver name 123.SET. If you are creating two or more driver sets, you must name each driver. For example, if you have a graphics plotter, you could name your second driver set PLOT.SET.
5. When you exit the Install program, 1-2-3 automatically saves your driver selections for you. If you need to make a change or correction to your existing driver set(s), enter the Install program and select the Change Selected Equipment option; then follow the on-screen instructions.

Installing 1-2-3

Two Floppy Disk Systems

1. Insert your Utility disk in drive A, and then type *install*.
2. When 1-2-3 prompts you to do so, replace the Utility disk in drive A with the Install Library disk. When the main Install menu appears, select First Time Installation; then create your driver set by following the step-by-step instructions that appear on your screen.
3. If you are creating only one driver set, use the default driver name 123.SET. If you are creating two or more driver sets, you must name each driver. For example, if you have a graphics plotter, you could name your second driver PLOT.SET.
4. Save your driver set(s) on your System, PrintGraph, and A View of 1-2-3 disks by following the on-screen directions. (Note: In Release 2.01, if you try to store additional drivers on your System disk, you may get an error message indicating insufficient disk space. Check your documentation for a way to free up space on the System disk.)
5. If you need to make a change or correction to your existing driver set(s), enter the Install program and select the Change Selected Equipment option; then follow the on-screen instructions.

Two Microfloppy Disk Systems (PS/2 Model 25 and 30)

1. Insert your Install disk in drive A, and then type *install*.
2. When the main Install menu appears, select First Time Installation; then create your driver set by following the step-by-step instructions that appear on your screen.

3. If you are creating only one driver set, use the default driver name 123.SET. If you are creating two or more driver sets, you must name each driver. For example, if you have a graphics plotter, you could name your second driver PLOT.SET.
4. Save your driver set(s) on your System disk with PrintGraph and the View of 1-2-3 with Translate disk by following the on-screen directions.
5. If you need to make a change or correction to your existing driver set(s), enter the Install program and select the Change Selected Equipment option; then follow the on-screen instructions.

Installing Copy-Protection on the Hard Disk

Normally, you must place the System disk in drive A as a key disk when starting the 1-2-3 program. The System disk is used only to verify that you have a legitimate copy of 1-2-3, and the rest of the 1-2-3 program is read from the hard disk. After 1-2-3 has started up, you can remove the System disk from drive A.

As an alternative, Lotus provides a program (COPYHARD) to write the copy-protection information onto your hard disk. If you use this special program during the Install procedure, you don't have to place the System disk in drive A to start 1-2-3. In fact, you can't use the System disk while the copy protection is installed on the hard disk because the copy protection on the System disk is altered.

If you did not write the copy-protection information onto your hard disk during installation, but later decide to do so, you can access the COPYHARD program by changing to your 123 directory and then typing copyhard. You can also access COPYHARD through the Install program; change to the 123 directory, type *install*, and then choose Advanced Options.

Installing 1-2-3

To restore the System disk to operation, you must remove the copy-protection information from the hard disk and restore the information onto the System disk. Do this process by using the Uninstall option (COPYHARD /U) of the hard disk copy-protect program; change to your 123 directory and type *copyhard /u*. You can also Uninstall COPYHARD by choosing Advanced Options from the Install program.

Think carefully before writing the copy protection onto the hard disk. If something happens to the hard disk, you may lose the copy-protection information.

Do not install the copy protection on your hard disk if you use a tape backup for your hard disk. If you do a file-by-file backup and then restore the files, you erase all the copy-protection information on the hard disk. If the copy-protection information is lost for any reason, you must use your Backup System disk to run 1-2-3 and seek a replacement for your nonfunctional System disk.

Preparing Data Disks

The final procedure in getting started with 1-2-3 is preparing data disks. For those who are unfamiliar with preparing disks, all disks must be properly formatted using the DOS FORMAT command before they can be used. By using the 1-2-3 /System command, you can access DOS without exiting 1-2-3 (see Chapter 2). Then use the FORMAT command at the DOS system prompt. For more information on how to format disks, see Chris DeVoney's *Using PC DOS,* 2nd Edition or *MS-DOS User's Guide,* 2nd Edition; both books are published by Que Corporation.

Replacing Your 1-2-3 System Disk

As mentioned previously, Lotus provides the Backup System disk in case your master System disk is lost or destroyed. For information on replacing your 1-2-3 System disk, refer to the Customer Assurance Plan that comes with the 1-2-3 disks.

429

Index

1-2-3 disks, installing, 413
@ symbol, 21, 88, 90

A

A-F ranges for graphing, 259
Abs key (F4), 59
absolute cell addressing, 133, 202-204
absolute/relative references, 203
Access System,
    /Quit command, 50
    1-2-3, 44-45, 48-49
    exiting, 48-49
    floppy drive, 45
    hard drive, 45
    Lotus, 45
    menu bar, 45, 47
accounting tools, 12
adapters for graphics display, 258
Add option, 119, 122-123
adding borders to worksheets, 228
addresses,
    within spreadsheet, 71
    cell, 20, 80-81
Align Print menu selection, 221, 223
aligning labels, 92-92
alphanumeric keys, 43, 54
Alt key, 59
alternative command selection, 135-137
arrow keys, 70
    in Edit mode, 72, 97
    view grid, 17
ASCII files
    importing, 128, 130
    text printing, 254-255
assigning labels, 139
automatic
    macros, 404-405, 407
    recalculation, 182-184

axes
    x-axis, 257, 267
    y-axis, 257, 267

B

backslash (\) key, 401
Backspace key, 59, 111
    Edit mode, 97
backup disks, 419-420
bar graph, 33, 259, 266, 269
    symbols, 276
    specifying data range, 273-274
basic
    keys, 70
    of 1-2-3, 4, 6, 19
borders, 219
Break key, 135
bugs, 389

C

Calc key (F9), 59
calculations
    editing, 24
    iterative, 25
capabilities
    graphics, 32
    of 1-2-3, 6
    spreadsheet, 28
cells, 9, 11, 20
    addresses, 20, 80-81, 133, 202-208
        absolute, 202-204
        changing with F4 key, 203, 207
        deleting, 175
        in formulas, 91
        mixed, defined, 203
        relative, 202-204
    contents
        copying, 192-193, 196-212

formatting, 152
listing, 252-253
moving, 192-195
printing, 250-254
protecting, 186-188
coordinates, 139
copy, 196-201
current, 60
described, 16-17
entries, 11
    as labels, 78
    as values, 78
    copying, 24
    editing, 96-99
formats, 152-159
    changing, 158
    list of, 159
    resetting, 157
freezing, 169, 172
jumping to, 71
number of, 70
pointer, 9, 69-70
    described, 16-17
    move with End key, 76-77
    view grid, 17
    with commands, 137
protecting, 25
ranges, copying, 122-123
references, 20
suppressing zero value, 179
changing
    a password, 115, 117
    column width, 166-167
characters
    in functions,
        (@) ampersand, 242-244
        (#) pound sign, 242-244
        (|) vertical bar, 242-244
    label, repeating, 94
    label-prefix, 93
    wildcard, 36
checking disk space, 105, 109

choosing file names, 107, 113, 128-129, 131
Clear Print menu selection, 221, 223
collating sequence, database sort, 355
color option for graphs, 29, 324-325
Column worksheet command, 153, 161
column-row structure, 34
column-wise recalculation, 183-184
columns
    deleting, 174-175, 177
    hiding, 178-180, 232-235
    inserting, 174, 176
    setting column widths, 166-167
    transposing, 208-210
combining files, 119, 122-123
Comma, cell format, 152, 154, 159
Command Language programs, 11, 39, 41, 389
command menus, 134
COMMAND.COM file, 418, 422
commands, 9-10
    /Copy, 24, 85, 178, 192, 196, 202-203, 208, 370
    database, 34-35
    /Data, 135, 334, 338
    /Data Fill, 13, 358
    /Data Query, 35, 362-363
    /Data Query Criterion, 367
    /Data Query Extract, 377
    /Data Query Find, 35, 368-369
    /Data Query Input, 366
    /Data Query Output, 370, 384
    /Data Query Unique, 35
    /Data Table, 156
    defined, 132
    /Delete, 135, 365, 384-386
    DOS CHKDSK, 105, 109
    DOS DATE/TIME, 213
    DOS FORMAT, 105, 109
    DOS FORMAT, 216

Index

DOS TYPE, 220
/Extract, 346, 364, 370-371, 377, 385, 387
file, 25
/File Combine, 118-119, 122
/File Directory, 125
/File Erase, 124, 126
/File Import, 128, 220
/File List, 125, 127, 213
/File Retrieve, 101, 110, 112, 114, 117-118, 213
/File Save, 51, 53, 104, 106, 108-109, 114-117, 212, 214-216, 350, 385, 387
/File Xtract, 118-121, 370
/Find, 365, 370, 377, 384
/Go, printing, 316, 329
/Graph, 28-29, 259-260, 322
/Graph Name, 261, 303, 305
/Graph Name Delete, 303
/Graph Options, 265
/Graph Options Color, 261
/Graph Options Data-Label, 284
/Graph Options Format, 290, 292-293
/Graph Options Grid, 291, 294-295
/Graph Options Legend, 288-289
/Graph Options Scale, 261, 296-298, 301
/Graph Options Titles, 279, 282, 300
/Graph Reset X, 281
/Graph Save, 103, 261, 302, 304
/Graph Type, 263
/Insert, 135
/Move, 178, 192, 15
/Options B&W, 261
/Print, 218-222, 225, 232
/Print File, 218-222
/Print File Options, 128, 252
/Print Printer Align, 237, 239
/Print Printer Clear All, 225
/Print Printer Clear, 250
/Print Printer Line, 236, 239

/Print Printer Options, 85, 228, 232-233, 252
/Print Printer Page, 236, 239
/Print Printer Range, 144
/Print Printer, 218-222, 228
/Quit, 50-51, 53, 212, 215, 351, 361
/Range, 133
/Range Erase, 145, 147-148, 154-155, 163-164, 175, 177
/Range Format, 152-153, 158, 250, 296
/Range Format Currency, 392
/Range Format Hidden, 156, 233
/Range Format Reset, 157, 233
/Range Input, 187
/Range Label, 93
/Range Name, 141, 146
/Range Name Create, 139, 142-143, 401
/Range Name Delete, 145-146
/Range Name Label, 139, 142
/Range Name Reset, 145-146
/Range Name Table, 149, 151
/Range Protect, 186-188
/Range Transpose, 208-210
/Range Unprotect, 186, 188-189
/Range Value, 208-209, 211
selecting worksheet, 135
spreadsheet, 11, 24-28
/System, 50, 52, 105, 109, 126, 133, 212, 215-217
/System, with PrintGraph, 307, 309
/Unique, 364, 384-386
View, 28
worksheet, 153, 161, 166-191
/Worksheet, 133
/Worksheet Column, 166
/Worksheet Column Display, 178, 181, 232
/Worksheet Column Hide, 156, 178, 180, 232-233
/Worksheet Column Set-Width, 345
/Worksheet Delete Column, 349

/Worksheet Delete Row, 346-347, 385
/Worksheet Delete, 174-175, 177
/Worksheet Erase, 156-157, 164-165
/Worksheet Global Column-width, 166-167
/Worksheet Global Default Other International, 157
/Worksheet Global Default Directory, 111
/Worksheet Global Default Directory, 125
/Worksheet Global Default Status, 225
/Worksheet Global Default Status, 246
/Worksheet Global Format, 153, 158, 296
/Worksheet Global Format Text, 85
/Worksheet Global Label-Prefix, 93
/Worksheet Global Protection, 186-188
/Worksheet Global Recalculation, 182
/Worksheet Global Zero, 179
/Worksheet Insert Column, 286, 347, 349, 358
/Worksheet Insert, 174, 176
/Worksheet Insert Row, 191, 346-348
/Worksheet Page, 191, 237
/Worksheet Row Display, 181
/Worksheet Row Hide, 180-181
/Worksheet Status, 134-135, 190
/Worksheet Titles, 169, 172
/Worksheet Title Both, 173
/Worksheet Title Horizontal, 173
/Worksheet Title Vertical, 173
/Worksheet Window, 168-171
control panel, 43, 60, 62, 136
controlling data display, 152
converting formulas to values, 208-209
/Copy command, 85, 178, 196, 202-203, 208, 370
copying
    cell entries, 24
    disks for backup, 419-420
    disks to hard drive, 416-417
    ranges, 122-123
COPYHARD program, 413, 427
creating
    a table of range names, 149, 151
    graphs, 256-301
criteria, defining, 35
criterion range, 333, 376, 380
Ctrl-Break sequence, 135, 225
Ctrl key, 71-72, 97, 135
Currency cell format, 152, 154, 159
current
    cell, 60
    graph, 303
cursor movement, 71, 134, 193
cursor-movement keys, 55, 69-70

D

/Data command, 135, 334, 338
data
    defined, 69
    disks, preparing, 429
    display, controlling, 152
    editing, 34
    entering, 73, 78-83
    management, 11, 332-387
    menu, 338, 340, 384
/Data Fill command, 13, 358
/Data Query command, 362-363
/Data Query Criterion command, 367
/Data Query Extract command, 377
/Data Query Find command, 35, 368-369
/Data Query Input command, 366
Data Query menu, 360-361, 363-366, 371
/Data Query Output command, 370, 384
/Data Query Unique command, 35

433

Index

data ranges for
    bar graphs, 273-274
    graphs, 263, 275-276
    line graph, 272, 274
    pie, 273, 277
    specifying, 276
    Stacked bar graphs, 273-274
    XY graphs, 273, 277
Data Sort menu, 350-352, 356
/Data Table commands, 156
database
    adding records, 346
    applications, 6, 10
    capabilities, 36
    commands, 34-35
    creating, 338-343
    defined, 333-334, 336-337
    deleting records, 346
    determining output, 339
    editing records during search, 368
    entering data, 342-343
    functions, 34-35
        @DAVG, 35
        @DCOUNT, 35
        @DMAX, 35
        @DMIN, 35
        @DSTD, 35
        @DSUM, 35
        @DVAR, 35
    management, 34-38
    modifying, 346-350
    modifying fields, 346-348
    output range, 370
    placement in worksheet, 341, 345
    planning, 338-339, 344
    Primary-Key, 350-355
    Secondary-Key, 350, 354-356
    records (editing), 368
    searching, 379-387
        AND conditions, 377-379, 381-383
        criterion range, 364-367
        exact match, 376-377
        formulas in criterion range, 376, 380
        input range, 364
        OR conditions, 378-379, 381-383
        requirements, 360-361
        string, 379, 381, 384
        unique records, 385
        wildcard criterion ranges, 376-377, 380
    size limitation, 335
    sorting
        collating sequence, 355
        one-key sort, 350-354
        restoring presort order, 355
        string capabilities, 354-355
        two-key sort, 355-360
    tutorial screen, 67
Date cell format, 152, 155, 159
date/time functions, 21, 89
debugging, 389
default
    addressing, 204
    directory setting, 125
    font, 324
    format, 152
    graph, 33
    graph display items (changing), 290-293
    page
        layout, 246
        length, 236, 238
    settings
        changing graph, 296-298
        footer, 242
        graph scale values, 296
        header, 242
        PrintGraph, 310, 312
        restoring graph, 290
definition of 1-2-3, 14-15
Del key, 59, 97

/Delete command, 135, 365, 384-386
/Delete worksheet command, 153, 161
deleting
    a password, 115, 117
    columns, 174-175, 177
    files, 124, 126
    graphs, 303
    range names, 145-146
    rows, 174-175, 177
demonstration disk, 414
directories, graph, 328
Disk full error message, 105, 124
disk space (checking), 105, 109
disks
    1-2-3, 413-414
    backup, 419-420
    copying, 419-420
    copying to hard drive, 416-417
    data (preparing for), 429
    formatting, 420
    preparing for installation, 415
    System, replacing, 429
displaying
    data, 152
    files with wildcards, 110, 112, 124
    graphic images, 314
DOS
    accessing from 1-2-3, 216
    CHKDSK command, 105, 109
    DATE/TIME command, 213
    FORMAT command, 105, 109, 216
    TYPE command, 220
drivers
    changing, 424
    files, explained, 422
    programs, installing, 422-427
    selecting, 125

E

Edit key (F2), 59, 96, 346-347
EDIT mode, 70, 72, 97, 111
editing
    capabilities, 24
    data, 34, 96-99
    file specifications, 111
electronic spreadsheet, 9-18, 20, 51
End key, 134, 71-72, 97
    cursor movement, 71-72
    move cell pointer, 76-77
    point to range, 193
enhanced keyboard, 72
enhancing default graph, 311, 313
entering
    a range, 138, 140
    data, 73, 78-83
    formulas, 78-83, 91
    functions, 88
    labels, 92-95
    numbers, rules, 79
entries, cell, 11
equations, 20
/Erase worksheet command, 153, 161
erasing ranges, 145, 147
error messages, 62, 105, 124
errors
    correcting, 24
    in formulas, 85, 87
    Esc key, 59, 97, 111, 135
    excluding spreadsheet columns from printing, 232-235
    ranges from printing, 233-235
    rows from printing, 232-235
exiting
    1-2-3, 50-54
    PrintGraph, 306-309

Index

extensions, file, 220
/Extract command, 346, 364, 370-371, 377, 385, 387
extracting information, 118, 121

F

field, defined, 333-334, 337
/File Combine command, 118-119, 122
file commands, 25
/File Directory command, 125
/File Erase command, 124, 126
File extensions, 25, 100-103, 220,
/File Import command, 128, 220
/File List command, 125, 127, 213
file names 213
    choosing, 107, 113
    rules for, 100, 102
file passwords, 114-117
/File Retrieve command, 101, 110, 112, 114, 117-118, 213
/File Save command, 51, 53, 104, 106, 108-109, 114-117, 212, 214-216, 350, 385, 387
file specifications, editing, 111
/File Xtract command, 118, 120-121, 370
/File Xtract Formulas command, 119, 121
files
    ASCII, importing, 128, 130
    .PIC, 302
    combining, 119, 122-123
    COMMAND.COM, 418, 422
    deleting, 124, 126
    description, 100
    displaying, 110, 112
    displaying with wildcards, 124
    driver, 422

    introduction to managing, 100
    listing, 124-125, 127
    naming, 104, 107
    PGRAPH.CNF, 330
    .PIC, 29, 302
    printing, ASCII text, 254-255
    .PRN, 218, 220
    protecting, 25
    retrieving, 101, 110-114
        password protected file, 114-117
        partial, 118
        subdirectories, 111, 113
        wildcards, 110-112
    saving, 50-51, 104, 106, 108, 212-216,
        partial, 118
        to floppy disks, 104, 108
    transferring, 128-130
        /File Import, 128, 130
        Translate Utility, 128-129, 131
    types of, 25, 124-125
financial
    functions
        described, 21
        help screen, 65
    modeling tools, 11
    spreadsheets, 10
/Find command, 365, 370, 377
Fixed, cell format, 152, 154, 159
floppy disk system, with PrintGraph, 306-307
font option, for graphs, 29
fonts
    default, 324
    defined, 324
    selecting, graphs, 324
footers
    default settings, 242
    defined, 219
format commands, precedence of, 153

format menu, 158
formats
    cell, 152-159
    changing, 152, 158
    default, 152
    International, controlling, 157
    resetting, 157
    setting, 153
formatting
    cell contents, 152
    the worksheet, 24
    disks, 420
formulas and functions, 20-24
formulas, 9, 20
    containing functions, 91
    converting to values, 208-209
    correcting errors, 85, 87
    entering with pointer, 83
    entering, 78-83
    mathematical operators in, 83-87
    option, 118
    overriding precedence in, 85
    parentheses in, 85
    preserving, 119
freezing titles, 169, 172
function keys, 29, 43, 55, 67, 203, 393
functions help screen, 65
functions
    data management, 89
    database, 34-35
    date/time, 21, 89
    entering 88
    financial, 21
    index, 89
    investments/depreciation analysis, 89
    LICS, 89
    library, 89
    limits, 88
    lists of, 89

    logarithmic, 89
    mathematical, 21, 89
    parts of, 90
    range, defined, 90
    scroll, 70
    special, 21, 89
    statistical, 35, 89
    string, 21, 89
    SUM, 21
    trigonometric, 89
    using, 88-91
    within formulas, 91

G

General cell format, 152-153, 159
getting started, 6, 42-50
Global settings
    checking status of, 190
    default, 190
/Global worksheet command, 153, 161
/Go command (printing), 316, 328
Go Print menu selection, 221, 223
GoTo Key (F5), 59, 71-72, 141, 144, 148, 169
graph axis indicators, 300
/Graph command, 28, 259-260, 322
/Graph menu, 262, 266-267, 272-273, 278, 281-287, 290
/Graph Name Command, 261, 303, 305
/Graph Name Delete command, 303
/Graph Option Scale command, 261
/Graph Options Color command, 261
/Graph Options command, 265
/Graph Options Options Data-Label command, 284, 286
/Graph Options Format command, 290

Index

/Graph Graph Options Format command, 292-293
/Graph Options Grid Clear command, 291, 295
/Graph Options Grid command, 291, 294-295
/Graphics Options Grid Horizontal command, 291, 295
/Graph Options Legend command, 288-289
/Graph Options menu, 260, 278, 282
/Graph Options Scale command, 296-298
/Graph Options Scale Skip command, 301
/Graph Options Titles command, 279, 282, 300
/Graph Reset X command, 281
/Graph Save command, 103, 302, 304
/Graph Type command, 263
graphics
    applications, 6
    capabilities, 28, 32
    display adapter, 258
    labels, 261
    printer, 258
    printing, 29
graphs, 10
    adding labels to, 278-280, 284-285, 287
    adding numbers to, 27
    bar, 33, 266, 269, 273-274
    changing
        defaults, 296-298
        scale values, 296-299
    choosing type, 270-271
    color option, 29
    creating, 256-301
    creating, 259
    current, 303
    data labels, 278-280, 284-285, 287
    data ranges, 263
    default, 33, 290, 296-298
    deleting labels from, 280
    deleting, 303
    directory, 328
    display image, 314
    enhancing, 264, 311, 313
    font option, 29
    hardware requirements, 258
    grids, 260, 291
    label spacing, 297-298, 301
    legends, 260, 281
    line, 33, 266, 268, 272, 274, 290
    line symbols, 275
    manual option, 29
    marking for printing. 310, 312
    naming, 261, 302-305
    pausing printing, 319
    pie, 3, 266, 269, 273, 277, 290
    plotting, 267
    printed
        adjusting size, 322
        appearance, 326
        changing location, 323
        choosing colors, 324-325, 327
        image, 314
        orientation, 322
        paper movement, 320
        previewing, 328, 331
        rotating, 322-323
        selecting fonts, 324, 327
        selecting, 329, 331
        size setting, 322-323
    printing, 256-301, 310-331
    replotting, 29
    scale values, 296-299
    selecting type, 266-271
    setting background grid, 291, 294
    size option, 29
    stacked bar, 33, 266, 269, 273-274
    storing, 303, 305

symbols, 260, 290, 292-293
titles, 260
type, 257
"what if", 28-29
using Titles option, 279, 283
XY, 269, 273, 277
grids, in graphs, 260

H

hardware requirements for graphs, 258
headers
    character functions, 242-244
    default settings, 242
    defined, 219
headings,
    freezing, 169, 172
help
    features, 64-67
    index screen, 65
    key (F1), 59
    screens,
    ready mode, 65
Hidden cell format, 152, 156, 159
hiding
    columns, 178-180, 232-235
    rows, 232-235
Home key, 71-72, 97, 134, 169,
horizontal
    Bar Graph cell format, 152, 155, 159
    screen splits, 168

I

Image options, 322, 317, 326
Image select options, 316
index functions, 89
indicators (default format), 152
information
    accessing, 4
    extracting, 118, 121

input range, defined, 333
/Insert command, 135
Insert key (Edit mode), 97
insert modes, 99
/Insert worksheet command, 153, 161
inserting
    columns, 174, 176
    rows, 174, 176
install library disk, 414
Install, from Access System, 45, 48-49
installation, two floppy disk system, 418
installing
    1-2-3, 412-429
    driver programs, 422-427
internally documented macros, 400-402
International Formats, 157
investments/depreciation analysis
    functions, 89
invisible commands, 39
iterative calculations, 25, 183

J-K

joining criteria, 35
justification (labels), 94
key actions (Edit mode), 72, 97
key fields, 333, 335, 337
keyboard macros, 38-41
keyboards,
    enhanced, 72
    learning, 54-60
    numeric keypad, 43, 70, 154-155
    types of, 54-60
keys
    Abs (F4), 59, 203
    alphanumeric, 43, 54
    Alt, 59
    arrow, 70, 72, 97

Index

backslash (\), 401
Backspace, 59, 111
Backspace (Edit mode), 97
basic, 70
Break, 135
Calc (F9), 59
Ctrl, 71-72, 135, 87
Ctrl (Edit mode), 97
cursor-movement, 69-70, 55
Del, 59, 97, 346-347
Edit (F2), 59, 96, 346-347
End, 71, 76-77, 134
Esc, 59, 97, 111, 135
GoTo (F5) key, 59, 71-72, 141, 144, 148, 169
Graph (F10), 10, 59, 278, 331
Help (F1), 59
Home, 75, 134, 169, 71-72
main menu command (/), 134
Num Lock, 55, 59
numeric, 72
period (.), 54
PgDn, 71-72
PgUp, 71-72
primary, 34
Query (F7), 59
Scroll Lock, 59, 70, 74
secondary, 34
Shift, 55, 59, 71-72
Shift-Prtsc, 148, 224, 226
slash (/), 24, 50
special purpose, 59
Tab, 59, 71-72
Tab (Edit mode), 97
Table (F8), 59
Window (F6), 59, 168

L

LABEL mode, 92
labels
   aligning, 92-93
   assigning, 139
   characters, repeating, 94
   cell entries, 78
   entering, 92-95
   in graphs, 261
   length, 94
   prefix characters, 93
   prefixes, controlling, 93, 95
letters assigned to columns, 16-17
library functions, 89
LICS functions, 89
limits of functions, 88
line graphs, 33, 259, 268, 275, 290, specifying data range, 272, 274
Line Print menu selection, 221, 223
lines in graphs, 260
listing
   files, 124-125, 127
   range names, 148, 150
lock key indicators, 60-61-62
logarithmic functions, 89

M

macros, 10
   debugging, 408, 410
   defined, 40-41, 389-391
   documenting, 400-403
   editing, 408-409, 411
   elements of, 392-394
   errors in, 409
   executing, 404, 406
   internally documented, 400-402
   keyboard, 38-41
   naming, 400-403
   planning, 396-399

  positioning, 396-399
  self-documented, 400-402
  special key representations, 395
main command menu key (/), 50, 134
main menu bar, 93
managing files, 100-131
manual recalculation, 183-184
Margins options, 246
margins, setting, 246
mathematical
  analyses, 34
  functions, 89
  in formulas, 83-87
  operators (order of precedence), 84
memory, required for program, 16
menu bar, 93
message area, 60-62
microfloppy, 44
mixed cell addressing, 203, 206
mode indicators, 60-61
modes,
  EDIT, 70, 111, 76
  insert, 99
  overstrike, 99
  POINT, 70, 148, 150
  READY, 70, 105
monitors, graphic, 258
Move command, 178, 192, 195
multi-page reports, 229-231

N

Name (F3) key, 110, 148
naming
  files, 104, 107
  graphs, 261, 302-305
  ranges, 24, 139, 141-142

natural recalculation, 25
Num Lock key, 55, 59
Numbers option, 128
numbers
  assigned to rows, 16-17
  entering, 79
numeric keypad, 43, 54-55, 72

O

on-screen graphs, 278
operations in 1-2-3, 68
operators, 20, 69
  mathematical, 84
  purpose of, 86
Options B&W command, 261
Options Print menu selection,
  description, 221, 223
output range, database, 333, 370
overstrike modes, 99

P

page breaks (setting), 237, 241
page layout,
  changing, 246-249
  default, 246
page length,
  default, 236, 238
  setting, 246
Page Print menu selection, 221, 223
page-break characters, 191
paging through worksheet, 71
parentheses in formulas, 86
passwords, 25, 114-117
  creating, 114, 116
  deleting, 115, 117
  file, 114-117

Index

Percent cell format, 152, 155, 159
period (.) key, 54
PgDn key, 71-72
PgUp key, 71-72
pgraph (to access PrintGraph), 306
PGRAPH.CNF file, 330
physical print environment, 318-320
.PIC file, 29, 259-260, 269, 302, 328
pie graphs,
    explained, 266
    selecting colors, 325
    shading, 277
    specifying data range, 273, 277
POINT mode, 70, 148, 150
pointer, 69-70, 83
pointing to ranges
    with End key, 193
    with expanding cursor, 193
preserving formulas, 119
primary key, 34, 350-355
/Print command, 218-222, 225, 232
print defaults, 219
/Print File command, 218-222, 228, 252
Print menu, 221, 225
print options,
    clearing, 250
    menu selections, 250
/Print Printer Align command, 237, 239
/Print Printer Clear All command, 225
/Print Printer Clear command, 250
/Print Printer command, 218-222, 228, 232-233, 252
/Print Printer Line command, 236, 239
/Print Printer Options Border command, 228
/Print Printer Options menu, 242-243, 246, 250

/Print Printer Page command, 236, 239
/Print Printer Range command, 144
PrintGraph menu, 316-317
PrintGraph Settings Hardware menu, 317-318, 321
PrintGraph, 29
    accessing, 306-309
    default settings, 310, 312
    exiting, 306-309
    floppy disk system, 306-207
    from Access System, 45, 48-49
    hard drive system, 306-307
    saving settings, 330
printing
    a range, 144
    cell contents, 250-254
    draft-quality reports, 224-225, 227
    graphs, 29, 256-301, 310-331
        adjusting size, 322
        appearance changes, 314, 326
        changing location, 323
        choosing colors, 324-325, 327
        marking for, 310, 312
        orientation, 322
        paper movement, 329
        previewing, 328, 331
        rotating, 322-323
        selecting fonts, 324, 327
        selecting, 329, 331
    size setting, 322-323
    selecting B&W option, 281, 288
    selecting Color option, 281, 288
    worksheet labels, 228-231
    spreadsheets, 232-235
    using Shift-PrtSc, 224, 226
    with continuous-feed paper, 236, 238
    worksheets, 25
.PRN files, 218, 220
programming language, 39
/Printer Options Other Cell-Formulas command, 85

protecting a worksheet, 115-116
protecting
    cells, 25
    files, 25

Q

Query key (F7), 59
Query menu, 385
QuickStart concept, 2
Quit command, 50-51,53, 212, 215, 351, 361
Quit Print menu selection, 221, 223

R

RAM (random-access memory), 16
Range command menu, 139
/Range command, 133, 145
/Range erase command, 145, 147-148, 154-155, 163-164, 175, 177
/Range Format command, 152-153, 158, 250, 296
/Range Format Currency command, 392
/Range Format Hidden command, 156, 233
/Range Format Reset command, 157, 233
/Range Input command, 187
/Range Label command, 93
/Range Name command, 141, 146
/Range Name Create command, 139, 142, 401
/Range Name Delete command, 145-146
/Range Name Labels command, 139, 142-143
/Range Name Reset command, 145-146
/Range Name Table command, 149, 151

range names,
    creating a table of, 149, 151
    deleting, 145-146
    length, 139
    listing, 148, 150
    with formulas, 144
Range Print menu selection, 221, 223
/Range Protect command, 186-188
range specifications, 138
/Range Transpose command, 208-210
/Range Unprotect command, 186, 188-189
/Range Value command, 208-209, 211
ranges, concept of, 132
    entering, 138
    erasing, 145, 147
    function, 90
    hiding, 233-235
    methods of entering, 140
    moving between (with F5), 141
    multiple names, 144
    naming, 24, 139, 141-142
    pointing to, with end key, 193
    pointing to, with expanding cursor, 193
    printing, 191
READY mode, 70, 105, 172
    help screen, 65
recalculating worksheets, 25, 183-184
records, 333-335
relational database, 34
relative cell addressing, 133, 202, 204
replotting a graph, 29
reports, 10, 229-231
    printing draft-quality, 224-225, 227
    setting print range for, 229
retrieving
    files, 101, 110-114
    partial files, 118

Index

row-column coordinates, 16
row-wise recalculation, 183-184
rows,
    as records, 36
    deleting, 174-175, 177
    hiding, 232-235
    inserting, 174, 176
    number assigned, 16-17
    transposing, 208-210
rules,
    file names, 100, 102
    for entering numbers, 79

S

saving
    files, 50-51, 104, 106, 108, 302
    graphs, 304-305
    partial files, 118
    PrintGraph settings, 330
Scale
    option, 296
    values, changing graph, 296-299
Scientific cell format, 152, 154, 159
screen
    display, 60-64
    modes (Sync), 168
    splitting, 168, 170-171
    tutorials, 66-67
scroll function, 70
Scroll Lock key, 70, 74
searching
    criterion range, 364-367
    input range, 364
    operations, 36
Secondary-Key, 34, 350, 354-356
selecting
    a drive, 125
    worksheet, 135

setting
    formats, 153, 246
    margins, 246
    page breaks, 237, 241
    print range for reports, 229
Shift key, 55, 59, 71-72
Shift-Prtsc, 148, 224, 226
size
    limitations of database, 335
    limits of spreadsheet, 11
    option (for graphs), 29
slash (/) key, 24, 50
sorting
    operations, 36
    options, 424
    data, 34
splitting the screen, 168, 170-171
spreadsheet
    applications, 6
    capabilities, 28
    commands, 11, 24-28
    data (procedures relating to), 10
    electronic, 20, 51
    financial, 10
    moving around in, 70-77
    size limit, 11, 16-18, 70
stacked bar graphs, 33, 259, 266, 269
    specifying data range, 273-274
starting 1-2-3,
    floppy system, 44, 46-47
    from DOS, 44, 46-47
    hard disk system, 44, 46-47
statistical
    analysis, performing, 34
    functions, 21, 35, 89
status indicators, 61-63
Status worksheet commands, 153, 161
stop printing (with Ctrl-Break), 225
string functions, 21, 89

string search, 379, 381, 384
subcommands, 259
subdirectories, retrieving files from, 111, 113
Subtract option, 119, 123
SUM function, 21
symbols, 260
   @, 21, 88
   bar graph, 276
   line graph, 275
Sync screen mode, 168
/System command, 50, 52, 105, 109, 126, 133, 212, 215-217, 307, 309, 414
system disk
   backup, 413
   replacing, 429

T

Tab key, 59, 71-72, 97
Table key (F8), 59
Text option, 128
Text cell format, 152, 156, 159
tick marks, 257
tildes (~), 389
Time format, 152, 155, 159
titles,
   chapter, 3
   freezing, 169, 172
   in graphs, 260
tools,
   accounting, 12
   financial modeling, 11
transferring files, 128-130
Translate Utility, 45, 48-49, 128-129, 131
transposing
   columns, 208-210
   rows, 208-210

trigonometric functions, 89
tutorial screens, 66-67
   database, 67
   labels, 67
   text, 67
tutorial (from Access System), 45, 48-49
typing method for selecting commands, 137

U

Uninstall option, 428
/Unique command, 364, 384-386
Unsync screen modes, 168
utility disk, 414

V

values, 69
   cell entries, 78
   option, 118-119
vertical screen splits, 168
View command, 28
View (from Access System), 45, 48-49

W

"what if" analysis, 22-23, 28-29
wildcard
   displaying file with, 124
   file retrieval, 110-112
   in database search criterion, 376-377, 380
Window key (F6), 59, 168
/Window worksheet command, 153, 161
/Wordsheet Insert command, 174, 176
/Worksheet column command, 166
/Worksheet Column Display command, 178, 181, 232

Index

/Worksheet Column Hidden command, 156
/Worksheet Column Hide command, 178, 180, 232-233
/Worksheet Column Set-Width command, 345
/Worksheet command, 133
worksheet commands, 152-157, 160-165
/Worksheet Delete Column command, 349
/Worksheet Delete command, 174-175, 177
/Worksheet Delete Row command, 346-348, 385
/Worksheet Erase command, 164-165
/Worksheet Global Column-width command, 166-167
/Worksheet Global Default Directory command, 111, 125
/Worksheet Global Default Other International command, 157
/Worksheet Global Default Status command, 225,246
/Worksheet Global Format command, 153, 158, 296
/Worksheet Global Label-Prefix command, 93
/Worksheet Global Protection Disable command, 187
/Worksheet Global Protection Enable command, 186-188
/Worksheet Global Recalculation command, 182
/Worksheet Global Zero command, 179
/Worksheet Insert Column command, 191, 286, 347, 349, 358

/Worksheet Insert Row command, 191, 346, 347
Worksheet menus, 132-135, 172
/Worksheet Page command, 191, 237
worksheet ranges, 138-151
/Worksheet Row Display command, 181
/Worksheet Row Hide command, 180
/Worksheet Status command, 134-135, 190
/Worksheet Title Both commands, 173
/Worksheet Title Horizontal command, 173
/Worksheet Title Vertical command, 173
/Worksheet Titles command, 169, 172
/Worksheet Window command, 168-171
worksheets,
  area, 60
  adding borders to, 228
  commands, 166-191
  creating, 132-134
  default format, 152
  editing data in, 96-99
  formatting, 24
  labels (printing), 228-231
  paging through, 71
  printing, 25
  protecting, 186-188
  recalculating, 25, 182-186
  size of, 16-18
  steps for protecting, 115-116
  unprotecting, 186-188
  viewing, 17

X-Y

x-axis, 257, 267
XY graph, 266, 269
  specifying data range, 273, 277
y-axis, 257, 267

More Computer Knowledge from Que

LOTUS SOFTWARE TITLES

1-2-3 QueCards	21.95
1-2-3 QuickStart	21.95
1-2-3 Quick Reference	6.95
1-2-3 for Business, 2nd Edition	22.95
1-2-3 Business Formula Handbook	19.95
1-2-3 Command Language	21.95
1-2-3 Macro Library, 2nd Edition	21.95
1-2-3 Tips, Tricks, and Traps, 2nd Edition	21.95
Using 1-2-3, Special Edition	24.95
Using 1-2-3 Workbook and Disk, 2nd Edition	29.95
Using Lotus HAL	19.95
Using Symphony, 2nd Edition	26.95

DATABASE TITLES

dBASE III Plus Applications Library	21.95
dBASE III Plus Handbook, 2nd Edition	22.95
dBASE III Plus Advanced Programming, 2nd Edition	22.95
dBASE III Plus Tips, Tricks, and Traps	21.95
dBASE IV Quick Reference	6.95
dBXL and Quicksilver Programming: Beyond dBASE	24.95
R:BASE Solutions: Applications and Resources	19.95
R:BASE System V Techniques and Applications	21.95
R:BASE System V User's Guide, 2nd Edition	19.95
R:BASE User's Guide, 3rd Edition	19.95
Using Clipper	24.95
Using Reflex	19.95
Using Paradox, 2nd Edition	22.95
Using Q & A, 2nd Edition	21.95

MACINTOSH AND APPLE II TITLES

HyperCard QuickStart: A Graphics Approach	21.95
Using AppleWorks, 2nd Edition	21.95
Using dBASE Mac	19.95
Using Dollars and Sense	19.95
Using Excel	21.95
Using HyperCard: From Home to HyperTalk	24.95
Using Microsoft Word: Macintosh Version	21.95
Using Microsoft Works	19.95
Using WordPerfect: Macintosh Version	19.95

APPLICATIONS SOFTWARE TITLES

Smart Tips, Tricks, and Traps	23.95
Using Dollars and Sense: IBM Version, 2nd Edition	19.95
Using Enable, 2nd Edition	22.95
Using Excel: IBM Version	24.95
Using Managing Your Money	19.95
Using Quattro	21.95
Using Smart	22.95
Using SuperCalc4	21.95

WORD-PROCESSING AND DESKTOP PUBLISHING TITLES

Microsoft Word Techniques and Applications	19.95
Microsoft Word Tips, Tricks, and Traps	19.95
Using DisplayWrite 4	19.95
Using Microsoft Word, 2nd Edition	21.95
Using MultiMate Advantage, 2nd Edition	19.95
Using PageMaker on the IBM	24.95
Using Sprint	21.95
Using Ventura Publisher	24.95
Using WordPerfect, 3rd Edition	21.95
Using WordPerfect 5	24.95
Using WordPerfect Workbook and Disk	29.95
Using WordStar	18.95
WordPerfect QueCards	21.95
WordPerfect Quick Reference	6.95
WordPerfect QuickStart	21.95
WordPerfect Tips, Tricks, and Traps, 2nd Edition	21.95
WordPerfect Advanced Techniques	19.95

HARDWARE AND SYSTEMS TITLES

DOS Programmer's Reference	24.95
DOS QueCards	21.95
DOS Workbook and Disk	29.95
IBM PS/2 Handbook	21.95
Managing Your Hard Disk, 2nd Edition	22.95
MS-DOS Quick Reference	6.95
MS-DOS QuickStart	21.95
MS-DOS User's Guide, 3rd Edition	22.95
Networking IBM PCs, 2nd Edition	19.95
Programming with Windows	22.95
Understanding UNIX: A Conceptual Guide, 2nd Edition	21.95
Upgrading and Repairing PCs	24.95
Using Microsoft Windows	19.95
Using PC DOS, 2nd Edition	22.95

PROGRAMMING AND TECHNICAL TITLES

Advanced C: Techniques and Applications	21.95
C Programmer's Library	21.95
C Programming Guide, 2nd Edition	19.95
C Quick Reference	6.95
C Self-Study Guide	16.95
C Standard Library	21.95
Debugging C	19.95
QuickBASIC Quick Reference	6.95
Turbo Pascal for BASIC Programmers	18.95
Turbo Pascal Program Library	19.95
Turbo Pascal Tips, Tricks, and Traps	19.95
Using Assembly Language	24.95
Using QuickBASIC 4	19.95
Using Turbo Prolog	19.95

Que®

Que Order Line: **1-800-428-5331**

All prices subject to change without notice. Prices and charges are for domestic orders only.
Non-U.S. prices might be higher.

Using 1-2-3 Just Got Easier—
With 1-2-3 QueCards!

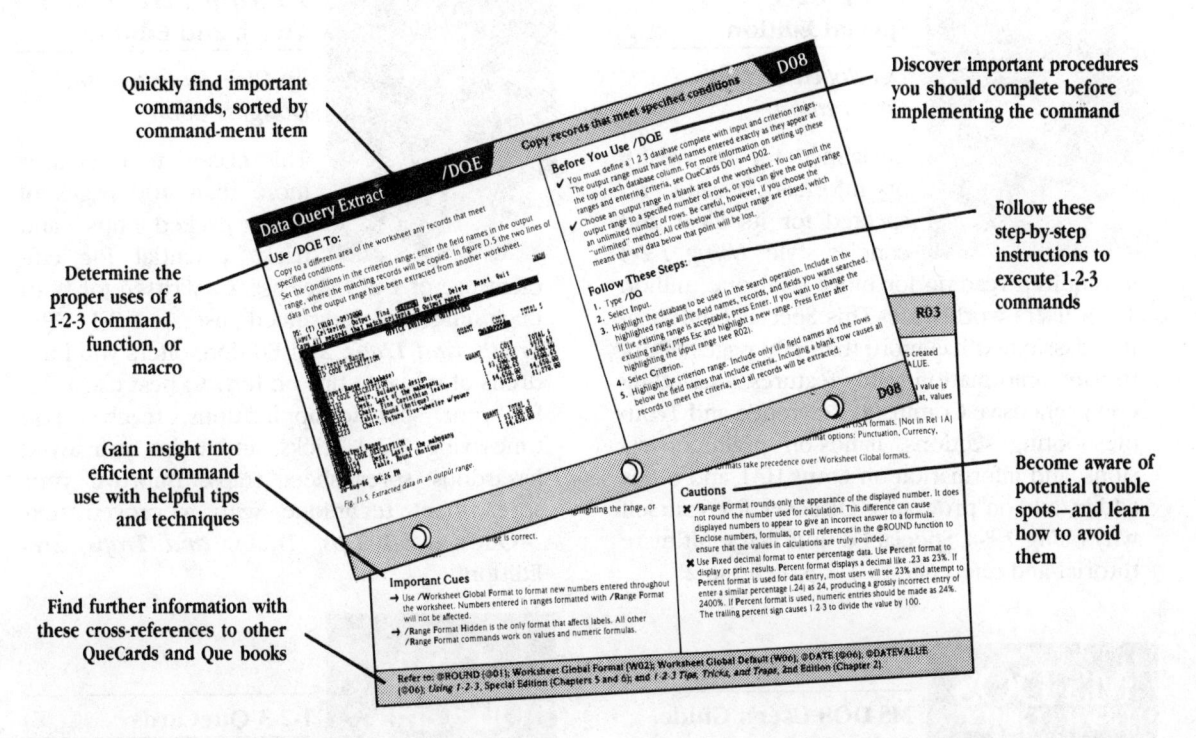

Quickly find important commands, sorted by command-menu item

Discover important procedures you should complete before implementing the command

Determine the proper uses of a 1-2-3 command, function, or macro

Follow these step-by-step instructions to execute 1-2-3 commands

Gain insight into efficient command use with helpful tips and techniques

Become aware of potential trouble spots—and learn how to avoid them

Find further information with these cross-references to other QueCards and Que books

1-2-3 QueCards—the rapid 1-2-3 reference! Each QueCard is a detailed reference to a particular 1-2-3 command, @function, or macro. With QueCards, you can determine instantly how to use a 1-2-3 command—as well as learn helpful hints and tips on avoiding treacherous traps. When you can't remember 1-2-3 commands, you need **1-2-3 Que Cards**!

1-2-3 QueCards—the easy-to-use 1-2-3 reference! QueCards are removable 5" x 8" cards, housed in a convenient 3-ring binder. You can use QueCards with the built-in easel or remove the cards and place them next to your computer keyboard. Put hard-to-remember 1-2-3 commands at your fingertips with **1-2-3 QueCards!**

When you want a convenient, comprehensive reference to 1-2-3, you want **1-2-3 QueCards**! Priced at only $21.95, **1-2-3 QueCards** belong next to *your* computer.

Look for **1-2-3 QueCards** at over 7,500 bookstores and computer stores nationwide, or call 1-800-428-5331, ext. 888, to order direct from Que!

SELECT QUE BOOKS TO INCREASE YOUR PERSONAL COMPUTER PRODUCTIVITY

Using 1-2-3, Special Edition

Developed by Que Corporation

Acclaimed for its wealth of information and respected for its clear and concise style, *Using 1-2-3* is required reading for more than one million 1-2-3 users worldwide. This Special Edition of the classic text has more than 900 pages of up-to-date information and features, including comprehensive Command Reference and Troubleshooting sections, hands-on practice sessions, and information on Lotus HAL and other add-in/add-on programs. Discover for yourself why *Using 1-2-3*, Special Edition, is the ultimate tutorial and reference to 1-2-3, Release 2!

1-2-3 Tips, Tricks, and Traps, 2nd Edition

by Dick Andersen and Douglas Cobb

This classic text features more than 400 pages of power-packed tips and tricks essential for efficient use of 1-2-3, Release 2. Written for both beginning and advanced users, *1-2-3 Tips, Tricks, and Traps*, 2nd Edition, offers you hundreds of valuable tips on how to best use 1-2-3 for your specific applications, teaches you timesaving 1-2-3 tricks, and helps you avoid hazardous spreadsheet traps. Improve your spreadsheet technique with a proven text —Que's *1-2-3 Tips, Tricks, and Traps*, 2nd Edition!

MS-DOS User's Guide, 3rd Edition

by Chris DeVoney

This classic guide to MS-DOS is now better than ever! Updated for MS-DOS, Version 3.3, this new edition features several new extended tutorials and a unique new command reference section. The distinctive approach of this text lets you easily reference basic command syntax, while comprehensive tutorial sections present in-depth DOS data. Appendixes provide information specific to users of DOS on COMPAQ, Epson, Zenith, and Leading Edge personal computers. Master your computer's operating system with *MS-DOS User's Guide*, 3rd Edition—the comprehensive tutorial/reference!

1-2-3 QueCards

Developed by Que Corporation

An exciting new concept in personal computer reference materials! QueCards are 5″ × 8″ cards housed in a sturdy 3-ring binder. The cards can be either used with the built-in easel or removed and placed next to your computer keyboard. Each QueCard shows the proper usage of a particular 1-2-3 command, macro, or @function. Convenient section tabs make it easy to find the particular command you need. Put hard-to-remember commands at your fingertips with the ideal 1-2-3 reference—*1-2-3 QueCards*!

ORDER FROM QUE TODAY

Item	Title	Price	Quantity	Extension
805	Using 1-2-3, Special Edition	$24.95		
62	1-2-3 Tips, Tricks, and Traps, 2nd Edition	19.95		
73	1-2-3 QueCards	21.95		
838	MS-DOS User's Guide, 3rd Edition	22.95		

Book Subtotal _____

Shipping & Handling ($2.50 per item) _____

Indiana Residents Add 5% Sales Tax _____

GRAND TOTAL _____

Method of Payment

☐ Check ☐ VISA ☐ MasterCard ☐ American Express

Card Number _____ Exp. Date _____

Cardholder's Name _____

Ship to _____

Address _____

City _____ State _____ ZIP _____

If you can't wait, call **1-800-428-5331** and order TODAY.
All prices subject to change without notice.

FOLD HERE

Place
Stamp
Here

Que Corporation
P.O. Box 90
Carmel, IN 46032

R870—1-2-3 QuickStart

REGISTRATION CARD

Register your copy of *1-2-3 QuickStart*, and receive information about Que's newest products. Complete this registration card and return it to Que Corporation, P.O. Box 90, Carmel, IN 46032.

Name _____ Phone _____

Company _____ Title _____

Address _____

City _____ State _____ ZIP _____

Please check the appropriate answers:

Where did you buy *1-2-3 QuickStart*?
- ☐ Bookstore (name: _____)
- ☐ Computer store (name: _____)
- ☐ Catalog (name: _____)
- ☐ Direct from Que _____
- ☐ Other: _____

How many computer books do you buy a year?
- ☐ 1 or less   ☐ 6–10
- ☐ 2–5   ☐ More than 10

How many Que books do you own?
- ☐ 1   ☐ 6–10
- ☐ 2–5   ☐ More than 10

How long have you been using 1-2-3?
- ☐ Less than 6 months
- ☐ 6 months to 1 year
- ☐ 1–3 years
- ☐ More than 3 years

What influenced your purchase of *1-2-3 QuickStart*?
- ☐ Personal recommendation
- ☐ Advertisement   ☐ Que catalog
- ☐ In-store display ☐ Que mailing
- ☐ Price   ☐ Que's reputation
- ☐ Other: _____

How would you rate the overall content of *1-2-3 QuickStart*?
- ☐ Very good   ☐ Satisfactory
- ☐ Good   ☐ Poor

How would you rate this book's graphics-based approach to learning 1-2-3?
- ☐ Very good   ☐ Satisfactory
- ☐ Good   ☐ Poor

How would you rate this book's organization of topics?
- ☐ Very good   ☐ Satisfactory
- ☐ Good   ☐ Poor

How would you rate the "pointer" method of referencing topics?
- ☐ Very good   ☐ Satisfactory
- ☐ Good   ☐ Poor

What do you like *best* about *1-2-3 QuickStart*?

What do you like *least* about *1-2-3 QuickStart*?

How do you use *1-2-3 QuickStart*?

What other Que products do you own?

For what other programs would a Que book be helpful?

Please feel free to list any other comments you may have about *1-2-3 QuickStart*.

_____
_____
_____
_____
_____

FOLD HERE

Place
Stamp
Here

Que Corporation
P.O. Box 90
Carmel, IN 46032

Put Essential Information at Your Fingertips...

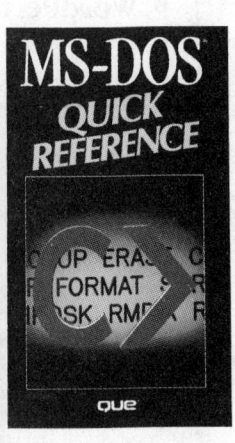

With the Que Quick Reference Series!

When you need a convenient reference to your favorite applications, choose the **Que Quick Reference Series**. Each Que **Quick Reference** is a low-priced, easy-to-use reference to common program commands and functions, and contains the high-quality information you expect from Que. Essential information in a compact format—the **Que Quick Reference Series**!

ORDER TODAY! CALL 1-800-428-5331, EXT. A105

YES!

Please send me the following Que **Quick Reference** books:

Qty.	No.	Title	Price
	865	MS-DOS Quick Reference	$6.95
	862	1-2-3 Quick Reference	$6.95
	866	WordPerfect Quick Reference	$6.95
	868	C Quick Reference	$6.95
	869	QuickBASIC Quick Reference	$6.95

Return this card to:
Que Corporation
11711 N. College Ave.
Carmel, IN 46032
For even faster service, call toll-free:
1-800-428-5331, ext. A105

Name _____
Title _____
Company _____
Address _____
City _____
State _____ ZIP _____
Home Phone _____
Work Phone _____
☐ MasterCard ☐ VISA ☐ American Express
Card Number _____
Signature _____

Please include 50¢ per item shipping and handling.
All prices subject to change without notice.
Prices and charges are for domestic orders only.
Non-U.S. prices might be higher.

- MS-DOS
- 1-2-3
- WordPerfect 5
- C
- QuickBASIC 4

If you use any of these popular applications, you should be using the Que Quick Reference Series!

Whether you use a laptop or a desktop personal computer, the **Que Quick Reference Series** provides immediate access to information often buried in traditional texts. These portable references help you quickly determine the proper use for important commands and functions, without wading through pages and pages of inapplicable information. When you need essential information fast, turn to the quality information contained in the **Que Quick Reference Series**!

MS-DOS Quick Reference
Gain immediate control of MS-DOS 3.3 with this compact reference.
Includes information on:
- DOS commands and error messages
- EDLIN commands
- Batch Files

Order #865, $6.95

1-2-3 Quick Reference
The instant 1-2-3 reference.
Includes information on:
- Fundamental 1-2-3 commands
- Essential @functions
- Important macros

Order # 862, $6.95

WordPerfect Quick Reference
The easy-to-use reference for all users of new WordPerfect 5.
Includes information on:
- Essential commands
- Common tasks and applications
- Uses of program function keys

Order #866, $6.95

C Quick Reference
The portable reference to programming with the forthcoming ANSI C standard.
Includes information on:
- Essential commands and keywords
- Important concepts
- Proper programming protocol

Order #868, $6.95

QuickBASIC Quick Reference
The convenient reference to the functions and keywords available with the QuickBASIC 4 compiler. Includes information on:
- Essential commands & keywords
- Important concepts
- Proper programming protocol

Order #869, $6.95

COMING SOON:
dBASE IV Quick Reference
Order $867, $6.95

ORDER TODAY! CALL 1-800-428-5331, EXT. A105